AGING IN MASS SOCIETY

AGING IN MASS SOCIETY

Myths and Realities

Jon Hendricks
C. Davis Hendricks
University of Kentucky

Winthrop Publishers, Inc.
Cambridge, Massachusetts

Library of Congress Cataloging in Publication Data

Hendricks, Jon
   Aging in mass society.

   Includes bibliographies and index.
   1. Aged — United States.   2. Aging.   I. Hendricks,
C. Davis   II. Title.
HQ1064.U5H44   301.43'5'0973   76-57716
ISBN 0-87626-032-6

Acknowledgments

Chapter 2: Portions of Chapter 2 appear in Hendricks, Jon, and Hendricks, C. Davis.
   "The Age-Old Question of Old Age." *Aging and Human Development, in press.*
Table 3.1. Petersen data copyright © 1969 by Macmillan Publishing Company, Inc.
Fig. 4.1. Copyright © 1959 by The University of Chicago.
Fig. 4.2. Copyright © 1960 by the American Association for the Advancement of
   Science.
Fig. 4.5. Copyright © 1962 by Scientific American, Inc. All rights reserved.
Fig. 5.1. Reprinted by permission of S. Karger AG, Basel.
Fig. 5.2. © 1972 by Russell Sage Foundation, Basic Books, Publishers, Inc., New York.
Fig. 6.3. Reprinted by permission of S. Karger AG, Basel.

For our Parents

and in memory of
Don Kent

Contents

Preface

To speak of the elderly in America is to refer to a diverse group already numbering nearly 23 million and growing faster than any other segment of the population. Although interest in the aging process has quickened considerably over the past decade, a great deal of nonsense pervades cultural perceptions about what it is like to grow old. Often the pronouncements upon which such views are based are not buttressed by empirical evidence, and even when they do contain a glimmer of fact, few truths are so hard and fast they cannot be changed. Part of the reason so many myths abound is that the complexities of aging reflect a two-way street, running between age as a physiological aspect of life and age as a social and psychological facet of our existence. Unraveling the nature of this interaction is as challenging as it is interesting. Whenever the topic of aging is broached, a multitude of substantive concerns crop up, and inevitably the explanations proffered are as diverse as the questions asked. In other words, there are no easy answers to why people age the way they do.

The current volume is intended to provide a comprehensive description of the dimensions of aging. It takes as its point of departure the proposition that it is meaningless to talk about any element of aging without having at least a nodding acquaintance with the others. Further, to appreciate the relative character of aging in today's world, it is prudent, if not essential, to have some grasp of where the elderly stand in other times and in other places vis-à-vis the larger social order. In addition, before one can attempt to describe and in some measure interpret the assumed facts about age, one must gain an understanding of the conceptual frameworks employed in gathering those facts. It is only in this way that change or accommodation can be forthcoming. Clearly there is no denying that an interdisciplinary approach to the study of aging is a tall order, one in which the attempt to collect loose ends is a monumental and unending task. As perplexing as this can be, it may turn out that, for the time being, the questions raised are even more salient than any of the tentative answers. Accordingly, the primary goal of this work is to offer a contextual overview of aging in modern mass societies, knowing full well no definitive conclusions can be forthcoming.

Part I will introduce the reader to the study of aging and to its links to historical and social currents. The fluid boundaries of age will be explored through a discussion of historical, demographic and cross-cultural patterns. Here, as well as in subsequent sections, comparisons with other countries should be viewed as illustrative of the relativity of the issues involved, rather than as in-depth delineations of aging around the world. Part II presents a survey of the theoretical frameworks of gerontologists, both physiological and social. In order to appreciate the interrelatedness of various components of the aging process, it is important to recognize the broad outlines of the conceptual apparatus utilized in the doing of gerontology. Part III zeroes in on certain crucial issues impinging on the daily lives of older people. Beginning with an examination of psychological, sensory and intellectual characteristics, it moves to a look at the myriad realities of everyday life confronting the elderly. Along the way, the discourse pauses to consider such diverse questions as health, finances, retirement and politics, and concludes with an examination of the special nature of minority-group aging. All who read these words will find themselves among the ranks of those euphemistically labeled senior citizens. Part IV is a brief section covering the future of aging tomorrow and the day after, forecasting what lies ahead. For readers who find themselves sufficiently challenged by what has been said to consider gerontology as a vocation, the final chapter includes a summary of the career prospects realistically available over the next few years.

Scattered here and there throughout the text are words printed in **boldface** type. These are terms that are sometimes used in a technical sense and, besides being defined in the body of the discussion, are listed in the glossary. Key *italicized* words will also appear from time to time. While these may be technical or used in a particular manner, for the most part their meaning should be clear from the context. Appended to each of the chapters is a list of pertinent readings. Each contains all references utilized in the preceding section, and in some cases also includes literature we considered germane, even if not actually cited. In several instances these reading lists are rather lengthy. However, it seemed to be in the best interests of intellectual curiosity to have a ready reference to turn to should a particular question spark the imagination.

While we have endeavored to avoid polemic arguments and moralistic statements, it is our fervent hope that the challenges stated herein will attract new scholars and practitioners to the field of gerontology.

The dividing line between original ideas and one's intellectual heritage is ambiguous at best; indeed, where one leaves off and the other begins is difficult to say. In the course of our intellectual development we have been graced with a number of helpful friends, colleagues and mentors, all of whom gave unsparingly of themselves. It presents a nearly impossible task to enumerate the many ways in which we are indebted to them. Truly we would not be where we are if not for them, though this in no way implies we are all that contented with the here and now.

Our appreciation to Don Kent is beyond measure. For several years he shared with us not only his passionate involvement with gerontology, but also his strength, love and concern.

At what we now realize were important turning points in our careers, Joseph Kockelmans and Alex Simirenko played pivotal roles. For their emotional support when it was needed most, we thank Jim Brown, Tom Garrity, Bob Straus and Willis Sutton. To our colleagues in gerontology who have been both friends and critics we offer our gratitude. In addition, the publisher's reviewers were most helpful. Special mention must be made of the trailblazing effort of Bob Atchley, who has made our task considerably easier. We would also like to acknowledge *Aging and Human Development* for permission to reprint portions of Chapter 2.

We are of two minds about how best to acknowledge those people without whom our work would never be exposed to the public eye. It seems they should come both first and last, having been central to all our endeavors. To the two women who served as clerical assistants, confidantes and warm friends we are sincerely appreciative. Mable Belt labored through the earlier drafts, working with hieroglyphics that would have driven a cryptographer mad. Carolyn Anderson stood ready to help whenever necessary. She cheerfully typed the final draft, which was also liberally annotated, and generously compiled the index. Not only were they critical yet supportive, they both regarded the project as their own.

Finally, the mistakes must be attributed to someone, but unfortunately we have no candidates other than ourselves. Although it may not always be apparent, we have tried to keep you, the reader, foremost in our minds. We welcome you to the study of a fascinatingly complex, socially responsive and emotionally provocative topic. We expect you will find the rewards manifold. Further, we wish we could see, feel and hear your reactions, for it will be your responses that shape our future paths.

AGING IN MASS SOCIETY

Part I

LOCATING THE AGED IN THE MODERN WORLD

Chapter 1

The Spectrum of Aging

What is it like to grow old? An innocuous enough question, certainly one asked by every generation since mankind gained the power of reflection, yet one even the wisest sage would be hard pressed to answer. To begin with, becoming old is by no means a singular process; rather, it is characterized by a complex interweaving of biological, psychological and social elements. Within each of these realms, what we call aging may occur at different rates, evolve in separate directions and manifest itself in distinct patterns. In this regard it should be stressed that although most of us tend to rely on chronological age to describe someone's stage of development, used in this way age is little more than a convenient index of a number of interrelated processes; in and of itself it has little intrinsic meaning. Furthermore, even a preliminary attempt to explain how a given individual negotiates the course of life requires looking beyond the circumstances of the solitary person. Few of us customarily evaluate the events that transpire in our lives in terms of general societal trends, yet this is exactly what is called for in analyses of aging. Before we can say whether Joe's or Ann's experiences in later life are typical or unprecedented, much less offer a solution to any obstacles they might face, we must know something about the lives of those who find themselves in analogous positions. Without assessing the roles played by societal and environmental factors, any solution of their problems can scarcely amount to more than a temporary bromide, masking the symptoms, but doing little to affect the causes of distress. So long as the disadvantages associated with old age are viewed as somehow unique to one's own personal situation, the obligation for ameliorating harmful conditions will not be seen as part of society's responsibility. It is only with the recognition that we will all soon face similar fates, and that countless numbers of elderly cannot be held individually accountable for what happens to them, that there can be any hope of successful intervention for the sake of the aged in the modern world.

Visibility of the Aged

Every society known to history has numbered among its members a certain proportion of people older than the vast majority. How these people were viewed hinged on the resources they commanded that could be utilized by the larger group, or the extent of resources, usually tangible, such as an abundance of food stuffs, that could be diverted to those aged no longer able to tend entirely to their own needs. As will become clear in subsequent chapters, even though the numbers of elderly were small, documents surviving from ancient civilizations show evidence of a heated debate over questions such as, "Does age carry with it whatever attributes we as a society esteem?" or "Is old age a time of debilitating changes running counter to our dominant values?" However, it was not until the dawn of the modern era that the **age distribution** of most societies began to reflect a significant aggregation of older people. As a consequence of medical, technological and economic advances, a decline in mortality occurred, so that for the first time sizeable numbers of people were living into their sixth decade or beyond.

Gradually technology spread into a variety of productive realms, making it possible for people to spend less time engaged in various work pursuits with no reduction in per capita output. Yet these very innovations carried with them a demand for workers with new skills and capacities that in effect helped establish a surplus of older workers and eventually led to the institutionalization of retirement policies as we know them today.

Prior to the end of the nineteenth century, the increasing proportion of the aged, along with their pressing needs, had awakened the social consciousness of several European governments. By the 1880s, social service programs had been inaugurated in Germany and Denmark, and, by the early decades of the present century, similar schemes had spread across the continent and to as far away as New Zealand. While each country openly acknowledged societal responsibility for providing a basic economic security for older people, both the content and extent of the support varied widely. In many instances, health insurance was included as an integral component of the package, although in the United States few people were willing to admit the need for such services until quite recently. Older people had a long time to wait before becoming a truly visible component of the American scene. Even though the federal government had already begun to assume a protective role over the rights of children, calls made in the political campaigns of 1900 by the Social Democrats and again in 1912 by the Progressives for similar federal responsibility on behalf of the elderly apparently fell on deaf ears. At the time, America was in the midst of an expansionist era and its priorities lay elsewhere. Successful political debates failed to incorporate or even to consider humanitarian principles regarding older people for three decades into the twentieth century.

The American Depression and Concern for the Elderly

What finally propelled the federal government into action on behalf of the elderly was in large part the result of the Depression of the 1930s ("Federal Action," 1975). For the first time in history, the American dream of an ever brighter tomorrow was challenged by the stark realities of economic blight. Always before it had been possible to relegate all manner of problems to the dusty corners of the country's conscience, by claiming that such issues would be resolved once a foothold on progress had been won or else by asserting they more properly fell within the purview of personal and familial obligations. In the process of determining the dimensions of the economic displacement brought on by the collapse of the stock market, researchers for the federal government discovered there was an inordinately high proportion of older people among those most severely affected with no place to turn for solace. Traditionally, families had been expected to come to the aid of their elderly, but with double digit unemployment rampant during the 1930s it was beyond the capacities of ever greater numbers of families to provide for their aged relatives. It was not that a whole new range of difficulties suddenly emerged; rather, problems previously defined largely in personal terms were now redefined as consequences of events over which individuals had little or no personal control. Although the fruits of medicine and technology were beginning to lengthen life, social change was effectively undermining whatever advances had been wrought. Under the circumstances it was perhaps only just that old people should take their place alongside children and adolescents as an age group with particular needs deserving of special attention (Philibert, 1965; Neugarten and Moore, 1968).

In analyzing the forces that have focused attention on the problematic aspects of aging and the enactment of protective legislation for older people, several authorities have suggested they resulted from a combination of ideological factors brought to the public's awareness by the practical realities of the years preceding the collapse of 1929 and the Depression. Spengler (1969), for example, outlines the spread of a kind of collectivistic redistributive ideology during the first three decades of the century that supported public assistance programs for various indigent groups, the elderly included. Added to this was a transformation of conventional religious injunctions of charitable deeds toward the less fortunate into a kind of secularized belief that gradually came to be translated into a political doctrine. Still further, support came in the form of an espousal of Keynesian fiscal principles by New Deal programs advocating expanded public spending to prime the pumps of private enterprise in order to reestablish fiscal and social stability. These same principles also lent credibility to the notion of providing for the economic well-being of older people. Supplementing these three value shifts was a variety of very real conditions, including the undeniable hardships of the Depression and the heightened visibility of the elderly. Part of that visibility arose from the growing number of the older Americans. Indeed, as is shown in Figure 1.1, from 1900 to 1930 their proportion grew faster than the overall population, a trend that has continued unabated to the present day. Another facet of the conspicuousness of older people's economic difficulties revolves around the process of urbanization. At the turn of the century the United States was still predominately rural, with the bulk

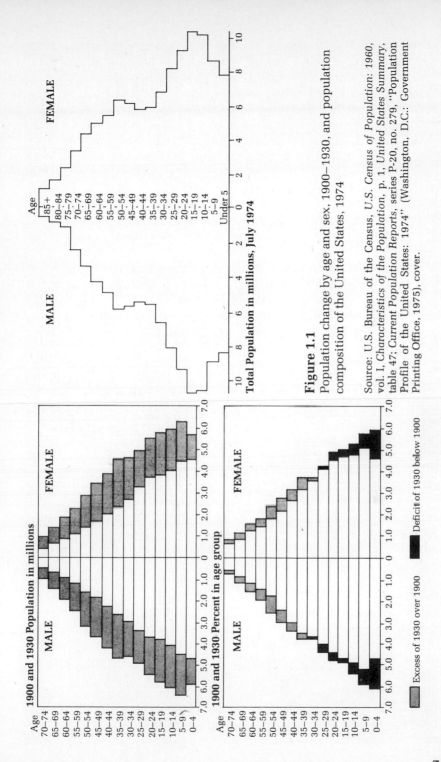

Figure 1.1

Population change by age and sex, 1900–1930, and population composition of the United States, 1974

Source: U.S. Bureau of the Census, *U.S. Census of Population: 1960*, vol. I, *Characteristics of the Population*, p. 1, *United States Summary*, table 47; *Current Population Reports*, series P-20, no. 279, "Population Profile of the United States: 1974" (Washington, D.C.: Government Printing Office, 1975), cover.

of the population living on or near the country's farms. By 1920, though, a change had occurred. America had become an urbanized nation, with a majority of its people now concentrated in towns of at least 2500. Because the younger segments of the population were both more willing and able to relocate, the obvious population movement for younger people was to the cities. However, for those elderly who did find themselves living out their later years in urban areas, a preponderance of financial and personal difficulties were cast in bold relief. This is not to say rural environments did not pose their own risks; it is merely to note that because of their dependence on salaried employment, with the concurrent adoption of formal retirement policies, the problems associated with growing old in a rapidly changing society were more evident among urban residents.

Rounding out the list of actual conditions that played an important role in highlighting the plight of older people, Spengler points to three complementary economic trends. As the burgeoning wartime economy of the early 1940s returned disposable per capita income to pre-Depression levels and beyond, there was relatively little opposition to expansion of the Social Security taxes first imposed in 1935. Consequently, payments to retired workers were allowed to increase, while current wage earners saw visions of substantial benefits awaiting them upon their own retirement. As the federal government became more intimately involved in public assistance programs, and as poverty guidelines were developed, it also became evident that older people were not only more likely to have incomes below established subsistence levels but were over-represented among the long-term unemployed. Last, the effects of the inflation that has plagued the country since World War II have obviously eroded the buying power of those on fixed incomes to a greater extent than those who were or are in a position to negotiate their financial situations. In conjunction with the foregoing trends becoming indisputable components of the American experience, Spengler and others suggest that they are probably sufficient in themselves to insure continuing attention to the needs of the elderly.

Age Grading

Age is so pervasive an element of social organization that anthropologists are now convinced it is a universal feature in the assignment of social roles, rights and responsibilities. This is to say, age is never merely a biological fact of life; everywhere it takes on cultural meanings that inevitably color the social definitions of people and the things they do. In this respect there is very little difference between modern and preindustrial societies except insofar as the nature of the criteria used in the distribution of roles has changed. In an earlier time it was possible to rely on *functional age* or performance capacities to evaluate people. The behavior expected of individuals by society was more closely based on their own age-related attributes than on their membership in any particular age-status group. Certainly there were age norms stipulating appropriate behavior, just as there were identifiable age groups, yet membership came about as a consequence of achieved status rather than on an automatic basis. With the increasing complexity of modern bureaucratic societies, functional determination of age group membership has been supplanted by a more diversified formal set of criteria which, although it may be arbitrary, does serve to insure a continuous progression of individuals through socially valued roles. In modern as well as in preindustrial societies, age norms, however they are derived, exercise considerable constraint on all members of a given category. This does allow people and society in general to anticipate the broad contours of their lives with a measure of precision (Eisenstadt, 1956; Bengtson and Haber, 1975).

Age-Appropriate Behavior

If asked to provide a list of our friends, most of us would find upon inspection that the ages of those people whose names we wrote down cluster fairly close around our own age. That this should be the case for young as well as for old ought not to come as a surprise, since by far the greatest proportion of interaction takes place among individuals from socially homogeneous groups who share a comparable position vis-à-vis the larger social system (Rosow, 1967). As we move through life, this tendency to associate most with those who are approximately our age and of similar circumstances is one of the means by which we all learn what is expected of us. These **age norms,** as they are called by social scientists, have an inexorable influence on how individuals behave. For the most part they do not designate in detail how a person is to carry out a particular social role; instead they provide a general definition of acceptable behavior within a given complex of roles. For example, norms regarding parental conduct do not specify an exact manner for discharging the responsibilities of being a parent, though they do prescribe what we usually consider suitable responses. It ought to be emphasized, however, that expectations of age-appropriate behavior are seldom formulated in isolation — that is, without reference to earlier and later age grades or reciprocal roles. Continuing with the parental example, anticipations of how the parents of young children will act are based in part on the relative youthfulness of the parents themselves, plus the dependent position of their offspring. At a later time, when both parents and children are more mature, slightly different behavior is expected, until finally each child becomes an adult and still further redefinitions take place. At each juncture, parents as well as offspring find themselves interacting most with others who are at a like stage in the life cycle, taking cues from one another as to what are acceptable attitudes and actions. It is only when the entire process is viewed as a whole, lasting throughout life, that the meaningfulness of age-graded expectations becomes apparent (Eisenstadt, 1956).

Although age norms circumscribe the implicit boundaries of desirable conduct, and hence are most noticeable in their transgression, researchers have found a marked consensus in people's conceptions of appropriate behavior (Neugarten et al., 1968). This is not to claim that everyone moves through life locked into an invariable chronological timetable in which there are no opportunities for individual description or modification. Indeed, there is a whole array of social factors, many of which are seemingly endemic to the social order, that plays a part in the timing of the life cycle. At the outset, socioeconomic status has a profound effect on considerations of social age. Generally speaking, members of disadvantaged socioeconomic classes pass what most people view as life's transition points at earlier chronological ages than their counterparts in the more affluent social classes. Thus, they establish independent households, marry, have children, cease having children and so on at relatively earlier ages. Similarly, they see themselves as middle-aged or old a few years in advance of men and women in the upper socioeconomic categories. Patterns of education and labor force participation also have an effect on determinations of social age; for example, students nearing their late twenties who are still enrolled in school are often thought of as younger, by themselves as well as by others, than their age mates who terminated their education earlier and have since established families or careers. In addition, there are indications that sex, ethnicity and racial background are contributing factors in the timing of the aging process. As will be seen in Chapter Thirteen, members of various minority groups in the United States do not necessarily age in a style exactly analogous to the majority white population. Among the most commonly observed differences are perceptions of the chronological age at which people undergo various changes in social age (Neugarten and Moore, 1968; Bengtson and Haber, 1975; Drevenstedt, 1976).

Despite the significant effects these variables have on assessments of social age, their impact, at least singly, is not so great as to deny the possibility of individualized variations. As one concomitant of the pluralistic nature of modern life and the numerous institutional spheres in which we participate, each with its own timetable, the succession of people through a well-regulated age-status system is not nearly as coordinated as it may have been in less complex societies. Today, because of fairly distinct boundaries perhaps basic to the various spheres of life, it is entirely conceivable for many people to experience a kind of asynchronous movement through the life cycle. This process is by no means as mysterious as it may at first sound; returning again to the earlier example of parenthood may be a useful way to clarify **age-status asynchronization.** Since most people marry for the first time in their early twenties, it is not at all unusual for them to have completed the procreative phase of the family life cycle before their occupational careers have taken root. Hence, in terms of family life, they are at a later stage of development than they are in their work lives. Likewise, for those women who do not work outside the home, family responsibilities may be essentially complete at an age when their husbands are considered to be too young for certain executive positions. Or alternatively, both partners may find themselves grandparents when they themselves have barely crossed the threshold of middle age. Of course these are not the only examples of asynchronization. Equally valid illustrations arise in the cases of those who delay starting their families, remarry and begin another set of family relationships, or embark on a second career at a point in life later than is customarily the case (Cain, 1964).

Interestingly enough, people are often fully aware of subtle variations in age-appropriate behavior and if asked can provide a reasonably accurate assessment of their own adherence to the norm. Neugarten and her associates have used the concept of *social clocks* to describe the marking off of various units of the life cycle. They have found that in most instances people recognize whether they are passing some transition point ahead of or behind schedule and, depending on their timing, often modify subsequent behavior to bring themselves closer to what they see as typically the case (Neugarten et al., 1968; Neugarten and Datan, 1973). While they may desire to approximate the norms with regard to certain aspects of aging, it appears most people feel somehow exempt from strict adherence to the general normative patterns of aging. In a sense, age norms are conceived by most of us as compelling strictures for others but lacking in any specific hegemony over our own lives. Why this should be the case is one of those paradoxes gerontologists have so far been unable to resolve. Nevertheless, it may be an age-related phenomenon, since, in comparison to middle-aged or older people, younger age groups often see themselves as more at variance with what they think of as the norm (Bengtson and Haber, 1975).

Rites of Passage

As people encounter the sequence of age-graded roles, **rites of passage** are one of the mechanisms used by society to denote their movement from one phase of the life cycle to the next. Originally such rites were celebrated by highly ritualized ceremonies and had as their function the provision of an institutionalized means for facilitating the cessation of certain behavior and the introduction of a new set of expectations. Readily familiar examples are the use among certain tribal peoples of circumcision or clitorectomy rites to initiate young males and females to adult status, or of Bar Mitzvahs, debutante balls, high school graduations, formal inaugurations and so on in modern social systems to indicate the transition to new statuses. In fact, rites of passage need not be so formalized in order to qualify, exclude or limit what is expected within particular age-related roles. Advancing through grades in school, joining new clubs or associations, even buying a house, can be seen as ways in which people are socially redefined, though these latter forms obviously lack much of the symbolic significance of ceremonial transitions. Usually such status shifts imply increasing maturity and responsibility, each helping in its own way to prepare the person for still later transitions, thereby insuring some semblance of continuity to the passage through life's stages without the distraction of major disjunctures (van Gennep, 1960; Rosow, 1974).

Becoming socially defined as an "older person" presents something of an exception to the foregoing pattern of rites and transitions. Like all antecedent changes, the movement into old age entails delicate alterations in social relationships which are, however, much more nebulous. Formal rites of passage, the occasional retirement dinner notwithstanding, are seldom features of the initial phases of the later years, since this period is most often experienced as an unscheduled gradual passage. Although today reaching one's sixty-fifth birthday is in a sense a rite, in many respects a redefinition is likely to have been imminent for a number of years. It should also be noted at this point that one reason the specter of institutionalization is so emotionally potent among older people might well be because it does signify so clearly what most perceive to be the final transition in the life cycle. Unlike all previous transitions, instead of expanding one's alternatives, old age tends to have a constricting influence over the structure of opportunities in a way that causes some people to feel alienated from important social roles. Part of this explanation lies in the simple fact that institutional supports implicit in all previous transitions are lacking in the passage into old age. For what is often the first time in their lives, people are confronted by the attrition or absence of predetermined institutional alternatives so integral to their sense of self-worth. Men perhaps more than women experience varying degrees of role discontinuity as they move into old age, since little or nothing in their backgrounds is preparatory to what life in the later years is like. We do not mean to suggest that retirement necessarily leads to situational depression; a blanket statement such as this would not only be inappropriate, but, without relevant information regarding attitudes toward work, leisure and self-concept, it would prove incorrect. It is merely to point out that the gradual tapering off of domestic chores among most women allows them more time to adapt to the changing expectations of later life (Rosow, 1974).

Stereotyping the Elderly

Either because of a lack of information or the absence of anticipatory socialization, old age occupies a unique place in the life cycle, at least insofar as it is surrounded by more misconceptions than any other phase. The tendency to develop stereotypes, oversimplified and often erroneous generalizations about various groups or categories of people, is apparently a common aspect of daily life. If nothing else, it serves to protect us from being overwhelmed by a welter of particulars. However, such categorizations as form the basis of stereotypes are frequently derived from limited knowledge and allow no room for individual variation. Americans, or members of any modern society for that matter, are not distinctive in their systematic denigration of certain classes of people. Nor is youth atypical in its perception of old age as a time of negatively valued change. Unfortunately, even the elderly themselves are influenced by the characteristically unfavorable image of older people. Not only are the phrases and adjectives they use to describe their contemporaries generally deprecating, but their own self-concepts reflect the very ambivalence they perceive in the attitudes of those with whom they interact. In every instance, the views people have toward both minority groups and specific age stages are shaped by the ideals of the culture in which they live and the stigmatizing of that which is at odds with those ideals. In an era that eschews traditional authority and values youth, freedom and the rapid dissemination of new ideas, old age is unlikely to be accorded very high prestige (Slater, 1963; Rosow, 1974). /

Ageism and Common Stereotypes

Gerontologists have coined the term **ageism** to refer to the pejorative image of someone who is old simply because of his or her age. Like racism or sexism, it is wholesale discrimination against all members of a category, though usually it appears in more covert form. Threatened cutbacks in Social Security, failure to provide meaningful outlets or activities, or the belief that those in their sixties and beyond do not benefit from psychotherapy are all examples of subtle, or in some cases not so subtle, appraisals of the old. Part of the myth, a fundamental if implicit element of ageism, is the view that the elderly are somehow different from our present *and* future selves and therefore not subject to the same desires, concerns or fears. Even our attempts at humor reveal the existence of largely negative attitudes about the elderly, with those referring to older women suggesting a particularly pernicious "double standard" (Palmore, 1971). Why should ageism have become a national prejudice? Probably because of the emphasis on productive capacity and technological expertise, or perhaps out of a thinly veiled attempt to avoid the reality that we will all one day grow old and die. Not to be dismissed is the fact the early gerontological research that filtered into the public consciousness and reinforced existing misconceptions was based largely on institutionalized older people, who, however important they may be in their own right, are still a scant minority among the elderly (Butler and Lewis, 1973).

Indicative of the range of commonly held stereotypes about the elderly is the belief that most older people are living isolated lives beset by serious health problems, causing them to be emotionally distraught. Just as widespread are the ideas that women experience psychological trauma with the onset of the so-called empty nest years, while retirement spells certain morale problems for men. That older people are no longer sexually active, that, in fact they are no longer even interested, is another generally held view unsupported by the facts. Surely some or all of these themes can be observed among those over 65, but they can be found in any other age group as well (Palmore, 1969; Maddox, 1970). The realities of aging simply do not fit the stereotypes; however, despite the accumulation of new information the myths continue to thrive.

Again, even older people who may not be experiencing the difficulties attributed to old age see themselves as exceptions to an otherwise dreary picture. By the nature of our misconceptions we do the elderly a great disservice, tending to cast them as just another problem rather than as a potential resource for resolving society's dilemmas (Harris, 1975).

To ascertain the public's attitudes toward aging and to measure the gap between the expectations and the experience of being old, the National Council on the Aging commissioned what may be the most extensive study of its type yet to be conducted. In all, over 4250 interviews were held with a representative cross-section of American adults by members of the Harris polling organization. As a group, only about 2 percent of the respondents could conceive of the years after 60 as the best in life, while approximately one-third of those 18 to 64 and an even larger percentage of those over 65 saw them as the least desirable. It might be worth commenting, though, that while the majority in both instances did not perceive the later years to be any worse than, say, the teenage years, younger people consistently volunteered more negative views than did those who were actually over the age of 65. The discrepancy between the two age groups emerges dramatically in Table 1.1. As is clear, young adults expect the problems identified to be far more serious than they are for the elderly who actually experience them. As an illustration, somewhat less than one-fourth of the older respondents report fear of crime to be one of their most serious concerns, yet over twice as large a percentage of the general public thought crime constituted one of the biggest problems in the lives of the old. Granted, some older people might have been reluctant to admit to problems because of what it would suggest about their personal abilities; still, when other responses were included in the definition of problem areas, the differences did not disappear, though, for the most part, the magnitude of the gap closed and the problems identified were less overwhelming than most of us might think.

Despite the dire expectations about what life is going to be like, Harris and his associates found that for every older person who feels his or her life is worse than he or she thought it was going to be, there are at least three age mates who claim they are pleasantly surprised — it is better. Not unusually, there are those in every age category who are dismayed that things are not working out as they had hoped; the elderly can hardly be considered an exception. On the whole, income and racial background have been identified as having a greater impact on life satisfaction than does age. The more affluent respondents were not only more likely to

Table 1.1

Differences Between Personal Experiences of Americans 65 and Over
and Expectations Held by Other Adults About Those Experiences

	VERY SERIOUS PROBLEMS EXPERIENCED BY THE ELDERLY THEMSELVES (PERCENTAGE)	VERY SERIOUS PROBLEMS THE PUBLIC EXPECTS THE ELDERLY TO EXPERIENCE (PERCENTAGE)	NET DIFFERENCE
Fear of crime	23	50	+27
Poor health	21	51	+30
Not having enough money to live on	15	62	+47
Loneliness	12	60	+48
Not having enough medical care	10	44	+34
Not having enough education	8	20	+12
Not feeling needed	7	54	+47
Not having enough to do to keep busy	6	37	+31
Not having enough friends	5	28	+23
Not having enough job opportunities	5	45	+40
Poor housing	4	35	+31
Not having enough clothing	3	16	+13

Source: L. Harris and Associates, *The Myth and Reality of Aging in America*
(Washington, D.C.: The National Council on the Aging, Inc., 1975), p. 31.

express satisfaction with their current situation, but were more positively disposed toward the prospect of growing old. Though the sample does not differentiate among racial or ethnic groups other than between black and white, it appears as if there is a paradox among minority respondents revolving around the phenomenon of rising expectations. Older blacks feel more satisfied with their lives than do their younger counterparts, though a similar pattern tends to emerge among all respondents who are at the bottom end of the lower income scale. Regardless of financial levels, the black respondents felt less adequately prepared for old age than did the whites, yet, racial characteristics aside, most people over 65 express regrets for not having planned better for their later lives (Harris, 1975). Had they been more aware of what they would face and less insulated from the facts by the common tendency to shut the later years off from the rest of the life cycle, even those problems they do encounter might have been greatly ameliorated.

The Study of Aging

Lying as it does on the borderland of many disciplines, *gerontology*, the systematic exploration of the aging process, encompasses a broad territory. Its representatives include scientists who prefer to focus their attention on plants and animals, as well as those who are concerned with the aging of human beings. Not all areas of interest have proceeded apace, research in the biological or clinical aspects of aging having a longer history than studies of the behavioral and social facets. Social gerontology, a label coined around 1950 to describe the study of the ways in which social and cultural factors enter into the aging process, is perhaps the most recent of the subspecialties to have achieved widespread recognition. Still, it has only been within the past three decades that all areas have flourished and become firmly ensconced on the academic roster. Because the mission of gerontology is not simply concerned with advancing our understanding of the ways in which people age, it cannot confine itself within the walls of our colleges and universities. To fulfill its quest, gerontology is also an applied discipline addressing itself to the practical and immediate effects of aging. Its practitioners attempt both to counsel those who are encountering difficulties and to forestall maladjustments for the bulk of the elderly. Although gerontologists are fully aware that aging does not begin when people pass some magic point, they do tend to confine their focus to changes occurring in the second half of life — if only because the complexities preclude an adequate grasp even of that period. Perhaps, since the physical manifestations of aging are the most obvious, it was inevitable that they were the first to attract the attention of early gerontologists.

Historical Foundations

As an analytical field of endeavor, the study of aging is still young — barely out of its adolescence. But from time immemorial, oracles, pundits and philosophers alike have puzzled over the secrets of prolonging life, and by the thirteenth century the body of humanist literature on the subject was sizeable, though repetitious. One of the most astute of the early views of aging and one that parted company from the rest was that propounded by Roger Bacon. Writing in the thirteenth century, Bacon explicitly acknowledged the interaction of heredity with physical health, resulting in the increasing vulnerability of the organism over time. With the popularization of scientific analysis in the seventeenth century, systematic inquiry into the process of growing old began to quicken. Yet what little information was collected for the most part resulted as a by-product of other studies. Even so eminent a scholar as Francis Bacon, responsible for proposing what is still regarded as the scientific method of inquiry, paused in the midst of his many intellectual pursuits to write *The History of Life and Death,* dwelling on the possible causes of aging. Bacon suggested that hygienic practices were likely to be a major contributing factor; thus, by improving the citizenry's hygiene, significant advances in life expectancy would be forthcoming (Freeman, 1965). His prominence undoubtedly served to spur the interests of other scientists, and it was not long before Halley, the noted astronomer, began collecting actuarial statistics to construct what was to be the first scientific analysis of life expectancy. Within the century, others joined their ranks. Foremost among them was the Belgian astronomer-mathematician, Quetelet. Curious about what he perceived to be the normal distribution of various human characteristics, Quetelet compiled a list of the ways in which a wide range of abilities, skills and strengths varied by ages. While his focus was occasionally wide of the mark by contemporary standards, his attention to changing physical capacities was the forerunner of the kinds of physiological analyses discussed in the second half of Chapter Four. Meanwhile, a Russian physician named I. Fisher was also seeking answers to questions of longevity by investigating the importance of physical attributes, mental status and enviromental factors. Both Fisher and a younger colleague, P. Yengalytchev, concluded that exercise, hygiene, diet and timely medical attention were essential in order to survive to an advanced age (Birren and Clayton, 1975; Chebotarev and Duplenko, 1972).

The first of the large scale surveys assessing differences in age-related abilities was undertaken near the end of the last century. In the 1880s, Francis Galton collected data on 17 physical measures from a sampling of 9000 visitors to the International Health Exhibition in London. With his findings on the reaction time, visual and auditory acuity, grip strength, and so on for individuals ranging in age from 5 to 80, Galton was able to demonstrate rather conclusively that physical characteristics do differ by age. At roughly the same time another Russian scientist, S. P. Botkin, conducted a mass examination of almshouse residents in St. Petersburg. Based on a sample of nearly 3000 of the city's poor, 85 percent of whom were over the age of 65, Botkin sought to discriminate normal from pathological aging. The guiding premise was unique in itself, but, even further, Botkin and his colleagues included data on marital status, number of children, hereditary factors and use of alcohol plus other social variables that might conceivably influence longevity. Among his findings, which have been verified time and again, Botkin noted older men had a higher incidence of atherosclerosis than older women, women tended to live longer, heavy alcohol use inhibited longevity and married people outlived their single cohorts. Perhaps most importantly, Botkin drew initial distinction between chronological and biological age (Birren and Clayton, 1975; Chebotarev and Duplenko, 1972).

Advancement of Gerontology

During the early years of the twentieth century, multidisciplinary interest in aging continued to spread at a gradual but ever increasing rate. Beginning in the early 1900s, Elie Metchnikoff, a transplanted Russian, began to publish his research concerning the role of intestinal bacteria. On the basis of work he conducted in England, Metchnikoff concluded incorrectly — it might be noted — that autotoxicity of the lower intestinal tract was a cause of foreshortened life expectancy; therefore, purging the bowels of all bacteria should lengthen life. We now know the alimentary bacteria that Metchnikoff saw as so detrimental perform an important function in the assimilation of nutrients. Nevertheless, his studies were not entirely in vain, since they awakened further interest and eventually led to the establishment of the International Club for Research on Aging. Founded by Lord Nuffield and one of Metchnikoff's students, V. Korenchevsky, the club sought to attract the attention of the worldwide scientific community to the study of aging. By the 1920s, Americans were also becoming active in the study of aging. G. Stanley Hall's *Senescence, the Last Half of Life* (1922) was a pioneering effort in which Hall presented his own views on old age bolstered by the analysis of a questionnaire he had administered to a sample of older people. Before the decade was out, several other innovative books also appeared, and, in San Francisco, Lillian Martin set up the first Old Age Counseling Center, whose proclaimed goal was to advise people on how to age successfully.

By the time the club dispatched Korenchevsky to the United States in 1939 to create a North American branch, his efforts were almost anticlimactic. Prior to his arrival the cause of gerontology had already become somewhat of a social movement, gaining adherents among lay people and scientists alike. The 1930s witnessed popular campaigns that helped pave the way for Social Security, the initiation of occasional course offerings in major universities and the publication of a number of landmark treatises. Among these E. V. Cowdry's edited volume *Problems of Ageing* (1939) caused quite a stir, bringing together as it did the most creative thinkers of the time, and setting the stage for the rapid growth of gerontology over the course of the next two decades. During the 1940s, activity on the front lines of gerontology increased dramatically. The war years interrupted a series of innovative, highly publicized conferences that conferred scientific respectibility on the field, but within a year of the war's end, the Gerontology Society was founded and the first issue of the *Journal of Gerontology* made its appearance. Responding to increasing attention and pressure, even the federal government became involved, launching the first of a series of agencies that culminated nearly 30 years later in the 1974 birth of a National Institute of Aging (Philibert, 1965; Birren and Clayton, 1975).

The development of gerontology has been exponential. What was a trickle of five or six books augmented by some 100 articles in 1940 has since turned into an enormous flood of scores of books and over 5000 articles yearly (Kent, 1972). So extensive has the bibliography become that a recent attempt to compile a listing of the titles published during the period 1954–1974 resulted in approximately 50,000 entries, certainly too many for any one student to ever assimilate and a number exceeding the literature of all previous years combined (Woodruff, 1975; Birren and Clayton, 1975). The availability of social services and practical programs designed for older people has gone through an equally remarkable period of expansion. Although it is nearly an insurmountable task to ferret out the many types of programs, facilities and services being provided the elderly, experts predict far and away the greatest manpower needs in the coming decade will be among those practitioners who staff programs where they are in daily contact with older people. An overview of personnel requirements is provided in Chapter Fourteen; suffice it to say at this point that if estimates of roughly 330,000 people currently working with the elderly for the provision of basic services is an accurate indication of recent growth rates, there has been a tremendous improvement since the end of World War II (U.S. Senate, 1975).

Conceptual Hurdles

The increasing attention being paid to the aging process by lay people, politicians and scholars must be seen as something of a mixed blessing. On the one hand it ensures continuing support for research and practical intervention, while on the other it has the potential of introducing biases that are difficult if not impossible to overcome. Knowledge is always a matter of interpretation and perspective — as anyone who has been embroiled in a disagreement can readily testify. Despite our willingness to turn to the "facts" to settle questions about aging or anything else, facts can never speak for themselves. The ways in which the inquiry is phrased always delimit in advance several features of the answer supplied. They determine, for instance, which dimensions of the situation will be included as significant variables, ruling out others as unimportant or beside the point. Since gerontology is both a cultural and a scientific enterprise, its focus necessarily reflects the society in which it takes root. Professionals, whatever their stripe, bring with them to their work in gerontology some elements of those attitudes learned long before their scholarly interests in aging were awakened. An example drawn specifically in terms of aging research can amply illustrate the point. Because the dominant stereotypes of older people emphasized the darker side of aging, early social gerontology tended to concentrate on those things the elderly were bad at. Thus, instead of looking for attributes that could conceivably be enhanced by age, earlier studies examined almost exclusively the declines or disadvantages assumed to be inherent in the aging process. Between those whose accentuation of the negative aspects of aging lent reinforcement to society's preconceptions and those who were content simply to accumulate descriptive statistics about the elderly, it has taken the last two decades to make it clear that a great number of what were once taken to be characteristics of aging may actually stem from a combination of physical, social and individual variables not causally linked to age per se (Bromley, 1966; Busse and Pfeiffer, 1969).

The methodological techniques employed by gerontologists have undoubtedly contributed in part to the beclouding of what are age-related characteristics and what are artifacts. Traditionally, researchers have most often relied on cross-sectional survey methods; that is, drawing a sample of older and younger respondents, and then providing a descriptive comparison of the ways in which the elders differ from their younger counterparts. The validity of age differences discovered in this manner is beyond question; however, the conclusion that such differences are a consequence of aging is now recognized as untenable. In point of fact, the discrepancies between the age groups may be due to the effects of a particular historical-social milieu on the respondents. Educational attainment offers a good illustration. Observed differences in the number of years of school for older and younger people can in no way be construed to be an indication that a person's educational attainment declines with age. On the contrary, all it implies is that at the time the respondents in the older generation were of school age, educational opportunities that have subsequently become the norm were unavailable. It would not be any more appropriate to evaluate a group of 80 year olds in order to predict what life will be like 20 years hence for those who are now in their early sixties. In other words, cross-sectional analyses cannot distinguish between changes occurring because of age and those growing out of cohort or generational differences in experiences or any of a wide range of other external factors. Longitudinal research, such as the studies conducted since the mid-1950s at Duke University and elsewhere around the country, is one means of avoiding the pitfalls of cross-sectional techniques, but it too has its limitations. Following the same individual or group of people over a period of time permits gerontologists to more closely identify *age changes* that are developmental in nature, yet it is still possible to confound the results with environmental changes between the times the evaluations are made. As gerontologists have become more theoretically and methodologically concerned, alternative research strategies have evolved that offset some of these problems. In the course of the next few years, gerontological research is likely to take yet another turn as it incorporates new data-gathering perspectives (Schaie, 1976).

Another major hurdle gerontologists must face if they are to provide a reliable and meaningful picture of aging involves the provision of unifying conceptual frameworks. If the data collected in the many aging studies are to be in any sense cumulative, rather than merely expanding our store of descriptive details, it is necessary to go beyond the facts and to trace the linkages between various facets of aging. Thus far, those working in the field have been slow to act on the need for an integrative overview, whether out of expediency due to the fervor generated by short-run pragmatic accomplishments or because of the nature of their training in a single academic discipline. Consequently, research findings are too often noncomparable, and the impact of their work falls short of its potential (Seltzer, 1975). With the flourish in theoretical activity witnessed in the last few years, integrative perspectives capable of lending some order to the disparate findings of the field may not be too far in the future. Although there are no straightforward avenues to so complex a goal as explaining why men and women age the way they do, recognition of the importance of interdisciplinary training and the pointlessness of concentrating on any isolated aspect of aging without making reference to others will go a long way toward resolving the lack of a holistic grasp of the issues. So, too, will an appreciation of historical and cross-cultural variables in terms of their influence on individual, cohort and societal aging help enhance the explanatory power of gerontology (Philibert, 1965).

Summary

Growing old is a dynamic process encompassing complex bodily changes, redefinitions of social identities and adjustments in psychological functioning. By itself chronological age has little meaning, although it does serve as a convenient indicator not only of physiological change but of social status as well. It is not likely that any appreciation of what it means to age can be complete if the light of analysis is focused only on a given individual or social group. If they are to offer an explanation of why aging occurs the way it does, students of gerontology must be willing to adopt a broad perspective, one that cuts across time, space and academic boundaries. Throughout history there has been a scattering of concerned people and scholars who have attempted to intervene in the lives of the elderly, to improve their lot relative to the rest of the population. However, it was not until late in the nineteenth century that societal concern began to grow in Europe, and not until the 1930s that Americans began to acknowledge that the situations in which the elderly were involved were not entirely of their own making. Out of the pattern of shifting values and practical questions, gerontology has emerged as something of a social movement as well as a systematic area of inquiry.

All societies employ age as a social variable by which they prescribe and evaluate what is considered to be appropriate behavior. On account of this universal tendency for age status systems to develop, most of our social interaction takes place within homogeneous age categories. People move through the life cycle adopting and abandoning one set of age-determined roles after another, preparing at each step for what is to follow and learning the cues about how to act in the process. Gradually, they pass into that nebulous era of old age. Unlike all previous transitions, this one is seldom anticipated, not in the sense that it always spells difficulty, but rather, that little of what has gone before serves to prepare people for what it is like to be old. Partially because it represents something most people view as alien to their ideas and values, old age is surrounded by a mirage of inappropriate stereotypes. Unfortunately, these sometimes carry over into the realm of scientific inquiry, as the negative conclusions of early gerontological research point out so readily.

As long as there have been old people, there has been speculation about aging, yet in terms of systematic codification, gerontology is still a relatively young field. Its forerunners can be traced back through the centuries, though it is only in the last hundred years or so that the problems of the aged have been addressed as legitimate in their own right. Academic interest in the United States dates from within a decade or two of the enactment of Social Security, but in the few years that have since passed, research has developed at an ever accelerating pace. Social gerontology is conceptually an even more recent arrival than interest in the physical aspects of aging; many of its founders are still living and actively contributing to its nurturance. The growth and expansion of the study of aging has not been without its problems however. Theoretically and methodologically it has taken a number of years to recognize that many of what were once defined as age-related declines may have been artifacts of particular historical times or research procedures. To overcome the hurdles that have impeded gerontologists of the past, many of whose judgments came close to being canonized as inevitable truths, contemporary students of aging must take a more holistic approach. We must turn our attention not only to social and cultural variables but to the physiological and psychological factors impinging on all humans traveling the paths of growth, development and aging.

Pertinent Readings

BENGTSON, V.L. and D.A. HABER. "Sociological Approaches to Aging." In *Aging: Scientific Perspectives and Social Issues,* eds. D.S. Woodruff and J.E. Birren, pp. 70–91. New York: D. Van Nostrand Company, 1975.

BIRREN, J., and V. CLAYTON. "History of Gerontology." In *Aging: Scientific Perspectives and Social Issues,* eds. D.S. Woodruff and J.E. Birren, pp. 15–27. New York: D. Van Nostrand Company, 1975.

BROMLEY, D.B. *The Psychology of Human Ageing.* Baltimore: Penguin Books, 1966.

BUSSE, E.W., and E. PFEIFFER. "Introduction." In *Behavior and Adaptation in Late Life,* eds. E.W. Busse and E. Pfeiffer, pp. 1–9. Boston: Little, Brown and Company, 1969.

BUTLER, R.N., and M.I. LEWIS. *Aging and Mental Health.* St. Louis: C.V. Mosby Company, 1973.

CAIN, L.R. "Life Course and Social Structure." In *Handbook of Modern Sociology,* ed. R.E.L. Farris, pp. 272–309. Chicago: Rand McNally & Company, 1964.

CHEBOTAREV, D.F., and Y.K. DUPLENKO. "On the History of the Home Gerontology Movement." In *The Main Problems of Soviet Gerontology,* ed. D.F. Chebotarev, pp. 3–40. Kiev: U.S.S.R. Academy of Social Sciences, 1972.

CLARK, M., and B.G. ANDERSON. *Culture and Aging.* Springfield, Ill.: Charles C. Thomas Publisher, 1967.

DREVENSTEDT, J. "Perceptions of Onsets of Young Adulthood, Middle Age, and Old Age." *Journal of Gerontology* XXXI, 1 (1976): 53–47.

EISENSTADT, S.N. *From Generation to Generation.* New York: Free Press, 1956.

"Federal Action for Aging Began in 1930's: What Has Happened Since." *Aging* 247 (1975): 13–15.

FREEMAN, J.T. "Medical Perspectives in Aging (12–19th Century)." *The Gerontologist* V, 1, pt. II (1965): 1–24.

GRUMAN, G. "An Introduction to Literature on the History of Gerontology." *Bulletin of the History of Medicine* XXXI, 1 (1957): 78–83.

HARRIS, L., and ASSOCIATES. *The Myth and Reality of Aging in America.* Washington, D.C.: The National Council on the Aging, Inc., 1975.

KENT, D.P. "Social Policy and Program Considerations in Planning for the Aging." In *Research Planning and Action for the Elderly,* eds. D.P. Kent, R. Kastenbaum and S. Sherwood, pp. 3–19. New York: Behavioral Publications, Inc., 1972.

MADDOX, G.L. "Themes and Issues in Sociological Theories of Human Aging." *Human Development* XIII, 1 (1970): 17–27.

NEUGARTEN, B.L., and N. DATAN. "Sociological Perspectives on the Life Cycle." In *Life Span Developmental Psychology,* eds. P. Baltes and K.W. Schaie, pp. 53–69. New York: Academic Press, 1973.

NEUGARTEN, B.L., and J.W. MOORE. "The Changing Age-Status System." In *Middle Age and Aging,* ed. B.L. Neugarten, pp. 5–21. Chicago: University of Chicago Press, 1968.

NEUGARTEN, B.L., J.W. MOORE and J.C. LOWE. "Age Norms, Age Constraints and Adult Socialization." In *Middle Age and Aging,* ed. B.L. Neugarten, pp. 22–28. Chicago: University of Chicago Press, 1968.

_____. "Sociological Aspects of Aging." In *Behavior and Adaptation in Late Life,* eds. E.W. Busse and E. Pfeiffer, pp. 33–69. Boston: Little, Brown and Company, 1969.

PALMORE, E. "Attitudes Toward Aging as Shown by Humor." *The Gerontologist* XI, 3 (1971): 181–86.

PHILIBERT, M.A.J. "The Emergence of Social Gerontology. *Journal of Social Issues* XXI, 4 (1965): 4–12.

ROSOW, I. *Social Integration of the Aged.* New York: Free Press, 1967.

_____. *Socialization to Old Age.* Berkeley: University of California Press, 1974.

SCHAIE, K.W. "Age Changes and Age Differences." In *Sociology of Aging: Selected Readings,* eds. R.C. Atchley and M.M. Seltzer, pp. 50–53. Belmont, Calif.: Wadsworth Publishing Company, 1976.

SELTZER, M.M. "The Quality of Research Is Strained." *The Gerontologist* XV, 6 (1975): 503–07.

SLATER, P. "Cultural Attitudes Toward the Aged." *Geriatrics* XVIII, 4 (1963): 308–14.

SPENGLER, J.J. "The Aging and Public Policy." In *Behavior and Adaptation in Late Life,* eds. E.W. Busse and E. Pfeiffer, pp. 367–83. Boston: Little, Brown and Company, 1969.

U.S. SENATE. "Training Needs in Gerontology." 94th Cong., 1st sess. Washington, D.C.: United States Government Printing Office, 1975.

VAN GENNEP, A. *The Rites of Passage.* Chicago: University of Chicago Press, 1960.

WOODRUFF, D.S. "Introduction: Multidisciplinary Perspectives of Aging." In *Aging: Scientific Perspectives and Social Issues,* eds. D.S. Woodruff and J.E. Birren, pp. 3–14. New York: D. Van Nostrand Company, 1975.

Chapter 2

The Age-Old Question
of Old Age

It might be easily believed that aging is a singular process, occurring throughout the life span, bringing the inevitable into reality. However the notion that at birth an individual steps onto a predetermined path leading at some point to death obscures the complexity of life's processes, which differentially affect every person. As pointed out in the previous chapter, these processes transpire on all conceivable levels: cellular, biological or physiological, psychological and social. Aging is thus the combination of a variety of events that impinge universally on the life span of all of us. Many theories of aging exist, for many phenomena must be explained; nonetheless, the processes of aging can never be assumed to take place in isolation. Although our aging theories discuss general trends, it should also be recalled that individuals of the same chronological age may appear markedly different with respect to any standard for their particular age group.

The difficulties in estimating the natural effects of aging stem from the competing, often conflicting levels at which one might identify some manifestations of senescence. *Senescence* refers to the increasing vulnerability of an organism progressing through its life span. While one of the classic texts in gerontology was primarily composed of articles in the biological and medical sciences, almost one-fifth of its chapters were devoted to locating aging and the aged in their psychological, social and historical environments (Cowdry, 1942). Yet in spite of our early cognizance of the multidisciplinary character of gerontology, the fact remains that gerontologists often overlook the fundamental, dynamic interplay of the various analytic levels in their day-to-day research and writing. Any study of aging must rely on the cooperation of several disciplines for the provision of its data and conclusions. This, of course, is easier said than done. Nevertheless, it is necessary to adopt a broader focus in order to reach a better understanding of both the interrelated facets and the foundations of aging in mass societies.

Describing Age

First on our agenda is an exploration of aging patterns throughout history. This task has been facilitated by an examination of data gleaned from literary or archaeological sources and other descriptive narratives. The principal question to be addressed is, "How have aging processes and the aged individual been defined in the past?" In other words, "What changes have been noted both societally and individually in the nature and length of senescence?" It is to these and related aspects of aging that we now turn.

Though we can be assured that some proportion of every population in history lived to reach old age, the criteria used in the determination of old age are not always uniform or clear. Before proceeding to the historical discussion, it is essential to draw a distinction between two concepts — life span and life expectancy. *Life span* is the maximum length of life potentially attainable. The human life span appears to be somewhere in the neighborhood of 120–150 years (Thomlinson, 1965), and there is little evidence to suggest the maximum has changed much over recorded history. A measure of far greater interest to students of gerontology is *life ex-*

pectancy, the average number of years lived by any *cohort* of individuals born in the same period. At any given age, remaining life expectancy is determined by demographers from a mathematical model called a *life table,* which specifies the probability of surviving from one age to another. Life tables are calculated on the basis of *age-specific death rates* operative at a particular time; these in turn are based on *crude death rates* compiled for each age group in the population (Dublin et al., 1949).

There has been an enormous increase in the absolute numbers of the world population and in human longevity since 1650. Until that time population growth was only sporadic and gradual at best. The significant expansion in the absolute size of populations and the proportion of elderly in each has profound implications for every society, whether it is characterized by industrialized and urbanized, transitional, or traditional patterns of organization such as hunting and gathering or sedentary agriculture. Even so, the dimensions of the population explosion of the past few centuries cannot be fully understood unless we look at the nature of the population and of longevity in earlier societies. The chief difficulty confronting any attempts to examine historical cultures is the near absence of systematic, accurate and reliable data. Many civilizations kept no written records, and for those that did, relevant data are sparse and often contradictory. Much of what is known about humanity's early history is conjectural in nature; the missing links are forged from assumptions that seem logically consistent with information already available.

Aging in Historical Context

Very early history is thought to be characterized exclusively by small, nomadic populations, which eked out their existence by means of hunting and gathering. These societies were seldom able to accumulate any surplus, requiring large amounts of land to support small numbers of people, and consequently could not sustain any noticeable population growth. Survival was fraught with risk and danger as any natural disaster, be it drought or epidemic, carried with it the potential decimation of the group. Our prehistoric predecessors probably had a life span of 40 years, though average life expectancy was undoubtedly less. According to analyses of the skeletal remains of several African tribes, the normal length of life was approximately 18 years (Lerner, 1970). Anyone managing to live beyond 25 may well have boasted of a greater than average degree of wisdom, charm or both, perhaps rightfully so. Other calculations suggest ordinary Neanderthals roaming the earth 150,000 to 100,000 years ago might have lived into their late twenties, while 95 percent of their comrades died before age 40 (Thomlinson, 1965). It has been hypothesized that as climatic conditions stabilized, longevity improved a bit; though an estimated 90 percent of those living from 35,000 to 8000 years ago still died before age 40, with the remainder succumbing by age 50. One of the major drawbacks in utilizing data for these historical periods is that analyses of skeletal remains and burial inscriptions rarely reveal population boundaries, the nature or extent of the particular sample under examination, or the societal factors that may have affected burial practices (Dublin et al., 1949; Richardson, 1933).

Societies with sedentary occupations, agriculture and some domestication of animals first came into existence about 10,000 to 7500 years ago. Until 1000 B.C. agriculture was not well developed; that is, extensive cultivation of land had not yet taken place, and population growth continued to be severely limited by available food supplies. High mortality rates were attributable in many instances to periodic famine and frequent malnutrition, each a characteristic of unstable supplies of food. Then as now, the pressures of high death rates meant families necessarily produced more children than they desired in hopes that a few would survive into adulthood. For these reasons, very early societies exhibited not only high mortality but high fertility rates as well. Although people eventually began to settle in villages and cities, their numbers grew almost imperceptibly. The development of more sophisticated tools and the agricultural revolution gradually enabled them to form more densely populated aggregates, yet it was not until well into the industrial revolution that populations multiplied at a significant rate. In fact, it was only after the midseventeenth century that humanity's lot began to improve enough to raise in any essential way its standard of living. Since that time, assured food supply, changes in food production, better housing conditions, and more progressive medical and sanitation facilities have contributed to population growth, declining mortality rates and substantial increases in longevity. The most compatible union of these factors has been witnessed by the countries of Northern and Western Europe and of North America. For various reasons, death rates among these populations declined long before the norms encouraging high birth rates changed. Previously, high birth rates were mandatory for population survival, but following the industrial revolution large families began to present some disadvantages; children came to be viewed as consumers rather than as productive members of the family. The spread of industrialization has been closely associated with declining fertility rates and a subsequent leveling off of the population growth in Western Europe and North America.

Pre-Christian and Early Christian Aging

Extensive written documents surviving from the time of the Greeks provide valuable resources for those interested in studying their longevity. Through analysis of their precise and detailed descriptions of disease, various literary works and burial inscriptions, researchers have been able to determine probable life expectancy in Greece. Again, it should be noted the data must be interpreted cautiously, for it is often speculative in nature. Not only do many monuments fail to reveal their dates of construction, but burial customs varied by region, social class and age. Members of the military and middle classes seem to have been very attentive to personal information, while other groups left only decorative shrines or no mark at all. Similarly, perhaps due to their subordinate positions in society, the records for women, children and older people are particularly erratic. For all groups, however, it is not uncommon to find ages rounded to the nearest five or ten year interval, especially when death occurred after age 30 (Macdonell, 1913; Richardson, 1933; Durand, 1960). Despite these manifest limitations, Greek literature and epitaphs offer approximate information with which we can reconstruct a fairly reliable picture of Greek life and health.

Evidence derived from a compilation of available sources indicates an increment in life expectancy between 3000 B.C. and 1300 A.D. of roughly eight years for men and four years for women. Studies of skeletons excavated from Greek tombs suggest an increase in body size, a decline in arthritic debilities and an improvement of dental conditions took place during the same period. It should go without saying that a number of factors, such as nutrition, living conditions and medical practices, must have evolved considerably for these advances to have come about. Although gathering historical evidence from graveyards presents the researcher a project laden with adversity, sepulcher inscriptions from burial sites laid down about 400 B.C. suggest the average length of life was around 30 years. Extrapolations from these and other sources point to a survival curve approximating that shown in Figure 2.1, where less than half of the Greek population during the Hellenistic and Roman eras reached what we would today consider young adulthood.

As a consequence of the extremely high infant mortality rates throughout history, life expectancy at birth has always been somewhat less, proportionately, than during adolescence. If a person managed to survive the innumerable diseases of childhood, he or she

Figure 2.1
Survivorship curve for the Greek population of the Hellenistic and Roman periods

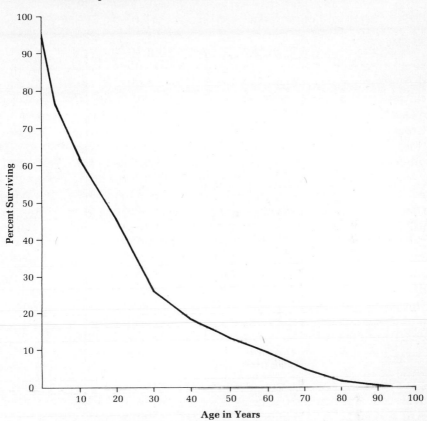

Source: J.L. Angel, "Human Biology, Health, and History in Greece from the First Settlement until Now," *American Philosophical Society Yearbook*, 1954, pp. 171–72. (Adapted from numeric data)

could expect to reach life's peak during the teenage years. Accordingly, Figure 2.2 demonstrates graphically the approximate life expectancy of a 15 year old during various historical periods. The fluctuations are due to all manner of events that have an impact on life expectancy, perhaps the most important being infectious diseases. Historical accounts are replete with descriptions of the havoc wrought by pestilence, plagues and wars on societies around the world. For illustration we need only recall the pestilences chronicled in the notes of Marcus Aurelius during the second century after Christ; Justinian's plague, which raged for more than half of the sixth century after Christ; and the Crusades of the twelfth and thirteenth centuries. Interestingly enough, the twelfth century is sometimes re-

Figure 2.2
Expectation of life at age 15 for various historical eras

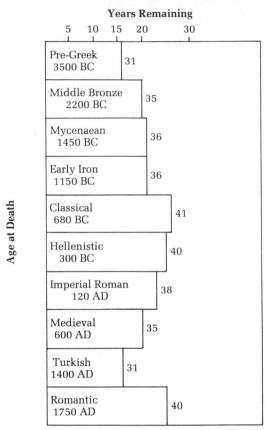

Source: J.L. Angel, "Human Biology, Health and History in Greece from the First Settlement until Now," *American Philosophical Society Yearbook*, 1954, p. 171.

ferred to as the "savage twelfth," not because of the wars waged, but on account of the deathly plagues that swept over Europe. More lives were claimed by disease than by the combined forces of the human combatants. Indeed, pestilence rendered life so precarious in the Middle Ages that "soul and body" poems, depicting the grisliness of slow death, were commonplace. These poems, with their graphic descriptions of putrefactive processes, survive as some of the most insightful annals of an era when death was never far removed.

Like their earlier Greek counterparts, the ruins of Roman burial sites prove useful in the collection of mortality estimates, especially for males. Roman inscriptions are similarly uninformative about the deaths of children, women and old people in all but the higher social classes. As with the Greeks, ages from Roman monuments are prone to slight exaggeration since they too were recorded in multiples of five. Following the death of Christ, life expectancy remained rather low for the next 400 years or so. The results of one study indicate the citizens of Rome experienced a shorter life expectancy on the average than their provincial brethren (Nordberg, 1963). Approximate longevity for residents of Rome and three of the provinces is presented in Table 2.1. The colonists in Africa apparently far outlived the other groups, possibly a consequence of a self-selecting process — that is, only the hardiest migrated to the strenuous agricultural outposts in northern Africa. Assuming the data for Rome are accurate, the high mortality rates, stemming in part from problems with sanitation and food supplies, paralleled those reported for urban areas during the Middle Ages and early industrial periods in Europe.

Examination of early Egyptian mummies furnishes additional support for the conclusions regarding Roman life expectancy. However, since children and lower class adults were seldom given this form of burial, there is once again a dearth of information upon which to base generalizations about their life expectancy. Nonetheless, we do have a fairly complete picture of longevity for upper class adults. At birth a male could expect roughly 22 years of life, but if he survived infancy to reach five or so, at least another 25 or 26 years stretched ahead of him. The Egyptian man who attained age 25 would be likely to live to the ripe old age of 48, give or take a few years. Further corroboration is lent to these figures by anthropological reports of modern day aboriginal tribes, provided we are willing to grant their comparability with ancient Greek, Roman or Egyptian societies (Cook, 1947).

Table 2.1

Expectation of Life in Years at Selected Ages for Three Roman Areas, 1–400 A.D.

AGE	ROME		HISPANIA AND LUSITANIA		AFRICA	
	MALE	FEMALE	MALE	FEMALE	MALE	FEMALE
Birth	22	21	40	34	48	46
5	22	19	36	30	45	43
20	20	14	26	21	36	33
40	18	15	21	17	28	26

Note: All values approximate; data converted from graphic representation.

Source: W.R. Macdonell, "On the Expectation of Life in Ancient Rome, and in the Provinces of Hispania and Lusitania, and Africa," *Biometrika* IX (1913): 370, 373, 376.

Despite inconclusive evidence about life expectancy, several distinct themes emerge from Greek literature regarding old age. Aristotle, in the second book of his *Treatise on Rhetoric*, offers a classic condemnation of later life. He presents youth and old age as opposite extremes, youth being a time of excess, old age a time of overreactive conservatism and small-mindedness. Of the young, Aristotle has this to say:

And all their errors are on the side of excess and too great earnestness . . . for the young carry everything to an excess . . . and, in their trespasses, they trespass on the side of wantonness, and not of malice. They are likewise prone to pity . . . for they measure others by the standard of their own guiltlessness. [Bk. II, ch. XII]

In describing the curse of the elderly, or euphemistically, "those advanced in life," Aristotle articulates themes all too apparent in much of today's literature and drama touching on the question of old age. Characteristically, he remarks, the elderly err

. . . in everything more on the side of defect than they ought. And they always "*suppose*," but never "*know*" certainly; and questioning everything, they always subjoin a "*perhaps*," or a "*possibly*." And they talk of everything in this undecisive tone, asserting nothing decisively . . . moreover they are apt to be suspicious from distrust, and they are distrustful from their experience. And on this account they neither love nor hate with great earnestness . . . they both love as though about to hate, and hate as though about to love . . . men of this age appear to be naturally temperate, for both their desires have relaxed, and they are enslaved to gain. And they live more by calculation than by moral feeling; for calculation is of expediency, but moral feeling is of virtue. [Bk. II, ch. XIII]

Aristotle advises his readers to bear these traits in mind when evaluating men for public office. Though he recognizes the possibility of great virtue among the elderly, he warns, in *Politics*: "That judges of important causes should hold office for life is a disputable thing, for the mind grows old as well as the body" (Bk. II, ch. IX).

Perhaps the best-known competing theme appears in the writings of Cicero. It is not old age per se that is a cause of all the reprehensible qualities detailed by Aristotle, but rather one's character.

If one is lacking in valuable personal qualities, it holds true at earlier as well as later ages. It may only be that such shortcomings are revealed more clearly in one's later years. In Cicero's (1923) view, certain facets of an individual's character, such as intellectual or moral qualities, are actually enhanced by age. With time, prudence cannot help but replace brashness. Yet he, too, likens advancing years to a disease that needs to be combatted and resisted. The most favorable qualities of age stem from the transformation of personal attributes.

> It is not by muscle, speed, or physical dexterity that great things are achieved, but by reflection, force of character, and judgment; in these qualities old age is usually not only not poorer, but is even richer . . . . the crowning glory of old age is influence . . . . when the preceding part of life has been nobly spent, old age gathers the fruits of influence at the last.[VI.17, XVII.61, XVIII.62]

Several lesser Greek authors reiterate Cicero's portrayal of the heady impetuousness of youth tempered by old age which, if an elder was wise and gracious, allows a greater influence upon social affairs. However, the occasional accolades do not dim the prevailing negative temperament ascribed to old age by the majority of writers. A fairly typical view emerges from the Greek legend of Tithonus, a man who had been blessed with eternal life by the God Zeus as a favor to Aurora, Tithonus' lover. Unfortunately, Aurora neglected to include in her request that Tithonus also be given perpetual youth; consequently, he was damned to live forever as an increasingly enfeebled old man. Writing in 20 B.C. Horace again echoed such descriptions of old age. He encapsulates and underscores the dominant view in this caricature of an old man, reproving "his desire for gain, his miserliness, his lack of energy, his greediness for longer life, his quarrelsomeness, his praise of good old days when he was a boy, and his condemnation of the younger generation" (Coffman, 1934).

Middle Ages and the Renaissance

By the thirteenth century, estimates of male life expectancy at birth in England range from a high of 35.3 years to a low of approximately 33 years in the second quarter of the fourteenth century (Russell, 1948). However, as was the case with the historical documents previously considered, generally only the upper social classes are represented in the records. Another factor to be taken into account is that, due to high childhood mortality, the records usually available include only those who managed to survive childhood. Nevertheless, several studies of medieval population trends, including mortality rates, have been carried out. Such diverse resources as family archives, official registers and legal documents dealing with inheritance have yielded valuable information about both the social and health situations of the elderly. The contemporary literature also provides a glimpse of the most pervasive themes on aging. An examination of the secular peerage from 1350 to 1500 reveals that at least one-fifth of every 25 year cohort born after 1350 died by violence, with slightly less than one-quarter of those who actively engaged in battle living to celebrate age 50. By comparison, the remaining nobles, whose deaths were attributed to natural causes, fared considerably better; over half lived beyond age 50. These rates are generally inflated above the norms likely to be representative of the general populace, since to have been included on the rolls, peers must have reached age 21. Approximate life expectancies may be calculated for each successive decade: life expectancy was estimated to be 29.3 years at age 20, 23.8 at age 30, and to reach nearly 10 years for those who survived to age 60 (Rosenthal, 1973). In addition, persons of noble birth nearly always experienced greater longevity, due in part to better food, living conditions and personal health maintenance. Not to be dismissed is the fact that, unlike the rest of society, the aristocracy presumably had the mobility to flee if contagion or wars should suddenly threaten. They also had the resources to escape periodic malnutrition, the effects of inclement weather and the chronic problems of insufficient heating or inadequate clothing.

Throughout history we see repeatedly the complex interplay between longevity and societal factors ranging from legal statutes to education and religion. As pointed out above, the law specified that those individuals who might be elevated to the peerage must be 21 years of age. This custom is linked to high fertility among many eligible families, since without a son who survived adolescence, the title together with all its privileges had to be passed to collateral relatives. Losing the peerage entailed not simply a loss of status, but, of at least equal significance, of the accoutrements so important for living a comfortable and long life. Due to the frequent and widespread mortality in preindustrial England, large extended families may not have been as common as we normally assume. Although estimates vary, roughly half of the people did live in households of six or more members, while the remainder lived in smaller households (Laslett, 1969). In all likelihood, many of the religious practices characteristic of the era arose in order to assist the multitudes in their search for the strength with which to rationalize the high rates of child mortality and to provide solace for the inexorable experience of death in every family.

These statistics begin to reflect a brighter picture as humanity experienced continuing gains in longevity after the Renaissance. Mortality among the 50–70 year old population has declined by half in the modern era (Peller, 1948). Even granting mortality rates for the aristocratic classes are inevitably lower than for the population as a whole, nonetheless Table 2.2 portends patterns that will gradually affect the rest of the society. The proportion of people dying before age 50 has steadily decreased in recent centuries, while the expectation of life for those already 50 years old has improved at a corresponding rate over the years. Upper class males who were 50 years old in the sixteenth century might expect to live 12.0 years longer to age 62; by the nineteenth century their descendants could anticipate an additional 18.7 years of life after age 50. Life expectancy for women has shown a similar upswing; the 14.6 years remaining for 50 year old females in the sixteenth century increased to 21 years by the nineteenth. Interestingly enough, however, the declining mortality rates over the past several centuries have been observed primarily in the early years of life; mortality has been cut by as much as 90 percent for ages under 15 years, 85 percent for those under 44 years, yet only 35 percent for the ages above 65 (Bogue, 1969). Infant and child mortality had traditionally been extremely high as a result of medical techniques inadequate for dealing with infectious diseases. The dramatic reductions in fatalities beginning shortly after the industrial era occurred as a consequence of the inroads against these, rather than the degenerative diseases to which the aged succumbed. As will be seen in Chapter Seven, the situation today is not markedly different. The elderly continue to die as a result of chronic conditions not yet within the reach of advanced medical techniques. In the sixteenth and seventeenth centuries the risk of dying increased greatly from decade to decade of one's life; however, from the seventeenth century onward life chances began to improve throughout the middle years, even for women in their childbearing years.

Table 2.2
Percentage of Individuals Dying Between the Ages of 50–70 in the European Ruling Classes

CENTURY	MALE	FEMALE
16th	82.5	69.1
17th	72.4	70.7
18th	65.9	56.3
19th	56.1	45.7

Source: S. Peller, "Mortality, Past and Future," *Population Studies* 1, 4 (1948): 439.

It is often assumed that the European colonists who set out for distant corners of the earth were hardy but short-lived pioneers. An interesting challenge to this assumption has been offered by recent research focused on the Plymouth Colony in America. The figures on longevity from 600 residents of the seventeenth century settlement presented in Table 2.3 disclose a quite considerable life expectancy for men reaching their twenty-first birthday. At age 21 a man might expect to live to 69.2 years, nearly equivalent to twentieth century expectations. A woman could look forward to 62.4 years of life, unusually high considering the hazards attendant on childbirth during the sixteenth and seventeenth centuries. Of those in the Plymouth sample, a third of the women and one-tenth of the men died between the ages of 20 and 50. Subsequent investigations of other colonies in Massachusetts lend some support to the notion that the pilgrims were indeed long-lived (Greven, 1966). Despite such an improvement in life chances, the endless process of migration and expansion continued to take a toll on both social structures and personal relationships, especially family ties. That the elderly in the colonies continued to anguish over their prospects is evident from the testamentary dispositions in the wills that have come to light during later research. Almost without exception, stipulations were made requiring the heirs to care for their elderly benefactors or imposing similar constraints on the legatees.

As mentioned in Chapter One, implicit in every society's age stratification system is the realization that age is a basic determinant of what individuals can and should do. It is often the case that these attitudes and norms are clearly stated in the popular literature of an era, a pattern quite evident during the later Renaissance and Elizabethan periods in England. The descriptions of old age by Aris-

Table 2.3

Average Life Expectancy and Percentage Dying During Subsequent Decade for Specified Ages in Plymouth Colony

AGE	MALE	(PERCENT DECEASED)	FEMALE	(PERCENT DECEASED)
21	48.2	(1.6)	41.4	(5.9)
30	40.0	(3.6)	34.7	(12.0)
40	31.2	(7.8)	29.7	(12.0)
50	23.7	(10.2)	23.4	(10.9)
60	16.3	(18.0)	16.8	(14.9)
70	9.9	(30.5)	10.7	(20.7)
80	5.1	(22.4)	6.7	(16.0)
90+	—	(5.9)	—	(7.6)

Source: John Demos, "Notes on Life in Plymouth Colony," *The William and Mary Quarterly* XXII, 2 (1965): 271.

totle and Horace created a strong tradition from which Renaissance writers drew. Pope Innocent III, writing early in the thirteenth century, dramatically enlarges upon Horace's themes in his depiction of old age. Old men are "easily provoked, stingy and avaricious, sullen and quarrelsome, quick to talk, slow to hear, but not slow in wrath, praising former times, despising the moderns, censuring the present, commending the past" (Coffman, 1934). Elizabethan writers of sixteenth century England were subtly conditioned by the same heritage. Combining the characteristics so long associated with youth and old age with the ancient Hippocratic notion of somatic humors then of scientific currency, they systematically identified the particular humor distinguishing each period of life. With a good deal of exactness, Elizabethan medical science described four humors or fluids which, if balanced, were presumed to be the source of perfect health. Youth, which lasted until age 25, was associated with the warm phlegmatic humor in childhood, shading into the sanguine humor of young adulthood. Middle age, perhaps lasting until 50, was linked to a choleric humor, viewed as the probable source of the dysphoria of the middle years. Finally, old age, begun in choleric humor, became in one's dotage a cold melancholic state (Sims, 1943). Appropriate remedies for the physical symptoms of each age were often elaborated in discussions of the four humors. In spite of this additional, allegedly novel, "scientific" conception, the traits associated with each period of life were merely restatements of the themes articulated during earlier eras.

While other examples exist, Shakespeare's plays provide brilliant illustrations of the conventional attitudes of his time toward all subjects, age included. Both Shakespeare and his contemporaries emphasized in their writings the deterioration of physical prowess among the aged. Advancing age was marked by the loss of teeth, hearing and virility; the whitening of hair; the presence of wrinkles, offensive odor, runny nose and eyes, and dimness of sight. If these were not enough, the elderly often experienced the dulling of mental powers. Shakespeare (1959) speaks explicitly of the ages of man in *As You Like It*. The passage in the second act beginning "all the world's a stage . . ." depicts the maladies of age. Says Jacques,

> . . . The sixth age shifts
> Into the lean and slippered pantaloon,
> With spectacles on nose and pouch on side,
> His youthful hose, well saved, a world too wide
> For his shrunk shank, and his big manly voice,
> Turning again toward childish treble, pipes

And whistles in his sound. Last scene of all,
That ends this strange eventful history,
Is second childishness, and mere oblivion,
Sans teeth, sans eyes, sans taste, sans everything. [2.7.160–61]

While the Elizabethans shared a tradition of negative views toward the elderly, they nonetheless recognized old age as one among many afflictions that could affect human behavior. Old age was seen as but a single defect in one's character. This view is radically altered by the stylized Restoration comedy of manners (1660–1700). Age is cast as one of the few certain determinants for assessing a player's role; players were either young or old, there was no middle ground. Although denying one's age becomes the subject of ridicule, there is yet no redeeming grace to be found in the further reaches of life. Women were old after 30, men nearly over the hill. The "Struldbrugs" encountered by Gulliver in his travels are reminiscent of the myth of Tithonus; they never die, though they suffer the calumnies of declining years. Sir Francis Bacon, introduced in Chapter One, certainly a gerontologist by inclination if not by training, delineates the qualities intrinsic to both youth and age. In the Aristotelian tradition, Bacon (1883) avers, "men of age object too much, consult too long, adventure too little, repent too soon, and seldom drive business home to the full period, but content themselves with a mediocrity of success . . . [yet] age doth profit rather in the powers of understanding, than in the virtues of the will and affections."

The negative qualities of old age do transcend the virtues; however, "a young man is affected with a laudable emulation, an old man with a malignant envy . . . a young man is given to liberality and beneficence, and humanity; an old man to covetousness, wisdom for his own self, and seeking his own ends" (Strong, 1952).

A contrasting view was published late in the sixteenth century by one of the few stalwarts of Cicero's persuasion. Gabriele Paleotti picks up the standard unfurled by Cicero to conclude "wisdom, maturity and a cooling down of certain emotional currents give old age its peculiar form of creativeness unobtainable at other life periods" (Stern and Cassirer, 1946). Obviously not all literature is of a singular theme. Though many authors were troubled by questions of mortality, their concern was often manifested through a consideration of the prevailing quality of life. One need only think of the works of such writers as Boccaccio, Victor Hugo, Charles Dickens and Daniel Defoe to quickly appreciate the wealth of information about health, disease and epidemics that has been passed down through our literature. Many theories abound in society relating the causes and cures of disease. Cicero articulated the prominent Greek view that old age was itself a disease to be ardently battled. Similarly, the epidemics which periodically raged across Europe skyrocketed mortality rates and spurred a great deal of literary reflection about death and aging. From a variety of sources we learn that life in urban areas was subject to poor working, living and health conditions. Hardship was no stranger to the residents of the period. Popular literature and scientific journals alike retold the story of Thomas Parr, a rural peasant known far and wide for his longevity, reputed to be 152 years old at the time of his death. It seems old Parr had been invited to London to be presented to the court of Charles I, whereupon he promptly died. No less a physician than William Harvey, father of anatomical studies, conducted the autopsy and attributed Parr's death to the unaccustomed variety of food and drink and to the city's foul air, proof positive for zealous critics that cities were unhealthy places in which to live (Zeman, 1949).

The Modern Era

With the rise of science during the later Renaissance and early Enlightenment, a greater emphasis on record keeping brought about a closer scrutiny of life expectancy. The well-known English astronomer Halley constructed what is believed to be the first scientific life table. Halley's careful study of the actuarial records compiled by the industrial city of Breslaw in southern Poland revealed normal life expectancy for late seventeenth century residents to be somewhat more than 33 years. Demographic investigations of other European cities supported Halley's findings, demonstrating the similarity of longevity patterns across the continent. By the turn of the twentieth century, careful recording of vital statistics disclosed that ten or more years had been added to general life expectancy. At the brink of the current century Swedish males enjoyed the greatest life expectancy at birth, nearly 51 years.

Prolongation of life was fostered in large measure by the complex changes accompanying the industrial revolution. Yet, frequent condemnations of early industrial societies are levied because of their assumed negative contributions to individual mortality. No doubt evidence can be adduced to support both positions, since in either case urbanization played an influential role in the higher death rates of industrial areas (Wrigley, 1969). It is true that contagion raged in densely populated urban slum areas just as had occurred prior to the presence of factories. However, in rural areas and smaller towns, even those undergoing rapid industrialization, mortality statistics were appreciably lower (Dubos, 1959). In keeping with our supposition about the quality of life, Figures 2.3 and 2.4 reveal that old Genevan families consistently fared better than their aristocratic peers elsewhere in Europe. Throughout modern history, citizens of Switzerland have experienced a general standard of living unmatched by those of her neighbors. The figures also illustrate the steady upward trend in life expectancy for all aristocratic families from 1550 to 1900. As we shall see in the following chapter, the increase was much less rapid in those countries not yet undergoing industrialization.

Figure 2.3

Expectation of life at age 20 for European aristocratic males between 1550 and 1900

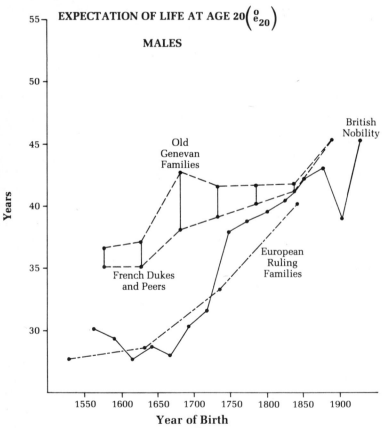

Source: T.H. Hollingsworth, "The Demography of the British Peerage," *Population Studies*, Supplement, XVIII, 2 (1965): 68.

It has become something of a cliche in gerontological literature, as well as in our daily conversation, to note that the elderly were better off before industrialization and by comparison have a rather pathetic lot today. Developmental models of the transformation of primitive societies to stable agricultural and ultimately industrial societies involve the notion that the aged are accorded maximum prestige during the agricultural phase. For it is at this stage that the elders exercise their greatest control over younger men through their possession of wisdom, skills and, more importantly, property rights (Slater, 1964). When societies begin to expand their industrial base at the expense of the agricultural domain, the elderly are presumed to suffer a loss of prestige. With the rise of industrial production,

Figure 2.4

Expectation of life at age 20 for European aristocratic females between 1550 and 1900

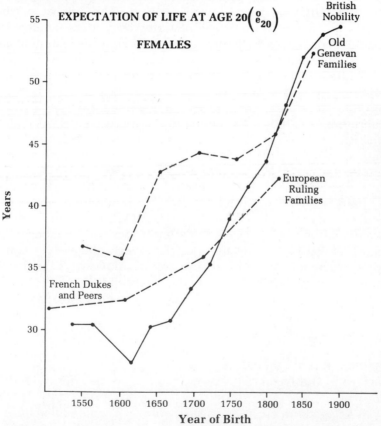

Source: T.H. Hollingsworth, "The Demography of the British Peerage," *Population Studies,* Supplement, XVIII, 2 (1965): 68.

workers begin to produce goods with which they are not able to identify. Educational functions are gradually removed from familial or apprentice relationships to a formal, structured sector of society. The nature of wealth changes from land or tangible property to other intangible forms, and the heightened emphasis on productivity leads to a degradation of the status accorded older, supposedly slower, workers. Despite these trends, a number of researchers have called attention to the pervasive gerontocratical leanings of the maturing political arena, with its corresponding age-graded seniority systems. When civic and religious leaders placed a positive value on age as a criterion for higher echelon positions, the role of age as a scientific category was likewise accentuated. It quickly becomes apparent in studying the treatment of the elderly through history that societal reactions to old age reflect fluctuations in mortality and longevity. For example, Latin affixed seven descriptive labels to the stages of life, though by the time French became the more popular language, only three different names were utilized. The impact of these changes is evident in the usage of terms by writers ranging from Aristotle to de Beauvoir; their evaluation of later life is undoubtedly conditioned in each case by language and social order.

While it is indeed the case that many of the supportive aspects of the preindustrial world are lacking in today's society, it is quite likely the ambivalent position of older people today predates the modern era. It is only when humanity is not preoccupied with the necessities of survival that a humane treatment of nonproductive members can be realized. In their exhaustive review of historical attitudes toward old age, Kastenbaum and Ross (1975) depict the conflicting themes that have recurred throughout time. They suggest the approach-avoidance dilemma many attribute to modern society is in fact common to nearly all societies for which we have records. In commenting on the negative overtones ascribed to old age, these authors assert the heterogeneity of the elderly themselves and the limited resources shared by all age groups, along with the discrepancy between the realities of the later years and the ideal of eternal youth or early death, may be partially responsible for what appears to be a universal orientation.

Socioeconomic Factors and the Prestige of the Aged

Many gerontologists and anthropologists contend that throughout history the safest haven for the aged has been the family (Simmons, 1945). Though the relationship between older people and their families will constitute much of the discussion in Chapter Ten, mention must be made at this point of several important historical themes. Among the many factors having a significant influence on family relationships is the nature of the economic forces operative within a society. That is, the model of economic organization in a society sets predictable limits on the types of families found within its boundaries. Three categories of economic organization are often delineated to distinguish among family types, namely, nomadic, agricultural and industrial. Research has shown that individual existence in hunting and gathering societies is precarious and marginal; thus, the elderly may be sacrificed or may ask to be sacrificed to insure the survival of the group. Even so, the aged are the source of knowledge of the society's cultural heritage due to their greater familiarity with cultural traditions and to the frequent lack of written records. Their memories serve as depositories of information essential for the well-being of the group; consequently, their status is unquestioned as they wield control over the distribution of knowledge. Since much of the information in such societies takes on a sacred and traditional aura predicated on ritualized exchange, the elderly possessing the requisite knowledge are treated in a like manner. Yet because the transfer of knowledge is dependent on individual memories, a great deal of historical fact about other, more remote times is jeopardized as temporal proximity is lost. When this happens over an extended period, oral transmission of information may ultimately lead to both social and cultural isolation.

It was not simply older men with a great deal of valued social knowledge who were revered in early social orders. Among hunting and gathering societies the necessity for self-sufficient females to protect hearth and offspring while the male members of the group secured food elsewhere provided aged females an element of prestige not always accorded them in more settled cultures. Again, the reasons lie with the wisdom learned over a lifetime of dealing with the exigencies of a harsh environment. Nonetheless, life was precarious in all its aspects. By their very nature however, agricultural societies are more stable in every respect, from their territorial to their social organization; accordingly, they often develop strict traditions that define the rules of inheritance, power, and the rights and responsibilities of family members. In a society where stratification derives from an ability to work the land and where property rights are inherited and immutable, children become an important source of security for older people in general (Blood, 1972). The concentration of power in agricultural societies that do have fixed property rights and permanent residence usually lies in the hands of the older men of the community. Their authority is heeded because they have the knowledge necessary to reap the fruits of the land, not to mention the fact that they retain title to property throughout their own lifetimes (Slater, 1964). Aged men appear to have the most prestige in the patriarchal families of herding or agricultural societies. Despite this, as the situation of aged parents in classical Greece so clearly points out, the balance was delicate, with sons often forcing their fathers to retire from active participation in family affairs (Lacey, 1968).

The generally higher esteem accorded the elderly in agricultural societies is also supported by observations of the role of the aged in traditional China. Advancing age for the Chinese was sweetened with the promise of prestige and authority. Elders were assured of care by other family members and of a sense of immortality through close interaction with one's descendants. Their greater years of experience brought wisdom in the sphere of interpersonal relationships, and if value is placed on "tranquility, moderation, and simplicity," the aged had a head start in the cultivation of such attributes (Chandler, 1949). Similar attitudes toward old age were held in Japan. The precepts of Confucianism accentuate reverence, support and deference for parents and elders. Prior to Western influences China, Japan and much of the Orient shared a rather different conception of time, where the cyclical predominates over the linear, and this possibly added to the greater ease with which society accepted old age. While these themes may still be apparent in modern Japan, there has been a conflicting reaction to the aged throughout the last several centuries. As familiar as the ambivalence of classical Greek conceptions of age is to the West, is the Japanese *Obasute* theme which stands in contrast to Confucian tenets. Roughly translated *Obasute* refers to "discarding granny," a reflection of the pressures accompanying the precarious existence of nomadic tribes that prompted them to devalue their dependent aged. The Confucian themes have persevered, though reality has seldom been as glorious as we would have it in ancient Japanese society (Plath, 1972).

The very stability that tended to be supportive of an extended family system and the positive qualities accorded the elderly in historical China or Japan are not found in the modern Western world. Here societies place greater emphasis on competition, change and mobility. While the roles to be played by the aged are largely altered in the face of rapid industrialization and urbanization, it is only in industrialized countries that the possibility of more egalitarian family relationships is realized. In advanced industrial societies, the family loses much of its economic importance as its members must turn outside for functional roles in the larger community. With increasing yet differential longevity, widowhood becomes a basic reality shared by many women in the contemporary world. Widowhood denotes the termination of one of a woman's basic roles, at least traditionally. Those women currently among the elderly who find themselves widowed late in life are unlikely to remarry because of both social pressures and the decreasing availability of eligible men. It has occasionally been suggested that much of the social isolation of today's older people could be avoided if a polygynous marriage arrangement for the elderly were positively sanctioned by society (Reiss, 1971). This seems highly improbable, however, since it would involve a reversal of norms extant throughout the majority of an individual's productive life.

Summary

Indeed, the most accurate characterization of population growth in the modern era is an explosion. Until 1650 societies experienced sporadic, at best gradual, population expansion. Those conditions inimical to the aggregation of people contributed likewise to foreshorten life expectancies. A combination of uncontrollable infectious diseases, poor nutrition and the unreliability of available food supplies, and inadequate health and medical knowledge effectively operated to suppress even the potential for attaining a ripe old age among most peoples. The normal duration of life hovered around 35 years until after the Middle Ages, though this figure must be offered hesitantly due to the often incomplete and speculative data. Life chances among the upper classes provide a partial glimpse of the patterns of fertility and morality found later among the rest of society. It is perhaps surprising in light of the brevity of life that prevailing literary references to old age echo Aristotle's critique of the conservativeness and calculating greed of old men. Cicero is one of the few who have maintained that old age per se is not indisputably linked to particular character flaws. Rather, if anything, a good man in his aging will achieve a measure of wisdom, tolerance, grace and influence rarely found in youth. Interestingly, the dominant imagery of old age appropriated from the past by lay people and scientists alike is closer to the view of Aristotle than to Cicero.

The Renaissance, heralding the inauguration of the modern era in Europe, also marks the beginning of vast changes in population structure. The rise of science and the spread of industrialization were to revolutionize societies. The earliest manifestation of the new order was a diminishing death rate. Since birth rates declined much more gradually, populations rapidly expanded. The initial beneficiaries of lower mortality rates were children and women of childbearing age; hence, some years elapsed before a significant proportion of the population attained what we now regard as old age. The combination of lowered death and birth rates brought about the eventual aging of entire populations in industrialized societies. As will be seen in the following chapter, those nations not touched by the industrial revolution exhibit strikingly different population structures. Longevity in the modern world is a direct consequence of the scientific and technological advances of the past two centuries. In conclusion, this passage from Emerson (1886) on the illusion of time and old age seems a befitting way to introduce a discussion of the status of the elderly in twentieth century mass society.

> Nature lends herself to these illusions, and adds dim sight, deafness, cracked voice, snowy hair, short memory and sleep. These also are masks, and all is not age that wears them. . . . Nature is full of freaks, and now puts an old head on young shoulders, and then a young heart beating under four score winters . . . . Youth is everywhere in place. Age, like woman, requires fit surroundings. Age is comely in coaches, in churches, in chairs of state and ceremony, in council-chambers, in courts of justice and historical societies. Age is becoming in the country.

Pertinent Readings

ANGEL J.L. "The Length of Life in Ancient Greece." *Journal of Gerontology* II, 1(1947): 18–24.

ARIES, P. *Centuries of Childhood: A Social History of Family Life*. Trans. Robert Baldick. New York: Alfred A. Knopf, 1962.

ARISTOTLE. *Treatise on Rhetoric*. Trans. Theodore Buckley. London: George Bell and Sons, 1883.

———. *Politics*. Trans. Benjamin Jowett. New York: The Modern Library, 1942.

BACON, F. "Of Youth and Age." In *The Essays Or, Counsels, Civil and Moral*. London: The Chesterfield Society, 1883.

BLOOD, R.O. *The Family*. New York: The Free Press, 1972.

BOGUE, D.J. *Principles of Demography*. New York: Wiley, 1969.

CHANDLER, A.R. "Aristotle on Mental Aging." *Journal of Gerontology* III, 3 (1948):220–23.

———. "The Traditional Chinese Attitude towards Old Age." *Journal of Gerontology*, IV, 3, (1949): 239–44.

CICERO, De Senectute, De Amicitia, De Divinatione. Trans. William Armistead Falconer. London: William Heinemann, 1923.

COFFMAN, G.R. "Old Age from Horace to Chaucer, Some Literary Affinities and Adventures of an Idea." *Speculum* IX (1934): 249–77.

COOK, S.F. "Survivorship in Aboriginal Populations." *Human Biology* XIX, 2 (1947): 83–89.

COWDRY, E.V., ed. *Problems of Ageing: Biological and Medical Aspects.* 2nd ed. Baltimore: The Williams & Wilkins Company, 1942.

COX, E.H. "Shakespeare and Some Conventions of Old Age." *Studies in Philology* XXXIX (1942): 36–46.

deBEAUVOIR, S. *The Coming of Age.* Trans. Patrick O'Brian. New York: Warner Paperback Books, Inc., 1973.

DUBLIN, L.I., A.J. LOTKA and M. SPIEGELMAN. *Length of Life: A Study of the Life Table.* Rev. ed. New York: Ronald Press Co., 1949.

DUBOS, R. *Mirage of Health: Utopias, Progress, and Biological Change.* Garden City, N.Y.: Anchor-Doubleday and Co., 1959.

DURAND, J.D. "Mortality Estimates from Roman Tombstone Inscriptions." *American Journal of Sociology* LXV, 4 (1960):365–73.

EMERSON, R.W. "Old Age." In *Society and Solitude: Twelve Chapters.* Boston: Houghton, Mifflin and Co., 1886.

GREVEN, P.J., JR. "Family Structure in Seventeenth-Century Andover, Massachusetts." *The William and Mary Quarterly* XXIII, 2 (1966): 234–56.

HOLLINGSWORTH, T.H. "The Demography of the British Peerage." *Population Studies,* Supplement, XVIII, 2 (1965): iv–108.

KASTENBAUM, R., and B. ROSS. "Historical Perspectives on Care." In *Modern Perspectives in the Psychiatry of Old Age,* ed. J.G. Howells, pp. 421–49. New York: Brunner/Mazel, Inc., 1975.

LACEY, W.K. *The Family in Classical Greece.* Ithaca, N.Y.: Cornell University Press, 1968.

LASLETT, P. "Size and Structure of the Household in England Over Three Centuries." *Population Studies* XXIII, 2 (1969): 199–223.

LERNER, M. "When, Why and Where People Die." In *The Dying Patient,* eds. O.G. Brim Jr., H.E. Freeman, S. Levine and N.A. Scotch, pp. 5–29. New York: Russell Sage Foundation, 1970.

MACDONELL, W.R. "On the Expectation of Life in Ancient Rome, and in the Provinces of Hispania and Lusitania, and Africa." *Biometrika* IX (1913): 366–77.

MIGNON, E. *Crabbed Age and Youth: The Old Men and Women in the Restoration Comedy of Manners.* Durham, N.C.: Duke University Press, 1947.

NORDBERG, H. "Biometrical Notes: The Information on Ancient Christian Inscriptions From Rome Concerning the Duration of Life and the Dates of Birth and Death." *Acta Instituti Romani Finlandiae* II, 2 (1963).

PEARSON, K. "On the Change in Expectation of Life in Man during a Period of circa 2000 Years." *Biometrika* 1 (1901): 261–64.

PELLER, S. "Studies on Mortality Since the Renaissance." *Bulletin of History of Medicine* XIII (1943): 427–61.

____. "Mortality, Past and Future." *Population Studies* I, 4(1948): 405–56.

PLATH, D.W. "Japan: The After Years." In *Aging and Modernization*, eds. D.O. Cowgill and L.D. Holmes, pp. 133–50. New York: Appleton-Century-Crofts, 1972.

PRESS, I., and M. McKOOL, JR. "Social Structure and Status of the Aged: Toward Some Valid Cross-Cultural Generalizations." *Aging and Human Development* III, 4 (1972): 297–306.

REISS, I.L. *The Family System in America.* New York: Holt, Rinehart and Winston, 1971.

RICHARDSON, B.E. *Old Age Among the Ancient Greeks: The Greek Portrayal of Old Age in Literature, Art, and Inscriptions.* Baltimore: The Johns Hopkins Press, 1933.

ROSENTHAL, J.T. "Mediaevel Longevity and the Secular Peerage, 1350–1500." *Population Studies* XXVII, 2 (1973): 287–93.

RUSSELL, J.C. *British Medieval Population.* Albuquerque: University of New Mexico Press, 1948.

SHAKESPEARE, W. *As You Like It,* ed. R.M. Sargent. Baltimore: Penguin Books, 1959.

SIMMONS, L.W. *The Role of the Aged in Primitive Society.* New Haven: Yale University Press, 1945.

SIMS, R.E. "The Green Old Age of Falstaff." *Bulletin of the History of Medicine* XIII (1943): 144–57.

SLATER, P.E. "Cross-cultural Views of the Aged." in *New Thoughts on Old Age,* ed. R. Kastenbaum, pp. 229–36. New York: Springer Publishing Co., Inc., 1964.

STERN, K., and T. CASSIRER "A Gerontological Treatise of the Renaissance: 'De Bono Senectutis' by Gabriele Paleotti (1522–1597)." *American Journal of Psychiatry* CII, 6 (1946): 770–73.

STRONG, L.C. "Observations on Gerontology in the Seventeenth Century." *Journal of Gerontology* VII, 4 (1952): 618–19.

THOMLINSON, R. *Population Dynamics: Causes and Consequences of World Demographic Change.* New York: Random House, 1965.

WRIGLEY, E.A. *Population and History.* New York: McGraw-Hill Book Co., 1969.

ZEMAN, F.D. "Thomas Parr: The Old, Old, Very Old Man." *Journal of Gerontology* IV, 2 (1949): 160–61.

Chapter 3

Aging in Advanced
Industrialized Societies

As described earlier, significant improvements in human longevity did not take place until after the midseventeenth century; before that time, extension of life expectancy was slight indeed. The gradual increments eventually culminated in an unparalleled rise in life expectancy during the first 60 years of the twentieth century. The increase was of such magnitude in Western industrialized countries that individuals could expect to live 20 years longer if they were born in 1960 rather than in 1900. At the present time this rate appears to have slowed or stabilized, and future predictions suggest this will remain the case. To know whether or not this is a likely possibility requires a general overview of the dynamics of population changes.

The appreciable increase in longevity has been most noticeable among citizens of Western European nations, as well as in the United States. Several countries currently experience a more advantageous position in terms of life expectancy than the United States, among them France, Australia, Denmark, the Netherlands, New Zealand, Canada, Norway and Sweden. Since this rate of improvement has not occurred uniformly throughout the world, many Third World populations exhibit markedly lower life expectancies than their European counterparts. For example, during the period 1960–1970, life expectancy in advanced industrialized countries averaged over 65 years, while males in India could expect to live about 45 years, males in Iran 50 years, and the peoples of the African continent approximately 43 years.

Greater longevity has traditionally gone hand in hand with higher standards of living, reflected in a blending of medical breakthroughs with social advances. Those countries profiting most from improvements in these areas are represented by the lowest birth and death rates relative to the rest of the world. Although their combined population is small compared to the total world population, the hurdles confronting these societies portend those to be faced throughout the rest of the world as technological, economic and demographic profiles are modified. In 1970, the less-developed countries accounted for approximately 2542 million of the world's population, while the more developed numbered 1090 million — a ratio of 2.5 to 1 (United Nations, 1971). The increased longevity experienced by part of the world also brings with it a larger proportion of individuals at the upper reaches of the life span. As population compositions shift, many institutions within a society must respond in order to meet the demand for additional or new services. The apparently simple fact of improved life expectancy implies a complex interweaving of social and biological factors that contribute to the additional years of life and are in turn modified by those added years.

The twentieth century has also witnessed the widespread urbanization of the industrialized countries of Europe, North America and Japan, coupled with the gradual industrialization of Eastern Europe. The population structures of these and other advanced industrialized countries of the world differ from those in Third World societies, the former having a larger percentage of people in adulthood, greater longevity and a lower birth rate than the latter. The increased life expectancy is due in part to adequate or better nutrition, health care and educational programs, plus advanced medical techniques. Those scientific discoveries that have added years to average life expectancy have not, however, offered answers to the problems currently facing the growing proportion of elderly in these populations.

Demography and Aging

Population Age Structures

Demographers often classify populations on the basis of the percentage of people age 65 and over. Thus, a young population is usually considered to be one in which those 65 or over constitute less than 4 percent of the total population. Similarly, a mature population has between 4 and 7 percent of its members in this age group, while an aged population has over 7 percent 65 or older (United Nations, 1956). The age structure of a population is an important indicator of many societal patterns. Demographers have found those countries in the world with young populations are characterized by economic underdevelopment, are often agricultural in nature, and have relatively high birth and death rates combined with comparatively short life expectancies. Nations with mature age structures include those undergoing rapid industrial transition and those experiencing high birth rates, declining death rates and a gradual upswing in longevity. Typically, many Eastern European countries fall into this category. To date, countries with aged populations still account for only a small proportion of the world population. Generally speaking, these countries demonstrate the lowest birth rates, lower death rates and greater longevity than the rest of the world. The most aged populations are found in the advanced industrialized societies of North and West Europe. As should already be evident, the aging of populations is a relatively recent phenomenon associated primarily with the growth of industrialism and the facilities available in technologically sophisticated societies. Although the rapid expansion of the proportion of the population age 65 or over began in the midnineteenth century for Sweden and France, the remaining countries illustrated in Figure 3.1 did not display such patterns until the present century.

One might easily assume populations age because of declining death rates, but in fact this is not necessarily the case. For example, despite the fact French mortality rates have not been reduced to the level of the Netherlands, France nevertheless has an older population. Why should this be so? Contrary to popular expectations, declining mortality is not sufficient in itself to bring about an aged population. In the previous chapter we noted that a lower birth rate

Figure 3.1

Percentage of the population aged 65 and over for selected countries

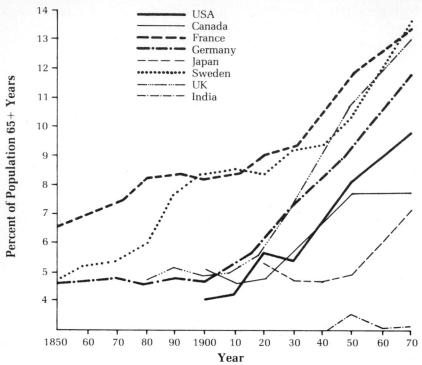

Sources: United Nations. *The Aging of Populations and Its Economic and Social Implications*. Population Studies, no. 26 (New York: United Nations, 1956); United Nations. *Demographic Yearbook, 1973*, 25th ed. (New York: United Nations. 1974). (Adapted from numeric data)

does not immediately follow on the heels of declining mortality. In industrializing countries, reductions of fertility lag behind those of mortality, creating in the interval something resembling a baby boom. The reasons for this are twofold: First, and perhaps most significant, improvements in medical technology have been most successful in combatting infectious diseases. Older people, however, are more likely to succumb as a consequence of the debilitating effects of chronic illnesses that sap their strength. Children on the other hand are more susceptible to the acute conditions of infectious diseases; hence, medical advances initially serve to inhibit aging of the entire population by swelling the numbers of the very young. Only after larger cohorts of children survive to adulthood does the age structure begin to shift upward. In all circumstances, the crucial variable is a declining fertility rate (United Nations, 1956). Today many Third World countries have experienced a drop in mortality with the introduction of sophisticated medical techniques, yet their population age structures remain quite young due to continuing high birth rates. Since fertility is so closely tied to a host of social practices, demographic data must be considered with an eye to the intricate association of biological, psychological and social factors. Finally, a variable of considerable importance, but one beyond the scope of the present discussion, is migration. Migratory movements can alter the population age structure in a variety of ways. One example, detailed later in this chapter, concerns the geographic relocation of young adults during the period of industrial expansion in the United States. Large scale international migrations, of less importance to today's industrialized societies, had, and to some extent have, a significant impact on societies that beckon in some way to younger, more mobile members of other cultures. Whether we select the colonization process by European powers, the influx of settlers in nineteenth century America or movement among Third World nations makes little difference. The crucial fact that must be assessed for each population in question is the intensity of the migratory movement, both for sender and receiver societies. Intensity must of necessity take into account age and sex distribution, but the interaction of migration with fertility and mortality involves even more complex and less certain relationships than the latter have with population age structures.

Age-Dependent Populations

Two important measures have been developed to furnish a basis for estimating the impact changing age structures have on a society. First, an *age-dependency ratio* provides an indication of the responsibilities carried by working adults for supporting non-productive age groups. The ratio represents an aggregation of the numbers of elderly and of children too young to be fully employed, compared against persons of working age to determine a ratio of dependency. Data similar to that upon which population pyramids are based are presented in numeric form in Table 3.1 in order to illustrate historic shifts in the age structure of the United States.

Dependency ratios in the table are computed using the format of the United States Census and are shown as a ratio of the combination of the elderly over 65 plus children under 15 to the working age population. Due to the tendency in recent years to delay entry into the labor market until after high school or college, the true dependency ratios from 1950 onward are most likely somewhat higher than those in the table. Likewise, dependency ratios for other countries would reflect their age norms for entry to and exit from the

Table 3.1

Percentage Distribution of Three Age Groups in the United States,
1880–1970, Index of Aging and Dependency Ratio

YEAR	14 YEARS OR UNDER	15–64 YEARS	65 YEARS AND OVER	INDEX OF AGING[1]	DEPENDENCY RATIO[2]
1970	28.5	61.7	9.8	34.4	62.1
1960	31.0	59.8	9.2	29.7	67.2
1950	26.8	65.3	8.2	30.6	53.5
1940	25.0	68.1	6.8	27.2	46.6
1930	29.3	65.1	5.4	18.4	53.3
1920	31.7	63.4	4.7	14.8	57.4
1910	32.1	63.4	4.3	13.4	57.4
1900	34.4	61.3	3.1	11.9	62.8
1890	35.5	60.4	3.9	11.0	65.2
1880	38.1	58.5	3.4	8.9	70.9

[1]Index of Aging $= \dfrac{\text{Population 65 years}+}{\text{Population 0–14 years}} \times 100$

[2]Dependency Ratio $= \dfrac{\text{Population aged 0–14 and 65 years }+}{\text{Population 15–64 years}} \times 100$

Sources: U.S. Bureau of Census. Census of the Population: 1970. Vol. 1, *Characteristics of the Population*, pt. 1 (Washington, D.C.: U.S. Government Printing Office, 1973); W. Petersen. *Population*. 2nd ed. (New York: Macmillan, 1969), p. 68. (Composite data)

labor market. Thus, in Sweden where retirement is legally set at 67, dependency ratios would be calculated for age categories different from those of India, where people are now retiring at 58. The point is, regardless of the age ranges utilized, the higher the ratio, the greater the burden placed on both the active work force and social institutions. For example, fixed and formal norms or laws governing retirement age and child labor mean fewer people available to perform the productive functions of a society. The implications of such age criteria are sometimes not fully expected. It is not uncommon to find retirement benefits the largest budgetary item in areas legally bound to offer social and economic support to the elderly. No better examples can be found than either West Germany or the city of New York. Both allocate major portions of their budgets to the elderly or, in the case of New York, to retired municipal employees. Probably few of us would challenge the right of the elderly to receive what individually turns out to be a rather nominal sum, while at the same time most of us endorse more monetary support for other institutional realms. The paradox arising is the increasingly difficult balance between greater availability of social services and reasonable burdens upon the working population.

The second index used in determining age structures is the *index of aging* (Valaroas, 1950). It contrasts the two ends of the life cycle, which were combined in the previous ratio. By comparing the number of people age 65 and over with those under 15, demographers are able to assess the extent to which the population as a whole is aging. Both the index of aging and the dependency ratio have been calculated in Table 3.1 to illustrate the long-term interaction of changing fertility and mortality patterns. The baby boom of the early 1950s is reflected by an upturn in the dependency ratio and a slight dip in the aging index for the 1960 census. If American population growth continues to slow, as it has for the past few years, to the point where birth and death rates are approximately equal, median age will advance from its current 28+ years to near 35, with a corresponding short-term decline in the dependency ratio. Demographers, economists and other social scientists find the information contained in these two indicators of age composition crucial in forecasting fundamental changes in our institutional structures. Some of these changes can already be seen; for the first time in three decades, elementary schools are not overflowing with students, while the pressure experienced by colleges in the 1960s from an excess of applicants is now beginning to slacken.

Quality of Life

Our evaluation of the relative position of the aged in society is made considerably easier in this century because of established census procedures in advanced industrialized countries. Although data are not always exactly comparable, a significant amount of information is available that enables researchers to provide a reasonably coherent description of the life situation of today's elderly. Any portrait of the elderly thus painted should also include a fine shadowing of the conditions that anticipated their current status. Since all segments of the population have grown, it is not enough to know there are more people over 65 now than ever before. The critical observer asks whether the *proportion* of elderly in mass society has shown a comparable increase. If the answer is yes, a glimmer of some of those factors influencing our social well-being begins to emerge.

The quality of life experienced by the elderly is directly related to their growing numbers, improving health status and changing societal values. As has been seen, the sheer numbers of people living beyond retirement age have multiplied dramatically since the turn of the century. The character of the lives they lead results from a wide spectrum of events and conditions impinging upon them. Among the more significant features to be discussed are sex and racial characteristics, residence and migration patterns, living arrangements, life expectancy, education, occupation, and income. Before moving on to a detailed explication of the role these factors play in the lives of the elderly, let us highlight just a few of the trends.

Throughout the industrialized world women live longer than men. At birth the differences in expected longevity are in the range of two to eight years. The actual expectations vary, depending on such variables as local circumstances or racial background. In the United States, both white and black females generally live longer than their male counterparts, with life expectancy for white males and black females being nearly identical. Among whites, females outlive males by over seven years, while for blacks the interval is nearly eight and a half years. After age 24 there are more women than men in the population, with the sex ratio becoming further distorted after age 65. Right now in the United States there are 72 men for every 100 women past retirement age, and by the year 2000 this number will likely decline to about 67 men per 100 women.

In addition to changes in the average length of life, the composition of the work force has also undergone several fluctuations since the turn of the century. Most of the industrialized countries of the world have followed the lead of Germany and Chancellor Bismarck in establishing legal retirement at age 65. As a plank in its 1932 platform, the Democratic party of the United States came out in favor of inclusive Social Security coverage modeled after Germany's. Following the election and the inauguration of the Democratic administration, the first Social Security legislation was enacted in 1935, setting forth a federal program of supplemental income insurance for all workers reaching age 65. While such formal retirement policies inevitably meet with some criticism, they do allow a smoother transition of the labor force and more open access to upper echelon positions by younger workers. Of course, they may also become the basis for age discrimination. In 1890, over two-thirds of older American males were employed; today that figure has dropped to approximately 25 percent. Among women, recent definitions of appropriate sex roles, periodic societal demands for workers and other economic incentives have contributed to a slight increase in the participation of older women in the labor force. The most dramatic change has occurred among women between 45–64 years of age. Their activity in the labor force has increased nearly fourfold, from 13 percent in 1900 to more than 48 percent in 1970. Over the course of the lives of today's elderly women, familial and household matters have constituted their chief responsibility, while their husbands were busy earning a livelihood outside the home. With the popularization of mandatory retirement, it was hypothesized by some gerontologists that men would find themselves deprived of what had been a major source of identity. Undoubtedly the psychological stresses attendant with the loss of a man's economic function are to be reckoned with, but as was pointed out earlier, recent longitudinal research has questioned their severity. It may well be that loss of work, although previously constituting a central life role, is not nearly as devastating to the individual as once assumed. Nevertheless, retirement necessitates some type of accommodation among older people. The problem is not limited to male workers; older women may also suffer emotional distress as they live out the last several years of life unaccompanied by either spouse or family. Seventy years ago, few couples had much time left to themselves after launching their youngest child into adulthood; recently, however, they have come to enjoy close to 15 years together after the marriage of their last child. In the United States at least, the wife then has an average of seven or more years in which she must cope with the realities of widowhood. If she is appreciably younger than her husband, and most wives are three to five years younger, this period may be even more extended.

Major population relocations have occurred as the emphasis on industrial production outdistanced that placed on agricultural. In the United States, the outmigration of young people from the Midwest has left behind vast areas where the proportion of the elderly in the population is far higher than the national average. Popular retirement states like Florida, Arizona and Nevada, or parts of California, also have an overrepresentation of the elderly. These shifts are reflected in the percentage of the country living in urban and rural environments. In 1900, over 60 percent of the population resided in rural areas; by 1970 this figure was cut to about 26 percent. The percentage of the elderly in smaller cities and rural areas is above the national average of one in every ten, as Table 3.2 illustrates. In urbanized regions, the elderly became concentrated in central city areas, as newer suburban neighborhoods attracted young, mobile families. Patterns not unlike those presented here have been observed in other industrialized societies of the world.

General Population Trends

Increasing Duration of Life

Earlier we noted the extent to which life expectancy has risen in the twentieth century. Primarily as a result of improvement in infant and child mortality, longevity has been on the increase throughout the world. But, as might be expected, the most striking advances are

Table 3.2

Percentage Distribution of Dependent Population by Residence: 1960 and 1970

| AGE IN YEARS | 1960 | | | 1970 | | | | | | | | |
| | TOTAL POPULATION | TOTAL URBAN | TOTAL RURAL | TOTAL POPULATION | TOTAL URBAN | URBAN AREAS* | | SMALLER CITIES | | TOTAL RURAL | RURAL | |
						CENTRAL CITIES	URBAN FRINGE	10,000+	2500–10,000		1000–2500	OTHER RURAL
Under 15	31.0	30.1	33.3	28.5	27.7	26.5	29.5	26.9	27.9	30.6	27.9	30.9
65–74	6.1	6.1	6.0	6.1	6.1	6.6	4.9	6.5	7.1	6.5	7.9	6.1
75+	3.1	3.1	3.3	3.7	3.7	4.0	3.0	4.3	5.0	3.8	5.6	3.5

*Not necessarily equivalent to Standard Metropolitan Statistical Areas.

Source: U.S. Bureau of Census. Census of Population: 1970. Vol. 1, *Characteristics of the Population*, pt. 1, United States Summary (Washington, D.C.: U.S. Government Printing Office, 1973), p. 269.

manifested by countries already industrialized or those currently undergoing industrialization. A summary of the latest available statistics on life expectancy at birth is presented in Table 3.3. A quick look at the table reveals seven countries where male infants can anticipate 70 or more years of life: Sweden, Norway, Iceland, Denmark, the Netherlands, Japan and Israel. As can be seen, without exception, females recently born in the countries listed will ordinarily live more than 70 years, and in many instances may expect to live as long as 75 years.

The greater longevity experienced in the United States is characteristic of trends found in other industrialized nations. Between the turn of the century and 1970, average life expectancy increased by half again its initial length, from 47.3 to 70.8 years. Detailed information depicted by sex and race is offered in Table 3.4. Overall, males born in 1970 should outlive their earlier counterparts by as much as 20 years; for females the extension is over 26 years. Contrary to what one might at first think, the gains achieved by nonwhites have been even more dramatic, as minority life expectancy in this century has almost doubled. Despite a reduction of one-half in the gap between the two groups, whites still live roughly seven years longer than their nonwhite peers. There is every reason to expect the gap will continue to shrink, however. A careful look at

Table 3.3
Life Expectancy at Birth for Selected Countries

| DATE* | COUNTRY | YEARS | |
		MALE	FEMALE
1973	Austria	67.4	74.7
1965–1967	Canada	68.7	75.2
1970–1971	Denmark	70.7	75.9
1966–1970	Finland	65.9	73.6
1971	France	68.5	76.1
1970–1972	Fed. Rep. Germany	67.4	73.8
1966–1970	Iceland	70.7	76.3
1972	Israel	70.1	72.8
1972	Japan	70.5	75.9
1972	Netherlands	70.8	76.8
1971–1972	Norway	71.2	77.4
1972	Sweden	71.9	77.4
1968–1969	U.S.S.R	65.0	74.0
1968–1970	U.K.	67.8	73.8
1972	U.S.A.	67.4	75.1

*Latest available figures

Source: United Nations. *Statistical Yearbook, 1974,* 26th ed. (New York: United Nations, 1975), p. 81–83.

Table 3.4

Expansion of Life Expectancy at Birth in the Twentieth Century for the United States*

YEAR	TOTAL YEARS			WHITE			NEGRO AND OTHER		
	TOTAL	MALE	FEMALE	TOTAL	MALE	FEMALE	TOTAL	MALE	FEMALE
1973	71.3	67.6	75.3	72.2	68.4	76.1	65.9	61.9	70.1
1970	70.8	67.1	74.6	71.7	68.1	75.4	64.6	60.5	68.4
1960	69.7	66.6	73.1	70.6	67.4	74.1	63.6	61.1	66.3
1950	68.2	65.6	71.1	69.1	66.5	72.2	60.8	59.1	62.9
1940	62.9	60.8	65.2	64.2	62.1	66.6	53.1	51.5	54.9
1930	59.7	58.1	61.6	61.4	59.7	63.5	48.1	47.3	49.2
1920	54.1	53.6	54.6	54.9	54.4	55.6	45.3	45.5	45.2
1910	50.0	48.4	51.8	50.3	48.6	52.0	35.6	33.8	37.5
1900	47.3	46.3	48.3	47.6	46.6	48.7	33.0	32.5	33.5

*Prior to 1960 excludes Alaska and Hawaii; prior to 1930 for death-registration states only.

Sources: U.S. Bureau of Census. *Statistical Abstract of the United States: 1975.* 96th ed. (Washington, D.C.: U.S. Government Printing Office, 1975), p. 59; U.S. Bureau of Census, *Historical Statistics of the United States, Colonial Times to 1957* (Washington, D.C.: U.S. Government Printing Office, 1960), p. 25.

the table discloses the emergence of a third trend. Since 1900, longevity among females has improved at a faster rate than among males. What was initially a differential of two years is now over seven years among whites. For nonwhites the magnitude is even more remarkable; the one year separation in 1900 grew to over eight years by 1973. Once again, very similar patterns can be found elsewhere in the industrialized world.

Expansion of the Elderly Population

Recalling Figure 3.1, it is clear that the percentage of people over 65 has steadily risen in all industrialized countries during the past century. While the proportion of elderly in the United States has doubled, their numbers have increased sevenfold. In the United Kingdom, the percentage of elderly in the population has nearly tripled during the same period to reach 13 percent in 1970. The percentage of older people in West Germany has doubled, in the Netherlands and Italy it is up by two-thirds, and in France, Sweden and Canada the percentage has increased half again as much over the course of this century. Despite these changes, only France and Sweden had a large enough proportion of their populations over 65 to exhibit aged population structures prior to 1900. Currently, each of the countries shown in the figure, with the exception of India, has an aged population structure, with 7 percent or more of its citizens 65 years of age or older; unless there is a highly unusual change in the current birth rates, it is unlikely that any reversal will take place in the foreseeable future.

Sex Ratio Among Older People

It stands to reason when women live longer than men, there will be an alteration in the sex ratio during the later years of life. After early adulthood the number of women living surpasses the number of men, increasing further each decade thereafter. The sex ratio among the elderly is determined by the complex relationship among fertility, mortality and migration patterns of the past. In Canada, for example, after the years of heaviest immigration, the usually observed sex ratio was eventually reversed. During the early period of immigration in the 1920s there were 97 men for every 100 women; by 1950 this changed to 101 men per 100 women, since the immigrants were predominately male. With heavy immigration a thing of the past, the ratio fell back to 87 men per 100 women by the beginning of the 1970s. Partially as a consequence of the fatalities of World War II and higher male mortality in general, Denmark's sex ratio is 82, Japan's 78, while the two Germanies, France and the

United Kingdom each have fewer than 65 males per 100 females in the ages over 65. As with population aging and the future proportion of the elderly, these trends are not apt to change significantly in the next few decades. Though demographers are uncertain about the causes, in the United States, younger whites have a higher sex ratio than blacks. However, at older ages the opposite is the case; there are 80 black males for every 100 females but only 72 white males per 100 females. The closer life expectancy among nonwhite men and women or an underrepresentation of older black women in the census have been suggested as factors in the higher sex ratio (U.S. Census, 1973b). As Chapter Ten describes, sex ratios and marital norms have broad ramifications for family life among the elderly, especially as it influences widowhood among older women.

Old Age and Urbanization

Differences in the distribution of elderly in urban and rural areas were illustrated in Table 3.2. At that point we commented on the heavier concentration of older Americans in central cities as contrasted to suburban fringes, their preponderance in smaller towns and so on. Here, too, similar developments have taken place in other industrialized countries. Even among those experiencing the slowest population growth, urbanization has proceeded at a rapid rate in the present century. Sweden and France, for instance, have had nearly stable growth rates for years, yet both have expanded their urban populations significantly, France by 15 percent and Sweden by over 30 percent. As younger people move to urban areas they leave behind parents and elders, eventually resulting in a disproportionate number of elderly in rural regions. In recent times this trend has been accompanied by younger workers settling in the newer, outlying suburban neighborhoods, thus contributing to an overrepresentation of older people in the inner city.

Urbanization is one by-product of the technological and economic changes fostered in part by the process of industrialization. The increasing size of our urban population is just one ecological manifestation of the technical and organizational requirements of industry. As more sophisticated means of production are created, new skills and knowledge are called for. Middle-aged and older workers have already established their occupational competence, and their educations were usually obtained in the distant past. As new opportunities become available, younger workers experience a selective mobility, both occupational and geographic. One of the apparent consequences of industrialization is a higher value placed on smaller family units that are more readily mobile, plus an emphasis on productive independence regardless of one's previous contributions. These themes will become familiar in Chapters Eight and Nine as the meaning of work and retirement, for both individual and society, is more fully explored.

Family Relationships and Living Arrangements

It is frequently, though perhaps erroneously, asserted that extended families were commonplace in preindustrial Europe and North America. Recent evidence has called into question assumptions regarding the prevalence of three generation families living under one roof, suggesting that such arrangements were temporary and seldom widespread or, in the case of the United States, more often nonexistent. Setting this issue aside for the time being, let us consider factors that are associated with feelings of loneliness, estrangement and unwanted dependence that are crucial for the morale and sense of well-being voiced by today's elderly. From an examination of Table 3.5, it can be seen that in nearly all cases, twice as many elderly men as women are married, while two to three times as many women are widowed. The large number of widows reflects both higher male death rates and societal attitudes toward remarriage. Not only do older men remarry more frequently than women, they may even secure a small measure of status from what we euphemistically term May-December unions, frowned on, to say the least, for older women. Traditional values and attitudes may tend to inhibit divorces among those people who grew up in an earlier era; with the exception of Swedish and Danish women, less than 3 percent of the elderly admit to being divorced.

The information presented in the table does not reveal the whole story of the loneliness and isolation facing older citizens. From age 50 onward, death begins to take its toll on married couples. In the United States today a majority of the women over 65 are widows, with more than one out of three living alone in the family home. Even though the figures on marital status among the elderly have scarcely changed over the last decade, living arrangements reflect the potential of greater hardship. The proportion of women living with their children has declined by 10 percent in the last ten years, so that today only 15 percent of the older women and 7 percent of the older men are living with either their children or other relatives. It is not at all unusual to find the elderly themselves quite militant in defending their independence; in fact, a large majority say they view too much help from their adult children as a form of charity they would just as soon do without. The cultural emphasis on individualism and self-help most definitely carries over into

Table 3.5
Marital Status Among the Elderly in Selected Countries

| COUNTRY | PERCENT* | | | |
SEX	SINGLE	MARRIED	WIDOWED	DIVORCED
Canada				
Male	11.1	69.1	19.4	0.4
Female	10.3	39.1	50.3	0.3
Japan				
Male	1.0	75.7	22.1	1.2
Female	1.8	31.2	65.8	1.7
Denmark				
Male	7.6	67.1	22.2	2.4
Female	14.6	37.0	44.4	3.5
France				
Male	7.1	72.7	18.6	1.5
Female	10.8	33.6	53.4	2.1
Sweden				
Male	13.1	65.2	18.7	2.9
Female	18.5	36.5	40.9	3.8
U.K.				
Male	7.3	70.7	21.6	0.4
Female	15.6	34.3	49.6	0.5
U.S.				
Male	7.1	73.1	17.1	2.7
Female	7.3	36.2	54.2	2.3

*Data based on latest available information — 1965–1971.

Sources: United Nations, *Demographic Yearbook, 1973* (New York: United Nations, 1974), pp. 420–52; U.S. Census, *Current Population Reports*, series P-23, no. 43 (Washington, D.C.: U.S. Government Printing Office, 1973), p. 26. (data adapted)

one's later years. For the recently retired or for the affluent elderly, living alone may not present as many problems, but for the vast majority, independence is like a commodity that becomes ever scarcer and costs more dearly the older they get. In light of the fact that generally neither adult children nor parents relish the prospect of living together, it is surprising so few elderly actually live in institutions of any kind. Estimates vary according to the methods used in data collection, but presently only about 5 percent of the older population are institutionalized. In keeping with these statistics, we might expect a slightly higher percentage of women to live in institutions, if only because there are more women than men living. As it turns out, about 3.6 percent of the elderly men, compared to 4.6 percent of the women 65 or over, live in institutions; however, the further into old age one lives, the more likely he or she is to become institutionalized (Kastenbaum and Candy, 1973). While it might seem easy to dismiss the institutionalized elderly as being an insignificant percentage of the older population, the fact cannot be escaped that well over one million elderly people live in varying degrees of dependence and indignity in homes which constitute a multimillion dollar industry. We shall return for a further examination of current living arrangements and possible alternatives in Chaper Ten.

Participation of the Older Worker

We have all experienced a sense of belonging when we are actively involved in events or when we feel we are carrying our own weight. Just as young workers are often anxious to show they are ready and able to do a job, old workers are equally desirous of showing that they too can perform occupational tasks assigned to them. Despite mandatory retirement ages, the total number of years spent in the labor force has increased over the current century. In large measure the extension is due to longer life expectancies, which have more than offset the concentration of active work life to the period between ages 20 and 65. The work role is of considerable importance to the identity of most older workers, regardless of the popularity of complaining about one's job. Whether or not work per se is critical for our sense of worth, many meaningful relationships do derive from our work situations over the course of our lifetimes; loss of the work role also means loss of or change in many of these relationships and much of the structure in our lives.

Seventy years ago, over 60 percent of all American men continued working past age 65. Today retirement has become less flexible, less a matter of individual choice, so that only about one out of five older men is still employed. A number of variables have contributed to a clearer demarcation of our working lives. In addition to the patterns of urbanization introduced above, compulsory education, technological advances, less self-employment, mandatory retirement policies and pension programs have all encouraged a movement away from the lifelong sunup to sundown routine of agricultural and early industrial societies. A lack of uniformity in census enumerations makes reliable comparisons somewhat problematic, but some general trends among the industrialized countries of the world can be described. There has been a decline in the numbers of older workers on the order of 10 percent or more every 20 years since the turn of the century. For those who do continue working, the first five years after formal retirement age constitute the most active period, with participation rapidly decreasing thereafter.

Data on the employment of middle-aged and older workers in the United States are provided in Table 3.6. As is evident, participation in the labor force by older men has declined steadily over the years. There is a narrow gap between white and nonwhite participation rates after age 65, though nonwhites are faced with slightly fewer opportunities to work after retirement age. However, the rates for women tell a different story. Overall, older women have continued to work at a more or less stable pace since 1900. There has been a gradual decline in the number of nonwhite women who remain in the work force, but the changes have been relatively minor. It is among middle-aged workers that significant changes have taken place. The slight decline for middle-aged men in no way offsets the fourfold increase of women working during their middle years. As children grow up and leave home, today's women are entering the labor market as never before. Since a great many of these women perform clerical or service work, there is little likelihood of lessened participation in the future, unless American industry were to change drastically. At the same time, unemployment among middle-aged males is on the rise with further movement away from agricultural, semiskilled or self-employed occupations. The consequences such patterns will have on later life are not yet known, but the loss of work roles for men and the legitimation of work among women in the second half of life promises to alter the face of aging in the years ahead.

Table 3.6

Changes in Labor Force Participation by Age Group and Sex, United States, 1900 to 1990

| | PERCENT | | | |
| | MALE | | FEMALE | |
DATE	45–64 YEARS	65+ YEARS	45–64 YEARS	65+ YEARS
1990*	84.5	19.3	51.9	8.3
1980*	85.5	21.2	50.4	8.6
1974	83.7	21.5	47.3	7.8
1970	87.2	25.8	48.2	9.2
1960	89.8	32.2	43.0	10.5
1940	89.4	42.2	20.0	6.0
1920	90.7	55.6	16.5	7.3
1900	90.3	63.1	13.6	8.3

*Projected

Sources: U.S. Bureau of Census, *Statistical Abstract of the United States: 1975.* 96th ed. (Washington, D.C.: U.S. Government Printing Office, 1975), p. 344; U.S. Bureau of Census, *Historical Statistics of the United States, Colonial Times to 1957* (Washington, D.C.: U.S. Government Printing Office, 1960), p. 71.

Age and Education

One of the correlates of most technological societies is a compulsory education system. As societies become more complex, higher levels of education are deemed necessary if a person is to make his or her way. Our recent history has been such that today there is an inverse relationship between age and education among adults; generally the older one's age, the less formal education obtained. As standards of living improve, educational opportunities increase, so that future generations of older citizens will be better educated. Between 1940 and 1974, the average educational level among Americans 65 and over has climbed from 8.1 to 9.0 years of school; by 1980 the average will increase another year or more. During the same interval, the number of elderly who had graduated from high school rose from one in ten to three in every ten. Over the next decade the proportion of older citizens who are high school graduates should reach 43 percent. Interestingly enough, many of the attitudes thought to be characteristic of older people are not related so much to their age as to their education. A number of the existing stereotypes concerning rigidity, conservativeness and so on will be challenged as a larger proportion of our older population attains a higher level of education. A second but related factor is the length of time that has elapsed since a person's education was completed. The further removed from his or her training an older person becomes, the more old-fashioned or rigid his outlook appears. By altering the structure of educational opportunities in the United States and other industrialized countries, one of the major artifacts of older people's attitudes could be overcome. As those born during the postwar baby boom finish school, many previously crowded facilities may well be put into service for continuing adult education. There are some indications that as more adults take advantage of midlife education or retraining opportunities, new attitude configurations will emerge among the elderly.

Economic Conditions of Retirement

Confusion over future economic benefits is almost universal among individuals facing retirement. Unlike many European programs, Social Security has never been intended as the sole source of support for retiring American workers. It comes as a grim surprise to many that Social Security often provides an income that falls below federally established poverty levels. Even when they expect their incomes to be diminished by one-third to one-half, many older people find they have overestimated the purchasing power of the amount they receive. For workers still supporting families, retirement income in recent years has averaged slightly over $5,000, or just about half of their previous income. Single individuals no longer living with spouse or family average considerably less, in the neighborhood of $1,950 a year. It is hardly surprising, therefore, that, according to federally established guidelines, nearly one of every five older citizens is impoverished. In 1974, governmental standards decreed older two person families must have received over $2,958 and single individuals $2,352 to achieve the bare minimum standard of living. As is clear in Table 3.7, race and sex play a crucial role in determining an older person's financial resources. As a general rule, whites receive slightly more and blacks a little less than the average income for older Americans. In all cases, unrelated individuals are much more likely to face life with inadequate incomes than married couples. Women more often have insufficient incomes than men, and as can be seen, this disparity is exacerbated by race. If income is used as one criterion of minority group status, the elderly no doubt

Table 3.7
Americans 65 Years or Older Below Low Income Level,* 1974

RACE	FAMILIES		UNRELATED INDIVIDUALS	
	MALE HEAD	FEMALE HEAD	MALE	FEMALE
ALL RACES				
Total	6925	1108	1455	5047
Number below low income level	616	114	390	1675
Percent of total	8.9	13.0	26.8	33.2
WHITE				
Total	6410	909	1233	4641
Number below low income level	493	74	292	1405
Percent of total	7.7	8.1	23.7	30.3
BLACK				
Total	454	187	195	381
Number below low income level	108	69	86	262
Percent of total	23.9	36.8	44.3	68.8

*Numbers in thousands.

Note: 1974 total low income thresholds (weighted average) were $2352 for unrelated individuals 65+ years, $2958 for two person families with head 65+ years old.

Source: U.S. Bureau of the Census, *Current Population Reports.* Series P-60, no. 99 (Washington, D.C.: U.S. Government Printing Office, 1975), pp. 16–17. (data adapted)

face serious problems analogous to other minority groups stemming from often inadequate financial resources. As will become clear in Chapter Thirteen and elsewhere in our discussion, those individuals already members of minority groups are placed in even greater jeopardy once they reach age 65. Galloping inflation promises to take a large chunk off the top of the Supplemental Security Income program enacted in 1974 to alleviate the most glaring income inequities facing senior citizens. The topic of income in later years is examined again in greater detail in Chapter Nine.

Despite the hard realities, the idea of a golden old age, a time of leisure marked by few responsibilities and a secure income, is a long sought after goal for many. The lack of retirement counseling proves to be a major culprit in the difficulty of adjusting to the actual experiences of old age. Even with financial security, some retired men do suffer some measure of psychological distress when they are finally deprived of their work role. Researchers on both sides of the Atlantic have noted the dissatisfaction that often pervades the lives of men no longer necessary to economic production (Townsend, 1963; Havighurst, 1969). And yet, other research has found that retirement is by no means a dreaded event for a large number of individuals (Streib and Schneider, 1971). In a cross-national study of Britain, Denmark and the United States, Shanas and her associates (1968) discovered that nearly one-quarter of the older Americans said they retired because they could afford to, as compared to 15 percent of the British and Danish workers who voiced similar views. Their research also revealed that half of the retired Danes found "nothing" to enjoy about retirement, while only three in ten Americans felt a similar malaise. In Britain and the United States, occupational level is one of the strongest factors associated with appreciation of retirement; those individuals retiring from white collar occupations were consistently more positive in their attitudes toward retirement than their blue collar age mates. Actual retirement benefits vary from country to country depending on such things as previous earnings, equity, current earnings and so on. In the United States, although established as a form of universal prepaid retirement insurance, Social Security payments are based in large measure on the individual's own contributions. Extensive low paid employment or work in jobs not covered by the social insurance scheme comes back to haunt the applicant seeking old age benefits. In the Scandinavian countries, and to some extent in Great Britain, previous earnings play a lesser role in determining the scale of retirement payments to those over age 65. Regardless of the elderly person's financial plight, the emphasis on equity, or individual contributions, over the adequacy of retirement income relieves the

American government of much of the financial burden facing those countries providing uniform benefits for all retired workers. In many cases, the staggering sums allocated each year decrease the amount available for other humanitarian programs. It presents a dilemma from which we cannot escape with easy answers.

Summary

The twentieth century has witnessed an astounding growth of the elderly population in the industrialized societies of the world. This aging of populations generally occurred after 1920, as the proportion of individuals 65 and over doubled or in some cases tripled. The sizeable numbers of elderly today owe their existence to a period of fairly high birth rates coupled with falling death rates. Life expectancy has increased in a corresponding manner in this century; on the average, gains are in the neighborhood of 20 years. Today most men can look forward to at least 65 years of life and women to 70 or more years. Many observers view enhanced longevity as one index of social progress, leading them to conclude humanity's lot has generally improved. In a sense it provides a measure of our mastery over the ever-present forces of nature that eventually terminate life. These factors alone create a range of health, economic and social issues confronting both individuals and institutions concerned with the well-being of the elderly. It was noted, however, that expansion of elderly populations and average duration of life signal only the beginning of changes in contemporary industrialized societies. Mortality rates have improved differentially, to the extent that elderly women outlive men by seven or eight years. In addition, modifications in sex ratios in the later years have implications for the living arrangements and family status of older men and women alike. The problems encountered by the disadvantaged elderly are compounded by their ecological and social isolation. Along with the impact of modern technology, the twentieth century has ushered in the urbanization of industrial populations. As a consequence of movement to urban areas, and later to suburban neighborhoods, there is a surfeit of older persons concentrated in inner cities, small towns and rural areas. At the same time, the status accorded the elderly in once stable societies has given way in some instances to societal disregard and personal alienation.

The social world of the elderly is affected by a number of diverse factors. Marriage and companionship are of singular import in the procession of age. Once individuals reach the mid-60s, their life chances are markedly better if they are married. The greater life expectancy of women leaves many more widows than widowers during the last years of life for whom the psychological ramifications of bereavement and despair are of serious measure. Despite these and other losses and debilities, only about 5 percent of the elderly currently live in institutions, though a much larger proportion will have some personal experience with institutional life prior to their deaths.

Adequate income is clearly one of the most effective hedges against the liabilities of age. Yet affluence is relatively rare among older people; on the average, older couples are able to muster about half the financial resources they previously received. Single older people are even worse off; their income is less than one-half that received by older couples. As one might expect, lower income levels among the elderly stem in part from the same factors that contribute to low income among other members of the population. Most influential are education, race and sex. While one in five older Americans lives in poverty, according to what may arguably be politically expedient standards, the rate among young and middle-aged adults is approximately one out of ten. Working is clearly an element in income maintenance. Older women have been active in the labor force at a fairly stable rate for the last few decades, though the rates for men over 65 have been falling at a steady pace. Future employment patterns will undoubtedly reflect the different traditions now being established by young adults.

Pertinent Readings

BURGESS, E.W., ed. Aging in Western Societies: A Comparative Survey. Chicago: University of Chicago Press, 1960.

COHEN, W.J. "Income Maintenance and Medical Insurance." In Aging in Western Societies: A Comparative Survey, ed. E.W. Burgess, pp. 76–105. Chicago: University of Chicago Press, 1960.

COMFORT, A. The Process of Ageing. New York: Signet Books, 1964.

THE COMMISSION ON POPULATION GROWTH AND THE AMERICAN FUTURE. Population and the American Future. Washington, D.C.: U.S. Government Printing Office, 1972.

COWGILL, D.O., and L.D. HOLMES. Aging and Modernization. New York: Appleton-Century-Crofts, 1972.

GLICK, P.C., and R. PARKE, JR. "New Approaches in Studying the Life Cycle of the Family." Demography II (1965): 187–202.

HAVIGHURST, R.J., J.M.A. MUNNICHS, B. NEUGARTEN and H. THOMAE, eds. Adjustment to Retirement: A Cross-National Study. Assen, Netherlands: Royal VanGorcum, Ltd., 1969.

KASTENBAUM, R., and S.E. CANDY. "The 4% Fallacy: A Methodological and Empirical Critique of Extended Care Facility Population Statistics." Aging and Human Development 4, 1 (1973): 15–22.

MERING, O. VON, and F.L. WENIGER. "Social-Cultural Background of the Aging Individual." In *Handbook of Aging and the Individual*, ed. J.E. Birren, pp. 279–335. Chicago: University of Chicago Press, 1959.

PETERSEN, W. *Population*. 2nd ed. New York: Macmillan, 1969.

ROSOW, I. *Social Integration of the Aged*. New York: Free Press of Glencoe, 1967.

SHANAS, E., P. TOWNSEND, D. WEDDERBURN, H. FRILS, P. MILHJ and J. STEHOUWER. *Old People in Three Industrial Societies*. New York: Atherton, 1968.

STREIB, G.F., and C.J. SCHNEIDER. *Retirement in American Society: Impact and Process*. Ithaca, N.Y.: Cornell University Press, 1971.

TIBBITTS, D., ed. *Handbook of Social Gerontology: Societal Aspects of Aging*. Chicago: University of Chicago Press, 1960.

TOWNSEND, P. *The Family Life of Old People*. Baltimore: Penguin Books, 1963.

UNITED NATIONS. *The Aging of Populations and Its Economic and Social Implications*. Population Studies, no. 26. New York: United Nations, 1956.

_____ . *The World Population Situation in 1970*. Population Studies, no. 49. New York: United Nations, 1971.

_____ . *Demographic Yearbook, 1973*. 25th ed. Special Topic: Population Census Statistics I. New York: United Nations, 1974.

_____ . *Statistical Yearbook, 1974*. 26th ed. New York: United Nations, 1975.

_____ . U.S. BUREAU OF THE CENSUS. *Historical Statistics of the United States, Colonial Times to 1957*. Washington, D.C.: U.S. Government Printing Office, 1960.

_____ . *Census of the Population: 1970, Characteristics of the Population*. Vol. I, pt. 1. Washington, D.C.; U.S. Government Printing Office, 1973a.

_____ . *Current Population Reports*. Series P-23, no. 43. "Some Demographic Aspects of Aging in the United States." Washington, D.C.: U.S. Government Printing Office, 1973b.

U.S. PUBLIC HEALTH SERVICE, NATIONAL CENTER FOR HEALTH STATISTICS. "Socioeconomic Characteristics of Deceased Persons." PHS Pub. no. 1000 — Series 22, no. 9. Washington, D.C.: U.S. Government Printing Office, February 1969.

VALAORAS, V.G. "Patterns of Aging of Human Populations." In *The Social and Biological Challenge of Our Aging Population*. Proceedings of the Eastern States Health Education Conference. New York: Columbia University Press, 1950.

Part II

THEORIES OF AGING

Chapter 4

Physiological Changes
Over Time

After the previous two chapters, critical readers have no doubt asked themselves why we observe such stable modes of aging over lengthy periods of time. The answer is because *all* organisms, be they plant or animal, age in species-specific patterns. Despite wide individual variations in any number of attributes, the life span of a human being is more or less predictable within narrow limits. While biologists are not yet prepared to give definitive answers as to why we age as we do, they have already furnished some valuable leads. The purpose of this chapter is to review the most promising hypotheses set forth to account for aging at the biological level. Since physiological theories in themselves are not sufficient, we will also describe some of the functional changes that our bodies undergo over the years. Consideration of the more important pathological conditions that are identified as those diseases frequently found among older age groups will be deferred until a discussion of health and medical characteristics of the elderly in Chapter Seven.

Becoming Old

The incidence of death among age cohorts increases steadily over the course of time. Nonetheless, most of us tend to think of the aging process as something beginning after the age of 50. Nothing could be further from the truth. As we sit here reading these words, no matter what our current age, we are becoming older. In fact, in certain respects we have been aging since birth, or even before in the case of brain cells. We attained our maximum number of brain cells before we were born and have been losing them ever since. Of course, we have so many, over 20 billion, that we are unlikely ever to notice the losses under normal conditions. What we lose in actual number of functioning cells, we compensate for through experience and learning. Though the physical growth of our brain (measured by weight) ceases about the time we graduate from high school or enter college, as shown in Figure 4.1, we do not become any less intelligent with age except in cases of *pathological* change.

Specialists who study the human body distinguish between developmental and aging phases of life. Throughout our early years, the rapid bodily changes undergone are largely adaptive in nature. They help us meet the challenges of our environment and respond in ways necessary to maintain life. At some point, which differs by individual and even by various organ levels within the same person, a gradual deteriorative process begins to lessen our ability to adapt. This slow decline increases our vulnerability to stress, thereby making the probability of effective threats to life more likely. Physiologists refer to the deteriorative process as *senescence*. The superficial physical symptoms of senescence are usually easy to recognize. Our skin wrinkles from increasing dryness, our hair turns gray and falls out, we tend to gain weight, we need brighter light to read and require stronger glasses, we begin to notice or perhaps worse, fail to notice, some loss of hearing ability, and we feel stiff after relatively little exercise. These signs are just the obvious manifestations of changes going on inside our bodies from the smallest cells to the most complex organs. As described in more detail later,

Figure 4.1
Brain weight, by age at time of death

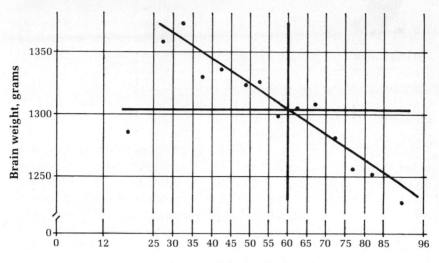

Age at time of death

Source: W. Bondareff, "Morphology of the Aging Nervous System," in J.E. Birren, ed., *Handbook of Aging and the Individual* (Chicago: University of Chicago Press, 1959), p. 137.

the causes have not yet been pinpointed, partly because of the youthfulness of the discipline of gerontology and partly because senescence is a multifaceted process that does not lend itself to easy analysis.

The physical changes so fundamental to aging never occur in isolation; they have psychological and social significance as well. These components both effect and are affected by the physiological changes taking place all the time. Strictly speaking, such changes reflect an interrelationship between extrinsic factors and internal or intrinsic events. External factors are considered to be those emanating from outside the organism. Included here are a variety of social and economic variables such as class, occupation, geographic locale, marital status, eating habits and nutrition, epidemics, viruses and diseases, exposure to radiation in the form of x-rays plus a host of other environmental agents that subject the individual to differing kinds and degrees of stress. These may hasten the aging process greatly, although many also serve to retard it. Intrinsic factors, on the other hand, are those inherent in an organism. As mentioned in the previous chapter, sex is one of the most significant intrinsic factors affecting longevity.

While the distinction between internal and external factors is frequently more analytic than real, physiologists find it useful insofar as it delimits the parameters of their research. One example of the difficulties inherent in the dichotomy is the cumulative result of evolution. As organisms, humans may have developed adaptive responses to environmental pressures exerted during their reproductive life. Later, these same responses may actually become liabilities, interfering with necessary functioning. To help distinguish between internal and external changes that occur with the passage of time, Strehler (1962) proposed the following guidelines for changes attributed to the aging process itself. First, age-associated changes must be observed *universally* among all older members of the species. This clearly rules out diseases and hereditary aberrations which might be characteristic only of particular subgroups. By way of illustration, for many years scientists thought *atherosclerosis,* what most of us call hardening of the arteries, was a condition common to all older people. If this were true we would expect to find very few exceptions; however, not only are many individuals in our own culture free from atherosclerotic disease, but among whole groups of people, such as the Mali tribes in Africa and Yemenite Jews, the disease is unknown. External factors such as nutrition and stress are now considered to account for most atherosclerosis. This leads to the second criterion: the changes must be *intrinsic* to the organism. In the event of an all-out atomic war, every living thing on earth would experience genetic damage, but the resulting mutations could not be classified as intrinsic. Under these circumstances we might mistakenly identify the effects of atomic radiation as intrinsic in successive generations.

Having read the last few pages, the final two dimensions of age changes should be fairly apparent. Because our physiology is so complex, we would expect a large number of events must take place before aging sets in. Hence, the third criterion is that physiological aging will be both *gradual* and *progressive.* If, as some scientists now assume, aging begins at the molecular or cellular level, we can imagine how many years might pass before changes become clinically observable. Such things as heart diseases, strokes or cancer take place relatively quickly when compared to other bodily processes, thus they can be excluded from the aging process, although they are responsible for a large percentage of the deaths in middle and old age. If senescence is a *debilitating* process, then clearly the final criterion is one of declining functional capacity that makes death more probable. The deleterious changes associated with senescence reduce an organism's adaptability to a given environment. While these four criteria are essential for the identification of inner mechanisms of aging, we cannot afford to ignore their inescapable association with social factors.

Over 150 years ago a man named Benjamin Gompertz formulated a mathematical model to predict mortality rates for use in his insurance business. According to Gompertz, our probability of dying increases throughout our adult life at an exponential rate, roughly doubling every eight years. From a simple mathematical equation Gompertz plotted the theoretical curve depicted in Figure 4.2. Actual mortality has been shown to closely approximate Gompertz' projections so frequently that his model is used today as a standard against

Figure 4.2
Gompertz plot. Mortality rate as a function of age, United States, 1939–41. Between age 30 and 90 the data obey the equation $R = R_o e^{at}$. R_o (the initial mortality rate at time o) and a (the increase in the mortality rate over time) are constants which depend on the population; e is the base of natural logarithms and t is the age in years.

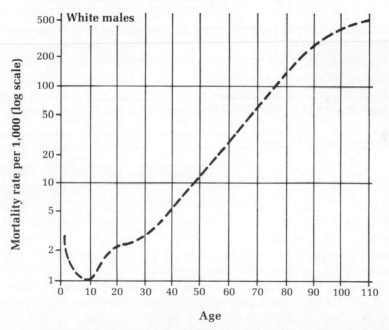

Source: B.L. Strehler, "Dynamic Theories of Aging," in N.W. Shock, ed., *Aging — Some Social and Biological Aspects* (Washington, D.C.: American Association for the Advancement of Science, 1960), p. 286.

which theories of mortality may be measured. While chronological age and physiological age do not always coincide, they are close enough that chronological age is to date the best predictor scientists have at their disposal for determining the probability of death.

Biological Theories of Aging

Since time immemorial people have searched for a magic elixir to ward off old age. Potential candidates have ranged from the proverbial tiger testicle recipes, or rejuvenizing contact with sexually active adolescents, to contemporary *procaine* (Gerovital H-3) agents. Legions of Ponce de Leons have sought the elusive formula, but regardless of whatever else they found, a cure for aging is still remote. Today scientists continue the search with an eye to the inner mechanisms of our bodies, beginning with the processes transpiring at the cellular level. When focusing on the system or organism, physiologists are looking for both the causes of biological decay and the minimum level at which organs in the body are capable of maintaining life. It is interesting to wonder how many of us would have the desire to prolong life if it meant living with the infirmities of advanced age for an additional number of years. To avoid the plight of the mythical Greek Tithonus, however, we must first learn the causes of aging in order to retard its advent. Only then will an extension of our normal life expectancy be a logically reasonable and sought after goal.

Entropy, Energy and Aging

Before turning to the explanations of biological aging, it will be useful to introduce a concept that had profound influence on early discussions of aging. During the nineteenth century, attempts to understand the apparent order of the universe became formalized in two laws of thermodynamics. The first of these held that energy can neither be created nor destroyed; hence, there is a limited amount of energy in the universe. The second contends that this energy became increasingly unavailable to do work or maintain order. Though we shall not discuss it in great detail, it is the second law that is important for our purposes, for out of its corollaries came the concept of *entropy*. While entropy is one of the most elusive concepts in science, suffice it to say that unless a system, any system, is already in equilibrium, it takes a greater amount of energy to maintain a stable state through time than would be necessary if its component elements became disorganized. An important variable controlling the speed with which the system loses its ability to do work, including the maintenance of its integrity, is the amount of energy originally involved. The degradation of the system, once begun, is irreversible, continuing until no further energy is available for its use, at which time the system can be said to have achieved equilibrium. This tendency for disorganization due to energy loss as a function of time is referred to as entropy. Increasing entropy has been thought to be a common characteristic of all systems, whether mechanical, cybernetic or human. Therefore, it is easy to understand how a physiologist might find the notion of entropy attractive in explaining aging and the ultimate disorganization of life's processes which we call death. The first physiological "theories" formulated to shed light upon biological aging were significantly influenced by the idea of a finite store of energy causing the eventual disruption of bodily equilibrium or, alternatively, by a variation of the then innovative germ theories, which, insofar as aging was concerned, focused primarily on the putrefaction of intestinal wastes. It should be borne in mind, however, that what we presently label as theory must meet far more stringent criteria than those specified in the formative period of the discipline. Among the early theories, two of the most prominent reflect in varying degrees the idea of entropy and are sometimes referred to as the *rate of living* and the *wear and tear* or *stress* theories.

Early Biological Theories

During the 1920s, biologists advanced the proposition that animal organisms have a fixed amount of energy available to them; after it is used up, death is quick to follow. The *rate of living* theory (Pearl, 1928) has received considerable attention in the intervening years but is currently regarded with disfavor. From a common sense point of view, such a theory seems plausible. Many organisms do appear to have a certain amount of energy stored within and once it is exhausted they die, much the way a fire dies after the wood is burned. If the theory were accurate for all activity, we would anticipate higher mortality rates among those organisms or individuals who engaged in the most exercise throughout their lives. In point of fact the opposite is the case. Regular exercise or work seemingly maintains the body rather than hastens its demise. Lessened functional capacity is indeed one cause of death, yet the losses that occur have nothing to do with any finite energy reserves. Another version of the rate of living theory sometimes set out is the *exhaustion* theory, usually discussed in terms of mechanical analogies like watch springs. While metabolic rates do seem to affect longevity — with those creatures having lower metabolisms living longer than those with higher rates — contemporary metabolic explanations do not include this fixed energy concept.

Another general proposition related to the foregoing hypothesis is offered by a more contemporary view subsumed under the rubric of stress theory (Selye and Prioreschi, 1960). It is unique by virtue of the fact stress theory perceives no difference between the consequences of normal aging and those of pathological conditions. It should be made clear, however, the theory does not encompass any kind of sociopsychological strain, but refers instead to physical wear and tear from sudden and unexpected stressors over which we have no control. Rapid temperature changes, chemicals or other irritants, exhaustion, and so on are typical stressors experienced by our bodies. Experiments conducted on both tissue samples and intact animals reveal a three stage reaction pattern that the theory contends resembles aging. The only difference is one of time frame; the stress syndrome identified in the laboratory is assumed to be a telescoped version of what happens over the lifetime of an individual. The three stage process of alarm, resistance and exhaustion presumably leaves us indelibly scarred with fibrosis tissue that accrues with successive stressful events. Old age is then that period in which we are no longer capable of fighting off various insults as a result of the accumulation of wear and tear. Like the concept of fixed energy, the stress hypothesis is not now a widely accepted causal explanation of the aging process.

Recent Biological Theories

When concerned with molecular and cellular levels, physiological accounts of aging become considerably more complex and technical. While the discussion here shall provide a topical review of the most popular of these, the task of detailed analysis must be left to specialized biological and physiological courses or texts. Perhaps as an artifact of our disciplinary training, each of the theories addresses itself to one particular aspect of the problem; this could lead one to the erroneous assumption that there is a single cause of aging. Scientists are beginning to realize any explanatory framework ultimately emerging from the years of research will be one that crosses narrow academic divisions — previous efforts to compartmentalize bodily areas for investigation have proven unsuccessful in determining macrolevel changes. The differences among the following theories are often more apparent than real; the sensitive reader will perceive a great deal of overlap and complementarity among them.

A look through a high-powered electron microscope would show our bodies to be made up of a variety of cell types, plus a ground scaffolding material that holds the cells in place. Basically these can be classified into two types of cells: *mitotic* cells such as those found in our skin, which divide or copy themselves, and *post-fixed mitotic* cells, which are incapable of duplication. Both types have a structure similar to that shown in Figure 4.3. Once we attain a maximum number of the nondividing cells, as, for example, in the central nervous system, which is composed of post-fixed mitotic cells, we face an ever-dwindling supply. Although scientists have been able to duplicate the chemical composition of the cell, they have not yet been able to produce one in the laboratory. Apparently there is something about the way the components are organized that presently eludes us. In terms of its function, the cell has been called a molecular factory, since it carries out the processes necessary for sustaining life. In order to do so the cell must first support and maintain itself. Only then can it contribute to the maintenance of the organism. However, for numerous reasons, cells die. It was once believed that mitotic cells were capable of reproducing themselves for an indefinite period; therefore, by implication, as far as aging was concerned, only the death of nondividing cells was of any consequence. Scientists now know that both types of cells have a maximum life span not appreciably longer than that of the whole organism. They also know that cells produced late in life show *morphological* differences from similar cells produced by a younger organism. The most significant cellular alterations occurring over time are summarized in Table 4.1.

Since nondividing cells cannot be replaced, scientists have sought a life maintenance level for post-fixed mitotic cells below which the probability of the immediate death of the organism increases drastically. Cellular deterioration or *cell necrosis* could be the consequence of normal changes over time in catalytic chemical components of the cell, or cells might cease their activities because of rearrangements of the genetic material in the nucleus, or decline might be the result of pathological conditions; in practice it is extremely difficult to distinguish among them. In any event, once a certain degree of loss has occurred, the chances of death begin to increase. Though we know spinal *ganglia*, certain cells along nerve tracts, and brain cells decline in very old age to roughly 60–80 percent of their number in younger organisms, these reductions do not appear to be the initiators of aging. Nonetheless, cellular modifications are particularly important for aging. To meet its two principal tasks, a cell must first produce the energy required by its internal components to sustain life, maintain its own and the organism's

Figure 4.3
Diagram of a typical cell

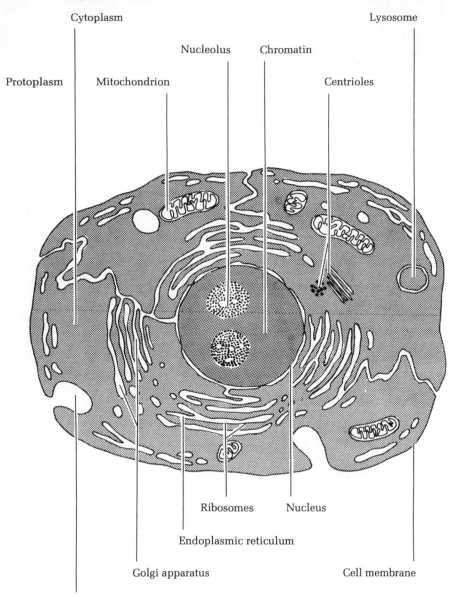

Source: Adapted from E.E. Chaffee and E.M. Greisheimer, *Basic Physiology and Anatomy* (Philadelphia: J.B. Lippincott, 1969), p. 17.

Table 4.1
Summary of Cellular Alterations in Aging

COMPONENT	ALTERATION
Nucleus	Clumping, shrinkage, fragmentation and dissolution of chromatin
	Increased staining
	Intranuclear inclusions
	Nuclear enlargement
	Amitotic division
	Invagination of nuclear membrane
Nucleolus	Increased size and number
Cytoplasm	Accumulation of pigments
	Accumulation of fat
	Depletion of glycogen
	Hyaline droplets
	Formation of vacuoles
Mitochondria	Decrease in numbers and alteration in shape
Golgi apparatus	Fragmentation
Endoplasmic reticulum	Loss of Nissl substance

Source: S. Bakerman, ed., *Aging Life Processes* (Springfield, Ill.: Charles C Thomas, 1969), p. 10.

chemical stability, and, in the case of mitotic cells, accurately reproduce itself. If for any reason the coordination of these subtasks is interrupted, then cellular deterioration is likely to follow. We will examine some of the factors thought to bring about a disruption in normal cellular functioning, but first we must comment briefly on the life span of dividing cells.

As mentioned earlier, biologists previously assumed mitotic cells were capable of duplicating themselves in near perpetuity under optimum laboratory conditions. Nourished by a correct medium, their life span, if not indefinite, was certainly longer than that of the host organism. The original research was surrounded by such acclaim, including a Nobel Prize, that subsequent challenges were attributed to faulty procedure and dismissed. Rather perplexing is the fact that until the late 1950s no such studies were carried out using human tissue; all research findings were based on animal samples, especially chick embryos, and generalized to humans. Almost serendipitously, as a spin-off from cancer research, it was discovered that human cells grown in culture doubled just as had been foreseen; yet after a number of doublings, the rate of division began to decline, eventually coming to a halt, and the cells died. The researchers titled the deterioration of the replicative process and the eventual cessation of cell division the Phase III phenomenon. They also found that tissue samples drawn from younger donors lived longer in vitro than those from older donors. In a series of carefully controlled experiments, the youngest cells were observed to attain a maximum of 50 doublings before death, while older cells doubled proportionately less, depending on the age of the host. This in itself was enough to alter much of the thinking about physiological aging. Interrupting cellular division by freezing cells in liquid nitrogen at temperatures as low as −190°C or by other means and then returning them to the normal range does not alter the remaining number of doublings, suggesting there is indeed a built-in limit to life (Denny, 1975). Doubtlessly the many subtle variations that go hand in hand with Phase III open the door to age changes in the organism long before its cells have lost their reproductive capacity (Hayflick, 1974).

Out of these data have come two related theories that give added weight to cellular level explorations for the causes of aging. The first, relevant to either mitotic or post-fixed mitotic cells, posits that our *genetic programing* may simply run out over time. Evolutionary forces actually play a role in the survival of a species up to, but not beyond, the reproductive period, since there is no way to pass along those attributes that prove to be adaptive in the later phases of life. Thus, the refinement of genetic instructions to the organism has an effect only on early portions of the program. Looking back at Figure 4.3, we see something labeled chromatin on the nucleus of the cell. These are loosely coiled strands that split lengthwise in dividing cells and must be present in all cells; most of us are probably more familiar with the term chromosomes. Human beings have 46 chromosomes in every body cell. They are in turn composed of thousands of tiny genes that ultimately determine what a cell will be and how it will function. For reasons as yet unknown, our genetic clocks may run down over the years, giving rise to the Phase III phenomenon.

The second hypothesis derived from knowledge of the construction of chromosomes was subsequently refined into two further explanations. With the discovery of deoxyribonucleic acid (DNA) in the early 1950s, it was also revealed that certain conditions brought about an alteration in the extremely precise arrangement of the chemical components of DNA. Basically DNA is a spiral ropelike ladder consisting of four compounds paired together much like tongue and groove flooring. The order the components take constitutes what we call the genetic code. These components, however, can be damaged by events in such a way that the message they provide will be incorrect. *Somatic mutation,* as the theories regarding genetic instability have been named, is applicable to both types of cells, possibly contributing to the demise of post-fixed mitotic cells and carried on to the next generation in mitotic cells. Cells of an inferior character seem to appear more frequently in older individuals and may be caused by any of a range of mutagenic influences on the body. Mutations may be the consequence of a "hit" that changes the structure of DNA or may result from cross-linkages between molecules within other parts of the cell. Exposure to radiation is one of the most familiar causes of mutations.

In addition to molecular mutations, mitotic cells may become inoperative due to *copying errors* in repeated divisions. For a message to be transmitted to the cell or larger parts of the organism, DNA depends on the ribonucleic acid (RNA) stored in the nucleolus portion of the nucleus. The synthesizing or manufacture of protein enzymes is the chief task of the nucleolus, with a duplicate copy of the mechanism transferred during cell division. Since changes in the structure of RNA have been observed in samples from older donors, it is hypothesized that these may be a result of slight but progressive modifications in copying. Such "error catastrophies" (Orgel, 1970) may so alter the protein produced by newer cells that they are incapable of recognizing essential components of themselves; this forces the body's immunologic apparatus to work against itself. Cancer is the best known example of aberrant cells produced within our own bodies. This *autoimmune* phenomenon has also been found to increase with age (Sigel and Good, 1972), but as yet scientists do not know whether it results from copying errors or from aging of the immune system itself. The prevalence of rheumatoid arthritis, a consequence of autoimmunity, is itself testimony to the impact of these inner mechanisms on the lives of the elderly.

Before concluding the discussion of physiological explanations of the aging process, a few words must be mentioned about two additional theories. The first focuses on the accumulation of age pigment within the cell, familiar to most of us as those "liver spots" we see on the skin of older people. The second concerns one of the most abundant forms of protein in our bodies — collagen. Collagen is present in all connective tissues such as ligaments, tendons or muscles, in the walls of arteries and in the ground substance holding our cells in place. It, too, is probably well-known to any of us who have had the misfortune to buy one of those "tough old birds" who mysteriously wander onto the poultry counter from time to time.

Around the turn of the century, two physiologists noted the accumulation of dusky brown particles in cells and tissue. They eventually decided these were the by-products of the body's assimilation of nutrients and designated them "clinkers." Subsequent research revealed a progressive deposition of the substance over time as a function of age, which today is referred to by the more appropriate name of age pigment, or *lipofuscin*. In the past few decades, intensive study of the changing chemical morphology associated with aging has shown lipofuscin granules to be composed of a number of chemical elements normally present in the body, combining to form lipofuscin as a consequence of chemical reactions necessary for metabolization of nutrients. We know it is found universally, first in the cytoplasm of nondividing cell lines, and that it is a reliable indicator of age; as yet, however, there is no conclusive information about its causal relationship with aging. We also do not know if it is the consequence of copying error or some other phenomenon. It appears that lipofuscin begins to mass together early in life in active organ systems like cardiac muscle and brain tissue, and gradually spreads, ultimately showing up on the skin. It is not, however, found in all tissue, nor is it deposited at a constant rate in the same tissue; rather, it is related to the functional specialization of a tissue's cells. For example, after age ten, lipofuscin is deposited at a constant rate in both healthy and diseased heart muscles. If we lived to be 90 years old it would occupy approximately 6 to 7 percent of the intracellular volume in our *myocardium* (Strehler, 1962; see Figure 4.4). Microscopic examination of the accumulation of age pigment in brain and nerve cells has shown similar progressive patterns. As further evidence of its relationship with aging, lipofuscin deposits are found extensively in cases of progeria, a rare form of premature aging among children (Timiras, 1972).

The collection site of lipofuscin in the cytoplasm of the cell is particularly important, since it is presumably involved in the inactivation of the Golgi, which are responsible for the export of substances from the cell. It may possibly have the same effect on the mitochondria, the transducers that furnish the enzymes and the energy for other essential processes. Finally, lipofuscin may also be associated with the lysosomes; the two have similar chemical components. Lysosomes produce the enzyme necessary for the digestion of nutrients and the dissolving of worn out cell parts. The enzyme they contain is so powerful that lysomes have been called "suicide sacks," for if the enzyme were to be released accidently, the entire cell would be destroyed. If the appearance of age pigment does indeed interfere with the respiratory and energy-releasing functions of the cell, its implication for aging is most significant (Strehler and Mildvan, 1962).

While we shall discuss nutrition in greater detail later, we should be aware that both disease and dietary habits are among the external factors contributing to the formation of age pigment. Lipofuscin has been associated with a deficiency of vitamin E and an oversupply of fatty acids. Further, the majority of us tend to eat too

Figure 4.4
Relationship between age and pigment content of human myocardium

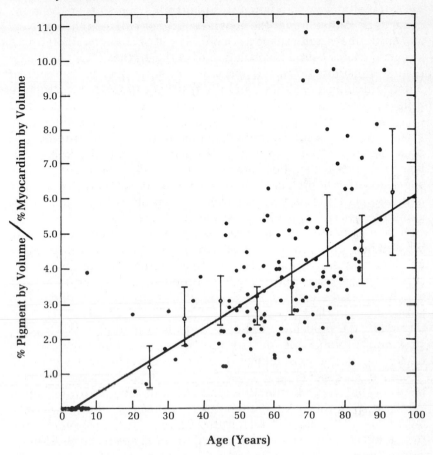

Source: B.L. Strehler et al., "Rate and magnitude of age pigment accumulation in the human myocardium," *Journal of Gerontology* XIV, 4 (1959): 433.

much for our own good — in the neighborhood of 1100 excess calories daily. Coupled with the fact that we eat more than we need, the manner in which we ingest our food makes a difference. Eating small amounts spread over several meals leads to a relatively innocuous oxidative process with few intermediate by-products. However, if we sit down and gorge ourselves with our usual intake of 3300 calories in one sitting, an accumulation occurs that leads to a buildup of harmful by-products. (Bjorksten, 1969).

Caloric intake may also contribute to the gradual biochemical vulcanization that bonds together certain cells and tissue (Bakerman, 1969). Since this cross-linking is observed most frequently in the extracellular protein found in collagenous fibers, its analysis has come to be known under the general rubric of *collagen theory*. Normal epidermal scar tissue is a good example of collagen fiber; it was known decades before the isolation of collagen that scars show age-related transformations. The formation of scars over the wounds of older individuals is slower, and the resultant tissue has a structure different from that found on younger people. Collagen composes 30 to 40 percent of body protein; it is found in the viscous gelatinlike ground substance surrounding the cells, in the walls of arteries and in connective tissue. Together with elastic and reticular fibers, collagen provides the support that holds the cells in place; it serves as a shock absorber to protect vital organs and it allows for the expansion and contraction of tissues. However, like an old rubber band, collagen undergoes modification of its elastic properties over time.

The characteristic changes in skin provide some indication of what is happening to the collagen throughout our bodies. As collagen becomes denser and replaces other components in the ground substance, cells experience greater difficulty acquiring nutrients and expelling wastes, because the ground substance has lost much of its permeability. A lack of elasticity in the walls of our circulatory system spells the probable onset of atherosclerosis, higher blood pressure and innumerable related problems. Muscular effectiveness declines with age, most noticeably after the age of 50, partly as a consequence of degenerative alteration in collagen fibers. Likewise bones become more brittle, due to changes in the marrow collagen. While it is improbable that alteration in collagen is the sole harbinger of aging, the pattern of cross-linking, and its role in impairing functional capacities, justify its inclusion among primary physiological explanations of the aging process (Bjorksten, 1969; Verzar, 1964).

Functional Impairment and Age

The significance of the foregoing theories lies in their ability to explain the progressive loss of biological integrity over life. They provide us with a perspective on the underlying mechanisms of more widespread physiological changes. Alone they are hardly sufficient to tell us why one person dies at 45 and another lives to be over 100. Longevity is a consequence of the reciprocal influences of normal physiological aging and a wide range of social and environmental factors. Generally speaking, our bodies are at their most vigorous when we are 12 years old, but at any time, fitness depends on the dynamic interplay between intrinsic and extrinsic resources. We tend to forget that chronological age is a convenient indicator of functional capacity, not an absolute measure. It is not at all unusual in clinical examinations of the elderly to find a man of 70 with the eyesight of someone 20 years his junior, yet with the kidney function of one considerably older. In this case, chronological age would clearly fail to provide an adequate index of the man's overall fitness.

Although it is true that technological advances and urbanization have alleviated many of the stresses that confronted our ancestors in harsher environments, stress remains a relative concept. It is axiomatic in discussions of physical capacities that function depends on use; if we are not called upon to perform, it is hardly possible to fully develop our resources. Today, few if any of us must compete with wild animals for our food. Yet if we did, and managed to survive until later life, the vital capacity of our lungs would not decline as it does leading a sedentary life. Many social and economic factors impose differential pressures on functional capacity. Overall, our ability to survive stressful episodes encountered from time to time in the normal course of events depends on the relative severity of the challenges, as well as on our reserve capacities. While measures of functional level show a linear decline with age, most of these reflect decrements under resting conditions. In addition, the participants in such studies have usually been drawn from elderly institutionalized patients. As we shall see in Chapter Ten, this group may not be at all representative of the elderly in general. Similar observations of other groups or tests run during brief periods of maximum effort might show different patterns. Under stress situations we would expect to see a more precipitous decline, a greater displacement of normal levels plus extended recovery periods (Shock, 1960b). A great deal remains to be uncovered about the physiological characteristics of the aged.

Changes in Body Composition

Regardless of the extent to which modern society mitigates the hard reality of physiological decline, one cannot avoid the gradual inevitable loss of life processes. Alterations at one level trigger changes at another; ultimately, body composition and the functioning capacity of organ systems undergo debilitating transformations. Some of the major changes in body composition are set forth in Table 4.2. It must be kept in mind the figures represent statistical averages and should not be taken as indicative of what is necessarily in store

Table 4.2

Comparison of a Tentative "Reference Man"
Aged 70 with One Aged 25

	AGE 25 *	AGE 70†
Fat (%)	14	30
Water (%)	61	53
Cell Solids (%)	19	12
Bone Mineral (%)	6	5
Specific Gravity	1.068	1.035

*Brozek, J., Washington, D.C., Department of the Army, Office of the Quartermaster General, 1954.
†Fryer, J.H., in N.W. Shock, ed., *Biological Aspects of Aging* (New York: Columbia University Press, 1962), p. 59.
Source: S. Bakerman, ed., *Aging Life Processes* (Springfield, Ill.: Charles C Thomas, 1969), p. 8.

for a given individual. Also, the gradual expansion of adipose tissue does not result totally from weight gain, but also from an increase in fat cells relative to muscle and bone. Both males and females experience a decrease in body water content with age proportionate to the increase in fat tissue. Women, however, tend to have approximately 5 percent more fat than men at every stage of life.

The decline in cellular solids is an important index of aging since it represents a loss of protein as well as *parenchymal,* or metabolically active, tissue contributing to the ongoing needs of the organism. Until our later years, lean body mass, as parenchymal tissue is labeled, accounts for 35 to 45 percent of body weight, but this proportion diminishes over time with the increments in fat tissue. Recently, measures of potassium or specific gravity have replaced lean body mass as indicators of the changing ratio of working to nonworking cells. Potassium is vital to a wide range of adaptive response mechanisms; its loss over time is bound to result in changes in all manner of feedback mechanisms. As shown in Table 4.2, total mineral content exhibits only a slight decline with age, but as yet scientists are not prepared to say that this is actually a consequence of age itself. The relationship of mineral content with a number of other variables is simply too complex to provide definitive information. Alterations in fat content and minerals are reflected in specific gravity. Parenchymal tissue has a greater density than fat, so that we would expect a decrease in specific gravity over time for a given weight. The usual procedure is to compare normal body weight to weight while immersed in water. Doing so reveals an average decline of a little over 30 percent in specific gravity between early adulthood and later life.

After age 30 a wide range of physiological functions exhibit a linear decline of somewhat less than 1 percent each year. Lest we acquire too negative an image, it should also be noted that an equally large number of functions remain fairly stable under resting conditions until well past the seventh decade. There appears to be little change in the acidity, osmolarity or sugar levels of our blood unless strong displacing stimuli occur (Shock, 1960b). The reasons for this have to do with alternative control mechanisms that are not found for other functions. Yet people rarely die of "old age"; that is, they do not actually wear out. More often they succumb to specific demands that surpass their remaining reserve capacity. The differences among people, and among organs within an individual, are a constant source of medical and interpersonal strain for the older person. Of major significance is the fact that those functions dependent on the coordination of various organs show a greater deterioration with age than those of single organs. One example would be maximum vital capacity; though lessened, we seldom become aware of it unless exertion prompts a need for a rapid oxygen exchange. Only then do we discover that the muscles necessary for rapid breathing have also undergone decay, making it considerably more difficult to catch our breath than we remembered. In the following paragraphs, some of the more salient physiological changes known to affect us in middle and later life are briefly enumerated. Sensory losses having a more immediate impact on psychological states will be discussed in the following chapter.

Conduction velocity, or the speed nerve pulses travel along neural pathways, shows a decrement of approximately 15 percent over the course of normal aging. The impulses themselves may be thought of as electrical charges that spontaneously depolarize the electrical potential of the nerve cell. When this happens, the membrane becomes temporarily more permeable, allowing both potassium and sodium ions to move in and out in wavelike fashion. For a response to be initiated, an impulse must first travel from the receptor that a stimulus has excited to the effector. The impulse velocity is dependent on the size of the nerve fiber, the continuity of its insulation and the age of the organism. In larger fibers, the impulses jump from node to node, covering a distance more than equal to the length of a football field in less than a second (120 meters per second). In smaller, exposed fibers, it may take nearly one second for an impulse to travel from foot to hip (0.5 meters per second). Before a second impulse can travel the same pathway, a refractory period must elapse, allowing a repolarization of potassium and sodium ions. The decreasing impulse speed among the elderly may be partially due to alterations in the chemical balance between these substances. Regardless of localized regressive changes in nerve fibers, the elderly show an increased reaction time of considerable magnitude. Velocity factors alone are responsible for less than 10 percent of the slowing in reaction time. It has been hypothesized that the differences result from higher threshold levels or the breakdown in the integrative mechanisms of the central nervous system (see Figure 4.5).

Basal metabolism rate is an aggregate index of oxygen consumption. Since oxygen is utilized in oxidative and energy-producing activities, its use is particularly dependent on the amount of work called for. We would naturally expect to note higher rates for organs constantly in use versus those only called on to work periodically. A declining basal metabolism rate has been viewed as indicative of loss of parenchymal tissue and cellular activity plus a lowering of caloric requirements. If metabolism rates diminish by an average of 20 percent and caloric requirements by approximately 30 percent, the dysfunctional consequences of our eating habits can

Figure 4.5

Simplified linear decline of physiological capacities with age, value at age 30 = 100 percent

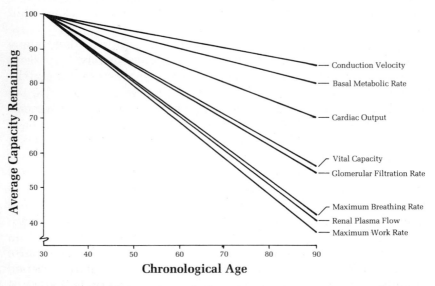

Source: Adapted from N.W. Shock, "The Physiology of Aging." *Scientific American* 206 (1962): 110.

easily be recognized. Intake exceeds demand, especially among older persons with lowered activity levels; therefore, obesity is the inevitable result (Freeman, 1965).

Cardiac function represents cardiac output per minute per meter of body surface. It declines at a constant rate directly proportional to basal metabolism. The reduction from early maturity to later life is paralleled by corresponding attenuation of other vascular capacities. The most noticeable among these are the elastic properties of the circulatory system and the redistribution of blood supplies. For example, the percentage of blood flowing to the cerebrum increases over time while that to the kidneys declines. Although physiologists have succeeded in plotting average decrements, the pervasiveness of cardiovascular diseases makes precise explanations of senescent changes extremely difficult. Diseases of the heart and associated interferences in blood flow are the number one cause of death among older persons. However, unlike the decrements in conduction velocity, cardiovascular decline is retarded by physical fitness (Brunner and Jokl, 1970).

Vital capacity and *maximum breathing rate* both reflect changing pulmonary capacities of the respiratory system. Insofar as they are coordinated, alterations in one presage changes in the other. Vital capacity is the maximum amount of air exchanged in breathing; the larger the residual volume, the shallower the intake and the more labored the breathing. Lung capacity itself is unaffected by age, but its proficiency is reduced by neuromuscular impairments. Maximum breathing rate is a measure of the amount of air moved through the lungs in a 15 second period while breathing as rapidly as possible. The inability to sustain rapid breathing, combined with lowered vital capacity, brings about poorer oxygenation of the blood. Our ability to perform work is predicated not only on muscular strength, but on adequate supplies of oxygen-rich blood and cardiac output. If oxygen intake declines or coordination between salient functions falters, it will be manifested in our ability to do work. Similarly, recovery time will be extended for older people subjected to displacing stimuli.

Glomerular filtration is the means whereby the kidneys filter water, salts, acids and wastes from the body's fluids, disposing of them by means of excretion. Research has pointed to a number of discrete homeostatic mechanisms of the kidney that undergo age-related changes quite apart from evidence of renal pathology. The accretion of calcium and collagen, autoimmunic responses, and alterations in renal blood flow interfere with optimum kidney function. Approximately one-fifth of the blood flowing to the kidney is filtered by the glomerulus. As the glomerular membrane becomes less permeable, percolation is inhibited, thereby checking the amount and concentration of the urine. The process of controlling fluid balances is very complex; even slight disturbances in the filtration rate have far-reaching ramifications for water and electrolyte balances. Clinical evidence from morphology and urinalysis suggest a decline of over 45 percent of glomerular permeability between maturity and our ninth decade.

Renal plasma flow is reduced by over half its original volume during the course of our adult lives. Both blood flow and filtration rates have been shown to drop by about 5 percent of the remaining capacity in each decade after age 30. Slightly less than one-quarter of the blood pumped by the heart flows to the kidney at maturity; however, the atrophy of the vascular tree, combined with tissue losses, serves to bring about reduction of this amount in successive decades. Involution of kidney structure and functional changes are considered basic senescent characteristics in human aging. As is the case with basal metabolism, appraisals of plasma flow serve as a comprehensive gauge for other renal functions as well.

Maximum work rate is also an inclusive measure of a number of coordinated activities. Muscular strength reaches a peak during our twenties, declining thereafter at a differential rate for various muscle groups and as a consequence of a range of social factors. But work performance is not dependent on muscles alone. Anaerobic work rate is an index used to ascertain efficiency and symmetry between the neuromuscular processes that have a role in the performance of physical tasks. Age changes evince a decline of 30 percent or more, accelerating rapidly after age 70 as greater incongruity among the various processes makes itself felt (Shock and Norris, 1970).

Numerous other functions are also vitiated over time. Blood cholesterol level increases, while glucose tolerance seems to be slightly reduced. Widespread changes in the endocrine system are reflected in a diminution of primary sex hormones, gastric acids and other enzymes, ACTH, thyroid hormones, steroid excretions, and so on. Considerable research has yet to be conducted before we can verify the relationship between normal physiological aging and declining functional capacities. For a number of processes, alternative mechanisms already exist; it is the ultimate goal of research to discover palliative measures for the remainder.

Summary

It is doubtful that many of us will wear out and die of actual old age. Rather, normal or pathological aging will impair our ability to respond to particular environmental challenges. This vulnerability is referred to by biologists as senescence. The theories of aging and senescence introduced were defined by the following parameters: aging must be inherent to the organism, common to all members of a species, gradually retrogressive and irreversible. However, as causes of death are seldom singular, theories of aging are generally evaluated in terms of their approximation to the exponential mortality curve or Gompertz plot.

As a consequence of numerous societal and pathological circumstances, wide discrepancies between chronological and physiological age are not at all uncommon. Chronological age, therefore, is but a façade, it cannot be relied upon as an accurate indicator of physiological aging. To obtain a better measure, some medical practitioners have proposed an index of biological age based on endogenous physiological deterioration. Initial explanations of biological aging focused on the accumulation of stresses or wear and tear that eventually led to exhaustion. These theories were closely linked to the notion of entropy — the degradation and eventual dissolution of all systems, human beings included. Subsequent theories concentrated on genetic designs or cellular level changes. Considerable attention has been given to the possibility of copying errors, mutations, finite doublings and autoimmunic responses as the causes of senescence. Other research has supported the hypothesis that the proliferation of age pigment or collagen substances may be an agent of cellular necrosis.

Cellular attenuation precedes the impairment of functioning and heightened susceptibility of the organism. While some processes do not diminish until quite late in life, we noted the linear decline endemic to vital systems. Those functions requiring symmetry between and among systems exhibit the greatest decay. Muscular atoxia, cardiac output or maximum breathing rate are good examples. Amelioration of physiological deterioration and prolongation of life are the ultimate goals of physiological research; as yet, however, these are beyond our grasp. In order to attain these goals, we need a better understanding of the psychological and sociological complexities of later life.

Pertinent Readings

ANDREW, W. The Anatomy of Aging in Man and Animals. New York: Grune and Stratton, 1971.
BAKERMAN, S., ed. Aging Life Processes. Springfield, Ill.: Charles C Thomas, 1969.

BIRREN, J.E., ed. *Handbook of Aging and the Individual.* Chicago: University of Chicago Press, 1959.

BJORKSTEN, J. "Theories." In *Aging Life Processes,* ed. S. Bakerman, 147–79. Springfield, Ill.: Charles C Thomas, 1969.

———. "The Crosslinkage Theory of Aging." *Journal of the American Geriatric Society* XVII (1968): 408–27.

BRUNNER, D., and E. JOKL, eds. *Physical Activity and Aging.* Baltimore: University Park Press, 1970.

COMFORT, A. *Ageing.* New York: Holt, Rinehart and Winston, 1964.

CURTIN, S. *Nobody Ever Died of Old Age.* Boston: Little, Brown and Co., 1972.

CURTIS, H.J. "A Composite Theory of Aging." *The Gerontologist* VI, 3 (1966): 143–49.

DENNY, P. "Cellular Biology of Aging." In *Aging: Scientific Perspectives: and Social Issues,* eds. D.S. Woodruff and J.E. Birren, 201–28. New York: D. Van Nostrand Company, 1975.

FREEMAN, J.T., ed. *Clinical Features of the Older Patient.* Springfield, Ill.: Charles C Thomas, 1965.

GOLDSTEIN, S. "The Biology of Aging." *New England Journal of Medicine* 285 (1971): 1120–29.

HAYFLICK, L. "The Strategy of Senescence." *The Gerontologist* XIV, 1 (1974): 37–45.

ORGEL, L.F. "The Maintenance of the Accuracy of Protein Synthesis and Its Relevance to Ageing." *Proceedings of the National Academy of Science* 67 (1970): 1476.

PEARL, R. *The Rate of Living.* New York: Alfred Knopf, 1928.

SELYE, H., and P. PRIORESCHI, "Stress Theory of Aging." In *Aging — Some Social and Biological Aspects,* ed. N.W. Shock, 261–72. Washington, D.C.: American Association for the Advancement of Science. 1960.

SHOCK, N.W. "Age Changes in Physiological Functions in the Total Animal: The Role of Tissue Loss." In *The Biology of Aging: A Symposium,* ed. B.L. Strehler, 258–64. Washington, D.C.: American Institute of Biological Sciences, 1960a.

———. "Some of the Facts of Aging." In *Aging: Some Social and Biological Aspects,* ed. N.W. Shock, 241–60. Washington, D.C.: American Association for the Advancement of Science, 1960b.

———, ed. *Biological Aspects of Aging.* New York: Columbia University Press, 1962.

SHOCK, N.W., and A.H. NORRIS. "Neuromuscular Coordination as a Factor in Age Changes in Muscular Exercise." In *Physical Activity and Aging,* eds. D. Brunner and E. Jokl. Baltimore: University Park Press, 1970.

SIGEL, M.M., and R.A. GOOD, eds. *Tolerance, Autoimmunity and Aging.* Springfield, Ill.: Charles C. Thomas, 1972.

STREHLER, B.L., ed. *The Biology of Aging: A Symposium.* Washington, D.C.: American Institute of Biological Sciences, 1960.

———. *Time, Cells, and Aging.* New York: Academic Press, 1962.

STREHLER, B.L., and A.S. MILDVAN. "Studies of the Chemical Properties of Lipofuscin Age Pigment." In *Biological Aspects of Aging,* ed. N.W. Shock, New York: Columbia University Press, 1962.

TIMIRAS, P.S., ed. *Developmental Physiology and Aging.* New York: The Macmillan Company, 1972.

VERZAR, F. "Aging of the Collagen Fiber." In *International Review of Connective Tissue Research,* vol. 2., ed. D.A. Hall. 243–300 New York: Academic Press, Inc., 1964.

Chapter 5

Theories of
Social Gerontology

As should already be evident, understanding the process of aging is impossible without consideration of the connections between aging on the physiological level and the social or cultural setting. For many years social gerontologists have worked alongside their biologically oriented colleagues to unravel the intricacies of becoming old, but only in the past two decades have they attempted to formulate integrative conceptual frameworks of their own to lend some order to the vast collection of empirical findings. Initially, gerontologists interested in either physiological or social aspects of the aging question proceeded piecemeal, focusing attention on problems the larger society defined as relevant, without any overriding concern for theoretical explanation. As the field has matured as a scientific endeavor, the separate branches developed at different rates by adopting the theoretical and methodological tools of earlier kindred disciplines. In Chapter Four we managed a brief glimpse at the biological theories currently in vogue as well as at those that have evolved over time. In the present discussion our concern will be with theories of social gerontology that have gained adherents since the first of them was formulated in 1960.

The Purpose of Theory

Theoretical Frameworks

The description of physiological theories in the previous chapter probably served to reinforce the preconception most people have of theoretical explanation as being the domain either of natural scientists surrounded by their specimens and a vast library or of life scientists in white lab coats carefully scrutinizing a computer printout of performance measures. Regardless of whether theory is defined by attempts at complete explanation and predictive accuracy or simply as a descriptive account of a particular event, theorizing is by no means limited to scientists. In point of fact, the theoretical process is considerably more widespread, constantly taking place in everyday life, from the time language is acquired to the development of a philosophy of life which gives it meaning. The process of naming, the most fundamental theoretical organization, is manifested by us all when as children we learn to identify objects by readily observable characteristics that help us discriminate one from another. Although general conceptual categories already exist in the structure of the language into which we are born, we each discover by experience increasingly diverse events that can be brought together under a general classification. Since others also learn to view the world in roughly the same terms, they, too, develop the same generalizations about it and are able to communicate what they see or feel. The structure of our language itself, therefore, serves as an implicit theoretical framework that not only circumscribes experience but acts as a filter through which individual encounters are perceived, modified, and categorized as examples of more general phenomena.

In a number of important respects, the theories formulated by social gerontologists can be viewed as extensions of the unreflective theorizing carried out in ordinary life. For one thing, gerontologists bring with them to the study of aging a certain taken-for-granted view of life based on their personal experience and the values of their culture. Furthermore, the "objects" upon which social gerontologists fix their attention are not at all like those of the natural scientists, who are free to impose a purely arbitrary order on their observations so long as it is logical and agreeable to fellow scientists. By contrast, the social scientist is faced with a pre-established system of meanings known to and utilized by the very people who are the focus of scientific investigation. It is important to bear in mind in examining the theories promoted by social gerontologists in their efforts to explain and understand the process of aging that the crucial dimensions of their conceptual frameworks are but reflections from the larger social matrix. At the same time, however, gerontologists strive to reach beyond the world of common sense to discover consistent patterns of aging in the social world.

Needless to say, the analysis of human behavior is infinitely complex and requires its own particular approach. Over and above any disciplinary orientation or field of investigation, all theoretical explanations share a common objective of making explicit the order behind what often appears as chaotic or individualistic events. By developing a system of interrelated propositions in a logical and verifiable manner, gerontologists subscribe to a similar goal with the intention of producing an integrative framework capable of providing a coherent explanation of why people age the way they do. In his introductory remarks to the first detailed explication of age stratification theory, Brim (1972) furnishes a concise statement of the need for conceptual integration that is equally applicable to other theories of aging. To begin with, an awareness of the *normative* character of aging in a social-cultural context brings about a broad appreciation of individual situations and the patterning fixed upon them by the institutional order in a given society. Once we have an impression of the relative nature of age-related norms, cognizance of their malleability should follow. The realization that aging does not necessarily have to be the way it is offers a justification for interceding in what is often taken to be a predetermined natural process. As Brim points out, the possibility for changing the manner in which we age has the potential of enhancing not only our personal lives but the general welfare of society as well.

Adjusting to Age

Prior to discussing the theories themselves, it is desirable to linger for a moment in order to touch on some of the difficulties involved in accounting for social patterns of aging. Not the least of these has to do with the wisdom behind or the need for a theory applicable to only the later years. There is less than complete agreement among gerontologists themselves that the social nature of aging requires its own explanation. Granted, theories do have a significant heuristic value, aiding as they do in the collection of data and the organization of existing information, plus giving direction for the implementation of policy changes. Still, the question remains as to *why* old age should demand its own, perhaps singular, interpretation. By the time people reach their later years, have they not already weathered innumerable personal changes and life course crises, which ought to leave them well prepared to face whatever ambiguities or anxieties they might encounter in their postretirement years? In one way, no, since for nearly every other age-related transformation in life, most people undergo what social psychologists call *anticipatory socialization,* the learning of a new role preparatory to actually assuming it. In addition, while it is true that adapting to change is a lifelong process, the adjustments made after one turns 60 or 65 are carried out against a backdrop of involutional changes in the physical and social realms. Whether or not it is essential or even possible to devise theoretical explanations is an issue that cannot be resolved here. Let us merely caution that some social scientists have noted the fallacy of inferring each new social problem demands a novel description. With regard to aging, some have suggested a perspective focusing on the nature of the transitional episodes throughout life may be sufficient to account for whatever change takes place during old age. In all fairness, it must be made clear the theories themselves do not seek to explain the totality of social aging; they generally limit themselves to expositions of how people adjust to advancing age. The means by which people reach a satisfactory structuring of their lives after the age of 65 are part and parcel of one of the more important unanswered questions about the life cycle. As older people become ever more visible on the national scene, it is predicted that even greater emphasis will be placed on providing an accurate prediction of what awaits us all in our later years (Havighurst, 1968; Maddox, 1970).

In constructing their explanations, social scientists are forced to treat all members of a category as though they are nearly identical. It is the only way by which any useful generalizations can be made, though in the case of human beings, they recognize the risks involved in making such an assumption. The aged do not, however, constitute a homogeneous aggregate; the same factors that are known to differentiate people at the earlier stages of life continue to operate unabated through the later phases. To adequately discuss the social and social-psychological processes integral to the way older people adjust to their situations, it is necessary to distinguish the consequences of aging per se from those more appropriately attributed to discontinuities in personal lifestyle or to situational constraints and generational effects. While there is no denying the importance of the latter, they do not actually reflect maturational age changes as much as they do differences between cohorts or individuals (Maddox, 1965; Schaie, 1967). To date, gerontological theory occupies an underdeveloped area within the field, but the last decade has been marked by a rapid growth and sophistication in the depiction of the social variables involved in human aging. The major theories all speak to essentially the same problem and, in a way, complement one another in many important respects.

Principal Theories in Social Gerontology

The propagation of explicit explanatory models in social gerontology can be dated from the first tentative statement of disengagement theory published in 1960, and particularly from the appearance the next year of Cumming and Henry's *Growing Old* (Cumming et al., 1960; Cumming and Henry, 1961). In the following years, scores of criticisms and reformulations appeared, including separate revisions by the original authors, before the controversy over the applicability of the theory finally began to subside. Although the disengagement model has now been largely discredited, it remains an important milestone in the theoretical literature because of the attention it generated and its role in bringing forth competing perspectives (Hochschild, 1975). An implicit emphasis on active involvement on the part of the elderly as a means of sustaining high morale had been an undercurrent in gerontological discussions for years, but did not receive deliberate explication until after the disengagement notion had sensitized researchers to the value of presenting detailed paradigms. It was inevitable, of course, that variations of these two approaches would prompt still further revisions. Perhaps the best known among these is the conception of an aged subculture formulated by Rose (1965) to account for the type of interaction commonly engaged in by older people. In the following sections each of these will be treated before turning to a brief discussion of a personality continuity theory, an ecological resource model and the recent age stratification perspective increasingly utilized by researchers to explain variations in life satisfaction and aging.

Disengagement Theory

The proposition of mutual disengagement represents the first major theoretical system attempted by social gerontologists. It was originally based on a cross-sectional survey analysis of 275 people ranging in age from 50 to 90, all of whom resided in Kansas City and were physically and financially self-sufficient. Reflecting the common sense observation that older people are more subject to ill health and to the probability of death than their younger counterparts, Cumming and Henry (1961) assert that a process of mutual withdrawal normally occurs in order to insure both an optimum level of personal gratification as well as an uninterrupted continuation of the social system. Since disengagement is thought to be a normatively governed phenomenon woven into the social fabric of mass society, they conceive of it as quite beyond individual whim or fancy, excepting some limited input into its timing. In setting forth the basic tenets of their theory, the authors refer to the aging process as:

... an inevitable mutual withdrawal or disengagement, resulting in decreased interaction between the aging person and others in the social system he belongs to. The process may be initiated by the individual or by others in the situation. The aging person may withdraw more markedly from some classes of people while remaining relatively close to others. His withdrawal may be accompanied from the outset by a preoccupation with himself; certain institutions in society may make this withdrawal easy for him. When the aging process is complete, the equilibrium which existed in middle life between the individual and his society has given way to a new equilibrium characterized by a greater distance and an altered type of relationship. [1961].

In spelling out the details of disengagement, Cumming and Henry clearly enunciate what is to be regarded as the inevitability and universality of the process. Society retracts because of the need to fit younger people into the slots once occupied by older people, no longer as useful or dependable as they were, and in order to maintain the equilibrium of the system. Individuals, on the other hand, choose to retreat because of an awareness of their diminishing capacities and the short time left to them before death. Although individual or cultural factors may alter the configuration of withdrawal, it is thought that older people everywhere will ultimately experience a severing of their social ties. As the number, nature, and diversity of the older person's contacts with the rest of the world contract, he or she will in effect become the sole judge of what is appropriate, freed as it were from normative control over commonplace behavior. Consequently, with the narrowing of the social life space, disengagement becomes a circular or self-perpetuating process in which there is a continuing shrinkage of interactional opportunities. Men, because of the instrumental nature of the roles with which they have primarily identified, will experience a drastic early constriction and identity crisis following retirement. In comparison, women, who have traditionally had ready access to socioemotional roles not as immediately subject to age-grading and organizational imperatives, encounter relatively fewer stresses. For a combination of experiential and developmental reasons, older people in general are likely to find themselves less motivated to preserve their social positions, while at the same time society will attempt to place younger people whose skills are not yet obsolete in positions held by those nearing retirement. A disjuncture may occur when either the individual or society is not yet ready to begin disengagement, although in most cases societal needs will take priority in initiating the process. When older people suffer severe adjustment problems, it usually implies a lack of synchronization between individual readiness and societal demands. However, as a corollary to the postulate of mutuality, Cumming and Henry did concede the possibility of reengagement should the individual choose to cultivate a new set of valued skills. Morale will obviously suffer as the disengagement process gains momentum due to the gaps between opportunities and orientation to previous roles, but once the elderly person is able to carve out new concerns and rearrange his or her priorities to fit the new station in life, high morale can conceivably be reestablished (Cumming and Henry, 1961).

Almost from the instant it appeared, disengagement theory engendered a running controversy among social gerontologists. For the most part, criticisms tended to converge around the presumed inevitability and inherent nature of the process. Questions were also posed about the functionality of withdrawal from either the individual or societal standpoint, plus the apparent lack of attention to personality factors and their effect on the whole process (Maddox, 1964; Atchley, 1971). Even Cumming and Henry have expressed misgivings in separate revisions of their original formulation. In her further thoughts on the theory of disengagement, Cumming (1963) backed away from an emphasis on the societal equilibrium and prescribed behavior to concentrate instead on the role of innate biological and personality differences as distinct from externally imposed withdrawal. She no longer viewed societal pressures as sufficient to account for disengagement, though she did reiterate her contention that men and women would undergo sex-linked stylized adjustment. Responding to the theory's critics, Cumming adds a caveat regarding what she terms the *appearance*, contrasted to the *experience*, of engagement. To those who would look simply at activity levels, Cumming suggests it is possible for disengaged people to appear involved, when in fact they are merely going through the motions of interaction, remaining oblivious to or simply shrugging off social sanctions on their behavior. The psychologically engaged, on the other hand, engrossed as they are in social intercourse, would still be responsive to feedback from others. At the same time, Cumming indicates a nascent attitudinal detachment, akin to a desocialization, may begin in middle age, far in advance of actual withdrawal and in the midst of what may for all intents and purposes look like the height of engagement.

Cumming also makes an important distinction between "impingers," those who take an assertive stance in their interaction, and "selectors," who are more passive, waiting for others to confirm preexisting assumptions about themselves, while recognizing only those cues that reinforce their views. In later years, impingers are thought to be more anxious about the prospect of disengagement, while the selectors have a capacity to use alternative mechanisms to insulate and maintain their personal orientations. Furthermore, Cumming repeatedly distinguishes men and women along a social dimension, not necessarily related to personality attributes as much as socialization, with men being the more ill-prepared to accommodate themselves to compensating forms of sociability in their later years. In either case, the remaining socioemotional roles assume added importance in maintaining self-conceptions or stimulation, helping both men and women resist shrinkage throughout much of the rest of life. Subsequent research has affirmed Cumming's emphasis on differential disengagement as an avenue for maximizing adjustment in various relationships (Williams and Wirths, 1965; Strieb and Schneider, 1971; Cumming, 1975). As far as the earlier definition of mutuality is important, Cumming (1975) redefines it as ". . . another way of saying the process is normatively governed and in a sense agreed upon by all concerned." She does repeat, nonetheless, her original contention of the interest mass society has in controlling its own vital affairs by removing crucial functions from the role repertoires of older people, though she does not explicitly address the part played by structural conditions.

Henry (1965) also amended his initial view of the disengagement model to lay greater stress on psychological dynamics. Like Cumming, he agreed that they had not satisfactorily resolved all the questions of the process, but rather than focusing on innate temperamental variables, he chose instead to adopt a developmental approach. In essence, Henry's later statement is practically synonymous with the position propounded by Havighurst, Neugarten and Tobin (1968), who also worked with the Kansas City data, but who arrived at a somewhat different conclusion from that originally implied by Cumming and Henry. Since a general overview of the developmental perspective is offered below and in Chapter Six, it should suffice at this point to say developmentalists conceive of personality as continually evolving, with adjustments at each successive stage reflecting earlier coping strategies as well as the matrix of environmental factors active at the moment. Most developmental psychologists also see a gradual turning toward greater *interiority* over the course of life; consequently, it is quite natural to expect older people to be less attentive to external events and more attuned to their own inner states. In Henry's restatement, the character of personality coping mechanisms and the focus on interiority are derived from previous experiences that determine the level of engagement or disengagement during subsequent stages of the life cycle. Those people who customarily have dealt with stress by turning inward and insulating themselves from the world will probably continue to manifest a pattern of withdrawal. At the same time, those who remain engaged are likely to have been similarly predisposed over the course of their lives. For this latter group, the nature of activities may change, but generally they will rely on their interaction to resist the centripetal movement inherent in the disengagement model. For all practical and theoretical purposes, Henry's revision of the kernel of disengagement theory can be read as an abandonment in favor of a more developmental approach.

The Activity Perspective

In the course of maturing, children gain a sense of themselves through their socializing experiences and via responses of significant others to various identities tried on in much the way adults try on clothing. By assuming various roles, children are able to participate in the larger world, thereby gradually carving out their own social identities. As adults, people continue to refine and refurbish their self-concepts in their performance of socially valued, or at least legitimated, actions, seeking out what is sometimes referred to as *consensual validation:* the affirmation of their personal sense of worth and integrity. Upon reaching that socially prescribed stage of life wherein they are commonly divested of many of the roles that have been so central to their lives for years, older people experience a narrowing of their social radius, a reduction of their activity levels and, consequently, a loss of or confusion in their sense of who they are. To offset these losses, preserve morale and sustain self-concepts, the activity theory of aging presumes, almost the converse of disengagement, that restitution, in the form of compensatory activities, must take place. By keeping active, it is presumed people will remain socially and psychologically fit. In the words of one researcher, the central thesis of activity theory can be summarized as: ". . . the greater the number of optional role resources with which the individual enters old age, the better he or she will withstand the demoralizing effects of exit from the obligatory roles ordinarily given priority in adulthood" (Blau, 1973).

The proponents of the activity orientation assert that disengagement theory may be applicable to a small minority of the elderly, usually the very old; but for the vast bulk of older people, the continuance of a moderately active lifestyle will have a marked preservative effect on their sense of well-being (Havighurst and Albrecht, 1953; Maddox, 1970). Despite recognition of the fact that not all activities provide sustenance for the self-concept, little attention has as yet been directed to the differences between types of activities or an individual's ability to exert any significant control over either the roles themselves or the performance of those roles. As a result, the theory has received only limited empirical support and has been criticized as an oversimplification of the questions involved. It may hardly be appropriate merely to substitute pastimes, geared to what is thought to be older people's interests and abilities, for those roles they surrendered as they moved beyond middle age. Busying one's self with enterprises meaningless in terms of dominant cultural values, presumably still subscribed to by older people, may not in itself contribute to adjustment (Phillips, 1957; Gubrium, 1973). On the other hand, both longitudinal and cross-cultural investigations of old age have repeatedly found a positive, but by no means incontrovertible, association between morale, personal adjustment and activity levels (Havighurst et al., 1969; Palmore, 1970).

The first full-bodied, systematic statement of activity theory did not appear until over a decade after the disengagement theory caused such a furor in gerontological circles, and even then its validation proved to be somewhat problematic. Following an explicit definition of the concepts implied, four postulates central to activity theory have been stipulated. First, the greater the role loss, the less the participation in activity. Second, as activity levels remain high, the greater the availability of role support for role identities claimed by the older person. Third, the stability of role supports insures a stable self-concept. Finally, the more positive one's self-concept, the greater the degree of life satisfaction. From these four propositions, six theorems were deduced that specify in detail the relationships implied by the theory. With such an auspicious statement of a theory never more than implied in the 20 years since it was initially suggested, it is indeed unfortunate that the data available to the investigators were insufficient to provide definitive support for the propositions basic to activity theory (Lemon, Bengtson and Peterson, 1972).

The Aged as a Subculture

Broadly speaking, both the activity and subcultural perspectives on the adjustment problems of the elderly share an underlying interactionist orientation that posits a close relationship among roles, social identities and the maintenance of self-concepts. However, while the activity approach assumes people continue to adhere to middle-aged standards and expectations as they move into their later years, the latter asserts the development of a distinctive aged subculture. Unfortunately, neither is able to explain the discontinuities assumed to exist between middle and old age. To help clarify the social relations between older people and the rest of society, some social gerontologists have offered the concept of an aged subculture similar in nature to those age status groupings discussed in Chapter One in order to account for differential adjustment. As conceived by Rose (1965), the initial advocate of this perspective, whenever members of one category interact more among themselves than with people from other categories, a subculture will be generated. In addition, he suggested there are a variety of demographic and social trends contributing to the genesis of an identifiable aged subculture that effectively cuts across all previous statuses to impart to the elderly a sense of group identity over and above earlier memberships. Among the specific factors mentioned by Rose are the sheer numbers of persons beyond the age of 65 who are still healthy and mobile enough to interact. With the growth of what some have termed aged ghettos, either retirement communities, inner city neighborhoods or residual rural congregations created when younger people migrate to urban areas, older people live in close proximity to one another. Legally established retirement policies now common in most industrialized societies have blocked major avenues for many older people to retain their integration with the larger society, thereby promoting a greater identification with an aged peer group. Social services designed to assist older people also tend to prompt recognition of their common situation at a time when many have an opportunity to engage in wide-ranging, non-work-related activities for the first time. Rose goes on to note that many attributes of an aged subculture may stem from biological changes, normative expectations and perceptions of older people held by the general population, or from generational differences in socialization, each making its own contribution to an age-graded segregation.

As Rose outlines it, individual involvement in an aged subculture depends on the solidarity of the age group itself, plus the nature and extent of contacts retained with the total society through families, the media, employment or the older person's own resistance to aging. In many instances, the statuses previously so important are not nearly as meaningful in the world of the older person, who is isolated from the spheres of life that imparted status originally. Good health and physical mobility serve to confer status within the aged subculture, while occupational, educational or economic prestige tend to be redefined as less influential than they were during earlier years. Commenting on the development of an aging self-concept, Rose avers that societal institutions, formalized retirement being foremost among them, have imposed an artificial boundary on what is socially recognized as old age. Concomitantly, an aging group consciousness has arisen, fostering an awareness of belonging to a particular group and not simply a chronological category. Participation in voluntary associations has also been a primary mechanism in the development of group self-consciousness, as has the greater publicity given to the elderly's common predicament or occasional victories. Although there are many who disagree with the idea of an aged subculture, claiming for instance that the elderly do not fit traditional definitions of minority groups, there is an accumulating body of evidence to indicate many of the elements in Rose's framework are indeed extremely powerful factors in delineating associational patterns sponsoring a communal consciousness (Streib, 1965; Rosow, 1967, 1974; Hochschild, 1973).

Whether the social stigma attached to being old or the elderly's own affinity for people their age provides sufficient grounds for a subculture to evolve to the point where older people become a voting bloc as Rose envisions is a question which presently cannot be answered, despite the admitted increase in militancy among older people. It is agreed, however, that there is certainly a strong relationship between peer group participation rates and the adjustment process of the elderly. From the standpoint of activity theory, the occasional person who expresses high morale but low activity levels is a deviant, while from a subcultural perspective he or she may simply be listening to an older drummer. If by engaging in activities governed by performance standards not suitable to their capabilities older people perceive the possibility of failure, they will in all likelihood readjust their interests to reflect their current status, joining with their age peers (Miller, 1965). Neither the disengagement model, the activity theory nor the idea of an aged subculture has so far proven to be as useful a predictive tool as social gerontologists are searching for, though their underlying utility as heuristic aids remains unquestioned.

Personality and Patterns of Aging

There is a sizeable contingent of social gerontologists who are of the opinion that no monolithic theoretical framework can explain successful aging patterns. To understand why some people have difficulties while others have none is thought to require an appreciation of the interplay between biological, social and personal changes as they come to expression in an individual's own coping style. To meet the tasks of living, people develop distinctive behavioral and psychological responses which those with whom they interact come to identify as their personality. Over time, characteristic patterns are built up on which people rely in the process of adapting themselves to the new situations and problems they encounter. In a sense, these patterns are stable features of one's self; yet they are dynamic, perpetually evolving, but always rooted in the past (Birren, 1964; Havighurst, 1968). As far as the adaptability of older people to the situations confronted in later life is concerned, those who focus on the persistence of personality traits assert:

> There is considerable evidence that, in normal men and women, there is no sharp discontinuity of personality with age, but instead an increasing consistency. Those characteristics that have been central to the personality seem to become even more clearly delineated, and those values the individual has been cherishing become even more salient. In the personality that remains integrated — and in the environment that permits — patterns of overt behavior are likely to become increasingly consonant with the individual's underlying personality needs and his desires. [Neugarten, Havighurst and Tobin, 1968]

Interestingly enough, even though personal adjustment is by definition a highly individualized process, gerontologists have been able to isolate a limited number of *personality types*. In an analysis of adaptive patterns observed among a panel of 87 older men —

ranging in age from 55 to 84 — Reichard, Livson and Peterson (1962) delineated five main types of character structure that describe the majority of men they studied. In each case, all the evidence available to the research team suggested the personalities of the panel members, though distinguished by age-specific criteria, had not changed appreciably throughout most of adulthood. Healthy adjusted men could be classified as members of either the mature, rocking chair or armored categories, while the less successful agers were more often characterized as either angry or self-haters. *Mature men* are those well-balanced types who maintain close personal relationships. Being realistic, they accept both the strengths and the weaknesses of their age, finding little to regret about retirement and approaching most problems in a relaxed or convivial manner without having to continually assess blame. *Rocking chair* personalities are passive-dependent agers who are content to lean on others for support, disengage and let most of life's activities pass by their doors. They fret neither about work nor about retirement, though generally they look upon work as pure drudgery, to be escaped if at all practical. Usually they possess some insight into their own feelings, acknowledging their admiration for women, whom they see as experiencing a different sort of life. *Armored men* are those with well-integrated defense mechanisms, which serve as adequate protection. Rigid and stable, they present a strong silent front and often rely on activity as an expression of their continuing independence. Insight is not one of the armored type's stronger qualities, nor are they able to tolerate people who are markedly different from themselves. Still, they represent an adjusted group within the confines of their own personality system. On the other hand, *angry men* are bitter about life, themselves and other people. Aggressiveness is a common response, as is suspicion of others, especially minorities or women. With little tolerance for ambiguity or frustration, they have always shown some instability in work and their personal lives, and now feel extremely threatened by age. Finally, the *self-haters* are similar to angry men except most of their animosity is turned inward upon themselves. Seeing themselves as dismal failures, being old only depresses them all the more.

Ironically, another typology very similar to this one was developed by a group of social psychologists working with the same Kansas City data utilized by Cumming and Henry. Viewing personality systems as a crucial dimension of life satisfaction, Neugarten and her associates utilized sophisticated statistical procedures in order to avoid the methodological criticism that was leveled at Reichard's findings. In a preliminary typology published about the time Cumming and Henry began to express doubts about their own theory, Neugarten, together with various colleagues, outlined four major personality types, each with its own subdivisions (Neugarten et al., 1964, 1968; Neugarten, 1972). In the original version separate patterns were developed for men and women, although subsequently these were combined into one typology resembling that developed by Reichard and her associates. Neugarten's types are labeled *integrated, armored-defended, passive-dependent* and *unintegrated*. In most respects her descriptions parallel Reichard's, with one important modification. Neugarten asked her respondents to evaluate themselves both in terms of their own earlier expectations and in comparison with age peers. Judging from their case histories, it does indeed appear likely, according to Neugarten's position, that aged personalities are most often merely the extensions of middle age coping styles into later years.

Emergent Theories in Social Gerontology

Social Environment and Aging

As the quest for a serviceable conceptual framework has expanded, still another contingent of the gerontological community has called for a closer look at the reciprocal relationship between aging and social environments. Generally speaking, the various approaches, though still in the formulative stages, assert contextual analyses that have not received the attention they deserve in studies of the aging process (Bennett, 1970). In essence, their view contends that the values and beliefs endemic to given situations exert an undeniable degree of suzerainty over individuals insofar as they constitute the cultural backdrop against which the elderly test their adaptability to change. Advocating the development of an ecological perspective that stresses the interaction between role alternatives and individual adjustment within social systems, Bruhn (1971) claims it ought to be possible to avoid the negative connotations often associated with chronological age. Whether or not a person does adapt to the inevitable changes of life depends on the nature of alternative exchange mechanisms available within the social environment. Without some idea of their range, it is impossible to evaluate adjustment. Although Bruhn's ecological posture stands out because of its anticipation of age stratification theory and because of its attention to aging as a dynamic process occurring in a system of structural and processural components, he is not alone in setting forth what will be called here a social environmental model. As conceived by another researcher, three elements are crucial to such a model: an emphasis on normative expectations derived from particular contexts, attention to individual capacities for interaction and a focus on the subjectively evaluated correspondence between ability and what is expected in a particular situation. If all three components are reasonably consonant, older people are much more likely to feel a sense of well-being. Yet since each is constantly changing at its own unique rate, adjustment is always contingent on maintaining supportive environments and individual resources for manipulating unfavorable situations (Gubrium, 1973,1974).

A useful framework for analyzing the role of personal resources in promoting successful aging is provided by those who conceive of aging as involving a rebalancing of exchange relationships. The thrust of the exchange model is relatively simple: interaction is predicated on all parties maximizing the rewards to be had from their association while minimizing the costs. In other words, people continue to trade in the realm of personal exchange only so long as the benefits of their interaction outweigh the costs. Should the rewards, whether material or nonmaterial, be devalued relative to what must be undergone or foregone in order to achieve them, social contact will subsequently cease. Naturally, an assessment of the costs entailed depends on an appraisal of alternatives for reaching the same goal or a viable substitute (Emerson, 1972). In terms of the interaction of older people, exchange theory explains their shrinking social networks as a realignment of their personal relationships brought about by a debasing of the influence that they are able to exercise over their environments. Without valued skills and finding themselves more often the recipient than the initiator of personal bonds, the only commodity older people have to bargain with in the social marketplace to win acceptance and support from others is compliance. Hence, for example, they may cultivate the appearance of "mellowness" in order to avoid alienating the affections of those upon whom they are dependent for their interpersonal ties (Blau, 1973). The link between the ability to control one's environment and a whole gamut of physiological and social factors needs to be specified in far greater detail; however, the exchange paradigm does at least permit a consideration of these in the adjustment process of the elderly (Dowd, 1975).

What has been labeled the social breakdown theory provides what may be the most systematic statement of the interdependence between older people and their social world. As initially drafted, the social breakdown syndrome referred to the negative feedback generated by a person already susceptible to psychological problems. Once the cycle is initiated, it serves to reinforce everyone's conception of incompetence, thereby insuring even further difficulties

(Zusman, 1966). A parallel is assumed by some gerontologists to exist among older people who encounter societal prejudices about aging. As is the case with anyone else surrounded by unfamiliar circumstances, role loss or drastic change without adequate preparation, older people reach out for some hard and fast cues to advise them as to how they should react. The very fact that they must reach out is then taken by all parties as an indication of failing capacity, a cause for concern. In order to elicit further interaction, older persons gradually, almost inadvertently, adopt some of the negative characteristics ascribed to them, thus slipping deeper into a dependent status as the cycle is repeated (Figure 5.1). In adapting the social breakdown model to explain aging in modern societies, Kuypers and Bengtson (1973) assert the continuing adherence to the middle age values of visible productivity, so prevalent in American society, practically assures an invitation to involvement in the breakdown syndrome.

There are, however, alternatives available that might lessen the probability of social breakdown. Intervention in the cycle through provision of opportunities for older people to enhance their sense of competence in appropriately structured environments free from the dominance of general societal values, engenders the possibility of breaking the spiral, or of replacing it with what Kuypers and Bengtson term a reconstruction syndrome. By improving environ-

Figure 5.1

The social breakdown cycle in old age

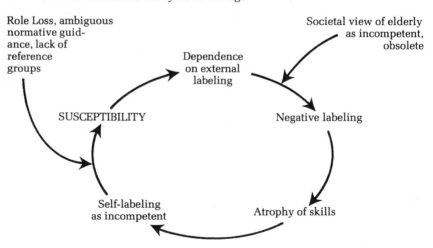

Source: J.A. Kuypers and V.L. Bengtson, "Social Breakdown and Competence: A Model of Normal Aging," *Human Development*, XVI, 3 (1973): 190.

mental supports while facilitating an expression of personal strengths, if in no other way than recognizing the tendency toward inferiority or allowing older people to make independent decisions, the forces leading to breakdown could be ameliorated within a positive interactive environment (see Figure 6.3). Shifting the focus from general theoretical explanations or the narrow emphasis on continuity of personality traits to one that attempts to align personal factors, including self-labeling, with a fluid responsive world will, according to those espousing a social-environmental model, allow for effective participation by older people. In the view of Kuypers and Bengtson, the place to begin is with a model having practical applicability at the individual level, since it is unlikely the larger society will furnish alternative environments when dominant values are what brought about the situation in the first place. Restructuring of the environment will be by no means simple, as all sponsors of an environmental approach realize, but even small gains will improve our chances for insuring a satisfying life among the elderly, paving the way for the eventual acknowledgement of the potential inhumanity of unresponsive societal institutions.

Sociology of Age Stratification

Age stratification theory adopts a somewhat broader stance than any of the foregoing explanations in an effort to illuminate the myriad linkages among age, personality and the social systems to which people belong. To speak meaningfully about the status of old age, or for that matter any age, the proponents of an age stratification model focus on the need to view age not merely as an individual characteristic, but as a dynamic component of every aspect of modern societies (Riley, 1971; Foner, 1975). It takes as its point of departure the seemingly straightforward observation that societies typically arrange themselves into a hierarchy of age strata complete with obligations and perogatives assigned to members as they move from one stratum to the next. The particular configuration of one's social roles is dependent on individual attributes, yet at the same time, it reflects certain parameters imposed by structural factors and by the composition of successive biological cohorts. Since each age stratum develops its own characteristic subculture as it moves through time, and because history itself presents subsequent cohorts with their own unique conditions, sequential generations manifest distinctive patterns of aging (Riley, Johnson and Foner, 1972).

The notion of *age grading* discussed earlier, long a familiar concept in the anthropological literature but infrequently applied to modern mass societies, forms the underpinning for the age stratification model. As shown in Figure 5.2, the age structure of a society is constructed from four primary elements. The first requirement is a population of disparate individuals who can be grouped together on the basis of chronological age or other developmental criteria into a series of *age strata*, a good analogy being seen in the levels of the population pyramids presented in Chapter One. As these cohorts move through life, innumerable forces impinge on them to alter the overall size and composition of each stratum and, indirectly, the population as a whole. Second, each stratum, because of actual physical, social or psychological factors, differs from the others in terms of the contributions it makes to ongoing societal needs. *Age-related capacities* of successive strata might vary as a result of the impact of cultural values on the definition of childhood and old age, technological change, or the influence of health factors on physical performance throughout life. Consequently, aging can be viewed either as a movement from one stratum to the next or as an indicator of physical abilities or motivations in other areas of life.

The third ingredient of the model is the patterning and distribution of *social roles*. Age may be a direct linkage—as when biological constraints limit when women may be pregnant, or when age criteria are legally established for voting, holding certain public offices, retirement and so on—or it may operate indirectly—as when there are socially prescribed parameters for given roles. Examples of the latter might include the sanctions regarding the appropriate age for high school students or for those desiring to enter medical school, or the appropriate age for a junior executive. Most often, age-graded roles appear as sets or constellations of roles simultaneously accessible to people within a certain flexible time frame; for instance, parents of preschool children are not usually found among the retired or those ensconced in the upper echelons of their occupations. In a general but very real sense, the criteria employed in establishing the distribution of age-related roles provide a reliable guide to societal priorities and values. Finally, there is an element of *age-related expectations* intrinsic to the ways in which people react in the roles they perform. Even when a role may not be closed to a person on the basis of age, age nevertheless influences the perceptions of competence and the finer shadings of performance. What is considered suitable behavior ranges along a sliding scale within the larger definition of the role, thereby allowing people to continue in roles for some time without experiencing serious disjunctures or incongruities.

As originally formulated, the age stratification model also posits a series of interrelated processes affecting the degree of articu-

Figure 5.2
Elements and processes in age stratification theory

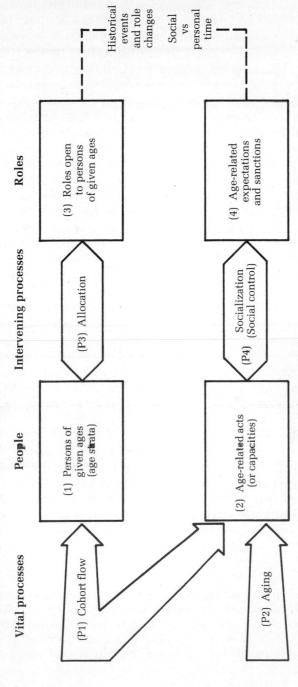

Source: M.W. Riley, M. Johnson and A. Foner, *Aging and Society, Vol. three: A sociology of age stratification* (New York: Russell Sage Foundation, 1972), p. 9.

lation between the structural elements and the rhythm or patterning of individual lives. The two most basic and vital processes are said to be cohort flow and what is termed aging. *Cohort flow* refers to all those factors that contribute to the shaping of the age strata; foremost would of course be fertility, mortality and migration. Perhaps the best way to illustrate the process of cohort flow is the metaphor used by the authors themselves of people stepping on an escalator at birth. How many and what types of people get on at any two points are never identical, although in every instance those arriving at the bottom at the same time move up in a collective fashion. However, they do not remain a completely stable group as they move along: some get off by leaving the area; others, particularly men, by dying; hence, proportionately more women continue the ascent after early adulthood . As they move along, some acquire social attributes that come to distinguish them from others, either enhancing or impeding their likelihood of staying on the escalator for the full ride. Eventually, fewer and fewer people are left on the moving stairs, until all of those who began together are dead. As successive cohorts pass by, they alter conditions to such a degree that later groups never encounter the world in exactly the same way.

Interrelating the ideas of age strata and cohort flow provides a means of conceptualizing the dynamic nature of age in determining social location, but it does not explicitly account for individual exceptions or for how mobility from one stratum to the next occurs. For this purpose the age-stratification model incorporates the concept of *aging* as an endemic process taking place on two levels. As portrayed in Chapter Four, physiological aging, although fundamental, does not occur in a vacuum; rather, it is influenced by innumerable exogenous factors. Some of these are already apparent, and more will be discussed later as we address the question of health among the elderly. It should be sufficient at this point to note that physical aging is by no means an isolated experience. At the same time, aging can be seen as a maturational phenomenon, a measure of acquired experience or knowledge, reflecting the extent of whatever personal resources are available to bolster and guide a person. According to age stratification theory, the nature of aging is inextricably bound up

> . . . by the individual's characteristics and dispositions, by the modifications of these characteristics through socialization, by the particular role sequences in which he participates, and by the particular social situations and environmental events he encounters. Hence, it follows that patterns of aging can differ,

not only from one society to another and from one country to another, but also among successive cohorts in a single society. [Riley, Johnson and Foner, 1972]

It is by no means possible to explain the multifarious differences between strata by reference to age alone; therefore, the age stratification model proposes the intervening processes of allocation and socialization to account for the disparities that arise. *Allocation* refers to the process of assigning and reassigning people of various ages to suitable roles. Even though the size and compositions of successive cohorts may change, the functional needs of society persist, necessitating occasional redefinitions of age-appropriate or essential positions in order to redistribute people in the system's role structure. As people age, they also adopt and abandon a sequence of roles. The process of deciding which people will fill what roles is not, however, always conscious, deliberate or immutable. Among the examples of allocative processes we could mention are the number of students admitted to college as determined by age, sex, income levels, race and so on, or the size of the faculty responsible for their instruction. Similarly, age is an important consideration in apportioning the role of parent for those who wish to adopt a child, in filling an executive position or even for securing certain kinds of fairly menial positions such as stock clerk in a grocery store. In the case of adoption, the age criterion for allocation is often abandoned when the number of children grows too large; or, in the case of new industries, executives may be appreciably younger than in more established spheres. In an overall sense, the criteria used for allocation of particular roles or role complexes reflect both social values and the vital processes inherent in aging.

Socialization, the other intervening process included in the theory, is a means of insuring a smooth transition of individuals from one age status to the next. Sociologists previously discussed socialization almost exclusively within the context of childhood, though it has been widely accepted for a number of years that it is a never-ending process, operative throughout life for every role assumed. The age stratification model views individuals as well as entire cohorts as molded by socializing agencies independently and together. Some researchers have suggested that in complex industrial societies, the criteria for role assignments have become increasingly ambiguous, and socialization processes weakened to the point of being inoperative. As a consequence, there is an undercurrent of asynchronization, sometimes called role strain or simply personal stress, built into the movement between age strata that requires special attention (Cain, 1964). An example which comes readily to mind is the need for preretirement counseling to facilitate the adjustment of older workers to their future and to the new roles which present themselves. Preretirement programs are reciprocal in nature, not only helping a person socialize out of the work role, in anticipation of future roles, but at the same time, having a latent socializing influence on company policies regarding older workers.

Finally, age stratification theory includes, but does not deal extensively with, a set of exogenous processes not directly linked to age structures, but which nonetheless influence the role available. Some role changes may reflect historical events, as in the relatively few blacksmith positions currently found for people regardless of age. Similarly, differences in timing between the life span of a social order and the timetables of individuals are thought to add to the strains experienced as part of aging. Although these external factors impinge on the way people age, they are not explicitly considered by the model. They do, however, serve to remind us that the age-specific elements in society never constitute a complete system, nor can any aspect of aging be adequately understood without reference to the complicated interplay among the factors involved. In spite of the numerous aspects of aging left untouched, the age stratification model offers the most comprehensive theoretical perspective yet developed. Perhaps one of the more significant omissions is any serious discussion of an actor's intentional participation in a process that cannot be mandated entirely by societal constraints. Further, while the authors assert that generations are not limited to mere chronological age groups — that they can be defined by attitudinal variation or perceptual factors — little is made of this important distinction. These unresolved questions do not negate the importance of the age stratification model for greatly expanding the scope of theories and their practical applications in social gerontology.

Summary

Social gerontology has not escaped the common plight confronting most disciplines that attempt to integrate the theoretical with the applied. Solutions nearly always appear couched in the language used to formulate the problems. To date, the theoretical frameworks are neither all that they should be nor what they could be, but the growth of explanatory models witnessed in the last decade or so definitely has laid the groundwork for significant advances in the near future. Our review of the theories promulgated by social gerontologists should provide ample evidence of the continuing search. The insufficiency of unitary models of adjustment to explain the multiple dimensions of aging that must be taken into consideration should also have become apparent (Maddox, 1970). Still, no theory can ever be completely rejected, only disregarded in favor of those that offer a greater utility in the real world of the elderly. As the conditions affecting older people change, gerontologists must construct new models or renovate older ones if their explanations are to be of any scientific or social consequence. Limited as some may be as explanatory devices, each new effort serves to sharpen the issues involved, so that one day deliberate intervention will become a viable means of making life more satisfying for older people.

As one of the original theoretical attempts, disengagement theory, with its assertion that aging is a process of quietly receding from view or at least of withdrawing from active participation, quickly met with criticism from all sides. Especially vocal were those activity theorists who contended older people do not change their minds about the importance of being involved even when they can no longer keep pace with the world around them. In an effort to account for differential adjustment among those who withdraw as well as those who remain active, Rose (1965) suggested the possibility of an aging subculture, very much the counterpart of the widely recognized youth movement associated with the late 1960s. By becoming their own reference group, by recognizing their common predicament, Rose claims older people will develop a new basis for adaptation, even to the point of evolving into a social movement with a political voice. Not content with any of these descriptions of why older people experience and react with the feelings they do, social-psychologically oriented gerontologists expressed reservations, asserting instead that it all depends on a person's psychological makeup and habitual methods of coping. It is true, they noted, that roles themselves may be discontinuous, but people are not; the repertoire of responses developed throughout a lifetime is not suddenly abandoned on the threshold of old age.

Filling the gap between theories that stress social factors and those emphasizing personal ones, the social environmentalists posit a reciprocal process wherein any acknowledgement of personal stress prompts the social environment to label an older person as incompetent, a label frequently internalized by the person. Which people end up their years overcome by despair depends on what kinds of environmental supports are available to them. Finally, the age stratification theory is an attempt to formulate a whole life conception of aging. A complicated model to say the least, age stratification views old age as a process of becoming socialized to new or revised role definitions, reflecting a fluid relationship between people, their social contexts and their opportunities. How much change must be accommodated by individual actors is difficult to predict; it is dependent upon an intertwined series of feedback loops revolving around the size of the aging population, the roles available and differences in the timing of individual and social needs. Before any of the theories reviewed or one yet to emerge adds measurably to our understanding of aging in the modern world, they must each be subjected to thoughtful testing in a variety of cultural contexts.

Pertinent Readings

ATCHLEY, R.C. "Disengagement Among Professors." *Journal of Gerontology* XXVI, 4 (1971): 476–80.

BENNETT, R. "Social Context — A Neglected Variable in Research on Aging." *Aging and Human Development* I, 2 (1970): 97–116.

BIRREN, J.E. *The Psychology of Aging.* Englewood Cliffs, N.J.: Prentice-Hall, 1964.

BLAU, Z.S. *Old Age in a Changing Society.* New York: New Viewpoints, a division of Franklin Watts, Inc., 1973.

BRIM, O.G., Jr. "Foreword." In *Aging and Society. Vol. three: A sociology of age stratification,* by M.W. Riley, M. Johnson and A. Foner, ix–xii. New York: Russell Sage Foundation, 1972.

BRUHN, J.G. "An Ecological Perspective of Aging." *The Gerontologist* XI, 4, pt. 1, (1971): 318–21.

CAIN, L.D., JR. "Life Course and Social Structure." In *Handbook of Modern Sociology,* ed. R.E.L. Faris, 272–309. Chicago: Rand McNally & Company, 1964.

CUMMING, E. "Further Thoughts on the Theory of Disengagement." *International Social Science Journal* XV, 3 (1963): 377–93.

———. "Engagement With an Old Theory." *Aging and Human Development* VI, 3 (1975): 187–91.

CUMMING, E., L.R. DEAN, D.S. NEWELL and I. MCCAFFREY. "Disengagement — A Tentative Theory of Aging." *Sociometry* XXIII, 1 (1960): 23.

CUMMING, E., and W.E. HENRY. *Growing Old: The Process of Disengagement.* New York: Basic Books, Inc., 1961.

DOWD, J.J. "Aging as Exchange: A Preface to Theory." *Journal of Gerontology* XXX, 5 (1975) 584–94.

EMERSON, R.M. "Exchange Theory, Parts I & II." In *Sociological Theories in Progress,* vol. II, eds. J. Berger, M. Zelditch and B. Anderson, 38–87. Boston: Houghton Mifflin, 1972.

FONER, A. "Age in Society: Structure and Change." *American Behavioral Scientist* XIX, 2 (1975): 144–65.

GUBRIUM, J.F. *The Myth of the Golden Years: A Socio-Environmental Theory of Aging.* Springfield, Ill.: Charles C Thomas, 1973.

_____ . "Toward a Socio-Environmental Theory of Aging." *The Gerontologist* XII, 3, pt. 1 (1974): 281–84.

HAVIGHURST, R.J. "A Social-Psychological Perspective on Aging." *The Gerontologist* VIII, 2 (1968): 67–71.

HAVIGHURST, R.J., and R. ALBRECHT. *Older People.* New York: Longmans, Green, 1953.

HAVIGHURST, R.J., J.M.A. MUNNICHS, B. NEUGARTEN and H. THOMAE. *Adjustment to Retirement.* Assen, The Netherlands: Van Gorcum & Comp. N.V., 1969.

HAVIGHURST, R.J., B. NEUGARTEN and S.S. TOBIN. "Disengagement and Patterns of Aging." In *Middle Age and Aging,* ed. B.L. Neugarten, 161–72. Chicago: University of Chicago Press, 1968.

HENRY, W.E. "Engagement and Disengagement: Toward a Theory of Adult Development." In *Contributions to the Psychobiology of Aging,* ed. R. Kastenbaum, 19–35. New York: Springer Publishing Company, Inc., 1965.

HOCHSCHILD, A.R. *The Unexpected Community.* Englewood Cliffs, N.J.: Prentice-Hall, 1973.

_____ . "Disengagement Theory: A Critique and Proposal." *American Sociological Review* 40, 5 (1975): 553–69.

KUYPERS, J.A., and V.L. BENGTSON. "Social Breakdown and Competence: A Model of Normal Aging." *Human Development* XVI, 3 (1973): 181–201.

LEMON, B.W., V.L. BENGTSON and J.A. PETERSEN. "An Exploration of the Activity Theory of Aging: Activity Types and Life Expectation among In-movers to a Retirement Community." *Journal of Gerontology* XXVII, 4 (1972): 511–23.

MADDOX, G.L. "Disengagement Theory: A Critical Evaluation." *The Gerontologist* IV, 2 (1964): 80–82.

_____ . "Fact and Artifact: Evidence Bearing on Disengagement Theory from the Duke Geriatrics Project." *Human Development* VIII, 1 (1965): 117–30.

_____ . "Themes and Issues in Sociological Theories of Human Aging." *Human Development* XIII, 1 (1970): 17–27.

MILLER, S.J. "The Social Dilemma of the Aging Leisure Participant." In *Older People and Their Social World,* eds. A.M. Rose and W.A. Peterson, 77–92. Philadelphia: F.A. Davis Company, 1965.

NEUGARTEN, B.L. "Personality and the Aging Process." *The Gerontologist* XII, 1, pt. 1, (1972): 9–15.

NEUGARTEN, B.L., W.J. CROTTY and S.S. TOBIN. "Personality Types in an Aged Population." In *Personality in Middle and Late Life,* ed. B.L. Neugarten et al., 158–87. New York: Atherton Press, 1964.

NEUGARTEN, B.L., R.J. HAVIGHURST and S.S. TOBIN. "Personality and Patterns of Aging." In *Middle Age and Aging,* ed. B.L. Neugarten, 173–77. Chicago: University of Chicago Press, 1968.

PALMORE, E., ed. *Normal Aging.* Durham, N.C.: Duke University Press, 1970.

PHILLIPS, B.S. "A Role Theory Approach to Adjustment in Old Age." *American Sociological Review* XXII, 2 (1957): 212–27.

REICHARD, S., F. LIVSON and P.G. PETERSON. *Aging and Personality*. New York: John Wiley & Sons, Inc., 1962.

RILEY, M.W. "Social Gerontology and the Age Stratification of Society." *The Gerontologist* XII, 1, pt. 1, (1971): 79–87.

RILEY, M.W., M. JOHNSON and A. FONER, *Aging and Society, Vol. three: A sociology of age stratification*. New York: Russell Sage Foundation, 1972.

ROSE, A.M. "The Subculture of the Aging: A Framework in Social Gerontology." In *Older People and Their Social World*, eds. A.M. Rose and W.A. Peterson, 3–16. Philadelphia: F.A. Davis Company, 1965.

ROSOW, I. *Social Integration of the Aged*. New York: The Free Press, 1967.

_____ . *Socialization to Old Age*. Berkeley: University of California Press, 1974.

SCHAIE, K.W. "Age Changes and Age Differences." *The Gerontologist* VII, 2, pt. 1 (1967): 128–32.

STREIB, G.F. "Are the Aged a Minority Group?" In *Applied Sociology*, eds. A.W. Gouldner and S.M. Miller. New York: The Free Press, 1965. Reprinted in *Middle Age and Aging*, ed. B.L. Neugarten, 35–46.

STREIB, G.F., and C.J. SCHNEIDER. *Retirement in American Society*. Ithaca, N.Y.: Cornell University Press, 1971.

WILLIAMS, R.H., and C.G. WIRTHS. *Lives Through the Years*. New York: Atherton Press, 1965.

ZUSMAN, J. "Some Explanations of the Changing Appearance of Psychotic Patients: Antecedents of the Social Breakdown Syndrome Concept." *The Millbank Memorial Fund Quarterly* LXIV, 1 (1966).

Part III

DIMENSIONS OF AGING

Chapter 6

Psychological Processes in Later Life

How well an individual adjusts to life's challenges depends on a wide range of biological, social and psychological processes. To complicate matters, few of these are either understood or easily controlled. In a rapidly changing society, which extols the virtues of youth and denigrates the elderly, it is small wonder that older people run the risks of psychological distress accompanying superannuation. Still, among the elderly, as with any other cohort, only a relatively small percentage can be considered to be suffering from serious emotional disturbances. Yet the fact that older people constitute a disproportionately high number of both the admissions to psychiatric facilities and the suicides committed yearly indicates the existence of increased or unexpected tensions in their lives. In order to discuss the psychological characteristics of old age in any meaningful way, it is necessary to review alterations in psychomotor capacities, developmental adaptation and what is commonly labeled psychopathology. Over the course of the life span, sensory and perceptual modalities are in a constant state of flux and, as changes occur, adjustments and compensations in the cognitive and intellectual realm are increasingly required. One of the central themes emerging from lifespan analyses of adult development and aging is the continuity of the adaptive responses in the face of losses accruing with each successive life stage. In addition, acceptance of the limitations imposed on physical abilities over time involves learning new skills and reorienting personal desires or expectations. Recognition of the fact that youthful capacities gradually fade, to be replaced by other attributes, is a crucial developmental task that must be accomplished if a person is to feel at all competent or satisfied in his or her later years.

Just as positive accommodations are cumulative, so too are responses that eventually become maladaptive, even though they might originally have been functional. The appearance of psychological disorders in later life has usually been a long time coming; they seldom spring full blown for the first time at an advanced age. Nor do they stem solely from an individual's psychological makeup; rather, they reflect stresses to which one is exposed and the availability of appropriate resolutions. The psychological problems of older people resemble those of the rest of society, except that older people have additional vulnerability to organic disorders not usually incurred by most younger people. To fully understand these, as well as the more normal aspects of the psychological dimensions of the aging process, it is important to appreciate the ways in which the various components change over the life cycle.

Sensory and Cognitive Functioning

Sensory Modalities

Sensory processes have received considerable attention in the investigation of the effects of age on mental capacities. Of the five basic senses psychologists customarily study, taste and smell will not be addressed here beyond noting they show age-related decrements that frequently result in an inability among the very old to distinguish among various foods or odors. While nutrition is closely related to the ability to taste and smell food appropriately, the relationship of these two senses is more removed from psychological functioning. The remaining three senses — sight, hearing and kinesthetic sense — are more pertinent, as they are apt to be directly related to psychological well-being. An individual's potential for interaction with the environment is grounded in his or her receipt of and response to sensory inputs. Fortunately, most people are endowed with sensory acuities far in excess of what is normally required for simple awareness. In addition to ample surpluses, initial losses are often minimized by compensatory mechanisms called into operation when a given modality no longer provides essential information. After a certain point, however, any further depreciation of sensory processes is likely to manifest itself in behavioral or psychological aberrations.

For stimuli to be consciously recognized, a two step process, more distinct in analysis than in fact, must operate. First, the stimulus must be of sufficient magnitude to activate receptor organs and associated nerve tracts. If the stimulus is below the organ's *threshold*, or if the receptors are not working properly, no stimulation message is received by the brain. Once a message does reach the brain, it must be catalogued according to preexisting experiences before recognition takes place and a response is formulated. Innumerable factors, ranging from the type of stimulus or disorders in higher order cerebral functioning to socially ingrained habits, may intervene between stimulus and response. The fact that a response to a given stimulus may be perfectly appropriate under certain conditions and inappropriate under others renders the search for invariable explanations a difficult, and at times impossible, task. Generally, threshold levels increase with advancing age; the more specialized the sense, the greater the increment of change over time. Of equal importance is the complexity of the response or the degree of stimulus discrimination required, so that those responses calling for the greatest articulation between systems usually show the largest decrements. On the other hand, habitual response patterns are less likely to deteriorate, provided no sudden changes interrupt these patterns.

Audition, or the ability to hear, is one of the most valuable of our senses; when it becomes impaired, it places people at a disadvantage of which they are only too painfully aware. Current estimates suggest approximately 7 percent of all middle-aged Americans suffer hearing losses of a magnitude that hinders social interaction. By age 65 or so the percentage has jumped to over half of all men and 30 percent of all women (National Center for Health Statistics, 1971). Normally, young adults can hear pure tones in frequencies up to 15,000 vibrations per second. Beginning around age 25, *presbycusis*, an age-related loss of the ganglion cells necessary for conduction, causes erosion of the upper threshold, and after age 65 or 70 sounds above 4,000 vibrations per second may be inaudible. Conversely, low range tones, below 1,000 cycles, do not appear to be appreciably affected by age. Volume, or loudness measured in decibels, is a more common measure of hearing. Humans can hear sounds between 0 db, well below the level of a whisper which averages about 8 db, to those in excess of 130 db, though pain and nausea are associated with the latter. Since the range of normal conversation is in the neighborhood of 60 db, severe hearing impairments are said to occur when lower thresholds exceed 35 db. The increasing amount of noise pollution found in most industrialized countries has led many experts to predict even more widespread hearing difficulties among future generations of elderly (Butler and Lewis, 1973).

Testing for hearing loss is usually carried out under controlled laboratory conditions using constant and variable pure tones, as well as speech uttered at different volumes. From all indications, the declining acuity exhibited by the aged in laboratory tests suffers still greater aggravation in the less favorable circumstances of daily routines. While many of the changes are a consequence of retrogressive alterations, diseases of the inner ear, vascular difficulties or environmental assaults, other variables such as sex or intelligence are also implicated. Across the age span, women, and those people who by virtue of their training pay close attention to speech patterns, experience the least hearing loss as they become older (Bromley, 1971). One of the most obvious results of severely impaired hearing is a sense of isolation and loneliness, quite possibly coupled with emotional distress. Butler and Lewis (1973) note that the emotional upsets attendant with reduced reality testing and decreased auditory perception may lead to reactive depressions and paranoid ideational states if impairments are sufficiently severe and continue for any lengthy period of time.

Visual acuity is a summary index of efficiency most often reported in terms of ability to discriminate test objects at a distance of 20 feet. Twenty/twenty vision means an individual can read an eye chart as well as normal people at that distance, with smaller ratios indicating progressively poorer eyesight. For example, vision rated as 20/70 means objects distinguishable at 20 feet with impaired eyesight can be discriminated at 70 feet by the normally sighted. Resulting from morphological changes in the eye, most declines become noticeable by late in the fourth decade, appearing slightly earlier for nonwhites than whites. Hence, seven out of eight people over age 45 find it necessary to wear glasses, compared to three out of ten younger than 45. Be this as it may, fewer than 20 percent of those over 65 cannot obtain corrected vision of at least 20/40, more than adequate for normal activities (Gordon, 1971).

A variety of ocular problems afflict older eyes, the most frequent being cataracts, glaucoma and macular diseases. In fact, cataracts are encountered so often that some researchers consider them to be merely an acceleration of normal aging processes. Throughout life, new fibers are generated in the crystalline lens of the eye, but older fibers are not dispelled, thus building up to gradually cloud over and harden. When this occurs, the lens becomes thicker, shows evidence of yellowing, and eventually becomes opaque. As a consequence, less light filters into the eye, compounding the visual difficulties caused by the gradual loss of the lens's ability to alter its shape, a trait essential for accurate focus on near as well as distant objects. As the eyes' power of accommodation diminishes, glasses are required. Cataracts themselves can usually be removed surgically without undue complications, although under present medical technology the risk of corneal scars dictates removal from only one eye at a time. The utilization of contact lenses and evolving surgical techniques presages radical improvement in cataract operations during the next decade. The "old duffer" squinting at a newspaper held out at arm's length has been a sight gag in movies for as long as filmmakers have attempted humor. But *presbyopia,* or the inability to change the eye's focal length, is so common during the last half of life that most people over age 40 know exactly what the "duffer" in the movies is going through. A similar decline in the eyes' ability to adapt to darkness tends to inhibit reading and driving at night among the aged. Nonetheless, carefully controlled illumination can minimize a large share of the problems that might otherwise interfere with a person's daily routine.

In terms of provoking emotional upsets, most gerontologists regard hearing loss as more significant than vision loss. Aside from the insecurity and trepidation that come with poorer eyesight, many visually impaired elderly are able to maintain interaction with their environment much more comfortably than those who cannot hear. This is not to deny the hardships imposed by severely restricted vision or blindness; nearly half of all blind people are over 65 years of age. It is simply that those with visual handicaps are not so completely cut off without supportive resources as are the deaf (Butler and Lewis, 1973). In either case, the psychological isolation is undoubtedly traumatic.

Kinesthetic sensitivity refers to a somatic sense that provides an awareness of the body's spatial location. It is mediated by receptors found in muscles, joints and the *vestibular* apparatus of the inner ear. Perhaps the most expedient way to explain kinesthetic sensitivity, without going into great detail, is by a series of examples. Few young people have any difficulty whatsoever in recognizing when they are sitting upright or are partially prone. Nor do they often err when called upon to locate their feet relative to their knees, such as when climbing on uneven terrain. Usually they are able to make generalized postural adjustments when getting to their feet, compensating for slight misalignments without giving the matter any thought. Many elderly, on the other hand, do not have the luxury of remaining blithely unconscious of controlling body position or movement, since the loss of their kinesthetic senses leaves them vulnerable to accidental falls and postural instability. For each of us, the sense of movement, touch and position depends in part on receptors located in muscles, joints and the skin. Further, the *proprioceptive* system, as kinesthesis is called by physiologists, relies on visual cues and on vestibular controls. Obviously all are important, yet few of us experience postural confusion in the dark, primarily because our limbs and muscles send their own messages to the brain, advising of their location relative to other parts of the body. Fluid balances in the semicircular canals of the inner ear also help maintain spatial orientation, acting much like the gyroscope or artificial horizon in an airplane that shows the craft's attitude relative to the earth's surface. Each of the three semicircular canals extends in a different plane, and each contains a liquid that activates tiny hair receptors that transmit a message to the cerebral cortex and the thalamus when equilibrium is disturbed (Barrett, 1972). For various reasons, some of which can be traced to sensory impairments and some to a breakdown of the brain's integrative capacities, the dizziness or vertigo reported by many elderly is attributed to dysfunctions in these two areas. The specific causes of kinesthetic malfunctions are yet to be discerned. Motion sickness or a rare disease known as Meniere's Syndrome are thought to present extreme examples of the nausea and locomotion difficulties encountered among older people.

Reaction Time and Psychomotor Responses

Declining sensory acuity and the often concurrent slowing of behaviors involving the central nervous system are seen most clearly in evaluations of psychomotor performance of older populations. The relationship is by no means simple or direct. As noted in Chapter Four, diminished conduction velocities, the speed at which impulses travel neural pathways, account for only a small fraction of the delay in reaction times that accompanies advanced age. Traditionally, reaction time has been defined as the lag between stimulation and the initiation of a response. Any assessment of reaction time is complicated by such factors as the nature of the signal, the complexity and type of response required, motor skills, testing artifacts involving experience, practice or the amount of irrelevant information, plus a whole range of social-psychological variables including attention or motivation. In contrast to many younger test recruits, older respondents appear willing to sacrifice speed in favor of accuracy, thereby exhibiting slower overall profiles, but more precise responses (Botwinick, 1967). It is most important to remember that laboratory test results are quite difficult to translate into equivalent performances in daily life, since the latter are generally influenced by unexpected and extraneous environmental inputs and are seldom limited to the narrow range of choices characteristic of test situations. Nonetheless, age decrements in performance tests of reaction time do have substantial implications in the practical realm. The rapidity with which decisions based on coordination of cognitive and motor capacities may be implemented seems to depend almost entirely on the functioning of the cerebral cortex where signal-to-noise ratios show a steady age-related deterioration. Some researchers have suggested poorer performances are a consequence of heightened ambient arousal states in the cortex of older persons that exceed the limits of efficient functioning. This necessitates a longer time period to discriminate between random impulses and those to which response is required. Without the pressure of time, evidence indicates that older people are as capable of acting effectively as their younger counterparts. Whether they do so in fact reflects as much personality and educational variables or emotional states as psychological motor skills per se (Welford, 1969). It is known that reaction time lengthens with lethargic or depressed moods, although continued activity may serve to stimulate possible improvements within certain limits (Botwinick and Thompson, 1968). Circulatory deterioration, depressed cerebral metabolism or suppressed brain rhythms also tend to correlate with slower reaction times and lessened mental functioning. Apparently the propensity toward cardiovascular problems may also serve as a retardant on simple reaction sequences that the elderly cannot overcome regardless of their exercise levels (Botwinick and Storandt, 1974).

Learning, Remembering, Forgetting

At the outset, it cannot be stressed too strongly that older people can and do learn. Studies seeking to ascertain learning capacities and memory in older people in the past have tended to reinforce the popular notion that in both cases the elderly operate at a disadvantage. Many of the earlier investigations have stumbled over conceptual and procedural pitfalls, confusing learning with the demonstration of knowledge, thus making broad generalizations extremely hazardous. It has been widely accepted that the older the respondent, the less likely he or she is to fare well on performance tests demonstrating learning or memory skills, provided intelligence levels are not disparate. Disagreements arise when it comes to the question of whether such tests are indeed measuring capacity factors or refer instead to artifacts of the test situation (Eisdorfer, 1967; Murrell, 1970). The ordinary slowing of reaction time with age for nearly all tasks, or the overarousal of the central nervous system may account for lower performance levels on tests requiring rapid responses. Under conditions that allow self-pacing by the respondent, the magnitude of the age decrements is lessened considerably. Still, the best evidence available does confirm the finding that, when all variables are taken into consideration, older people usually do less well on complex perceptual learning tasks. Seemingly, the reasons for this stem from an inability to employ appropriate strategies for organizing the material to be learned (Botwinick, 1967). If this is true, would not practice benefit the older person immensely? Certainly, but then people of all ages improve when given a chance to practice — to learn how to learn; the crucial point here is that given an opportunity, older people can improve their scores on learning tests (Taub and Long, 1972; Hultsch, 1974). With a chance to refresh their skills or to acquire new techniques for organizing materials, older respondents are able to enhance their performance scores.

The distinction between learning and memory is confusingly vague since the demonstration of learning necessarily involves the retrieval of data from the brain's "memory bank." Precisely where learning leaves off and memory enters the picture is yet unclear. In a seminal discussion of the issues, Botwinick (1967) points out that, though the exact division may be arbitrary and is frequently blurred, the two processes do represent independent phenomena. In attempting to answer the question, psychologists have developed a three stage model for analyzing memories: impression, retention and recall. To be remembered, it is fair to say, most events must be consciously recognized. One dimension is referred to as incidental memories, those which emerge upon questioning, concerning events the respondent did not even know he or she remembered until asked. Apparently, however, incidental memories are related to intentional memories. If the salient particulars of a situation cannot be recalled, then correspondingly few incidental aspects are remembered. Provided information is initially acquired, it must then be retained in what psychologists label primary or secondary storage before people can be said to have memory of it. Primary storage is a kind of temporary holding area where details are sorted, with those not passed into stable storage quickly forgotten. Finally, there is a retrieval or recall aspect, more analytically distinct than real. To recall information upon questioning, it is necessary to rummage around in the memory banks to reach correct answers. If for any reason the retrieval processes break down, then a person cannot be said to retain memory of an event.

Age-related memory deficiencies have been widely reported in the psychological literature. While short-term recall seems to decay with age, perhaps as a consequence of poorer sorting strategies, long-term memories of remote events do not show similar changes. However, the character of long-term memories needs to be carefully examined before any definitive conclusions can be drawn. It may well be that only "practical" long-term memories, those which are frequently recalled, can be readily remembered. Do unrehearsed memories also resist dissolution? The answer certainly has practical significance for all levels of mental functioning. In nearly every instance, well-educated, mentally active people do not exhibit the same decline as their age peers who do not have similar op- portunities to flex their minds. Nevertheless, with few exceptions, the time required for memory scanning is longer for both recent and remote recall among older people, probably more the result of social and health factors than any irreversible effects of age (Taub, 1973; Eriksen et al., 1973). In one 20 year analysis of mental functioning, women were found to retain an advantage over men as they moved further into old age. While the opposite might be expected to be the case, as men are customarily perceived as being more active, the researchers suggest the differences may stem in part from higher morbidity and earlier mortality among the men (Blum et al., 1972).

The exploration of how memories are forgotten is fraught with the complexities of social and psychological, as well as physiologi- cal or neurochemical, influences. For a social scientist to claim resil- ient memories are those that continue to be meaningful to a person's life is to offer only a partial explanation. The neurophysiologists are not much better off, having yet to agree among themselves on whether memories are "wet" or "dry" phenomena. Those who con- tend memory depends on brain chemistry currently debate those who are of the opinion that memories reflect electrical or morphologi- cal properties. While some biochemists tend to favor RNA coding as the source of memory, and enzyme agents as the cause of forgetting, preliminary research in which patients with memory difficulties received dosages of RNA have so far proved inconclusive (Botwinick, 1967). Even if scientists conclude that memories are chemical in nature, as opposed to either electrical or morphological, the challenge remains to explain gradual losses and incorrect recall under varying social conditions. Almost all researchers agree the older a person is the more likely he or she is to become forgetful. In the past it was assumed the sheer volume of memories accumulating over the life course interfered with one's ability to accurately recall any particular memory. In addition, habits competed with recently acquired information to increase the possibility that the latter would not be retained. Alternatively, some psychologists felt that remote memories were perhaps recollected only insofar as they affirmed contemporary self-images, while unpleasant memories were conveniently "forgotten." An example of such a process in its most extreme form can be seen in the development of psychological disorders that enable a person to block out particularly stressful events from his or her memory.

Age, Intelligence and Creativity

It has been only recently that the assumption of waning intelligence in later life has come under close scrutiny. Not the least of the reasons why this misconception has been so slow to yield to scientific analysis is that, like other psychomotor processes, intelligence can only be inferred from performance scores. Consequently, testing artifacts inevitably color the outcome. In two of the most popular tests, the original 1939 Wechsler-Bellevue Scale (W-B) and the 1955 update, the Wechsler Adult Intelligence Scale (WAIS), the concept of age is so central a component in determining intelligence quotient that scaling instructions clearly specify the age-related corrections necessary to render the scores of young and old people comparable. In spite of correction factors, when such standardized intelligence measures are applied in cross-sectional analyses of intellectual functioning, older participants customarily score lower than their younger counterparts. However, when testing procedures are altered to reflect the more pragmatic cognitive operations closer to those used in everyday life, older respondents often prove superior to young adults. In one test constructed by Demming and Pressey (1957) in the late 1950s, intellectual functioning was ascertained by the facility shown in using telephone directories and in understanding common paralegal concepts, and by the ability to secure essential social services. Even though middle-aged or older adults scored much higher on such practical performance measures, their achievement on conventional tests still followed the expected downward pattern (Botwinick, 1967). While there is no logical basis to assume that the poorer performance of older respondents is due to failing mental capacities rather than to cultural-environmental factors, all too often the former is presented as the sole explanation. Unfortunately, the traditional measures of intelligence have become powerful myths, unquestioned by young, middle-aged and older adults alike.

It is frequently forgotten that intelligence, as we normally speak of it, is a composite statistical measure of several distinct though interrelated capacities rather than of any single attribute. Intelligence is infinitely more than the score a person achieves on a test; rather, it is the ability to combine available information in the pursuit of a specifiable goal. Some psychologists have broadened the concept of intelligence to encompass effective utilization of all environmental factors (Eisdorfer, 1969). Performance, intelligence as estimated by psychological tests, is usually determined through a series of subtests that theoretically tap all dimensions of intellectual capacity. The WAIS, for instance, groups 11 subtests under the verbal and performance scales. On the Verbal series, oral answers are required to test Comprehension, Information, Vocabulary, Similarities, Arithmetic and Digital Span. Thus, on the Similarities test, individuals must explain why a series of paired objects seems to belong together. In response to an Information question about the origin of rubber, they must provide the simplest reasonable answer to receive a correct score. The Performance tests, which include arranging and completing pictures, assembling objects, block design or digital symbol tasks, require respondents to actually manipulate materials in accordance with instructions.

While there is increasing agreement that the distinction between psychomotor and cognitive skills is not nearly as rigid as originally assumed (Welford, 1969), older people usually perform better on verbal than on performance subtests. The discrepancy between the two normally expands with age, reflecting perhaps a stability in those capacities that are similar to routines frequently practiced over the course of adult life. Only a relative handful of individuals more than a few years removed from formal learning situations engage in the type of activities that constitute the central focus of timed performance tests. Accompanying the unfamiliarity of the requested behavior comes heightened anxiety and lowered motivation, both inexorably related to test results. On the other hand, the kinds of verbal skills measured by most intelligence tests are experientially quite like our familiar activities (Eisdorfer, 1969). Another reason early cross-sectional investigations of age-related intelligence changes tended to buttress popular stereotypes is the fact respondents were seldom tested on more than one occasion. Furthermore, with the greater incidence of health problems found among older people as a group and with health being a factor known to affect test performance, it is probable that a large number of older respondents experienced at least mild health problems at the time of testing. In contrast, longitudinal analyses of intellectual functioning provide many insightful clues to the reasons for age-related change. Generally speaking, though, the declines do not disappear; they are merely less exaggerated than cross-sectional research tends to indicate. Individuals who initially perform at superior levels exhibit much smaller decrements than their less well-endowed age mates. It should be emphasized that many people in fact show noticeable improvements on selected measures (Schaie, 1975).

For purposes of illustration, the longitudinal analyses of Schaie and his colleagues offer a penetrating look at intellectual functioning over the course of adult life. In 1956, a battery of psychological tests was administered to 500 men and women ranging in age from 21 to 70. Over 300 of those who were still available were retested in 1963 and finally again seven years later. On each occasion a series of cognitive profiles was obtained for individuals and then aggregated for each five or seven year age cohort. In an effort to discover what changes, if any, appeared as individuals became older, Schaie and his coworkers distilled 13 separate measures of intellectual functioning into four dimensions. Intellectual skills acquired by means of either formal or informal education were labeled *crystallized intelligence.* As on most IQ tests, Schaie assumes conceptual, verbal and arithmetic skills as well as logical thinking are reflected in this particular dimension. In practical terms, crystallized intelligence is thought to enable people to assimilate new knowledge or to learn quickly. *Cognitive flexibility* represents the ability to shift gears between accustomed modes of thinking or to accommodate changes in stimulus situations or a new set of instructions. *Visuo-motor flexibility* is thought to express competence in adjusting to unfamiliar routines on tasks involving both cognitive and motor capabilities. Finally, *general visualization* indicates an aptitude for working with visual materials, as evidenced by the ability to find a figure concealed against a similar background or to identify objects only partially displayed. Of the four dimensions, the last has been acknowledged by Schaie and company as less defensible than the others (Nesselroade, Schaie and Baltes, 1972; Baltes and Schaie, 1974).

Age-related patterns of intellectual performance over time are shown graphically in Figure 6.1. As can be seen, the original data,

Figure 6.1
Longitudinal patterns of intellectual performance by age

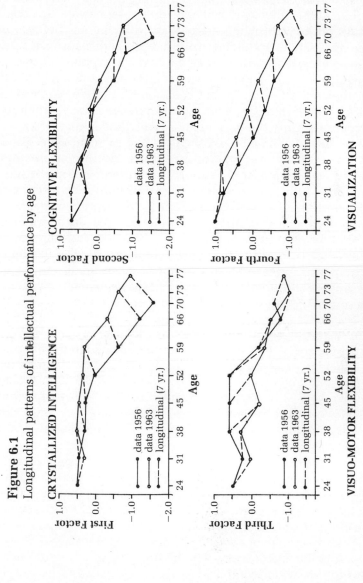

Source: J.R. Nesselroade, K.W. Schaie and P.B. Baltes, "Ontogenetic and Generational Components of Structural and Quantitative Change in Adult Behavior," *Journal of Gerontology* XXVII, 2 (1972): 225.

shown by the heavier dark line, appear to affirm a gradual deterioration in intellectual performance with age. Likewise, focusing only on the followup data collected seven years later might lead one to assert a definite age-related decline in intelligence. On all four dimensions, older adults seem to be at an increasing disadvantage when compared to successively younger respondents. Yet when each cohort is compared to its own earlier performance, shown by dashed lines, later scores turn out to be higher on two of the dimensions. Definite improvements in both crystallized intelligence and visualization aptitude are manifested across the age span. Cognitive flexibility is not strongly related to age. Among younger adults there was a slight decline in the ability to transfer between familiar modes of thinking, while older people demonstrated some improvements over their own previous scores. Only the dimension tapping visuo-motor skills reveals a marked age-related deficit. According to Schaie and his colleagues, the majority of downward trends found in cross-sectional analyses reflect the impact of generational differences, not of age itself. In other words, an age bias built into intelligence tests by the types of information or skill required is at the heart of much of the presumed decrements exhibited by older people. In short, intellectual abilities of older people do not decline, though they do become obsolete. To begin with, older people are usually further removed from their formal educational experiences; in most cases they left educational institutions earlier than today's generation, thereby missing out on certain important influences. Extraneous factors unrelated to intellectual talents are also more likely to affect older test takers; foremost among these is probably fatigue. Perhaps most significantly, the socially stultifying or impoverished circumstances in which the elderly sometimes find themselves may be tantamount to an intellectual handicap, interfering with optimal behavior (Schaie, 1974, 1975). As the situational constraints are removed and the educational levels of future generations upgraded, the relative intellectual declines historically thought to characterize older people will be moderated to a considerable extent.

Surpassing even intelligence as an illusive human attribute, creativity is equally perplexing and still more difficult to define or measure. Despite innumerable anecdotal accounts of famous artists who literally ward off death until the completion of their last great creative effort or who begin very late in life, like Grandma Moses, we know precious little about the effects of age on creativity. The work carried out by Lehman (1953) was the first of a series of exhaustive inquiries into peak creativity in a wide range of areas. The fact that Lehman himself repeated with each report of his study that he neither would nor could make any causal statements as to the relationship between chronological age and creative ability has not always prevented his readers from doing so. Using a technique involving the frequency with which a contributor was cited by others in his or her profession, Lehman charted periods of maximum productivity in both quantitative and qualitative terms for living and deceased persons. Exact ages vary by the field of endeavor, but generally the decade of the thirties was found to be a high point, succeeded by a long and gradual diminution of creative effort. Responding to Lehman's work, Dennis (1966) attempted to introduce the effects of life expectancy in evaluating creative production. Obviously there are more creative people alive at age 30 than at age 60 according to Dennis; hence, it is natural that the largest number of respected contributors would be produced at a relatively early age. If the analysis focuses only on long-lived creators, Dennis agrees that creative productivity reaches a plateau at approximately the age Lehman claimed, or perhaps a few years later, which is maintained until very late in life. However, combining long- and short-lived contributors tends to exaggerate the decline. As many gerontologists are quick to point out, Lehman and Dennis might be comparing apples and oranges — quality and quantity — since the number of contributions may not provide a valid or reliable index of the magnitude of the effort. Regardless of this important issue, an equally relevant consideration is the context in which a contribution is made or recognized. A creative effort too far out of step with current thinking may be dismissed as foolhardy, just as a comparably adventurous breakthrough, coming on the heels of a highly acclaimed, but more glamorous, achievement, may also go without recognition. In spite of these findings, such investigations do not shed much light on the creative possibilities encountered by the vast majority of people living their lives outside the professional limelight.

Clinical and community studies of creativity conducted by Butler (1974) have convinced him that, in addition to living in a healthy and supportive environment, creative people are essentially inner-directed self-teachers. He refers to such people as *autodidactic* individuals. They seldom accept reality solely as it is presented, and are always searching for underlying themes, only to cast them aside as soon as they are uncovered in favor of still more innovative proposals. Autodidactic persons may not make any hallmark contribution hailed by the community as a brilliant insight, yet they are continually sifting new "data," forever remolding into alternative models. In his own attempt to isolate associative patterns between creativity and age, Taylor (1974) also identified certain characteristics of creative individuals that are in agreement with Butler's general statement. According to Taylor's argument, creative people do indeed shape their environment, organizing it in response to specific quests. However, Taylor goes on to note they transform the problem at hand through the use of metaphors or analogy into one capable of a fruitful solution. Implicit in both Butler's and Taylor's analyses is the need for people of all ages, not simply the aged, to receive stimulation and rewards for their efforts lest they cease and fall back into routinized patterns. In American society, which has thus far paid scant attention to the lives or potential contributions of its elderly citizens, few creative outlets currently exist to provide an opportunity for older people to live to their utmost potential (Kogan, 1973).

Cognitive Ability and Impending Death

Recent evidence of a close relationship between cognitive abilities and impending death has generated considerable interest in gerontological circles. In their efforts to overcome the methodological problems posed by a dwindling sample in longitudinal studies, researchers have reanalyzed various intelligence tests' results for those who remained involved against those respondents who died during the course of the study. Some have observed that nonsurvivors scored noticeably lower on intelligence tests and other measures of mental functioning than did those participants who were still available at the time of the followup interviews. The first report of a *terminal drop* in diverse cognitive abilities in advance of death prompted others to return for a retrospective look at the test performance of deceased sample members, comparing their scores to those of the survivors. The results of a longitudinal investigation of twins in which surviving members scored better on intelligence tests than nonsurvivors (Jarvik and Falek, 1963) spurred further interest in the possibility of a decline in cognitive functioning prior to death. Not only was deteriorating health and impending death reflected in the measures of intellectual capacity, but projective and reproductive tests requiring interpretation of a fairly unstructured stimulus were also modified by the nearness of death. Two American psychologists studying elderly Germans found not only that the deceased had performed less well up to five years prior to their deaths, but, remarkably, that those respondents who were unwilling to become involved in the first retest also died at a rate in excess of those who had cooperated — perhaps intimating a cognizance of their own decline (Riegel and Riegel, 1972). Lending additional credibility to the notion of a terminal drop, reports issuing from the 11 year study of healthy older men carried out on behalf of the National Institute of Mental Health have confirmed the tendency for survivors to manifest markedly stable intellectual functioning. Combined with this is a social dimension in which survivors experience a near absence of emotional problems and a high degree of continuity in their personal lives. On almost all measures of IQ, morale and activity, the deceased participants scored lower and showed less consistency in their overall performances when compared to the group still alive after 11 years. Not surprisingly, a large number of the survivors coped with their circumstances through an instrumental orientation to life, though they exhibited few tendencies toward disengagement or withdrawal (Granick and Patterson, 1971). Contradictory findings have also emerged from the studies being conducted at the Duke University Center for the Study of Aging. Initially, published research not only affirmed the death-related declines identified previously, but the Duke investigators also associated the incidence of slower brain wave frequencies and depressed cerebral processes with the terminal decline in cognitive capabilities. Subsequent reports issuing from the Duke studies have suggested that what was at first seen as either a decline or drop may in fact stem from conceptual or methodological ambiguities (Palmore, 1974; Palmore and Cleveland, 1976). Obviously, considerable work on this intriguing phenomenon must be carried out before any definitive conclusions can be drawn.

Adjustment Over the Life Cycle

Age and the Developmental Process

The emphasis placed on psychosexual development by Freud and his followers as the foundation for later psychological patterns has served to sensitize psychologists to the notion of an unfolding developmental process. While Freud and his early psychoanalytic colleagues would probably disagree, few students of human behavior today are willing to grant that psychological makeup is totally fixed early in life or inevitably linked to psychological states. As one of the first to depart from Freud's position, Erikson (1963) attracted widespread attention to the proposition that personalities continue to evolve throughout the adult life course in a gradual yet continuous manner. Even those who doubt the validity of the specific stages postulated by Erikson or set forth in any of the other emerging life span models find a developmental framework useful in discussing qualitative changes in the attitudes and reactions to one's social world. The basic argument of nearly every developmental paradigm is that for individuals to remain reasonably satisfied over the course of life, they must undergo slight modifications in the ways they think of themselves or their environment. Although specific modes of adjustment depend on an individual's personality, world view and cultural milieu, developmental psychologists assume that people everywhere face similar developmental tasks in the process of adjusting to their changing life circumstances.

During the 1930s, a Viennese psychologist named Buhler set forth one of the first sequential models emphasizing the continuity of ego development in adulthood. From their inventory of autobiographical reviews, Buhler, and her student, Frenkel-Brunswik, outlined a five stage trajectory of psychological development intended to compliment the biological curve. The first two phases carry a person through the middle or late twenties with the establishment of an independent life style. The next phase follows no later than the late twenties and continues until the onset of middle age or the later forties. What clearly distinguishes this period is the achievement of vocational stability, along with a high degree of social involvement and community participation. In Buhler's scheme, it is this interval that is the watershed where potentials are approached and all previous gains are consolidated. Accordingly, it also serves as a reference point for the evaluation of subsequent changes. Reflecting the bias implicit in the model, the fourth phase is characterized as a time of physical or emotional crises that are most appropriately resolved in favor of new interests apropos diminishing physiological capabilities. Some retreat from what was earlier socially prescribed interaction is to be expected, leading to an eventual restriction of social life space and a turning inward of one's interests. Finally, the fifth phase is inaugurated sometime during the early or middle 60s and is marked by the onset of nagging illnesses and occupational retirement. As their social world continues to shrink, Buhler's developmental model asserts that many people become preoccupied with retrospective reexamination and recollections of previous achievements. Unfocused pastimes, largely forgotten since childhood, may once again be resumed and questions of a religious or philosophical nature frequently become dominant concerns (Frenkel-Brunswik, 1968).

Erikson's (1963) eight stages of ego development also encompass the entire life cycle, but his model tends to differ from Buhler's in the emphasis on a series of crises that must be overcome. Somewhat better known than the work of Buhler and her colleagues, Erikson's theory has served as an impetus for empirical refinements, though his original formulation of a lifelong sequence of development was derived primarily from his own clinical observations. According to Erikson, each stage consists of solving a developmental task in terms of one or the other of two possible choices. While the process is assumed to be universal, specific solutions are culturally bound, thus reflecting not only human nature, but a particular social milieu. Erikson's concern with childhood development is revealed in the first five stages, all of which are concluded prior to biological maturity. Following the resolution of *identity crises* during adolescence, young adults move into the sixth stage, one of *intimacy* in which they either create mutually satisfying relationships or find themselves *isolated*, and self-absorbed, with little regard for others. Throughout most of adulthood and into the middle years (Erikson does not give specific age parameters) the choice is between *generativity*, a reaching beyond selfish concerns to contribute something of lasting value, or *stagnation,* accompanied by feelings of boredom, self-indulgence and bodily preoccupation. The last stage is one of consummation, a time of *ego integrity* versus a sense of *despair*. On the one hand, successful resolution of the previous crises will leave one prepared for accepting life for what it is, without longing for an opportunity to begin anew. Older individuals who have a sense of integrity will of course realize the relative nature of all their evaluations, yet will nonetheless have a sense of confidence in the wisdom of their own choices. On the other hand, those who have not satisfactorily adjusted to changes that have occurred along the way will find themselves suffused with a sense of despair and foreboding over the prospect of the years of retirement and their ultimate demise. In short, they will be devoid of a sense of integrity, both psychologically and socially (Erikson, 1963).

Using Erikson's model as a foundation, numerous psychologists have formulated refinements that they feel more truly represent the life cycle. Viewing Erikson's last two stages as too gross a depiction of the majority of adult life, Peck (1968) subdivided the later years into middle and older age categories. In the middle years, four developmental issues must be confronted if favorable adjustment is to follow. Thus, individuals need to arrive at a point where they value intellectual pursuits, seek sociability free from sexual connotations, and are capable of keeping their emotional investments flexible while appreciating the possibility of new experiences, if they are to retain a sense of well-being. If adaptation is to be maintained in the years following retirement, Peck contends new sources of gratification must be elaborated along with an ability to transcend not only bodily functioning but personal skills in order to contribute to the lives of others. In another revision of sequential development, Gould (1975) moved even further afield from our earlier examples. Studying over 500 middle class adults ranging in age from 16 to 60, Gould outlined seven developmental stages in adult life with fairly distinct age limitations. As might be expected, people in the youngest categories continue to align themselves as members of the parental family unit. But in the next phase, between 18 and 21, some changes have taken place, so that, by the third phase, independent adult attitudes have become stabilized. The fourth phase, lasting from 29 until age 36, marks the beginning of self-reflection and deeper feelings, while the next phase, up to age 43, is characterized by some personal and marital unrest, although financial worries are no longer as overriding as they were previously. Life becomes stable once more in the sixth period, with friendships and emotional ties increasing in importance. By Gould's seventh phase, time has become the central issue, with typical concerns converging on the allocation of temporal resources and health. The particular manner in which these general tendencies are expressed quite naturally varies; however, there is a progressive building between the stages. It is unfortunate that Gould did not include later age phases in his research since the stages he does discuss provide empirical valida-tion of Erikson's heuristic suggestions (Gould, 1975). Many of the developmental perspectives emanating from Freud's psychody-namic model focus rather exclusively on optimal individual pro-cesses, unalloyed for the most part by considerations of historical or social trappings. Clearly human beings do not live out their lives unaffected by societal prescriptions. Older persons reared around the turn of the century tend to evaluate the stresses they encounter late in life in terms of the social philosophy and values of their youth, of which subsequent generations may not even be aware. Similarly, the lifespan models outlined by Buhler, Erikson or Peck do not take explicit notice of possible sex differences in develop-mental tasks. Both Neugarten and Lowenthal report from their respective studies that the dominant goals and problems faced by women and men may actually run at odds. Neugarten's (1968) research reveals women do not experience the same occupa-tional or health-related stresses as men; instead they must learn to deal with new-found opportunities for self-expression and a freedom from overriding family obligations. Indeed, in her cross-sectional analysis of aging, Lowenthal (1975) found that in most circumstances, sex differences proved to be greater than the differen-ces she discovered between developmental stages. In contrast to Neugarten's data, Lowenthal notes that women in their middle years faced more critical stresses and anxieties than men. As women reach the last phase of life, they leave behind many of the crises of the middle years, turning their attention to a new range of developmen-tal tasks. Men in their middle years are most frequently apprehen-sive over perceived financial strictures to be dealt with in the future and present occupational boredom; by retirement they have advanced to more immediately hedonistic concerns. According to Lowenthal, men and women also react differently to transitional crises; perhaps somewhat surprisingly, men tend to rely more on interpersonal relationships to see them through.

Psychological Disorders in the Later Years

Although no period of the life cycle is free from the specter of emotional distress, the later years constitute a time of especially high risk. Developmental stresses appear to be of a cumulative nature, often taking years to become clinically observable. Since psychological disorders are rooted in social factors as well as in internal psychological disruptions, depriving an individual of familiar and supportive social contacts is likely to add fresh burdens, while aggravating existing problems. Upon reaching what is considered old age, an entire cohort is sytematically exposed for the first time to a range of risks previously affecting people only on an individual basis. How people react to the stresses they encounter will depend on their personal skills and on supportive networks; for some it is conceivable that the challenges of becoming old may even engender new-found strengths. For the majority, however, weaknesses carried over from earlier life will be exacerbated in old age. The factors contributing to what is commonly thought of as mental illness are not well understood. In fact, the whole phenomenon of psychiatric deviance is as elusive as any in the argot of social science. Of necessity, then, our discussion will confine itself to a general overview of the psychological facets of the aging process. While a concise outline of the stresses that possibly foster the undermining of people's mental health would doubtlessly omit certain crucial issues, in his effort to bring some order to the classification of stress-induced factors, Rosow (1973), for one, has succeeded in presenting a usable summary. In addition to the cohort liability pointed out above, he contends the loss of roles experienced by the elderly often excludes them from absorbing memberships and devalues their potential impact on society. What makes the exclusion even more devastating to many is that their socialization has not prepared them for such a fate, nor are their new lives infused with clear structural guidelines that would allow an easy transition. The ill-defined circumstances in which most elderly find themselves naturally generate considerable strain, often leading ultimately to a profound sense of anxiety and malaise. Under similarly stressful and anxiety-provoking conditions, the majority of us would probably react in an analogous fashion. The difference would lie of course in the supportive networks to which we could turn for reaffirmation of our self-concepts. For a number of elderly, successive role losses have left them bereft of compensatory feedback so that they must rely solely on their personal resources to shore up their mental health. When physiological deprivations and poor health are compounded with the social adversities incurred by the elderly and the lack of understanding of their plight, it is no wonder they are susceptible to emotional upsets.

The acquisition of informative statistics on the incidence of mental disorders in old age poses something of a hurdle. In the United States the most inclusive data are collected in the Health Examination Survey, administered regularly by the National Center for Health Statistics. Besides inquiring about physical well-being, it contains a series of questions covering psychological distress and so-called "nervous breakdowns." Despite the indication from the findings of a slight progression in mental disorders by age, the definitions of these disorders used by various age groups are subject to innumerable factors beyond the control of such research efforts. To begin with, respondents may be unaware of any difference between *functional disorders*, those psychogenic problems without apparent physical cause, and *organic disorders*, stemming from physiological impairments of the brain or other areas of the body. Further, the range of mental disorders is so variable that respondents' personal evaluations are often difficult to interpret; certainly they cannot be compared to first time admissions to psychiatric units or other more definitive indicators. Even among psychiatrists and psychologists, diagnostic categories prove to be highly questionable; indeed, the nomenclature referring to psychological disruption among the elderly is especially vague. Be this as it may, the American Psychological Association reported in 1971 that at least 15 percent of the older population could benefit from mental health services. Some investigators claim that even this estimate is overly conservative when the number of elderly facing high risk situations is considered. Add in the million or so persons already residing in various kinds of institutions, plus the seven million who face severe stresses from living below the poverty line, and the two million who have chronic diseases, and the proportion of the population disposed to emotional disorders increases rapidly (Butler and Lewis, 1973). When all the forms of psychopathology experienced by the elderly both in and outside of institutions are tallied, the proportion of elderly who may be suffering serious mental distress could easily range from 25 to 60 percent. However, community surveys in the United States and Britain suggest figures of between 10 and 20 percent may be more reliable (Pfeiffer and Busse, 1969; Redick et al., 1973). As further testimony of the higher risks incurred by the elderly and of the likelihood of an age bias operating in the delivery of mental health services, we have only to note that in the United States older people comprise nearly 30 percent of the institutionalized mental patients, though they account for barely 2 percent of the individuals seen on an outpatient basis. Figure 6.2 indicates the range of mental disorders occurring, by age, in the United States.

Figure 6.2
Percent Distribution of Resident Patients in State and County Mental Hospitals by Diagnosis, United States, 1970

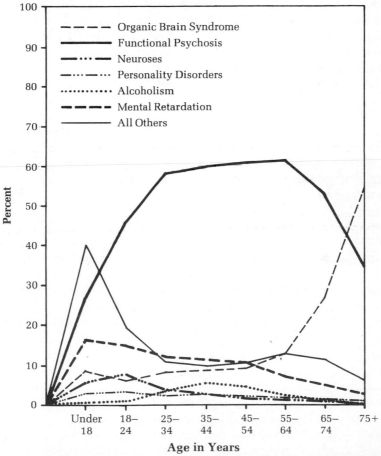

Source: U.S. Department of Health, Education, and Welfare, Public Health Service, "Age, Sex and Diagnostic Composition of Resident Patients in State and County Mental Hospitals — United States, 1961–1970" (Washington, D.C.: Government Printing Office, 1972), p. 10. (Converted from numeric data)

Despite the impossibility of drawing a hard and fast line between psychogenic and organic disorders, the typology does serve as a useful framework for classification and treatment. By far the majority of psychogenic problems, sometimes called functional disorders, found among the elderly are of long duration, resulting from earlier maladjustments that may go unnoticed until the later years. There are doubtlessly some people who do first manifest symptoms of psychological distress relatively late in life, but these probably constitute a small minority and are subsumed under a particular diagnostic label. Most practitioners agree that the reaction patterns developed over the course of a lifetime are fairly resilient, regardless of whether they are helpful, adaptive responses or dysfunctionally negative. Again, we find widely diverse estimates of the incidence of psychogenic disorders among older people. Some suggest up to half of all psychological disruptions are attributable to functional causes (Butler and Lewis, 1973; Bromley, 1971). At present, however, these figures must be viewed as rough approximations, since the whole question of psychological disorders in later life is being rephrased as we acquire new insights on the problem.

Affective disorders are the most common psychogenic illness found after the middle years. Generally speaking, affective disorders can be described as alterations in personality or normal mood states, keynoted by a growing lack of self-respect and unresolved turmoil. Many affective disorders are diverse forms of depressive reactions, though elation and bodily preoccupation may also occur. Depression, whether based on mild reactive responses to identifiable situational factors or on serious psychogenic states that have no apparent link with external events, is the single most frequent functional disorder. The symptoms of depression usually involve a mood of despair in which individuals withdraw from active participation in most interactions, concentrating their attention instead on depreciating their own self-worth and potential, though they remain capable of angry outbursts against real or imagined wrongs. A wide gamut of psychosomatic symptoms usually accompany affective disorders. Such irregularities as loss of appetite, sleeping difficulties, constipation and fatigue may all prove indicative of emotional upset. No doubt at least a portion of the anecdotal accounts reported in newspapers about older people repaying income taxes or debts outstanding for 20 years can be attributed to the feelings of guilt and retribution that are also facets of many depressive syndromes. Those relatively rare depressive reactions that crop up late in life seemingly without prior history are customarily diagnosed as a form of **involutional melancholia.** The label was used originally to refer to postmenopausal women who found themselves unable to muster normal emotional responses. It is now utilized for many affective disorders that appear for the first time during later life. Sensory deprivations such as deafness may often carry a psychogenic component, manifested in psychological distress as the sufferer becomes increasingly isolated. Hyperemotional reactions, including those classified as manic behavior, are a less common affective disorder, though they are observed frequently enough to be identified as similar in nature to the depressive mood states characteristic of younger people. Manic-depressive disorders seem to afflict women and professional people more often than men or blue collar workers, but whether this remains the case among older populations is by no means certain.

 Neuroses likely to be encountered among the elderly also follow the patterns exhibited for the rest of the population. With the possible exception of obsessive-compulsive traits, it is safe to say the neuroses experienced by the elderly have evolved over a number of years. Usually the symptoms of an obsessive-compulsive reaction involve an inability to shake off disquieting thoughts and a need to repeatedly engage in ritualized behavior. Not infrequently, the compulsive behavior acquires meaning as a purifying or protective act guarding the person against some dreaded consequence to which he believes himself vulnerable. Most often, neurotic reactions are marked by considerable anxiety and may be interpreted as the patient's futile attempt to grapple with unfavorable external circumstances beyond his or her control. **Dissociative** and **conversion neuroses** represent the serious breakdown of cognitive functioning and entail psychosomatic complaints of considerable magnitude. Some gerontologists are convinced that threatened displacements or depreciations of identity bring about neurotic reactions as a kind of defense against overwhelming psychological disjunctures. **Hypochondriasis** is another form of neurosis exhibited by the depressed, although one difference is that the depressed patient may be unable or unwilling to seek professional treatment, while the hypochondriac cannot gain enough attention. Somatic complaints reflect a preoccupation with bodily functioning and an exaggerated concern with normal aches and pains. According to Pfeiffer and Busse (1973), after middle age, women are more disposed to hypochondriasis than men, perhaps partially as a compensatory strategy against other role losses or threats of personal failure. All hypochondriacs seemingly use their complaints, at some time, as a means of controlling social interaction. There may also be a phobic component to hypochondriasis where food fads and excessive hygiene are adopted as safeguards against disease-causing germs.

Psychoses comprise a more serious category of psychological dysfunction since they reflect a break with normative definitions of reality and a disintegration of logical processes. Hallucinations and delusions of grandeur are the most stereotypic examples of psychotic breaks, but cases in which there is a complete personality alteration, as in the legendary psychotic who believes himself to be Napoleon, are no longer given as much credibility as previously. **Paranoid** states are characterized by the belief people have that they are being persecuted for some presumed wrongdoing. Unlike other psychotics, paranoids do not necessarily manifest disrupted intellectual capacities; once their initial assumptions are accepted, there is a logical development which follows. Paranoid reactions occur more often among already institutionalized elderly or those who are suddenly thrust into adverse situations. Sensory impairment, as in the loss of vision or hearing, or social isolation may also bring on paranoid fears. Fortunately, most paranoid reactions are of fairly short duration and often they do not even fall too far outside what is considered the normal range of suspiciousness. For this reason they are frequently difficult to detect, merging into ordinary experiences in such a way that, while seeming a bit strange, they may not be sufficiently out of line to attract attention. The diagnosis of **schizophrenia** covers nearly half of all patients admitted to mental hospitals in the United States. In Europe, when hallucinations, cognitive breakdown, abandonment of social facades and so on occur in later life, the disorder is labeled *paraphrenia*. Apart from the reference being applicable to elderly schizophrenics, other distinctions are probably nebulous. Schizophrenia, as one of the more intractable forms of psychotic disorders, has a poor prognosis. It is an extremely formidable task to attempt to communicate with patients who are at best only occasionally lucid and capable of responding to normal therapeutic contact. Few schizophrenics become so only at an advanced age; more often this disorder is of a chronic nature dating as far back as late adolescence, though it might remain secondary until declining physical health or some other crisis brings it to the fore.

Self-destructive behavior has traditionally been considered a form of emotional disorder requiring societal intervention in most Western cultures. The outstanding example of destructive behavior is, of course, suicide, and each year a disproportionate number of suicides are committed by people over the age of 65. The elderly number over a quarter of all self-inflicted deaths in the United States. Among white males, each decade brings a higher suicide rate, up to and including the very oldest ages. For white women the peak comes in early middle age, but here, too, the rate is on the increase. Blacks follow with only a slight decrease during the middle years, though suicide is becoming more frequent over all older age categories. Regardless of nationality, suicide rates increase by age despite slight variations in peak years. In almost all cases, divorced, widowed or single people are more likely to end their own lives. The same holds true for people who have recently experienced an unresolved crisis or are otherwise deprived of satisfying interpersonal relationships and feel depressed. Suicide is not the only destructive act older persons may direct against themselves. How else can we interpret the behavior of heavy smokers, drinkers or eaters who recognize the health and social risks they are imposing on themselves, yet continue their ways unabated? Neglecting medical attention or medication for a known illness is another less dramatic form of destructive behavior contributing to the shortening of life (Patterson et al., 1974). Psychic death or early withdrawal may also be detrimental to an individual's physical or mental well-being, and so long as they remain passive means to an end, society tends to ignore their destructive intent.

Whether functional psychological disorders are cause or consequence of chronic physical illness is still open to question, although it is known that among older people the two usually occur in close proximity. Thus far the discussion has focused on functional disorders, but a significant portion of the elderly hospitalized mental patients are victims of organic brain disorders rather than psychogenic responses to the stresses of age. In neither case, however, do the two types usually appear in pure form. People who develop organic impairments may later show neurotic or psychotic symptoms as their social world becomes even more intolerant and unresponsive. Psychological disruptions may also operate in the opposite direction, and functional disorders may be joined by organic complications, with the symptoms of each becoming intermingled. From either source, it is fruitless to address one without treating the other at the same time. Diagnostic problems are manifold, since clinical evaluations depend as much on cognitive functioning as they do on neurological signs. In both types of disorder, patients may fall well within the normal range of performance for people their age while experiencing organic or psychogenic damage to their well-being.

Any cerebral impairment that interferes with normal mental functioning may be diagnosed as one or another form of organic brain syndrome; hence, the range of symptoms is often quite diffuse. In many instances the symptoms displayed depend as much on previous psychological characteristics, stable social or physical environments, and related factors as they do on the extent of physiological damage. Apart from traumatic lesions, there is even some controversy among neurophysiologists about whether organic brain syndromes are qualitatively distinct from normal involutional changes or represent merely a hastening of the inevitable. A number of microscopic alterations appear naturally in the older brain, some being so common as to convince many people that they are inherently related to the aging process itself. The current weight of opinion in the United States lends its support to the pathological status, while many European neurophysiologists take the opposite view (Wang, 1969; Butler and Lewis, 1973; Dayan, 1973). In considering the genesis of organic disorders, it is important to recall the discussion in Chapter Four regarding the accumulation of lipofuscin in post-fixed mitotic cell lines such as compose brain tissue. This accumulation may inhibit cellular metabolism to a degree sufficient to cause degenerative alterations. It also ought to be remembered that progressive changes in the elastic properties of arteries occur throughout the body, disrupting the dispersion of life-sustaining oxygen and nutrients in the brain as well as the limbs. Accurate statistics on the prevalence of organic brain syndromes are unavailable largely as a result of the complex nature of the problem and the high number of incorrect diagnoses. We do know, however, that among older patients admitted to mental hospitals for the first time estimates of organic impairments reach 75 percent. In psychological terms *organic dementia* is usually characterized by disorientation, and intellectual and judgmental declines, along with a loss of memory and a lack of affective responsiveness. Organic brain syndromes are divisible into one of two types. If physiological damage is diagnosed as reversible, the patient is said to suffer from *acute brain syndrome*; in Europe the preferred label is acute confusional state. Physical changes stemming perhaps from similar causes, but which remain irreversible, are labeled *chronic brain syndromes*, or chronic confusional states. Although chronic brain patients may respond to palliative treatments, as a rule any remissions are only temporary.

Acute brain syndromes are often misdiagnosed, in part due to a symptomatology dominated by inconsistency — that is, near perfect lucidity one minute and mild or severe confusion the next. Misinterpretations of environmental cues and speech difficulties are common, as are easy distractability and occasional hyperactivity. Early medical attention is essential for a speedy, full recovery and must include treatment for the physiological causes as well as the maintenance of social involvement. The etiology of acute brain damage presents a complicated question, though cerebrovascular accidents that result in brief oxygen starvation, infections accompanied by high temperatures, malnutrition, alcoholism, other systematic illnesses such as kidney diseases and sensory deprivations are implicated. Pinpointing clear-cut neurological degeneration is a perplexing task, since, for the most part, diagnoses are accomplished by means of psychological testing. In severe cases involving cerebral trauma or serious infections, the detection of physiological impairments is not particularly difficult. The mild cases arising from chronic malnutrition or involving other brain disorders are more problematic and may go largely unnoticed or unattended. Social activity and environmental considerations are also intimately involved in the symptoms that are exhibited; thus, disadvantaged elderly are quite likely to manifest behavioral disruptions related to acute brain syndromes (Busse and Wang, 1974).

Chronic brain syndromes, by contrast, are defined as being irreversible, and until recently were thought to be entirely intractable. We now know, however, that many of the behavioral symptoms do in fact respond to treatment. There are two subtypes of chronic brain disorders identified with later life. **Senile psychosis** occurs when the aged brain undergoes anatomical involution, ventricles become enlarged, and there is generalized shrinkage and focal atrophy associated with the breakdown of brain cells. As the extent of the degeneration increases, senile plaques emerge in the cerebral cortex region. Some researchers hypothesize most all of us would eventually develop senile plaques provided we lived long enough, given that nine out of ten people aged 90 or over show at least some early indications of a diffuse loss and deterioration of nerve cells (Dayan, 1973). Patients with senile psychosis experience a pernicious decline in intellectual functioning and attention span, often beginning in their later sixties. Gradually they lose the more subtle shadings of emotional responses and show signs of impaired memories. As the disease progresses, emotional reserves seem to become fragile, with quick tempers and antisocial conduct becoming more pervasive until the patient finally becomes physically incapacitated. Under routine circumstances there is a preservation of certain skills, which facilitates some regularization of behavior, but unfamiliar tasks or surroundings cannot be dealt with and should be avoided as far as possible. Usually people die within five years of the observation of the disease. As a consequence of greater female longevity, the disease is more often found among older women than among older men (Bromley, 1971). Conversely, **cerebral arteriosclerosis** is likely to occur earlier, by age 65 or so, and more frequently among men. When cerebral blood flow is inadequate due to a hardening of the arteries or for any other reason, tissue death ensues as the processes of oxygenation and the exchange of nutrients and waste products are thwarted. Much of the dizziness, headaches and confusion experienced by older people is probably a result of tiny infarctions of brain tissue that, when they occur on a massive scale, we label strokes. Unlike senile psychosis, cerebral arteriosclerosis follows an intermittent cycle of improvement followed by the inevitable decline as additional areas of the brain are affected. In both forms of brain damage, psychotic symptoms identical with those associated with functional disorders appear, only to be commonly misdiagnosed. While hypertension is implicated as a possible cause of cerebral circulatory impairments, heightened blood pressure may sometimes prove helpful when there is a reduction in the oxygen content of the blood or when peripheral resistance in the circulatory system inside the brain prohibits ready diffusion of blood supplies. It is not unusual to find high blood pressure in patients whose cerebral arteries are encrusted with a mineral-like coating that impedes the diffusion of oxygen and nutrients through the artery wall. Metabolic upsets may also contribute to the development of arteriosclerosis and chronic brain syndromes.

The primary characteristic of organic brain syndromes of either type is a breakdown of psychological stability and intellectual functioning. Diagnoses have largely depended on evaluation of mental profiles until recent years, but the advent of sophisticated electroencephalographic (EEG) techniques and the identification of abnormal electrical patterns have begun to facilitate more precise diagnoses. In nearly all elderly people, dominant brain rhythms slow with advancing age, yet their relationship with psychological factors has only recently yielded to the probing of neurophysiologists. Still, the causes of differential brain deterioration have not been discovered. Nor can neurophysiologists currently tell us why some people develop what is labeled presenile dementia as early as their 40s while others remain mentally sound well past age 90. Another problem inhibiting the proper diagnosis and treatment of psychological abnormalities among older patients is that geriatric specialists have not been consulted by the American Psychiatric Association's Committee on Nomenclature, which is responsible for establishing diagnostic categories and symptom profiles. So long as the problems of older people are defined without benefit of an aging specialist, adequate treatment is impossible (But-ler and Lewis, 1973). With more refined diagnostic procedures, in-appropriate descriptions of "childish emotionality" will be realized for what they are — wrongheaded misinterpretations of the emo-tional upsets manifested by older people.

Treatment and Intervention

There is little doubt that much of the suffering endured by older people afflicted with psychogenic or organic disorders could be al-leviated by early rehabilitative treatment. However, preventive measures designed to avert the occurrence of psychological difficul-ties in the first place would be far more effective. In the majority of cases, the emotional upheaval that interferes with normal func-tioning does not take place in isolation, that is, without societal involvement. By changing, redesigning as it were, normative per-spectives regarding the status of the aged, entire generations might escape some of the high risks that challenge the ability of today's elderly to withstand stress. Primary prevention would, by definition, entail large scale efforts at reeducating people about what it means to age in terms of developmental goals. A concerted program aimed at offsetting traditionally negative images about aging would go a long way toward restoring a sense of competence to the lives of older people. Further, insuring adequate levels of income, providing re-sponsive medical attention and encouraging active participation in the decisions affecting their lives, while emphasizing personal worth developed from much more than productive contributions or youthful capacities, would surely mediate those factors that pres-ently increase the likelihood of emotional breakdowns. In terms of practical applications various elements of preserving or restoring optimal functioning appear in Figure 6.3.

Older people who are already experiencing emotional traumas cannot afford to wait for society to realize that their problems are not entirely of their own making; they are desperately in need of atten-tion now. Prompt recognition and treatment aimed at reestablishing equanimity in the lives of those whose mental health is threatened must reach beyond psychological intervention to encompass sup-portive environmental and social relationships. Historically psychiatry has reflected its Freudian biases regarding the minimal effectiveness of therapy for middle-aged or older adults. If we are to judge by the minority of older patients receiving private therapy, the prejudicial concept of "ageism" described in Chapter One has seem-ingly carried over to the practice of psychiatry. Despite this, private psychiatric care has proven to be very potent in treating the kinds of

Figure 6.3
Reducing the likelihood of psychological distress among the elderly

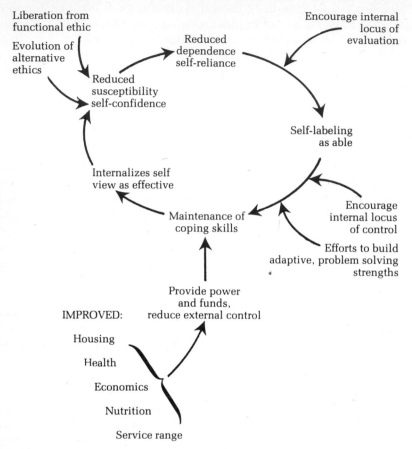

Source: J.A. Kuypers and V.L. Bengtson, "Social Breakdown and Competence: A Model of Normal Aging," *Human Development* XVI, 3 (1973): 197.

problems frequently found among older patients. Factors which have prevented psychiatric referral and treatment in the past include the patient's age, the psychiatrist's age, the diagnosis and the presence of complicating physical illnesses (Garetz, 1975; Butler and Lewis, 1973). The elderly themselves may also be hesitant about submitting to therapy because of personal prejudices and fears. Accordingly, the large majority who need mental health services are not receiving attention until their disorders have advanced to severe stages or until no other alternatives are available. Once an older person is institutionalized, his or her prognosis does not greatly improve. The same biases that operate in the general community are carried over to the institutional setting, where therapists express a view that reflects the dominant societal stereotypes (Kastenbaum, 1964; Fracchia et al., 1973). As will be seen in the following chapter, psychiatric coverage under Medicare as yet does little to furnish needed care. It is extremely limited, with no provisions for social services, counseling or support except those few supplied by a physician.

Secondary prevention aimed at lessening the extent of psychological impairments must necessarily be determined by the nature of the disorder. With affective disorders, most older patients will respond to either individual or group psychotherapy. Of course, the therapist must take into consideration the practical, defensive role many psychogenic disorders play. The question then becomes: If a defense is working, if a patient's ego is being protected, should we by means of therapy attempt to right the disorder? Since many anxious or depressed patients have a difficult time perceiving or verbalizing the cause of their complaints, it may be more efficient to wait for the spontaneous remissions that often occur. Antidepressive drug therapy may also prove advantageous, considerably easing conventional psychotherapy. In all psychogenic cases, however, the principal goal is the restoration of positive self-esteem in terms of one's available resources. In doing so, the situation of the older patient often calls for a more active involvement by the therapist than is usual for younger patients. Supportive interaction may be far more beneficial than rational analyses, partially because the existence of dependencies that brought about the crisis in the first place is usually an inescapable reality for all intents and purposes. Similarly, therapy that enables patients to continue normal routines is very important; allowing the patient to remain at home or with his or her family is not only reassuring, but provides an opportunity for reality testing not available in most institutional settings. What the patient may need most of all is a facilitator who will furnish an opportunity for a review of previous experiences, with the goal of bringing about a progressive realignment of disparate self-images (Butler and Lewis, 1973).

For patients with organic brain syndromes, secondary prevention requires both behavioral and neurophysiological therapy. Generally, mental functioning will respond as cerebral damage is controlled. Intervention must first concentrate on improving one's consumption of oxygen and glucose. Various drugs are now utilized that increase cerebral blood flow. Until the causative factors involved in organic disorders are better understood, specific therapy is yet to be achieved. Vascular disorders outside the brain are thought to be involved in the onset of dementias whose control seems to result in remission of organic symptoms or at least in a lessening of behavioral disruptions. While the physical causes of organic brain syndromes are not now amenable to treatment, attention to psychological well-being has proven most helpful. Although a great deal of patience and perseverance is required, efforts to maintain the older patient's contact with reality through traditional therapy, including occupational therapy or behavioral modification techniques, do ameliorate the extent of his or her disorientation.

Summary

The psychological characteristics encountered in an older population may best be understood as the culmination of a lifetime's selection of alternatives. Whether the focus is on a single person or a cohort, mental functioning reflects both strengths and weaknesses shaped by unique biographical developments, plus the experience of an entire generation. For example, the effects of social Darwinism, widely accepted prior to World War I, or of the Depression of the 1930s, are an integral facet of the way today's elderly view themselves and life. If as individuals they fared particularly poorly during the Depression, then their fears of old age may well stem from dread of the possibility of a similar fate. Increasingly, older people must grapple with limitations and disabilities that inevitably influence their self-concept and social interaction. By the time they reach their sixth decade, most people have experienced and accommodated themselves to sensory impairments that gradually encroach on normal activities. Normal developmental adjustments and the environmental conditions faced by the elderly also prepare the way for a kind of psychological retrenchment which, while it may not be ubiquitous, is certainly widespread (Back and Gergen, 1968). The myth of age-related declines in intelligence has only recently been challenged by new evidence. Schaie, as leader of a research team, has shown that intelligence and sensory declines do not go necessarily hand in hand. What had previously been identified as an age-related decline is now thought to be due to conceptual inadequacies or biases built into most psychological tests. While certain cognitive capacities involving motor skills are lost with age, these, too, have been grossly overestimated. When evaluation is made by cohort-appropriate means, the debilities simply do not appear. Of course there are individual exceptions; capacities may be modified by ill-health, by unfavorable social circumstances and, ultimately, by the nearness of death. In practical terms we must restructure the nature of formal educational opportunities to allow for and encourage later participation if we value optimal well-being for our elderly.

Although serious psychological illnesses are not inevitably associated with old age, their occurrence is sufficiently disproportionate to indicate the existence of special problems confronting the elderly. Social scientists have known for some time that factors such as social or economic status, educational levels, or marital ties are directly related to mental health. Depressive and hypochondriac reactions lead the litany of psychogenic complaints voiced by the elderly, but in many instances these are merely the manifestation of long-standing problems. Organic brain damage may be superimposed on any of the psychogenic disorders or it may exist independently; in either case, it precludes normal behavior and thought processes. It is not uncommon for lay people and professionals alike to use the term "senility" with reference to organic brain disorders. In point of fact, there is no such medical or psychological diagnosis. Chronic brain syndromes are usually what they are describing, though often the distinction between chronic and acute brain disorders lies in the accuracy of the diagnosis and the quality of the treatment. Acute damage will respond to proper treatment, returning the patient to near normal functioning. Chronic conditions, on the other hand, are intractable; while remissions are possible, they are but temporary, and institutionalization is a probable outcome. To say chronic brain syndromes are inevitably debilitating is not to claim that they or any other psychological disorder should not be given treatment. Using appropriate therapies, it is often possible to preserve socially valued behavior in the face of serious organic or emotional upset. Unfortunately, such treatment has been unavailable in the past because many misconceptions have stood in the way of the delivery of mental health services, adding further to the stigmatization of the elderly as beyond help. Gradually these negative perspectives are being overcome by more enlightened opinions, and future generations of elderly hopefully will receive the kind of treatments and support they need.

Pertinent Readings

BACK, K.W., and K.J. GERGEN. "The Self Through the Latter Span of Life." In *The Self in Social Interaction,* eds. C. Gordon and K.J. Gergen, 241–50. New York: John Wiley and Sons, Inc., 1968.

BALTES, P., and K.W. SCHAIE. "The Myth of the Twilight Years." *Psychology Today* X, 7 (March 1974): 35–40.

BARRETT, J.H. *Gerontological Psychology.* Springfield, Ill.: Charles C. Thomas, 1972.

BLUM, J.E., J.L. FOSSHAGE and L.F. JARVIK. "Intellectual Changes and Sex Differences in Octogenarians: A Twenty-year Longitudinal Study of Aging." *Developmental Psychology* VII, 2 (1972): 178–87.

BOTWINICK, J. *Cognitive Processes in Maturity and Old Age.* New York: Springer Publishing Company, Inc., 1967.

BOTWINICK, J., and M. STORANDT. "Cardiovascular Status, Depressive Affect, and Other Factors in Reaction Time." *Journal of Gerontology* XXIX, 5 (1974): 543–48.

BOTWINICK, J., and L.W. THOMPSON. "Age Differences in Reaction Time: An Artifact?" *The Gerontologist* VIII, 1 (1968): 25–28.

BROMLEY, D.B. *The Psychology of Human Ageing.* Baltimore: Penguin Books, 1971.

BUSSE, E.W., and E. PFEIFFER. "Functional Psychiatric Disorders in Old Age." In *Behavior and Adaptation in Late Life,* eds. E.W. Busse and E. Pfeiffer, 1–10. Boston: Little, Brown and Company, 1969.

BUSSE, E.W., and H. SHAN WANG. "The Multiple Factors Contributing to Dementia in Old Age." In *Normal Aging II,* ed. E. Palmore, 151–60. Durham, N.C.: Duke University Press, 1974.

BUTLER, R.N. "The Creative Life and Old Age." In *Successful Aging,* ed. E. Pfeiffer, 97–108. Durham, N.C.: Center for the Study of Aging and Human Development, Duke University, 1974.

BUTLER, R.N., and M.I. LEWIS. *Aging and Mental Health: Positive Psychological Approaches.* St. Louis: C.V. Mosby Company, 1973.

DAYAN, A.D. "Neuropathology of Aging." In *Textbook of Geriatric Medicine and Gerontology,* ed. J.C. Brocklehurst, 161–81. Edinburgh: Churchill Livingstone, 1973.

DEMMING, J.A., and S.L. PRESSEY. "Tests 'Indigenous' to the Adult and Older Years." *Journal of Counseling Psychology* IV (1957): 144–48.

DENNIS, W. "Creative Productivity Between the Ages of 20 and 80 Years." *Journal of Gerontology* XXI, 1 (1966): 1–8.

EISDORFER, C. "New Dimensions and a Tentative Theory." *The Gerontologist* VII, 1 (1967): 14–18.

——— . "Intellectual and Cognitive Changes in the Aged." In *Behavior and Adaptation in Late Life,* eds. E.W. Busse and E. Pfeiffer, 237–50. Boston: Little, Brown and Company, 1969.

ERIKSEN, C.W., R.M. HAMLIN and C. DAYE. "Aging Adults and Rate of Memory Scan." *Bulletin of the Psychonomic Society* I, 4 (1973): 259–60.

ERIKSON, E.H. *Childhood and Society.* 2nd ed. New York: W.W. Norton, 1963.

FELTON, B., and E. KAHANA. "Adjustment and Situationally Bound Locus of Control Among Institutionalized Aged." *Journal of Gerontology* XXIX, 3 (1974): 295–301.

FRACCHIA, J., C. SHEPPARD and S. MERLIS. "Treatment Patterns in Psychiatry: Relationships to Symptom Features and Aging." *Journal of the American Geriatric Society* XXI, 3 (1973): 134–38.

FRENKEL-BRUNSWIK, E., "Adjustments and Reorientation in the Course of the Life Span." In *Middle Age and Aging*, ed. B.L. NEUGARTEN, 77–84. Chicago: The University of Chicago Press, 1968.

GARETZ, F.K. "The Psychiatrist's Involvement with Aged Patients." *American Journal of Psychiatry* CXXXII, 1 (1975): 63–65.

GORDON, D.M. "Eye Problems of the Aged." In *Working with Older People*, vol. IV, ed. A.B. Chinn, 28–37. Washington, D.C.: Department of Health, Education and Welfare, July 1971.

GOULD, R. "Adult Life Stages: Growth Toward Self-Tolerance." *Psychology Today* VIII, 9 (1975): 74–78.

GRANICK, S., and R.D. PATTERSON, eds. *Human Aging II: An Eleven-year Followup Biomedical and Behavioral Study.* DHEW Publication No. (HSM) 71-9037. Washington, D.C.: U.S. Government Printing Office, 1971.

HULTSCH, D.F. "Learning to Learn in Adulthood." *Journal of Gerontology* XXIX, 3 (1974): 302–308.

JARVIK, L.F., and A. FALEK. "Intellectual Stability and Survival in the Aged." *Journal of Gerontology* XVIII, 2 (1963): 173–76.

KASTENBAUM, R. "The Reluctant Therapist." In *New Thoughts on Old Age*, ed. R. Kastenbaum, 139–45. New York: Springer Publishers, 1964.

KIMMEL, D.C. *Adulthood and Aging.* New York: John Wiley and Sons, Inc., 1974.

KOGAN, N. "Creativity and Cognitive Style: A Life-Span Perspective." In *Life-Span Developmental Psychology: Personality and Socialization*, eds. P.B. Baltes and K.W. Schaie, 146–78. New York: Academic Press, 1973.

KUYPERS, J.A., and V.L. BENGTSON. "Social Breakdown and Competence: A Model of Normal Aging." *Human Development* XVI, 3 (1973): 181–201.

LEHMAN, H.C. *Age and Achievement.* Princeton, N.J.: Princeton University Press, 1953.

LOWENTHAL, M.F. "Psychosocial Variations Across the Adult Life Course: Frontiers for Research and Policy." *The Gerontologist* XV, 1 (1975): 6–12.

MURRELL, F.H. "The Effects of Extensive Practice on Age Differences in Reaction Time." *Journal of Gerontology* XXV, 3 (1970): 268–74.

NATIONAL CENTER FOR HEALTH STATISTICS. Department of Health, Education and Welfare. "Health in the Later Years of Life." Washington, D.C.: U.S. Government Printing Office, 1971.

NESSELROADE, J.R., K.W. SCHAIE and P.B. BALTES. "Ontogenetic and Generational Components of Structural and Quantitative Change in Adult Behavior." *Journal of Gerontology* XXVII, 2 (1972): 222–28.

NEUGARTEN, B.L. "The Awareness of Middle Age." In *Middle Age and Aging*, ed. B.L. Neugarten, 93–98. Chicago: University of Chicago Press, 1968.

NEUGARTEN, B.L. et al. *Personality in Middle and Later Life.* New York: Atherton Press, 1964.

PALMORE, E., ed. *Normal Aging II.* Durham, N.C.: Duke University Press, 1974.

PALMORE, E., and W. CLEVELAND. "Aging, Terminal Decline, and Terminal Drop." *Journal of Gerontology* XXXI, 1 (1976): 76–81.

PATTERSON, R.D., R. ABRAHAMS and F. BAKER. "Preventing Self-destructive Behavior." *Geriatrics* XXIX, 11 (1974): 115–21.

PECK, R.C. "Psychological Developments in the Second Half of Life." In *Middle Age and Aging*, ed. B.L. Neugarten, 88–92. Chicago: University of Chicago Press, 1968.

PFEIFFER, E., and E.W. BUSSE. "Mental Disorders in Later Life — Affective Disorders; Paranoid, Neurotic and Situational Reactions." In *Mental Illness in Later Life*, eds. E.W. Busse and E. Pfeiffer, 89–106. Washington, D.C.: American Psychiatric Association, 1973.

REDICK, R.W., M. KROMER and C.A. TAUBE. "Epidemiology of Mental Illness and Utilization of Psychiatric Facilities among Older Persons." In *Mental Illness in Later Life*, eds. E.W. Busse and E. Pfeiffer, 199–231. Washington, D.C.: American Psychiatric Association, 1973.

RIEGEL, K.F., and R.M. RIEGEL. "Development, Drop and Death." *Developmental Psychology* VI, 2 (1972): 306–19.

ROSOW, I. "The Social Context of the Aging Self." *The Gerontologist* XIII, 1 (1973): 82–87.

SCHAIE, K.W. "Translations in Gerontology — From Lab to Life." *American Psychologist* XXIX, 11 (1974): 802–07.

_____ . "Age Changes in Adult Intelligence." In *Aging: Scientific Perspectives and Social Issues*, eds. D.S. Woodruff and J.E. Birren, 111–24. New York: D. Van Nostrand Company, 1975.

TAUB, H.A. "Memory Span, Practice and Aging." *Journal of Gerontology* XXVIII, 3 (1973): 335–38.

TAUB, H.A., and M.K. LONG. "The Effects of Practice on Short-term Memory of Young and Old Subjects." *Journal of Gerontology* XXVII, 4 (1972): 494–99.

TAYLOR, I.A. "Patterns of Creativity and Aging." In *Successful Aging*, by E. Pfeiffer, 113–17. Durham, N.C.: Center for the Study of Aging and Human Development, Duke University, 1974.

WANG, H. SHAN. "Organic Brain Syndromes." In *Behavior and Adaptation in Late Life*, eds. E.W. Busse and E. Pfeiffer, 263–88. Boston: Little, Brown and Company, 1969.

WELFORD, A.T. "Age and Skill: Motor, Intellectual and Social." In *Decision Making and Age*, ed. A.T. Welford, 1–22. Basel, Switzerland: S. Karger, 1969.

Chapter 7

Health Status
in the Later Years

Over the past hundred years, medicine has done more to improve the quality of life than in all previous centuries combined. Yet from the life tables presented in Chapter Three it is clear that the most significant breakthroughs have been observed for those illnesses likely to affect people in their earliest years. The control of infectious diseases brought dramatic declines in infant mortality. With improved sanitary conditions and public health information, maternal mortality quickly subsided as a prime contributor to the death toll during childbearing years. Intestinal disorders, a major cause of death in the last century, have all but disappeared as a consequence of new food-handling techniques and other hygienic measures. Unfortunately, these problems have been replaced by diseases unique to industrial societies, primarily disorders of the upper respiratory system. Changes in the causes of mortality and the course of the illnesses themselves also reflect wide-ranging alterations in the kind of society we live in and the work we do. In fact, one of the early pioneers of gerontological research, Elie Metchnikoff (1908), suggested around the turn of this century that industrialized civilizations directly influence the alimentary tract, interfering with natural intestinal functioning, and thereby increasing susceptibility to the degenerative diseases of later life.

Although Metchnikoff's theories of putrefactive processes subsequently fell into disrepute, his suspicions regarding the role played by chronic deleterious conditions have proven to be of considerable merit. Besides combatting those diseases likely to strike prior to biological maturity, medicine has scored its biggest victories over those conditions that have a specific *etiology* — that is, result from a single identifiable cause. Ironically, the illnesses that appear most often to accompany aging are not of this type, and therefore have not yielded to medical research as rapidly. Yet contrary to popular stereotypes, the later years need not be a time of continual ill health, however much the two seem to be inevitably linked in our thinking. Not very long ago "old age" itself was frequently noted as the cause of death for people who died after age 60, out of the belief that aging itself was a form of disease. A few countries still continue to refer to age as cause of death; in West Germany, for example, between 8 and 10 percent of the deaths of older people are officially attributed to "old age." Generally speaking, medical science no longer views illness and age as indistinguishable phenomena. Nonetheless, normal aging and the development of chronic diseases remain closely related.

The Dimensions of Health

It is not nearly as easy as we might first assume to define what it means for a person to be healthy, as opposed to ill. In an effort to lend some coherence to worldwide reporting, the following definition was offered at the inception of the World Health Organization, one of the humanitarian arms of the United Nations: "Health is a state of complete physical, mental and social well-being and not merely the absence of disease or infirmity" (1946). It does not require a trained physician to begin to see that such a conception entails as many problems as it was intended to solve. If the question is phrased in reference to older people, the answer takes on added complexity, since an older person's health presents much more of a composite picture than that of his or her younger counterparts. In formulating a response to what it means to be healthy, we must also clarify whether our question is in terms of individual health history, age peers, the population as a whole or previous generations of elderly persons. When younger people fall sick, it is most often as a consequence of exogenous factors and frequently of infectious disease. The course such illnesses follow is traumatic, with a definite onset, crisis point and self-limiting aftermath. In other words they are *acute* conditions. Later in life the causes of illness change, becoming essentially endogenous and nonspecific. They are of a *chronic* nature, developing slowly, without a marked crisis point, and lingering for extended periods. In contrast to acute conditions, chronic illnesses usually involve a number of bodily functions and cannot be attributed to a single cause, thereby confronting both the patient and the attending physician with a more obstinate problem. Another difference is that, unlike youthful illnesses, the pathological conditions of later years seem to be progressive, leading to increased vulnerability rather than protective resistance.

Implicit in the definition of what it means to be healthy is a sense of well-being and satisfaction. Indeed, research focusing on older people has revealed what appears to be an intrinsic relationship between diminished health and such social factors as marital status, socioeconomic position, education, activity level and general life satisfaction. One must exercise caution, however, before imputing causal relationships between health and social variables. A number of interactive issues must be considered before deciding whether older people act as if they are or at least consider themselves to be healthy. For one thing, normality is a relative evaluation; people are seldom perfectly healthy even in the absence of pathological symptoms. In Chapter Four it was remarked that one of the criteria of senescence is a heightened vulnerability to all manner of stress, including pathological lesions. This being the case, physicians faced with complaints of aching joints or lower back pain must determine if such symptoms are clinically significant or are merely an inevitable result of becoming old. It is not yet possible to say with any assurance how much of what is currently known about the health of older people is derived from intrinsic processes or how much is an artifact of the social position of the elderly. For years, medical scientists thought of arterial disease as a normal dimension of aging. It was even said rather often that people were only as old as their arteries, implying that every older person suffered from hardening of the arteries. As we will see later, this is simply not true.

Not only can individual exceptions be found in industrial societies, but entire groups of people show no evidence of atherosclerosis, the most common form of arteriosclerosis, suggesting arterial disease need not be an inescapable companion of aging.

Some recent investigators have indicated that advances in medicine may one day leave future generations of older people free from many of the degenerative diseases so extensive today. On the other hand, some scientists continue to view pathological disease as the fate of the aged regardless of future medical developments, apparently envisioning that, once present conditions respond to treatment, a new set of impairments will take their place. Whether or not this proves to be the case, the health status of older persons clearly represents the dynamic interplay of phenomena continually subject to change. One means of achieving a better understanding of health status among the elderly is to look at the ways in which the causes of death for various groups have been modified since the turn of the century.

Mortality Among the Elderly

Without giving the matter a great deal of thought, it is usually assumed that the illnesses from which human beings suffer have been fairly constant throughout history. No doubt those illnesses with which we are currently familiar have afflicted people for centuries, yet many of the diseases prevalent in the past no longer demand attention today. One example that comes readily to mind is rickets, so commonplace it was considered a normal fate in England 200 years ago. The severity of still other diseases has been reduced over the years, although the conditions themselves are still observable. Measles, for instance, rarely strikes fear in the hearts of any but the pregnant or the most timid, despite the fact that during the last century measles were frequently fatal, causing near epidemic numbers of deaths on occasion. By 1915 measles had given its place to diphtheria, influenza and other infectious diseases as primary causes of death. Historically, respiratory diseases, tuberculosis and bronchitis among them, have been closely associated with populations that have undergone rapid periods of industrialization, often appearing as a fatal condition among the older males in these populations (Susser and Watson, 1971).

Since the early 1900s there has been a substantial movement away from those infectious diseases that had been so intractable in previous years. In the industrialized nations of the world, improved sanitary and health conditions have been reflected by an upward shift in the age composition of populations. A concomitant change has occurred in the advent of those degenerative diseases usually characteristic among older populations as primary causes of death. As shown in Table 7.1, retrogressive chronic diseases have replaced infectious viruses and tubercular fatalities in the United States as the most commonly identified fatal illnesses. A comparison of modern American patterns with mortality in four other countries is presented on the right side of the table. While the rank order in the more industrialized countries parallels that witnessed in North America, current patterns among developing or Third World countries differ, in part because of their more recent industrialization. The second part of the table provides a representation of age-specific mortality found in later adulthood. Close inspection of the table will reveal a subtle variance in the major causes of death in the second half of life. For both middle-aged and older people, heart diseases, cancer and cerebrovascular lesions, predominantly strokes, appear as the most frequent causes of death, accounting for approximately 70 percent of the deaths among those over age 45. Fully 40 percent of the fatalities can be directly attributed to heart disease alone. As we move beyond the top three causes of death, fatal conditions sort themselves into distinct groups by age. Among the middle-aged, violent deaths from accidents, suicides or homicides take a rather significant toll. For the older category these are surpassed by fatalities that result when physiological defenses have been vitiated by age. As is evident, however, from the right side of the second part of the table, men and women 65 or over do not succumb uniformly to the same diseases.

While mortality data do provide a considerable store of information about the illnesses that most often result in death, they cannot reveal the extent to which the lives of the living are affected by these same or other conditions. It is necessary to look at the evidence gathered by health surveys to ascertain the incidence of those illnesses currently afflicting various segments of a country's population. Depending on whether the statistics are based on individuals who actually seek medical attention or are derived from a sample of all members of a designated group, the causes of *morbidity*, or a departure from full health, will vary somewhat. In either case, though, the diagnostic categories employed have some impact on the results; that is, symptoms will be perceived and listed in terms of a fairly well-defined range of expected conditions. Still, incidence surveys provide the most complete picture of the quality of health experienced by a majority of people.

In a very general way, age itself can serve as a reliable indicator of the prevalence of both acute and chronic conditions. As a rule of thumb it may be said that older people are more likely to suffer chronic conditions and less likely to be afflicted by acute illnesses at

Table 7.1

Comparison of Primary Causes of Death in the United States, 1900 and 1973, and in Selected Countries[1]

CAUSES OF DEATH UNITED STATES 1900	RANK	CAUSES OF DEATH UNITED STATES 1973	ORDER IN SELECTED COUNTRIES			
			UNITED KINGDOM 1972	FRANCE 1971	JAPAN 1972	KENYA# 1970
Influenza/ pneumonia	1	Diseases of heart	1	1	3	16
Tuberculosis	2	Malignant neoplasms	2	2	2	14
Gastroenteritis (incl. diarrhea)	3	Cerebrovascular diseases	3	3	1	5
Diseases of heart	4	All accidents	7	4	4	13
Cerebrovascular diseases	5	Influenza/ pneumonia	4	6	5	3
Chronic nephritis	6	Diabetes mellitus	8	8	8	***
All accidents	7	Arterio-sclerosis	6	7	9	*
Malignant neoplasms (all cancers)	8	Cirrhosis of liver	9	5	7	18
Early infancy diseases	9	Early infancy diseases	*	*	*	*
Diphtheria	10	Upper respiratory diseases**	5	9	6	7

[1]Latest available data.
*Data not comparable.
**Refers to bronchitis, emphysema and asthma.
***Not ranked among first 20 causes of mortality.
#In order the top ten causes of death are: whooping cough, enteritis-diarrhea, influenza-pneumonia, typhoid fever, cerebrovascular diseases, measles, upper respiratory diseases, other infective and parasitic diseases, smallpox, vitamin and nutritional deficiencies.

Sources: National Center for Health Statistics, Department of Health, Education and Welfare, *Facts of Life and Death*, 1967; U.S. Bureau of the Census, *Statistical Abstract of the United States, 1975*, Washington, D.C.: Government Printing Office, 1975; World Health Organization, *World Health Statistics Annual* (Geneva: World Health Organization, 1974); United Nations, *Demographic Yearbook* (New York: United Nations 1973), pp. 322-33.

any given time. Of the nearly 23 million people over the age of 65 in the United States today, fully 85 percent report the presence of at least one chronic condition, with approximately half of these people experiencing limitations in their daily activity because of poor health (U.S. Department of Health, Education and Welfare, 1972).

Table 7.1, continued.

CAUSES OF DEATH AGE 45 – 64	RANK	CAUSES OF DEATH OVER AGE 65	65+ MALE TO FEMALE RATIO
Diseases of heart	1	Diseases of heart	1.408
Malignant neoplasms	2	Malignant neoplasms	1.688
Cerebrovascular diseases	3	Cerebrovascular diseases	1.046
Accidents	4	Influenza/pneumonia	1.468
Cirrhosis of liver	5	Arteriosclerosis	.998
Influenza/pneumonia	6	Accidents	1.439
Diabetes mellitus	7	Diabetes mellitus	.809
Upper respiratory diseases	8	Upper respiratory diseases	6.273
Suicide	9	Cirrhosis of liver	1.819
Homicide	10	Kidney infections	.934

Source: National Center for Health Statistics, Department of Health, Education and Welfare, *Health in the Later Years* (Washington, D.C.: U.S. Government Printing Office, 1971).

The statistics themselves do not tell the entire story, however. In the early years of life only about six out of every 1000 people endure chronic conditions. During young adulthood, age 25 or so, the rate increases to 35, and by the fourth decade that figure has nearly tripled to 100 people out of every 1000. By age 65 this number has again doubled, and then doubled yet another time after age 75, until almost nine out of ten people over age 90 live with a chronic illness. While older people do continue to suffer at least one acute episode of illness every year, this represents a drastic decline from the actual number encountered at earlier ages. One significant change is that older people who contract an acute condition are disabled longer. A similar pattern emerges for accidents; they happen less often for older people, but result in longer periods of recuperation. Thus, nearly 29 percent of the young adult population fell victim to accidental injury in 1970, while only 19 percent of the group between 45 and 64 were injured through accidents. Although fatal accidents continue to decline among the elderly, the overall percentage of accidents creeps up slightly, to 21.3 percent. Unlike the younger groups, who are usually involved in traffic accidents, two-thirds of the injuries of older people are a result of accidents around the house, an important factor to keep in mind when planning living accommodations for older people. Among older women, accidents cause about four days of disability yearly, compared to about one day from accidents for men. As a consequence of their various health problems, both acute and chronic illness as well as accidental injury, older people have their activities restricted for nearly five weeks every year, up from the three weeks for people in the 45–64 age range.

Many elderly find the aftermath of ill-health poses a more threatening specter than do thoughts of even their own death. From the middle years onward, a large proportion of people live with at least one chronic health problem and the likelihood of more cropping up in successive years. The various respiratory ailments become the most frequent acute illnesses among older adults, accounting for 72 out of every 100 episodes of acute distress by age 45, dropping to 46 after age 65. Accidental injuries are second, representing slightly more than 21 and 16 of every 100 episodes in the middle-aged and older categories respectively. Diseases of the digestive tract are the third most common acute condition among older people; however, for the middle-aged they are preceded by infectious and parasitic diseases. Despite the many unanswerable questions, so far as researchers have been able to tell, the treatments indicated for the acute illnesses observed in older persons are identical to those indicated for other age groups. The primary difference among the age groups is the presence of chronic conditions that may complicate the course followed by acute illnesses.

Far more significant than acute conditions are the chronic illnesses reported by the elderly and the limitations they impose. Looking first at the limitations on daily living, it is not difficult to appreciate why older people face the possibility of becoming socially isolated. During the middle years there is a noticeable increase in the number of people who relate the incidence of constraint in their daily routine, although interestingly enough, half the people 65 or over go about their business seemingly undeterred by any limitations. The percentage of adults who feel constrained in day-to-day activities by chronic conditions is illustrated in Figure 7.1.

As revealed by the figure, the proportion of severely limited individuals increases dramatically with age — nearly fourfold just among the ages specified. Not shown is the fact that after individuals reach their midseventies, they are even more inhibited by the effects of chronic illnesses, thereby facing still greater barriers to social interaction. In light of potentially extensive health problems and diminished financial resources, it is small wonder that many older people express a great deal of anxiety over possible dependency. This is not to say that all older people experience the same health-related problems or that those they do cannot possibly be mitigated. Figure 7.2 provides a closer look at the information presented in the previous figure. Without any more detail than is here offered, it is

Figure 7.1
Percentage of adults with various degrees of limited activity, 1970

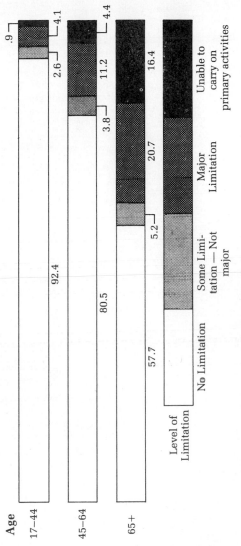

Source: *Limitation of Activity Due to Chronic Conditions, United States, 1970,*
Vital and Health Statistics, series 10, no. 80 (Washington, D.C.: U.S. Government Printing Office, April 1973), Table B, p. 5. (Converted from numeric data)

Figure 7.2

Percentage of specified categories suffering some activity limitation, United States, 1970

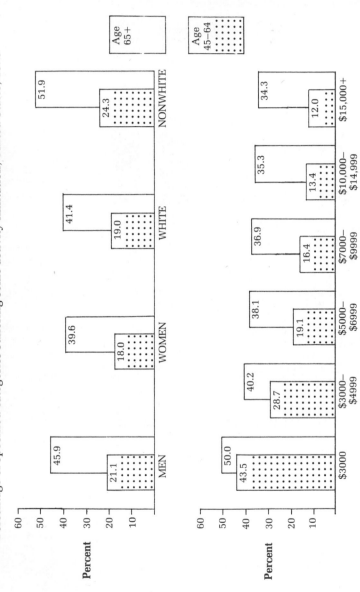

Source: *Limitation of Activity Due to Chronic Conditions, United States, 1970, Vital and Health Statistics*, series 10, no. 80 (Washington, D.C.: U.S. Government Printing Office, April 1973), Tables 1, 3, 4. (Converted from numeric data)

obvious that such factors as sex, race and income are important components of the overall health picture. With few exceptions, women, nonwhites and poorer people suffer more from ill-health in the process of becoming older. An understandable concern repeatedly voiced by inquiring older citizens is why optimal medical attention is not available to all as part of their retirement benefits.

Diseases of Later Life

The most frequently occurring chronic conditions afflicting older people are the various forms of heart disease, hypertension or high blood pressure, and the several forms of arthritis. In addition there are a great many other illnesses that cause varying degrees of distress. Foremost among the latter are cancer, diabetes, cerebral hemorrhages and circulatory problems. In Chapter Four, aging was emphasized as an intrinsic process distinct from the numerous pathologies so often associated with it, yet at the present time medical researchers have difficulty in separating the manifestations of either. Nevertheless, some knowledge of the diseases of the elderly is essential if the wide range of problems they engender is to be dealt with in terms of the whole person. Most scientists agree no one ever really dies of old age per se; rather, everyone does suffer and die from one or more specific diseases.

Heart Diseases

Cardiovascular diseases, including *myocardial* and valvular degeneration, hypertension, and atherosclerosis, surpass all other disorders in terms of both incidence and fatalities in industrialized societies. In fact, heart diseases are so common from the fourth decade of life and beyond that until recently they were thought to be synonymous with the aging process itself. While we now know this is not the case, it is not always possible to distinguish pathology from normal anatomical changes. Combined with the characteristic dehydration of bodily tissue, the normal aging heart shows an accumulation of subpericardial fat and lipofuscin, plus thickened, less efficient valves marked by widespread atrophy. Since the left atrium becomes larger over time, the heart's configuration is gradually altered, with cardiac output declining at a rate of 1 percent a year after age 30 (Freeman, 1965). The predominant change is the loss of reserve capacities and with it the heart's ability for rapid response under stress. Although the specific etiology of middle age myocardial degeneration remains a controversial question, the disease is manifested by progressive deposits of fatty tissue and gradual decay of the heart muscle. The changes that take place are functional as well as structural, thereby bringing about an eventual *infarction* or tissue death in the muscle. Whether functional impairment is a consequence of calcification within coronary vessels or a biochemical process, the end result is inadequate oxygenation of the active tissue. While the most commonly observed symptoms are pain, breathlessness and irregular rhythms, confusion accompanied by diminished blood pressure sometimes occurs. It should be obvious that careful clinical examinations are required for accurate detection, and even then alternative diagnoses are possible.

According to recent findings, heart diseases are responsible for over half the fatalities in North America, the Scandinavian countries and the United Kingdom. Cardiovascular diseases kill almost three times as many people as do various forms of cancer. While younger males are susceptible targets, prior to menopause women apparently have some hormonal protection, which when lost exposes them to a greater likelihood of experiencing coronary problems. The rate of male mortality from heart attacks during the second half of life ranges from a low of only 719 per 100,000 in the countries of southwestern Europe to a high of over 1225 in the United States and 1400 in Finland. Incidence among females is comparably broad, with a low of 376 in a few Scandinavian countries to over 520 in the United States. Even when not fatal, heart diseases take their toll; about 22 percent of all the disabilities found in men and 15 percent of those in women during the middle years are attributed to heart problems. With advancing age, mortality increases dramatically, doubling every decade or so for men and tripling for women. In some of the Scandinavian countries the rate among women climbs even more rapidly, approaching a fourfold increase per decade. Still, female deaths average only about half those of their male counterparts (Metropolitan Life, 1971). Some epidemiological investigations suggest that coronary heart diseases are closely tied to an affluent lifestyle resembling that found among the advantaged classes in most industrialized countries (Marks, 1967). The implication seems to be that rich diets, lowered activity levels and so on may heighten the risk of heart diseases, even though such factors may be partially offset by better quality medical care. If these same risk factors are present with a correspondingly lower level of medical services, higher mortality rates could be anticipated. In fact, studies carried out in the United States reveal that nonwhites are considerably more prone to heart diseases than whites, with rates up to twice that recorded for whites. No doubt this is due in part to the greater prevalence of high blood pressure, poorer dietary routines marked by higher fat consumption and extrinsic factors such as less adequate medical care (Susser and Watson, 1971).

Once a heart attack has taken place, approximately one-third of all victims succumb before they receive medical attention. Yet immediate care is essential, as another 20 to 30 percent are likely to die in the 24 hours following infarction. Continued survival beyond this point and eventual rehabilitation depend not only on the severity of the attack, but on the patient's ability to come to terms with the fear and anxiety heart attacks inevitably engender. The nature of relationships with significant others and personal security seem to play crucial roles in successful recoveries. Thoughtful communication among the victim, his or her spouse, and the attending physician should alleviate many uncertainties about vital questions such as probable longevity or sexual performance, thus speeding recovery and preventing recurrences (Croog et al., 1968).

Atherosclerosis

Arteriosclerosis is a general label for all arterial diseases; however, the form most prevalent in later years is called atherosclerosis. It is characterized primarily as a hardening of the *intima* or interior walls of major vessels and is considered the leading precursor of other retrogressive coronary changes. In a recent report on the worldwide distribution of heart diseases, the World Health Organization noted that atherosclerosis is a nearly universal health problem that singularly stands in the way of any appreciable prolongation of life. The same report also predicted in those countries where the incidence of atherosclerosis is not yet a widespread cause of death, rapidly changing social and technological conditions portend future increases ("World Health," 1967). Indeed, evidence indicates this was clearly the case historically both in industrialized countries and in those currently undergoing rapid industrialization. The disease cannot be considered an exclusively modern malady as it was described in explicit detail in ancient Greek medical literature. Examination of mummies also suggests it was known in Egypt and probably throughout the ancient world (Timiras, 1972). The extent to which heart diseases alone claim lives is overwhelming. In the United States over 600,000 die yearly from the various forms of cardiovascular disease, while over 28 million exhibit some form of the disease. Add in atherothrombotic diseases not involving the heart and the number of fatalities increases by another one-third. Despite a recent slight decline, middle-aged American men stand about one chance in five of developing clinically significant cardiovascular problems before they reach retirement age; aside from Finnish men, Americans have the highest cardiac mortality rates in the world. Like so many other generic cardiovascular diseases, atherosclerotic conditions discriminate on the basis of sex; they occur among American males at a rate three times the incidence among similarly aged females. And like other chronic illnesses, atherosclerosis need not prove fatal or disrupt normal routines; its prevalence approaches 100 percent among the very old in certain populations, seriously impairing their way of life.

Only among sufferers of diabetes or other high risk illnesses does atherosclerosis make much of an impact before late in the fourth decade, although its inception usually dates from early adolescence. Individuals with a family history of heart disease seem particularly prone to cardiovascular disorders, although the mechanism by which susceptibility is transmitted is still a puzzle to medical science. The most important factors that have been linked to heightened probabilities of arterial diseases are diets high in saturated fats, sedentary activities, obesity, cigarette smoking and psychological stress.

Over the past century, numerous theories have attempted to trace the pathogenesis of atherosclerotic conditions, but to date none have won uncontested acceptance. The appearance of fatty streaks in the inner wall of the arteries has prompted many investigators to conclude that the blood deposits fatty substances that are absorbed through the *endothelial lining* separating the actual blood flow from the intima of the artery. These in turn are trapped inside the artery wall rather than passing through with the nutritive substances. Ultimately a roughening and swelling occurs that promotes the formation of fibrous plaques in the *lumen* or artery channel. Once the irregularity has taken shape, further buildup follows, constricting the space through which blood may flow. The actual buildup is called a *thrombosis* and may eventually bring about a complete *occlusion* or closing of the artery. Under stress thromboses may break loose, floating through the artery until becoming lodged in one of the smaller branches. Since the artery is a living form of connective tissue, damage begins immediately after any individual cell dies, no matter what the cause. With tissue death comes calcification, loss of elasticity and lowered permeability. Which factors actually initiate the damage is a hotly debated topic among physiologists, and while it is agreed that certain preventive steps may inhibit the development of plaques, nothing can be done about reversing their effects until the process is more fully understood (Walton, 1973).

Hypertension

Hypertension, what most of us call simply high blood pressure, affects roughly the same percentage of older people as heart disease and, like other coronary problems, is much more prevalent among blacks. Part of the difficulty with diagnosing hypertension in older people is the general tendency for blood pressure to elevate throughout most of life, especially among women. Also, the issue of appropriate levels for a given individual poses problematic questions not easily resolved. In addition, blood pressure is affected by the presence of other illnesses, fever, obesity and even air temperature. In turn, hypertension may cause other bodily homeostatic functions to become unbalanced, contributing indirectly to death. Cerebral hemorrhage and cardiac failure appear to be the most frequent terminal conditions associated with high blood pressure, though *renal insufficiency* and *bronchopneumonia* are not unusual. Among the clinically significant symptoms are fluctuations in *systolic* and *diastolic* pressure, changes in the structure of certain parts of the eye and mental confusion, especially late in the day. Again, however, personal history and family background are important factors that must be taken into account (Howell, 1970).

Cerebrovascular Accidents

Cerebrovascular accidents, or strokes, rank as the third most common fatal affliction in the second half of life. Each year strokes claim over 200,000 lives in the United States and leave many times that number impaired. Although quite a number of traumatic events may cause brain damage, most of them stem from other circulatory difficulties. In referring to strokes, most practitioners mean cerebral hemorrhages caused by *embolisms* that have traveled to the brain occluding one of the cerebral arteries, or by a thrombosis that develops in the brain's own *ventricular* system. In either event, the result is a cutting off of oxygen-rich blood supplies to some part of the brain, with a subsequent degeneration of the affected sections. Part of the insidious aftermath of a stroke is loss of memory, speech aphasia, emotional problems, partial paralysis, loss of bowel control and so on. Epidemiological studies of stroke suggest they occur more frequently in industrialized countries than in the so-called underdeveloped nations and are more likely to strike nonwhites than whites, with both sexes equally prone, under comparable occupational conditions and activity levels. Nearly all research agrees, cigarette smokers impose a greater survival risk on themselves in terms of both strokes and other coronary difficulties than nonsmokers. While immediate medical attention may alleviate many complications and rehabilitation can help stroke patients overcome still others, the neural injury can never be undone. Recent investigations of the toxic effects of the chemical components present in neurotransmitters, but released in unusually large doses during and after infarction, may provide new avenues for minimizing stroke damage (Wurtman, 1974).

Various degenerative diseases of the brain are yet another form of pathology affecting the elderly. Cerebral atrophy, senile plaques, Parkinson's disease and numerous other disorders are generally lumped together under the label organic brain damage because of their diffuse character. As illustrated in Chapter Six, organic brain damage is difficult to diagnose, and many symptoms of functional disorders are incorrectly labeled as organic in nature. Many of the related cerebral conditions are long standing and only manifest themselves during stressful episodes in later life or when cardiovascular accidents trigger their appearance.

Cancer

While cancer is often referred to as a disease that confines itself to older people, it ranks near the top of the mortality list throughout life. In the United States this year roughly one out of six deaths can be attributed to one or another form of cancer. Nonetheless, certain types of cancer do appear to have age-specific mortality rates. Malignancies of the lungs, breast or cervix are more frequent at younger ages, while cancers of the stomach, intestinal tract, prostate, skin or kidney are more common in the elderly. Leukemias rank high in both young and old, but appear somewhat less often among middle-aged people. The highest incidence of fatal cancers takes place in the 40 to 60 age range, with women clustered in the younger years and men in the older. As yet, cancer remains an etiological mystery to medical researchers, but increasingly, the evidence points toward chemical or chromosomal abnormalities as precipitating factors. Mortality for women in earlier adulthood is higher than for men; however, following menopause a reversal takes place, again indicating that hormonal factors may provide some protection for women prior to menopause. Investigations of immunological mechanisms and their disruption in older individuals is thought to be another promising area. External agents have also been closely investigated. Lung cancer, for example, is many times more frequent in heavily industrialized urban areas and among smokers than in agricultural areas or among nonsmokers. The diverse pathological profile of the various malignancies has thus far inhibited the search for causes, and in all probability they will ultimately be found to be multiple in nature, thereby making their discovery all the more difficult.

Arthritis and Rheumatism

Arthritis and rheumatism are seldom identified as causes of death. Nonetheless, they are important conditions interfering with normal life for the elderly, appearing among half the middle-aged and in up to four-fifths of people in their seventies. Arthritis and rheumatoid ailments are second only to heart disease as the most common reason for disabilities after midlife, accounting for over one-fifth of the impairments of normal activities. Again, these rates seem to be sexually related, climbing even higher for women in extreme old age. Among nonwhite Americans, especially blacks, arthritis is much less frequent than for whites.

Arthritic conditions are of two general types: *osteoarthritis* and *rheumatoid arthritis*. It should be noted the demarcation between natural involution of bone material and osteoarthritis as a pathological state is blurred, since a gradual demineralization of bones is usually thought to be a normal aspect of aging. The most serious ailments are a result of the breakdown of bone structure in the lower back and in joints where the harder outer surface of bone cartilage wears away most rapidly. Dietary insufficiencies, alterations in bone metabolism, wear and tear, and even cold environments have been identified as probable causes of most arthritic conditions. Changes in collagen structure and ground substances are also assumed to be possible factors in the onset of arthritis, since this alteration allows bones to rub together, causing noticeable pain.

Rheumatoid arthritis is somewhat less frequently found among the elderly, and strictly speaking cannot be termed a disease of old age, occurring as it does any time after infancy. The majority of cases develop in early adulthood, but due to the disease's chronic nature, only become clinically significant later in life. Rheumatoid conditions are found primarily in smaller joints, where the membranes lining the joint cavity wear thin, allowing the ends of the bones to scrape against one another. In its active phase, bone marrow may also become involved, resuting in marked atrophy and muscular wasting. The role of the body's immunological mechanisms as a factor in the breakdown of connective tissue and the development of rheumatoid arthritis has been under investigation for many years and at present seems the most fruitful area for further studies (McKeown, 1965).

Diabetes Mellitus

Diabetes is another common ailment encountered in the elderly that may stem from changes in the body's collagen fibers, in this case resulting in the lessened permeability of cellular membranes through which glucose is transported. The exact incidence of diabetes in the general population is impossible to determine with any assurance, since many thousands of cases are so mild as to go unnoticed or untreated. However, current estimates are that 4.4 million persons in the United States have some form of diabetes. Ordinarily, diabetes is diagnosed in the middle years, where it is found more often in men. In the later years women experience a greater incidence. The exception to this is the presence of a family history of diabetes, in which case the onset may take place much earlier. As important as the disease itself is its disruptive effects on other organs, the heart, kidneys, arteries or the pancreas are the most significant organs damaged by its complications of circulatory and filtration processes. The symptoms of diabetes are so diffuse as to be unrecognizable from myriad normal age-related complaints, though unusual thirst and weight loss, especially among the obese, may prove indicative of its presence. Onset can be gradual or can result from severe illnesses and is usually confounded by environmental factors. The prevalence of diabetes is many times more common among people in their sixties and seventies, when it is most often fatal. Roughly 4 percent of the population over 65 is thought to be afflicted, and a similar percentage of all disabilities that limit normal routines can be attributed to this disease. Interestingly enough, when obesity is used as the criterion for incidence, most ethnic and cultural differences frequently pointed to tend to disappear. The Western rates, several times that of Japan, for instance, may be partially explained by the preponderance of overweight people in Western countries. In the United States, a wide range of variables contribute to a higher nonwhite mortality rate from diabetes.

Oral and Dental Problems

Oral and dental problems, decay, loss of teeth and periodontal diseases have not received the attention they deserve in light of their role in the elderly's sense of well-being. Recent upgrading of dental care, patient awareness and fluoridation should lessen premature endentuousness in the future, but among the middle-aged and elderly today, one-fourth to one-half of those in each age group have lost all their teeth. Of this number, roughly three-fourths of the middle-aged and over half of the elderly who have lost their own teeth have been fitted with dentures. Judging from the best nationwide data available, a look into the mouth of anyone over the age of 45 who still has his or her own teeth would reveal an average of 20 teeth either filled, missing or decayed. In the 45–64 year old age group, slightly less than half the permanent teeth are still in place, while in the group aged 65–79 an average of 25 teeth are missing. Periodontal inflammation affecting the gums and other tissues is the other major oral disease of the elderly, the consequences of which may be even more serious than caries. Regional variations exist, but according to the National Center for Health Statistics (1971), nine out of ten people over the age of 65 have some clinically significant form of periodontal disease. The percentage is nearly as high for the middle-aged, with 85 percent of the men and 76 percent of the women afflicted with painful gum diseases.

For a number of reasons, many older people seem to be hesitant to visit their dentist; in contrast to physician checkups, the number of dental visits declines with age. During the last year, if long-term patterns continue, up to three-quarters of the older group and half those middle-aged have not seen a dentist. Clearly, if socioeconomic background is related to a willingness to seek out all medical services, the same relationship will be true for dental care. Upper income whites are twice as likely as their poor or nonwhite age peers to visit the dentist.

Culture and Chronic Conditions

Comparative health surveys are very difficult to conduct in any way systematic enough to provide incontrovertible information. Nevertheless, even partial comparisons can shed a great deal of light on the health problems faced by older people, not only in industrialized countries of the West, but in Asia and the Third World nations. Accordingly, this brief overview is for comparative purposes, to enable the reader to reach a better understanding of the dynamic character of health conditions without offering an in-depth look at the countries surveyed. It is immediately apparent from a comparison of industrial and nonindustrial societies that the age structure of the latter differs in predictable ways from the former, where technological change long ago altered the people's relationship with nature and each other. As noted in previous chapters, nonindustrial societies are characterized by high mortality throughout life, but particularly during infancy. An inescapable consequence of living at near subsistence levels is long-term nutritional deficits that preclude large segments of the population from living long enough to collect retirement benefits they would be entitled to as residents of most industrial societies. Ironically, the opposite problem, too much food, shortens life expectancy in many technologically advanced societies. While the same chronic deleterious conditions can be found around the world, as is evident in Table 7.1, their rank ordering differs according to a complex of environmental and genetic factors.

With the age distribution of agrarian societies skewed toward the young, we would anticipate the most common diseases to be of a type more likely to strike early in life. Accordingly, fatalities from chronic illnesses characteristic of the second half of life will be significantly less frequent. Where rigidly endogamous marriages are culturally sanctioned, genetic predispositions toward certain problems also contribute to the pattern of diseases. Among Pima Indians, for example, diabetes rates are higher than for any other known group, affecting over half the adults before they reach their mid-thirties (Bourliere, 1973).

Japan provides an interesting example of a recently industrialized country that is undergoing many diverse changes, including among them health and mortality patterns. In some respects Japan resembles older industrialized giants, though it presents a different pattern in terms of the illnesses and the normal physiological parameters of age. Improved nutritional programs have recently given younger generations of Japanese a larger stature than their parents, but, like their parents, they do not normally experience a weight gain between ages 25 and 45, which is characteristic of people from European origins. Further testimony to the importance of diet and environmental factors for modifying constitutional elements is provided by the propensity among Japanese who have migrated to North America to develop cardiovascular diseases at a rate approximating that of Americans of European stock (Stamler, 1967). Traditionally, nearly all Asians have consumed a diet heavily vegetarian in nature, but supplemented by fish; as a consequence, their blood cholesterol levels have been lower than those found in people whose diets include a large complement of animal fats. On the other hand, higher salt intake in fish-consuming groups, as in Japan, does result in elevated blood pressure. Vegetarian peoples around the world show similarly low cholesterol levels. In such diverse groups as the bushmen of the Kalahara and the Ituri pygmies whose diets are extremely low in animal fats, blood cholesterols are reportedly near zero, with both arteriosclerosis and heart attacks rare occurrences (Bourliere, 1973).

Throughout most of Africa, coronary heart diseases are seldom ranked among the primary causes of death, although people do suffer from other illnesses closely tied to their way of life. For example,

Yoruba tribe members who have left the country to live in urban areas develop blood pressure and atherosclerotic patterns much more comparable to their black counterparts in North America than to those who remain in the country. Bantu or Kurumba tribe members who continue their traditional way of life show a much lower incidence of atherosclerosis than is observed for black Americans in the United States. South Africans also exhibit many urban-rural differences related to lifestyle, such as a higher incidence of both cancer and diabetes in the cities, where dietary consumption is influenced by the predominantly westernized patterns. Although peptic ulcers are uncommon ailments across Africa, other nutritional disorders are familiar, especially those closely related to protein consumption. In Masai tribesmen, intestinal infections and liver diseases are frequent conditions, while arteriosclerosis and heart diseases are nearly unknown. While oral hygiene is a concept little known in most African societies, both tooth decay and periodontal diseases are relatively rare events (Dubos, 1959). In northern India, in the provinces near New Delhi, medical research has provided additional insight into the relationship between diet and coronary diseases. As in Africa, the lower social categories in India traditionally follow diets that are low in animal fat; their more affluent neighbors on the other hand have adopted many Western ways of living, especially dietary habits, and have consequently shown a marked increase in calcification of the arteries and related vascular problems (Bourliere, 1973).

Control and Prolongevity

As the proportion of older people in the population continues to grow questions regarding control of illness and prolongation of life will become ever more pressing. As described above, the major breakthroughs in health care thus far have come about in the realm of acute diseases likely to strike during the first half of life. As long as variations in length of life occur, researchers are convinced that both the length of life and the quality of old age experienced by most people can be improved. For example, 65 year old white women in America may look forward, on the average, to another 16 years of life, while white men have no more than about 13 years left. Older nonwhite men and women both have even fewer years remaining to them than their white counterparts. The differences are due in large measure to socioeconomic characteristics such as occupation, income, education, marital status, and knowledge of and access to medical care rather than inexorable or intrinsic factors (National

Center for Health Statistics, 1971). It is for these same reasons that we may expect the quality of life, in terms of health, to be sufficiently optimized to allow the vast majority to experience as few illnesses and impairments as those in the most advantageous social categories.

Over the course of the last few decades many thoughtful investigations have focused on those long-term conditions that tend to shorten life expectancy. Some headway has already been made and more work is continuing; hence, it is no mere exercise in futility to hypothesize about the future. Examples of the extensions of life expectancy to be expected from the control of certain specified conditions are presented in Table 7.2. It is not, however, easy to make predictions about increments in life expectancy that might accrue if the primary culprits suddenly yielded to medical science. The main obstacle lies in the likelihood of alternative disorders replacing those eliminated as major causes of death. Tuberculosis provides an excellent case in point. At the beginning of this century tuberculosis ranked high as a lethal illness; today it is no longer particularly dreaded. People who might have succumbed to tuberculosis in the past are today recovering and living long enough to contract a fatal cancer instead. Again, however, mortality statistics do not completely reveal the vagaries of the problem. Another example is provided by diabetes. With the discovery of insulin therapy, diabetics no longer suffer either the symptoms of their disease or many of its complications. As a consequence, the incidence of diabetes is increasing among older people simply because they are still alive, not because the disease is any more prevalent than before. The same is

Table 7.2

Gains in Life Expectation from the Elimination of Some Major Causes of Death

CAUSE OF DEATH	YEARS GAINED	
	AT BIRTH	AT AGE 65
Cardiovascular-renal diseases	10.9	10.0
Diseases of the heart	5.9	4.9
Cerebrovascular lesions	1.3	1.2
Malignant neoplasms	2.3	1.2
Accidents (except automobile)	0.6	0.1
Influenza and pneumonia	0.5	0.2
Infective and parasitic diseases	0.2	0.1
Diabetes mellitus	0.2	0.2
Tuberculosis	0.1	—

Source: *Some Demographic Aspects of Aging in the United States,* Current Population Reports, series P-23, no. 43 (Washington, D.C.: U.S. Government Printing Office, 1973). (Note: Data based on 1961 Public Health Service estimates.)

true for any other illness that is neither fatal nor self-limiting; it will become more prevalent in older populations (Ford, 1968).

Improving Life Expectancy

Preventive medicine can go a long way toward improving the quality of life among older people. For epidemiologists studying the distributions of disease, prevention is discussed in terms of primary and secondary strategies. *Primary prevention* entails attempts to avert the onset of disease. It combines public health measures to lessen the occurrence of illnesses with the lowering of specific risk factors by modification of diet, activity level, personal habits, custom, health examinations and so on. *Secondary prevention* is intended to fend off the more severe states of existing maladies or their complications through the use of therapeutic drugs, palliative measures and counseling. A crucial component of secondary prevention of the disabilities likely to affect the elderly lies in an extensive reshaping of the negative attitudes, held both toward the elderly, and by older people themselves, described in Chapter One.

Nutritional Improvements

Even in the midst of plenty, malnutrition is a fundamental problem facing many older people. With a third to one-half of the health problems of the elderly stemming directly from nutrition (Subcommittee on Aging, 1973), modifying the habits of a lifetime is clearly one of the principal environmental considerations conducive to prolongevity. Acknowledging the multifaceted ramifications of both nutritional inadequacies and surfeits, the second White House Conference on Aging, responsible for recommending priorities of the 1970s, charged the federal government with the obligation to provide adequate nutrition for all the elderly in the United States. Inherent in the policy suggestions offered by the delegates and their advisory panels is the assumption that nutrition refers not simply to minimal requirements for vitamins, minerals or protein, but also to recognized upper boundaries of caloric intake. Despite the limits imposed on nutrition by poverty for roughly 20 percent of all older Americans, overabundance appears to play a major role in vitiating life for the remainder. Most people overindulge themselves to the point where they threaten the lives they might otherwise lead. If by some stroke of fate medical science discovered a way to prevent obesity, an average of over four years could be added to life expectancy at birth, just about double the extension to be realized from elimination of the various forms of cancer (Freeman, 1965).

How much to eat is a complicated question, depending on everything from activity levels to body surface area and lean body mass. Daily food consumption in the United States runs to around 3300 calories, far in excess of the amount that is advisable. According to the best estimates, few men require more than 2900 calories daily and few women need over 2100. With normal declines in metabolic rates averaging 3.5 percent every decade after maturity, caloric requirements in later years are reduced even further. At most, middle-aged men and women should maintain an intake of between 2400 and 1700 calories. Curtailments of between 8 and 10 percent per decade are recommended thereafter, for a total caloric reduction of over one-third between the ages of 25 and 70. By way of comparison, in sections of Kashmir and the Caucasus, or in the Ecuadorian village of Vilcabamba, where extreme longevity is commonplace and many people remain active for over 100 years, average daily food consumption comes to only 1200 to 1900 calories (Leaf, 1973).

In addition to how many calories, there is the question of what to eat. An adequate balance of protein and carbohydrates combined with essential vitamins and minerals is crucial. Dietary surveys in Europe and North America found the required 50 to 65 grams of protein daily are surpassed by nearly 40 percent of the younger people, while the elderly more often fall short of optimal amounts. Dramatic improvements in health would be observed if the average cholesterol intake of nearly 600 mg. was reduced by half. The elimination of egg yolks, probably the highest cholesterol food most people eat on a regular basis, would likely go a long way toward lowering blood cholesterol levels. Unfortunately, in most other cases foods high in cholesterol are also sources of essential protein, which must be retained for optimum diets. The elderly also find themselves with too little calcium, too few vitamins and an overabundance of fats and carbohydrates in their diets. The calcium is important to offset other declines that lead to the possibility of *osteoporosis*, while vitamins aid in maintaining the secretion of enzymes which normally diminish with age. Iron and B-12, for example, are beneficial supplements to the stomach's natural juices, aiding the absorption of nutrients and assisting in the production of amino acids used for energy and as the body's building blocks. One of the liabilities associated with vegetarian diets is the inadequate supply of high quality proteins and the increased incidence of liver diseases. On the other hand, too large an ingestion of saturated fats from animal sources adds to the lipids in the blood stream, exacerbating the risk of atherosclerosis and other coronary diseases. Further problems arise when the caloric intake at any one meal is too high, resulting in harmful metabolic by-products that add to the buildup of atherosclerotic plaques, even if total daily allowances are not exceeded. Currently, the recommended pattern is four or five light meals a day rather than one or two large repasts. There is preliminary evidence that suggests that to some extent, earlier dietary improprieties may be partially reversed by replacing saturated fats with polyunsaturated fats, with the possible result of limited regression of atherosclerotic plaques (Stamler, 1967).

Food should not be thought of simply as a source of nutrition or a means of avoiding hunger. It is also imbued with wide-ranging symbolic connotations inextricably interwoven with the rest of our lives. One of the reasons lifelong patterns are so resistant to change, and why even programs such as meals on wheels, which provide healthful meals, cannot ensure adequate nutrition, is the all too frequently neglected social significance of eating. Meals are social events, time for socializing. Isolated people who are often lonely are less likely to secure proper nourishment regardless of the availability of appropriate food merely because eating alone is emotionally distasteful (Pelcovits, 1972). Similarly, the habits of a lifetime are quite difficult to break. Changing them entails major emotional adjustments that few of us, particularly the elderly, are prepared or able to make. Among the other contributions to inadequate nutrition are ill-fitted dentures, troubles with swallowing, diminished sense of taste and smell, and the inability to shop or prepare food, all predisposing factors that seem to characterize the lives of many older people (Confrey and Goldstein, 1960).

Smoking and Physical Activity

Perhaps it seems a little glib to say that many heavy smokers die young, but it is true, nonetheless. Epidemiological studies of mortality among cigarette smokers have found that on the average they die ten years sooner than otherwise comparable nonsmokers (Granich, 1972). In the mid-1960s, the Surgeon General of the United States began reporting what others had suspected for some time, that cigarette smoking is a major risk factor not only in cancers, but is a probable cause indicated in pulmonary deficiencies, coronary heart ailments and cerebrovascular disease. During the younger years, the relative risk accompanying smoking is statistically greatest among males, primarily because of their heavier smoking habits. Generally speaking, it may be claimed that all smokers, regardless of age, are courting a likelihood of coronary heart disease some 70 percent greater than nonsmokers, with at least two-thirds of the smokers dying sooner than normally would be expected. The relationship between smoking and longevity is so strong that, for men in their sixties, smoking is the single most accurate predictor of remaining life expectancy (Palmore, 1974a,b). Smokers who are bombarded daily with exhortations to quit commonly offer the response that "it's too late." While the effects of cigarette smoking can never be completely overcome, there is sufficient data to suggest that discontinuing does indeed lessen the probability of heart disease and its complications (Inter-Society Commission, 1970).

Moderate physical activity such as that exerted in exercise regimes or manual occupations also appears to enhance longevity through a reduction of the risk factors contributing to heart disease. Physical conditioning among older people usually results in improvements in the cardiovascular system, the respiratory system, musculature and body composition — all of which help the person relax as well as work. Although it is improbable that many people leading sedentary lives could develop the skill or the stamina to go the distances recorded for Masi tribesmen or certain Central American Indians, walking at a rapid pace over reasonable distances reduces by one-third the work the heart muscle must do to keep the blood moving (Brunner and Jokl, 1970). Exercise is also an indirect aid in the consumption of lipids and in preserving the functional capacities of many organ systems besides those mentioned. Exercise regimes emphasizing rhythmic activity appear to be the most appropriate and beneficial for older participants.

Life Satisfaction

The existence of a symmetrical correlation between health and an overall sense of life satisfaction is acknowledged by most gerontologists (Maddox and Eisdorfer, 1962). While it can certainly be said that ill health leads to a diminished sense of contentment or that a positive outlook ranks high as a predictor of future morbidity or even longevity, the relationship is by no means straightforward. To begin with, investigators concerned with health must distinguish between self-assessment and actual clinical evaluations. The question of the correspondence between self-perception and physical evaluations of health status remains a rather complex issue (Haberman, 1969). The central focus is not really on whether anyone, including the elderly, can replace a physician's clinical observations with his own, but instead, on the consequences of positive or negative self-perceptions. In most cases, estimates made by the elderly themselves tend to overrate health, with approximately six out of ten people claiming better health than their physicians accorded them (Susser and Watson, 1971). Nevertheless, longitudinal studies of the elderly's ability to accurately describe their own physical health suggest that their ratings are primary determinants of satisfaction, and in fact may be more important than objective health status as far as future longevity is concerned (Maddox and Douglass, 1974).

When evaluating their personal health, the parameters the elderly take into account are their individual health histories, that is, are they as healthy as previously? How are they doing compared to others their age or to those who live in similar situations? If for any reason they conclude that they are at a disadvantage, observed clinical health begins to deteriorate regardless of how good it was. Apparently, objectively verifiable factors only enter into the elderly's sense of life satisfaction when they become subjectively meaningful in terms of self-evaluated health (Tissue, 1972). Among a complex range of social conditions that seem to provide a stable health picture are intact marriages, adequate financial resources, stress-free lives and a cohesive psychological profile (Pfeiffer, 1974). While health status tends to decline following major crises, as with the death of a loved one, we must exercise caution before making any generalizations. According to popular conceptions, retirement often results in more illnesses. After all, male mortality does reach a peak in the years immediately after men retire. Is it not also the case that a large percentage of older men claim ill health as a reason for not seeking additional employment in the postretirement years? Both statements are doubtlessly true, yet the best indications are that retirement has little direct effect on health. Whatever changes seem to occur among retirants also happen among those who have been able to continue working (Streib and Schneider, 1971). It may also be that claims of impaired health are really rationalizations for not seeking new jobs, functioning partially as a face-saving device to offset the displaced status accompanying retirement. As has often been pointed out, the sick role may actually serve as a replacement for the loss of primary roles that cannot be resumed. Intense social involvements providing a purpose and sense of confidence through furnishing alternative roles would go a long way toward upgrading self-reported health status among many elderly (Palmore and Luikart, 1974).

Health Care Services

Despite the prevalence of chronic conditions and the preponderance of elderly among recently hospitalized patients, geriatric medicine is seldom a core element of the curriculum at most medical schools in the United States. According to some estimates, only a small percentage of the newly minted doctors have ever been exposed to any advanced courses oriented to the health problems of the elderly (Sinex, 1973), a depressing commentary in light of the increasing number of elderly over the age of 65. In comparison to the programs and refresher courses designed for medical students and practicing physicians in the Soviet Union and many European countries, the United States has much ground to make up. Addressing the necessity of comprehensive health care, the 1971 White House Conference on Aging reiterated the need for a fully funded National Institute on Aging in order to upgrade professional education preparatory to meeting just the existing need for health care services (Subcommittee on Aging, 1973). Delegates to the 1971 conference emphasized that Medicare was intended from the beginning only as a supplement to augment individual resources, but in the face of woefully inadequate legislation and skyrocketing medical costs national health insurance is nearly mandatory if the health of the nation is to be maintained.

Providing the Elderly with Medical Care

Worldwide attempts to conquer disease and to improve health have obscured the conventional division between personal and social or governmental responsibility for health maintenance. In the years since World War II there has been a dramatic expansion of compulsory insurance programs throughout the world in an effort to secure unified protection aimed at segments or at all of a country's citizens. While the dilemmas cannot be minimized, functioning health insurance programs with varying degrees of coverage now exist in most of the industrial countries East and West, as well as in many of the Third World nations. In fact, with the passage of Medicare legislation in 1965, the United States became the last industrialized nation in the West to inaugurate some form of compulsory health insurance (Harris, 1966).

Only a basic overview of worldwide trends is possible here, since every convention of a nation's lawmakers is likely to result in new amendments to its health care system and any summary would have to be seen as only tentative, subject to annual update. Charitable medical service is as old as the medical profession itself, and voluntary "sickness societies" date at least from the time of the medieval guilds. Public hospitals also have a long tradition, dating back to public expressions of social consciousness first codified in Roman law. It was not until Germany instituted its wide-ranging social security program in the 1880s, however, that whole nations began to assume some of the expenses of medical attention

(Bridgman, 1972). By 1911, the United Kingdom had followed suit, offering state aid to certain specified segments of its population. The National Health Service established in 1948 finally extended universal coverage to every British citizen. The Scandinavian countries, Switzerland, the Soviet Union and others also enacted similar health care programs before or during the First World War. By the cessation of hostilities engendered during the Second World War, Portugal, Spain, France, Belgium, Ireland and other European countries had followed suit and joined the list. With spreading worldwide recognition of public responsibility over the past two decades, such schemes have become commonplace not only in the industrial world, but in Turkey, Greece, India, Japan, and certain African and Latin American countries as well. Obviously, not all health programs are equally comprehensive; however, the very fact of their existence is evidence of governmental acknowledgment that health care cannot rest solely on the shoulders of individuals. In 1972 cost comparisons for total public health insurance ranged from $50 to $250 annually on a per capita basis in industrial countries to between $0.50 and $10 in the Third World countries (Fendall, 1972).

Health Provisions in the United Kingdom,
the Soviet Union and Selected Countries

For purposes of comparison, a look at two of the health plans operating in major industrial countries might shed some light on the varying benefits offered. In the United Kingdom, health care is administered under a series of regional councils whose working capital comes from local taxes and central government rebates. The budget for all health expenditures during 1972 accounted for approximately 4.5 percent of the gross national product, with one of the largest single shares of the total going to eldercare (Elder, 1972). While most physicians serve as salaried employees in nationally sponsored hospitals, they may also tend private patients who desire care over and above the benefits they are entitled to under the National Health Service. As a general rule, British citizens receive coverage for all hospitalization; doctors, including a British invention, the neighborhood "drop-in" clinic; mental health services; retraining to deal with handicapping conditions; home nursing visits; community support personnel; and so on. Exemptions include dental and eye care, certain drugs and prescriptions, and privileged hospital accommodations or nursing care. The elderly are exempt from many of the exclusions, plus they are eligible for additional home health aids and visits not offered to the general populace. One innovative program the British scheme supports is a holiday plan available to the elderly and their families that enables adult children responsible for aged parents to take periodic holidays with an assurance that their parents will be fully cared for. The elderly are also eligible for domiciliary care benefits when they are no longer capable of fully independent living but do not require close medical attention.

Canada and Australia established national programs subsequent to the British scheme. Canadian philosophy regarding health services is somewhat closer to the model of the United States than that operative in Britain. Hospitalization and diagnostic insurance was offered for the first time in 1957, with federal monies earmarked for use in the provinces on a matching basis to cover specified kinds of hospital and laboratory services. The benefits were vastly expanded at about the time Medicare was enacted in the United States, and by 1972 coverage had become virtually universal. Saskatchewan was the first province to initiate compulsory insurance programs for all physician and hospital expenses, but gradually others have followed suit. With the enactment of the Canadian Medical Care Act of 1968, matching funds have become available to each province to provide expanded coverage for medical services not offered previously. In all likelihood, a potpourri of distinct programs will continue through the decade as a result of political disagreements and the separate control each jurisdiction exercises over its own plan; however, the coverage presently provided is more comprehensive than that of the Medicare program in the United States (Kohn, 1972). In Australia, voluntary national insurance was established in the early 1950s. As a consequence of 1970 legislation it was expanded considerably, but it remains a completely voluntary program. For an annual premium that breaks down to roughly one-third the per capita cost of providing services, individuals and families may receive coverage for a large majority of their medical outlays. For the elderly and certain other dependent people, much of the remaining cost is also waived. Personnel shortages currently impose hardships on elderly persons who require visitation or nursing home services, but recent information suggests the situation is improving (Robson, 1972). As is the case in the United States, the Australian government pays only approved charges, after which the individual may be billed for deductible expenses or for additional fees levied by the attending physician.

Soviet citizens and all visitors to the Soviet Union have received medical care ostensibly without charge since the 1917 Revolution, though nominal charges may still be imposed for dental and eye care or for drugs. Certain other costs may also be charged to the recipient, but large numbers of people are exempted from additional fees and over half the populace does not pay out-of-pocket medical expenses. Unlike many Western countries, the Soviet Union openly acknowledges individual health as vitally important for the best interests of the country. Accordingly, preventive health maintenance is routinely accessible to all. One component of the prophylactic measures designed to ensure a healthy work force is a nationwide health and holiday spa network where workers may go for health treatments, rest and recuperation. Health care expenditures reportedly make up about 7.2 percent of the budget in the Soviet Union, although exact comparisons with Western nations are tricky since Soviet economists do not use gross national product accounting schemes. In an effort to upgrade medical attention for the elderly and to maintain older citizens in their own residences for as long as possible, the Soviet Union has recently organized a number of "geriatric cabinets" composed of both elderly clients and health practitioners to insure use of the best locally available resources. Cabinet physicians are responsible for meeting the particular needs of the elderly in their districts and for providing postgraduate training for other medical personnel faced with caring for older patients (Vinogradov and Revutskaya, 1972).

Medicare in the United States

Theodore Roosevelt considered calling for national health insurance as a plank in his Progressive Party campaign, but unfortunately the outbreak of war shifted political priorities and the idea was abandoned. Crises coming in rapid succession precluded much attention to the issue of health services until 1950 when the Old Age Assistance Act (OAA) finally provided federally sponsored assistance aimed at lifting the burden of medical expenses from indigent elderly. With the exception of the Social Security Act of 1935, the OAA was the first federal program oriented to the special problems of the elderly; nevertheless, it failed to provide any assistance for the vast majority of older Americans, let alone the rest of the population. In 1957, the initial version of a series of proposed national health programs especially focused on the elderly was presented to Congress; however, a decade of wrangling and strident opposition from the American Medical Association and allied organizations was to pass before legislative action translated the ideas into law. The compromise Medicare bill, as it became known, underwent more than 80 revisions before it passed both houses of Congress in July 1965 to become effective with the next fiscal calendar (Townsend, 1971).

From the outset, it is clear that the backers of the Medicare legislation intended their program only to supplement, not to supplant, individual responsibility. Part A, providing basic hospitalization insurance, is automatic for all who qualify for Social Security or railroad pensions and includes their dependents under stipulated conditions. Subsequent amendments have now included kidney patients requiring expensive long-term care and paid subscribers over 65 who are not otherwise eligible for Social Security or railroad retirement. As of 1977, coverage under Part A begins after patients incur $124 in deductible expenses; then for the first 60 days all regular nursing services, inpatient drugs, equipment and so on are provided free of charge in hospitals or skilled nursing facilities. If hospital treatment is terminated in less than 60 days, and no further hospital care is required for a period of 60 days, the benefit period begins anew. If hospitalization continues beyond the initial period, a "coinsurance" charge of $31 is levied for another 30 days care, after which time patients begin to draw against a lifetime reserve of 60 days billed at a rate of $62 a day. Using the nonreplaceable lifetime reserve extends the total benefit period to a maximum of 150 days, or approximately five months of continuous hospitalization. If, after being in the hospital for at least three days, the attending physician prescribes treatment in an extended care facility, patients receive 20 days of nursing facility services without charge and then can obtain an additional 80 days at a 1977 rate of $15.50 per day. Once a patient is finally discharged, he or she is entitled to 100 home health care visits by qualified nursing or therapy personnel, if it is required by the condition that brought about the original hospitalization or one that developed along the way. Psychiatric inpatient care is a separate category, providing a maximum lifetime benefit of 190 care days. Every time Congress convenes it can amend the Medicare benefits; thus, in future years changes are highly likely to alter the above figures. At the present time, Part A does not provide for private duty nurses, the first three pints of blood, custodial care or convenience items such as a television set or telephone.

Medicare Part B is open for voluntary enrollment at a supplemental fee which is withheld from Social Security payments. The task of rejecting enrollment is the responsibility of the individual receiving benefits; about three months prior to his or her 65th birthday, each person receives a refusal card that must be returned within seven months or premiums are automatically withheld. If one does not enroll at the time Social Security benefits begin, open subscription is available during the first quarter of each calendar year, but a 10 percent penalty is assessed for each year the person was eligible but not actually enrolled. Once coverage is in force, subscribers are responsible for an annual deductible, with the government paying up to 80 percent of all other approved charges. Doctor's fees, office drugs or supplies, emergency room services, 100 house calls, prescribed treatments or equipment, ambulance, and chiropractic care are the principal benefits provided under Part B. At the present time optical and dental examinations, prescription drugs not administered in the physician's office, hearing aids, routine checkups and certain other medical expenses are not covered. One of two repayment plans may be utilized. If the government pays its 80 percent of the approved fees directly to the physician, the patient is billed independently for the remainder; however, if payment is sent directly to the patient, additional fees in excess of the approved rates may be levied by the physician. Whether payment is made to the physician or to the patient depends on who completes the necessary forms; with few exceptions, it is to the patient's advantage if the physician files, yet the paperwork involved tends to discourage physicians from routinely offering this service to their patients.

In overcoming the vigorous opposition, not to mention the $50 million spent by the American Medical Association and its affiliates to prevent passage of the bill (Townsend, 1971), one might assume that Medicare would be a well-reasoned and equitable scheme not easily criticized. Unfortunately, the compromise necessary to secure passage for even a nominal level of health insurance resulted in a program far from what its sponsors envisioned. With passage of some form of comprehensive, universal health bill nearly assured during the later 1970s, many of the current problems will hopefully be alleviated; however, until such time, the elderly will continue to face the unanticipated burdens of medical care. In the last ten years inflation has hit medical care particularly hard, with an increase of at least 59 percent in overall costs, greater than any other single personal item on the consumer price index, although not all medical expenses have escalated at an identical rate. Hospital costs have increased more rapidly than doctor's fees, which in turn lead dental expenses or the price of medicines. The greater costs have affected both the individual consumer and the federal government's health care funds, without any consequent improvement in either utilization levels or quality of service. In 1977 most American workers contribute 5.85 percent of their wages up to $16,500, a maximum of $965, for Social Security — Medicare benefits, payable in most instances only upon reaching 65. However, according to reports issued by the federal government, instead of complete coverage, retired workers find themselves paying over half of their medical expenses out of their own pockets during the very years that they are adjusting to 50 percent lower incomes. Adding up all deductibles, premiums and expenses, the average annual medical bill for people over 65 comes to three times that paid by the rest of the adult population (Mueller and Gibson, 1975). Medicare-Medicaid programs have appreciably aided with unexpectedly large medical expenses, but for the majority of the elderly medical care continues to be an onerous burden. Until alternative comprehensive approaches address themselves to the social causes of illness in old age, the needs of older Americans will remain largely unmet (Brody, 1973).

Summary

No period of life is free from illness or disability, though the types of health problems we face do change. In youth and in the middle years acute conditions are the most prevalent, only to be replaced in the later years by chronic ailments. Too frequently overlooked is the fact that an older person's ills have been a long time coming. The mild stiffness that robs the young of their jaunty step gives bad backs or trick knees to the middle-aged and finally settles in to debilitate the elderly. Through the course of life a host of social and economic factors influence one's health, shaping not only the significance attached to various conditions but the probable outcomes. In industrialized cultures people no longer fear the infectious epidemics that formerly killed large numbers before they could reach what we now consider middle age. Instead, respiratory ailments and degenerative diseases take their toll, often remaining constant companions in one's life for decades. What permits the health problems of the second half of life to be so resistant to medical science is their multiple etiology, stemming from diffuse and gradual alterations. As causes of death some diseases, cardiovascular impairments or malignant neoplasms among them, are more common than others, occurring among men and women, nonwhites and whites at differential rates. On the other hand, many nonfatal, or at least not necessarily fatal, illnesses may be found in nearly all elderly living in modern industrial societies; atherosclerosis is far and away the outstanding example. Provided some segment of the population is exempt from the health problems faced by the rest of the population, there is room to improve the quality of life experienced by the vast majority.

Around the world there is a developing awareness of the close ties between the health of a people and the welfare of their nation. Widely diverse health programs have evolved in specific economic and political contexts to help ameliorate the heavy burdens of medical care. In the United States, legislation currently makes available only a minimum level of health care. Unfortunately, the benefits envisioned have in most instances been more than offset by the spiraling inflation haunting the health field, a 12 percent increase in medical expenses in 1975 alone. The two parts of the Medicare program cover only narrowly specified expenses for periods in excess of the two to three week maximum stays most people spend when hospitalized. Yet actual expenses are distributed in such a manner that older people pay more than twice what the bulk of the population expends for their medical needs. The enactment of a universal health program in the decade of the seventies has been a long sought after goal, but to avoid the pitfalls of Medicare, even more careful planning and execution is needed.

Pertinent Readings

BOURLIERE, F. "Ecology of Human Senescence." In *Textbook of Geriatric Medicine and Gerontology*, ed. J.C. Brocklehurst, 60–74. Edinburgh: Churchill Livingstone, 1973.

BRIDGMAN, R.F. "International Trends in Medical Care Organisation and Research." In *International Medical Care*, eds. J. Fry and W.A.J. Farndale, 8–26. Wallingford, Pa.: Washington Square East Publishers, 1972.

BROCKLEHURST, J.C., ed. *Textbook of Geriatric Medicine and Gerontology*. Edinburgh: Churchill Livingstone, 1973.

BRODY, S.J. "Comprehensive Health Care for the Elderly: The Continuum of Medical, Health and Social Services for the Aged." *The Gerontologist* XIII, 4 (1973): 412–18.

BRUNNER, D., and E. JOKL. *Physical Activity and Aging*. Basel, Switzerland: S. Karger, 1970.

CONFREY, E.A. and M.S. GOLDSTEIN. "The Health Status of Aging People." In *Handbook of Social Gerontology*, ed. Clark Tibbitts, 165–207. Chicago: University of Chicago Press, 1960.

CROOG, S.H. et al. "The Heart Patient and the Recovery Process." *Social Science and Medicine* 2 (1968): 111–64.

DUBOS, R. *Mirage of Health*. Garden City, N.Y.: Anchor Books, 1959.

ELDER, A.T. "Medical Care in the United Kingdom." In *International Medical Care*, eds. J. Fry and W.A.J. Farndale, 75–107. Wallingford, Pa.: Washington Square East Publishers, 1972.

FENDALL, N.R.E. "Medical Care in the Developing Nations." In *International Medical Care*, eds. J. Fry and W.A.J. Farndale, 204–48. Wallingford, Pa.: Washington Square East Publishers, 1972.

FORD, A.B. "Distinguishing Characteristics of the Aging from a Clinical Standpoint." *Journal of the American Geriatrics Society* XVI, 2 (1968): 142–48.

FREEMAN, J.T. *Clinical Features of the Older Patient*. Springfield, Ill: Charles C. Thomas, 1965.

FRY, J., and W.A.J. FARNDALE, eds. *International Medical Care.* Wallingford, Pa.: Washington Square East Publishers, 1972.

GRANICH, M. "Factors Affecting Aging; Pharmacologic Agents." In *Developmental Physiology and Aging,* ed. P.S. Timiras, 607–14. New York: The Macmillan Company, 1972.

HABERMAN, P. "The Reliability and Validity of the Data." In *Poverty and Health,* by J. Kosa et al, 343–83. Cambridge, Mass.: Harvard University Press, 1969.

HARRIS, R. *The Sacred Trust.* New York: New American Library, 1966.

HOWELL, T.H. *Geriatrics.* Springfield, Ill.: Charles C. Thomas, 1970.

INTER-SOCIETY COMMISSION FOR HEART DISEASE RESOURCES. "Primary Prevention of the Atherosclerotic Disease." *Circulation* XLII (1970): A55–95.

KOHN, R. "Medical Care in Canada." In *International Medical Care,* eds. J. Fry and W.A.J. Farndale, 144–76. Wallingford, Pa.: Washington Square East Publishers, 1972.

LEAF, A. "Every Day is a Gift when You Are Over 100." *National Geographic* 143, 1 (1973): 93–118.

MADDOX, G., and E.B. DOUGLASS. "Self-Assessment of Health." In *Normal Aging II,* ed. E. Palmore, 55–62. Durham, N.C.: Duke University Press, 1974.

MADDOX, G., and C. EISDORFER. "Some Correlates of Activity and Morale among the Elderly." *Social Forces* XL, 3 (1962): 254–60.

MARKS, R. "A Review of Empirical Findings in Social Stress and Cardiovascular Disease." *Milbank Memorial Fund Quarterly* XLV, 2 (1967).

McKEOWN, F. *Pathology of the Aged.* London: Butterworths, 1965.

METCHNIKOFF, E. *The Prolongation of Life.* New York: G.P. Putnam's Sons, 1908.

METROPOLITAN LIFE INSURANCE COMPANY. *Statistical Bulletin,* vol. LII. New York: Metropolitan Life, 1971.

MUELLER, M.S., and R.M. GIBSON. "Age Differences in Health Care Spending, Fiscal Year 1974." *Social Security Bulletin* XXXVIII, 6 (1975): 3–16.

NATIONAL CENTER FOR HEALTH STATISTICS. Department of Health, Education and Welfare. "Health in the Later Years of Life." U.S. Government Printing Office, 1971.

PALMORE, E. "Health Practices and Illness." In *Normal Aging II,* ed. E. Palmore, 49–55. Durham, N.C.: Duke University Press, 1974a.

———. "Predicting Longevity: A New Method." In *Normal Aging II,* ed. E. Palmore, 281–85. Durham, N.C.: Duke University Press, 1974b.

PALMORE, E., and C. LUIKART. "Health and Social Factors Related to Life Satisfaction." In *Normal Aging II,* ed. E. Palmore, 185–200. Durham, N.C.: Duke University Press, 1974.

PELCOVITS, J. "Nutrition to Meet the Human Needs of Older Americans." *Journal of the American Dietetic Association* LX (1972): 297–300.

PFEIFFER, E. "Survival in Old Age." In *Normal Aging II,* ed. E. Palmore, 269–80. Durham, N.C.: Duke University Press, 1974.

ROBSON, H.N. "Medical Care in Australia." In *International Medical Care,* eds. J. Fry and W.A.J. Farndale, 249–64. Wallingford, Pa.: Washington Square East Publishers, 1972.

SINEX, F.M. "A View of Training from Within the Medical School: Attitudes, Status and Structure." Paper presented to Gerontological Society, Miami Beach, 1973.

STAMLER, J. *Lectures on Preventive Cardiology.* New York: Grune and Stratton, 1967.

STREIB, G.F., and C.J. SCHNEIDER. *Retirement in American Society: Impact and Process.* Ithaca, N.Y.: Cornell University Press, 1971.

SUBCOMMITTEE ON AGING. *Post-White House Conference on Aging Reports 1973.* Washington, D.C.: U.S. Government Printing Office, 1973.

SUSSER, M.W., and W. WATSON. *Sociology in Medicine.* London: Oxford University Press, 1971.

TAYLOR, W.J. "Medicare and Medicaid Fall Woefully Short." In *The Crisis in Health Care for the Aged,* ed. L. Summit, 56–57. New York: The Huxley Institute for Biosocial Research, 1973.

TIMIRAS, P.S., ed. *Developmental Physiology and Aging.* New York: The Macmillan Company, 1972.

TISSUE, T. "Another Look at Self-Rated Health among the Elderly." *Journal of Gerontology* XXVII, 1 (1972): 91–94.

TOWNSEND, C. *Old Age: The Last Segregation.* New York: Bantam Books, 1971.

U.S. DEPARTMENT OF HEALTH, EDUCATION AND WELFARE. Public Health Service, series 10. *Limitation of Activity Due to Chronic Conditions.* Washington, D.C.: U.S. Government Printing Office, 1972.

VINOGRADOV, N.A., and Z.G. REVUTSKAYA. "Problems of Health and Medical Care for Elderly and Old Persons in the USSR." In *The Main Problems of Soviet Gerontology,* ed. D.F. Chebotarev, 252–63. Kiev, USSR: USSR Academy of Medical Sciences, 1972.

WALTON, K.W. "Atherosclerosis and Aging." In *Textbook of Geriatric Medicine and Gerontology,* ed. J.C. Brocklchurst, 75–112. Edinburgh: Churchill/Livingstone, 1973.

WORLD HEALTH ORGANIZATION CHARTER. Geneva: World Health Organization, 1946.

"The World Health Situation." In *World Health Chronicle.* Geneva: World Health Organization, no. 21, 1967.

WURTMAN, R. "A New Look at Stroke." *Men and Molecules.* American Chemical Society, no. 701, May 1974.

Chapter 8

Work, Finances and the Golden Years

Today all segments of the work force have become aware of the instability of national economies, the tighter inflationary pinch and the precarious interdependence of world powers. Particularly relevant to older workers nearing retirement is the necessity of extending savings, pension or Social Security benefits at a time of financial insecurity to cover ever-lengthening lifetimes and the increasingly high costs of living. Many of the economic problems that previously seemed peculiar to the aged are now recognized as a facet of the lives of middle-aged or younger workers as well. Labor market fluctuations have a more pronounced effect on all workers whose skills have become somewhat outdated or those who lack special skills. Compulsory retirement programs not only encompass the majority of all workers, but have had a notable impact on the shifting structure of the labor force. Most people assume retirement to be the special province of those over 60 and, as a result, many find they have labored under mistaken or clouded perceptions of the hard realities. Almost without exception, everyone subscribes to and works for financial security that will furnish today's essentials as well as tomorrow's cushion. The questions, of course, are: How many ever realize this dream, and what are the changing criteria for its achievement? And yet, we must also focus on the import work has for those presently middle-aged: only recently has there been the possibility that endeavors other than work may become the central focus in our lives. Accordingly, this chapter addresses itself to work-related events as they affect the lives of middle-aged and older workers.

The impact of technology on industrial change is readily apparent in considerations of the present and future shape of work and leisure. Theoretically, with full and constant growth in productivity and a stable population, the work week could be cut to approximately 22 hours in the United States by 1985, or, alternatively, workers might work only 27 weeks of the year and retire as early as age 38 (Kreps, 1971a). Conversely, if work time remains constant, the gross national product might double by 1985 from the 1960 level. Neither will happen, of course, as productivity will not be exclusively channeled into more work or more leisure. Economic and employment fluctuations have made forecasters cautious to say the least, but a few projections might be ventured nonetheless. If productivity is relatively steady and allocated, say, two-thirds to accumulating goods and services and one-third to leisure, the work week of the average worker will conceivably decline to 37 hours by 1980 with annual vacations averaging three weeks or more. Although these estimates are weighted on the conservative side, the free time accruing from improvements in output per productive hour is quite large. Despite a spate of national or local holidays, the five day week still tends to predominate in most of the industrialized West. When annual vacations are included in the picture, most workers can plan on spending in the neighborhood of 240 days a year on the job. Figuring in 12 hours daily for eating and resting, we are left with a distribution of roughly 42 percent of our time devoted to work, with the remainder given over to other pursuits (Clague, 1971). On the face of it, most people might seem to be well prepared to deal with the enforced leisure of the retirement years.

As has been intimated, however, compulsory retirement sometimes imposes a degree of hardship that surpasses the efficiency considerations of the industrial stimulators. This being the case, most societies will probably soon face policy decisions concerning the allocation of the fruits of increased productivity. If additional production is directed toward leisure, in place of continued economic expansion, crucial issues will revolve around how much should be invested in retraining programs, how much to shortening the work week or the work year, and so on. Although the problems are especially salient in times of national economic instability, explicit articulation of possible solutions has customarily been confined to the many interest groups that seek to secure their own advantage, not infrequently at the expense of outsiders. Consequently, the potential for nationally coordinated planning has been thwarted to a major degree.

Work Patterns and the Life Cycle

In order to thoroughly discuss the life of older workers, some attention must be directed to an examination of career patterns. Much previous research has been focused on the features of occupational careers, from both psychological and sociological perspectives. In either case, several factors repeatedly surface in the literature dealing with work and occupations. The classic definition of *career* was offered by Wilensky (1961), that is, an orderly succession of related jobs, arranged in a hierarchy of prestige, through which individuals move in more or less patterned sequences. Careers are embedded in an institutional framework, so that the organization of the workplace and the differential system of rewards for productivity and mobility are particularly important. Mobility may be either vertical, upward or downward in social rank, or horizontal, involving a change in function without a change in reward, such as a clerk of some sort becoming either a shoe salesperson or a receptionist. The meaning attached by workers to their occupation, in terms of their own attitudes and commitment, would seem to contribute to the shape of career patterns. Hence, factors influencing careers are both individual and situational; neither can be understood in isolation.

One of the earliest developmental models in the study of careers was the "trait-factor" theory, which assumed a matching process took place between an individual's peculiar abilities and certain vocational opportunities. Many variations of this approach have been articulated, the basic assumption of all the models being that occupational choice reflects personality traits. Partly in response to this trend, a sociological paradigm was offered that posited occupational selection as beyond the immediate control of an individual (Osipow, 1968). One of the early studies of occupations in the United States found that the majority of workers sampled showed little upward mobility, among lower status occupations a significant proportion of children had followed in their fathers' footsteps, and that the reverse of the trend was observed for those of higher status. For both groups, jobs held during the floundering period, that time when the worker was finishing his education and holding a variety of odd jobs, were seemingly prophetic of subsequent career developments (Davidson and Anderson, 1937). A decade later, another study of work histories led to the description of several typical career patterns, each of which was based on a succession of five work stages. These stages were termed the preparatory, initial, trial, stable and retirement periods. The preparatory phase consists of all behaviors leading up to the selection of the first job. During the initial period workers are completing their education and hold a series of temporary jobs. For three years or so after completing their education many workers continue to shop around, but during this trial period they move toward their ultimate choice. The stable period represents the selection of a long-term occupation, although workers do not necessarily stick with one job, as is illustrated by people in the professional and white collar arenas, who change jobs but not occupations. The final state is defined as retirement, that period after individuals cease their usual full-time occupations (Miller and Form, 1951).

A similar developmental model of career stages has been promoted by Gusfield (1961). In his scheme, three phases of career growth are linked to two distinctive career shapes. The stages, paralleling those of Miller and Form, are the trial, stable and established career periods. From these Gusfield develops the directed and undirected career shapes. The directed career is stable and focused, established either immediately or through gradual development. This pattern is represented most commonly by professional and white collar workers. Blue collar workers, on the other hand, more often demonstrate the undirected career, which is characterized by lack of commitment, frequent change and impermanence. A final model which places more emphasis on psychological factors was proposed by Super (1957). It is Super's contention that basically an occupation is selected because of its potential for self-expression. While factors external to the individual determine the exact manner of expression, particular vocational behaviors reflect the individual's stage of life development, with self-concept becoming more stable as vocational activities also become stabilized. Four career patterns are assumed to exist, including the stable pattern, where an occupation is entered early and permanently; the conventional pattern, where several jobs are tried, one of which leads to a stable job; the unstable pattern, where a person holds a series of trial jobs which may lead to temporary stability followed by disruption; and a multiple trial pattern, in which case an individual pursues several relatively stable jobs. The shape of a worker's career is determined by his "vocational maturity," defined by Super as the acquisition of appropriate attitudes and the display of suitable behavior for his or her life stage.

These models are important to bear in mind during the following discussion of work and preparation for retirement. It might be anticipated that attitudes toward and eventual adjustment to retirement or to continued work will be conditioned by occupational background and by individual adaptation to the sequential development described in Chapter Six. For example, in light of Super's model, professionals who have exhibited a stable career may be less willing to accept retirement than blue collar workers with unstable patterns. The former have developed a higher degree of commitment to and identification with their occupations, creating possible resistance to retirement careers that do not incorporate a degree of continued involvement with the profession. If occupational choice does indeed reflect personality traits, factors associated with adjustment in retirement ought to differ among workers. Retirement counselors might well make use, then, of the probable attitudes associated with each occupation, career pattern and personality type. At the present time, however, little resembling a well-ordered approach to counseling predominates among preretirement programs. The stability and security pointed out by Miller and Form and by Gusfield also have an impact on later work life and on transition to retirement. Retirement may be viewed by workers as a welcome phase in their occupational careers, either because it is another logical step or because it puts an end to a succession of tangentially related jobs and an unstable career pattern.

Working Around the World

Trends in Western Countries

The distribution of adults actively involved in the labor force in six industrialized countries is illustrated in Table 8.1. In all cases, over 95 percent of the men between the ages of 25 and 55 participate in the labor force. Between 55 and 65 the percentage steadily declines, as the proportion of men still working or seeking work is cut by 43 percent or more in every country except Japan. As can be seen,

Table 8.1
Percentage of Adults Actively Involved in the Labor Force Over a 20 Year Period in Six Countries

AGE	USA 1950	USA 1970	JAPAN 1950	JAPAN 1970	FRANCE 1946	FRANCE 1968	WEST GERMANY 1950	WEST GERMANY 1970	SWEDEN 1950	SWEDEN 1970	UK 1951	UK 1971
Men												
20–24	81.9	79.2	90.5	83.5	91.2	71.3	93.4	86.1	90.0	62.0	95.3	90.5
25–39	92.9	94.3	96.3	98.6	96.7	96.3	96.0	} 94.6	97.5	} 90.5	98.1	98.0
40–54	92.7	93.1	97.0	97.9	95.5	94.4	95.7		96.8		98.3	97.9
55–59	86.7	87.0	92.4	94.2	85.4	82.4	87.4	87.8	92.5	88.4	95.4	95.2
60–64	79.4	73.3	} 65.2	85.8	76.3	65.7	73.0	} 35.6	79.7	75.7	87.8	86.7
65+	39.0	24.5		54.5	51.6	19.1	26.8		40.1	15.2	34.8	21.1
Total	78.9	74.7	83.4	84.3	85.5	73.2	63.2	58.9	65.2	54.7	87.9	81.6
Women												
20–24	43.2	55.4	64.0	70.9	59.9	62.4	70.4	68.8	57.3	53.3	65.5	60.1
25–39	32.5	46.0	49.1	49.6	48.9	44.8	42.2	} 47.7	30.2	} 51.0	37.1	47.8
40–54	33.9	52.2	53.2	63.1	51.0	44.6	35.1		30.0		34.2	60.5
55–59	25.9	47.6	48.2	53.8	46.1	42.3	29.4	35.5	26.3	41.4	27.7	51.0
60–64	20.5	36.2	} 27.2	43.3	40.2	32.3	21.2	} 10.1	18.9	25.7	14.4	27.9
65+	7.3	10.3		19.7	22.0	8.0	9.7		8.6	3.2	6.1	8.0
Total	29.0	40.5	48.6	50.9	46.2	36.1	31.4	29.9	23.2	29.9	34.5	42.8

Sources: *U.N. Demographic Yearbook, 1956* (New York: United Nations, 1956), pp. 319–38; *Year Book of Labour Statistics, 1974* (Geneva: International Labour Office, 1974), pp. 28–40.

the most active period for women is between ages 20 and 24, prior to their taking on the obligations of parenthood. Generally speaking, approximately half of all women are economically active up until age 60. Between 60 and 65 the percentage falls so that only one in three women work, and after age 65 the number drops still further, to one in ten or less. Again, Japan presents the sole exception; Japanese women work at nearly twice the rate of women in Western industrialized countries.

Comparing current participation rates to the rates exhibited over two decades ago provides some insight into the changing nature of work. As is evident in looking at the figures for males, the proportion of American men over 65 who are still active in the labor force has declined from 39 percent in 1950 to less than one-quarter in 1970. During this same period Japanese men over age 60 have increased their participation by 5 percent. The situation for Swedish men is analagous to the American pattern, with a nearly identical decline. British men also experienced a decline; however, the magnitude is less than that for their American or Swedish counterparts. The figures for France are somewhat misleading, since the earlier census taken in 1946 reflects the effects of a country still mobilized for a war economy. This accounts for some measure of the apparently large decline in the participation of older French workers, but much of the remainder is due to rapid industrialization and the simultaneous phasing out of older workers. Although male labor force participation rates since 1950 have remained relatively stable up to age 60, there has been a significant expansion of the proportion of women actively working during middle age over the past two decades. The most noteworthy changes have occurred in the United States, Sweden and Britain for middle-aged women between 40 and 60. This age group has increased its participation to the point that one out of two women now works outside the home. While the table shows French women have experienced a decline from their participation at the close of World War II, this probably reflects to a great extent the widespread mobilization of all segments of the population during World War II. Sweden, on the other hand, exemplifies the typical trend with clarity. Between 25 and 39, traditionally the child-rearing years, there has been a 13 percent increase in the proportion of women participating in the labor force. The number of middle-aged women between 40 and 55 has grown even more, up nearly 20 percent, while for those between 55 and 65 the increase was about 10 percent. In the oldest category there also has been some expansion of women active in the work force.

An essential component of any comparison of working patterns involves unemployment. In the United States unemployment is more frequent among the younger age groups, but in West Germany the highest rate is for workers of either sex over age 55 (Engelen-Kefer, 1973). In both countries, however, it is long-term unemployment that is more characteristic of older workers, resulting in large measure from their concentration in geographic regions or in occupations with diminished employment opportunities or in industries experiencing an overall reduction in personnel requirements. During nearly every kind of economic crisis the first to suffer are the youngest and the oldest workers, with the middle-aged relatively insulated. The patterns in Britain provide supporting data, where 84 percent of workers unemployed for over one year are customarily over the age of 40. Of the oldest workers who were unemployed, half had been out of work for more than six months in 1971 (Slater, 1972). But what of the benefits supposedly made possible by technological advancement? The major effect may very well be to compress active work life into a shorter period. Unless our planning includes contingencies for multiple career patterns, flexible and frequently utilized retraining programs, and legitimated leisure activities, the social problems attendant upon industrialized development and technological change will increasingly affect the middle-aged members of society.

Countries in Transition — Japan and the Soviet Union

Japan presents an interesting case of a non-Western country that has undergone rapid industrialization over a very few years. While the technologically sophisticated, highly productive realm of the Japanese economy is continually expanding, as compared to the United States a significantly larger proportion of workers are still employed in agriculture, fishing, forestry and unpaid family work. Following World War II, labor surpluses helped establish strict rules governing entry into industrial jobs. Combined with more recent pressures created by growing affluence, including a gradual erosion of the traditional status accorded the society's elders, many older Japanese are presently confronted by strains not previously experienced. With retirement coming between 55 and 60, plus meager pension benefits, it is no wonder many older Japanese are encountering considerable stress that may last over 20 years. The interaction of these factors has created an imbalance where there are often abundant job openings for younger workers, but largely restricted opportunities available to older workers.

Paradoxically, in recent years Japan has experienced something of a labor shortage, arising in part from the burgeoning labor demands of a booming economy. The shortage has facilitated some movement of middle-aged people into industry, as well as the post-ponement of retirement in a small range of industries, but whether or not this trend will continue is highly questionable. Although large industrial companies set retirement age at 55, the Japanese govern-ment's policy recently has been to encourage an extension of retire-ment age to 60 by offering a subsidy to all employers who agree to retain older workers. While the general trend toward retirement at 55 has yet to predominate, over four-fifths of those workers retiring at 55 manage to find supplemental jobs to bolster their finances until public pension benefits begin at age 60 (Fisher, 1973). The gap be-tween retirement and the onset of pension benefits is bridged not only by continued employment in many guises, but also by a wide-spread practice of awarding lump sums of money, amounting to about a month's salary in return for each year of service, to every re-tiring worker. Even though retirees often find this bonus inadequate as far as meeting their expenses until pension benefits begin, it is nevertheless of enormous symbolic importance to those nearing re-tirement. As in most countries, Japanese women move in and out of the labor force and subsequently are usually unable to obtain similar retirement allotments. They do qualify for public pensions at the age of 55, however. Recognition of the dimensions of the problem and the need for more adequate retirement benefits finally came in 1973, 50 years after pensions were originally introduced, when the rate of benefits was doubled (Stewart, 1974).

Similarly to Western countries, the Soviet Union has recently experienced innumerable growing pains as the pace of industrializa-tion gained momentum following World War II. For one thing, the number of people reaching retirement age has expanded considera-bly since 1940, up from a scant 6.8 to nearly 12 percent in 1970. In addition, Soviet workers are now eligible for retirement at earlier ages than allowed in Western countries, women at age 55 and men at 60, but these ages are flexible according to occupation, with the more strenuous jobs permitting earlier retirement. At present, just over one-third of the Soviet labor force is in the age range of 40 to 59. Despite the possibility of early retirement, due to severe labor short-ages, the use of retired workers who have valuable skills and ex-perience is widely endorsed; hence, many people continue to work beyond the age at which they could retire. While women number half of the overall labor force, they represent a majority in some oc-cupational spheres. In the public health field for example, over 85 percent of all workers are women. Seventy percent of the medical doctors are women, and women constitute approximately the same percentage of all school teachers.

The impact of a growth-oriented economy is clearly reflected in the Soviet programs over the past 20 years. In 1956, benefits of old age pensions were bolstered to such an extent that the percentage of older workers declined from 50 percent in 1956 to below 10 percent in 1962. In the decade since, however, the need for a larger labor force has prompted governmental programs aimed at encouraging older workers to remain on the job. If they continue to work, older workers may obtain full pension benefits in addition to any wages that they might earn. This has fostered an upswing in the number of men over 60 in the labor force since 1963 to 53 percent. About 17 percent of the Soviet women continue working past retirement age, but a large proportion assume the role of unpaid family workers so that their children can work without worrying about the care of their own homes or offspring.

The United States and Working Women

In Western countries, the number of women active in the work force has increased dramatically since World War II. More women of all ages now work than ever before, and more middle-aged and older women are returning to work than at any previous time. It has simply become too expensive for many women to remain at home since the salaries which they must pass up to do so have steadily risen. Although women are now entering the labor force in growing numbers, they remain clustered primarily in service and clerical jobs, traditionally considered the exclusive domain of women. The professions continue to be marked by unbalanced sexual segregation in many countries, though here again women are very slowly increasing their numbers. The gradual inroads made by American women in a variety of professional occupations from 1950 to 1970 are shown in Table 8.2. It should be clear from these and earlier data that the majority of working women are not pursuing careers at the highest professional levels.

Still another area of inequality is the difference between the average earnings of men and the salaries paid to women. In 1955 women who worked full time earned about 64 percent as much as men, with the median salary for American women at that time $2719, while for men annual income was $4252. By 1973 women's incomes had increased to a median of $6488, but, in comparison, men were paid $11,468; thus women's earnings fell to approximately 60 percent as much. Differential earnings by sex and race are clearly indicated by Figure 8.1 for selected years. Undoubtedly the lower salaries paid to women may be largely explained by their pre-

Table 8.2

Percent of American Women in Selected Professions Between 1950 and 1970

PROFESSION	1950	1970
Dentistry	2.7	3.5
Engineering	1.2	1.6
Law (including judges)	3.5	4.9
Managerial (in manufacturing)	6.4	6.3
Medicine	6.1	9.3
Clergy	4.0	2.9
College level instruction	23.2	28.2

Source: Department of Commerce, Bureau of the Census, *Economic Report of the President* (Washington, D.C.: U.S. Government Printing Office, 1973).

dominant employment in low pay, low prestige kinds of jobs. As shown in Figure 8.2, women tend to be employed in semiskilled positions in which earnings are marginal regardless of sex. An additional factor contributing to the earnings differential between men and women is the variable rate at which women participate in the labor force. Women who are not the head of a household and who have working husbands may move in and out of the work force as their personal situation dictates, conditioned, of course, by the receptivity of the labor market. Unfortunately, in doing so they are usually unable to build up the seniority or experience customarily demanded of higher paying positions. Most men and women exhibit differential work patterns. Men usually work continuously from the time they leave school until retirement; for women this pattern still remains the exception, with the majority demonstrating a bi-modal work history with the peaks coming early and late in their adult lives. Under the circumstances not only must they face sex discrimination but there is an added element of age bias reflected in the jobs, the salaries and the retirement benefits women receive. It was not until the years following World War II that the percentage of working women began to increase at a rapid rate. From the turn of the century until the outbreak of World War II the proportion of women in the labor force increased by 5 percent, while from 1940–1970 the increase was nearly 20 percent. As might easily be expected, the trend has not been the same for single, widowed, divorced or separated women as compared to married women. Since large numbers of the nonmarried women have always worked, the most significant upswing has taken place among married women. Unfortunately, it is those same women who move into and out of the labor market who are penalized for their desire to have families in addition to working.

Figure 8.1

Average earnings of American workers by sex and race, 1962 and 1973

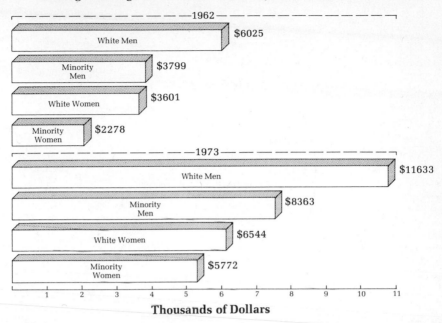

Note: Minority includes all races other than white.

Source: U.S. Department of Labor, Women's Bureau, *Women Workers Today* (Washington, D.C.: U.S. Government Printing Office, 1974).

The Meaning of Work

Worker Stereotypes

What is the relationship between a worker's age, job performance, satisfaction and self-esteem? In turn, how are these conditioned by the beliefs others hold about aging workers? As has been stated repeatedly, older people are not easily or neatly categorized. Chronological age is only one facet of a complex whole. It is often falacious, and perhaps foolhardy, to adhere to or even make generalizations about the performance of older workers. Nevertheless, one hears about the cycle of anxiety and frustration created

Figure 8.2
Occupational distribution for employed Americans by sex, 1973

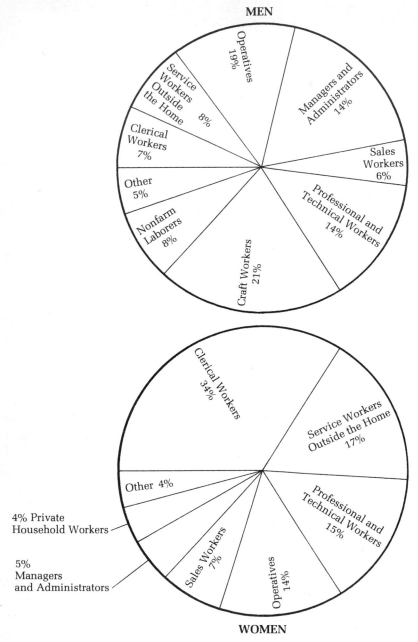

Source: U.S. Department of Labor, Women's Bureau, *Women Workers Today* (Washington, D.C.: U.S. Government Printing Office, 1974), p.5.

where older, unskilled, female or nonwhite workers somehow experience feelings of failure as an unavoidable concomitant of participation in the labor force. Although scant research can be found to support assumptions about emotional, cognitive or temperamental declines in the capacities relevant to performing an occupation, many pervasive societal stereotypes reflect negative appraisals, serving to undermine confidence and self-esteem among older workers. In addition, such stereotypes tend to create implicit resistance and prejudice among those responsible for hiring workers, with the result that older workers often find themselves rejected for employment or advancement on the basis of an age criterion alone.

Myths concerning older workers abound. While some changes in specific performance levels do occur over a person's work life, general performance rarely declines. Several factors are likely to account for the slight differences observed. As noted in Chapter Six, older workers who participate in experiments do less well on those tasks involving speed or time pressures than younger workers, partially because of their unfamiliarity with laboratory test procedures, and partially because of their desire to perform well. Also, when productivity is the unit of measure, the type of job may well have an effect upon a worker's output. In some retail positions, age is perhaps a less acceptable feature; thus, customers may not approach older clerks because of their own age biases. Differential productivity occurs less often among office or clerical personnel. Research conducted by the Bureau of Labor Statistics has consistently challenged the belief that older workers are less accurate or consistent than their younger colleagues or that their rates of absenteeism are higher. Not only are older workers more likely to remain on the job, they are less likely to incur job-related injuries. Despite the realities, people in charge of hiring or promotion have accepted the myths and negative stereotypes and attempt to avoid the alleged pitfalls of hiring workers over 40.

Whatever technical skills older workers lack may be fully compensated for by personal dependability, consistency or loyalty, traits in themselves that make their retention worthwhile. Related to the fundamental considerations of employment possibilities is job satisfaction and meaning in a worker's life. Ideas concerning midcareer retraining, portable pension plans and the transfer of certain general skills to diverse occupations are gaining popularity among those interested in promoting the adaptation of older workers to the changing nature of work. For some workers, especially men, impending retirement and loss of job or occupational role may signify the onset of a diminution in feelings of self-worth, respect or even masculinity, although these feelings do not characterize the majority. Even those workers forced out by mandatory retirement programs often cannot help but view their separation from the work arena as a personal failure or rejection (Palmore, 1972). People who elect voluntary retirement may do so unconsciously, in light of social pressure; they may feel they are saving face or, alternatively, that they are affirming their active participation in the decisionmaking process. The psychological price exacted from those workers who have thoroughly internalized the positive cultural attitudes toward work and production must indeed be high. Required to withdraw at an arbitrary age, they relinquish not only their central roles in the productive schema, but possibly the foundation of their identities. With industrialization has come a particularly heavy emphasis on productive accomplishments, so much so in fact that even nonwork activities are managed within the framework of a worklike orientation: often we fill our spare time with make-work pursuits, or with activities that more closely resemble work than leisure.

While these reactions may indeed hold true for some workers, they are not by any means universal. Associated with the increasing degree of industrialization and technological sophistication is a complex division of labor. In many instances, although it consumes a goodly portion of life, work does not contribute the most significant reinforcement or rewards in an individual's life. Many jobs are simply not inherently stimulating or satisfying to the people who must perform them. Rather, work has meaning in life because it facilitates interpersonal contacts or provides economic independence enabling the worker to engage in more meaningful pursuits. In spite of the fact that a worker might not miss the duties of his or her work per se, anticipating retirement carries with it the reality of a multitude of changes. Work gives or imposes a formal structure on an individual's life, with the free time usually defined as time left over from work. Work also provides a ready means by which people categorize one another, creating and demanding specific responses on the part of others. Obviously, both the work experience and prospective retirement bring common and unique experiences; thus there are few valid generalizations to be made about either large groups of older workers or early retirants. In a cross-national analysis of older workers in Britain, Denmark and the United States, Shanas and her colleagues (1968) found demographic factors were the most outstanding common characteristics among those who were able to continue working beyond customary retirement age. Most of these older workers were married men who had retained their health and were slightly younger than the majority of the retired population. An interesting difference between the United

States and Britain is that most of those who work past retirement age in America are white collar workers, while in Britain they are generally blue collar.

In our discussion of work in the second half of life, distinctions must be drawn not only by occupation, but by sexual, racial and marital status, too. To begin with, the types of jobs traditionally available and the amount of time spent working differ among men and women and among minority groups. Today women return to the labor force after their children are launched in school or leave home. A woman who works outside the home faces a special quandary, as she has a dual role that demands more of her time than is given up by either men or wives who work in the home. The typical relaxation or leisure time experienced by her domestic sisters or male counterparts is constricted for women who work at second jobs, for the latter must utilize a large portion of their time off to fulfill household obligations. Racial background and family status also contribute to differences among the work force. In 1974 in America, 46 percent of the white families had both spouses employed; among blacks the proportion is some 10 percent higher. For both groups, age is a factor in the frequency with which both spouses work. Slightly less than half of the white families with husbands between 25 and 55 had working wives, compared to a little over two-thirds of the black families. The gap begins to close after age 55, at which time both spouses are employed in four of every ten black and white families. In 10 percent of the white and 16 percent of the black families where the husband is over age 65 and employed, the wife continues to be employed as well.

Status Displacement

It is not uncommon for older workers who are having some occupational difficulties to experience what is called status displacement. Regardless of their skills, older workers who lose their jobs as a result of negative stereotypes, economic fluctuations or automation face a number of hurdles in attempting to locate new employment. By virtue of being middle-aged, they are usually tied down and have less geographic mobility than their younger counterparts who have not yet established residential stability. Unemployment tends to be lengthy, as personnel directors hesitate before offering job opportunities to older workers, partly due to the negative stereotypes mentioned earlier. Providing the prejudicial attitudes manifested by personnel officers are overcome and a job found, the older worker may frequently have experienced a change in occupation, slipping a rung or two in status, with a corresponding reduction in salary. Seemingly, newly acquired jobs are also most often with smaller businesses providing either services or retail trade (Dyer, 1973).

The other common type of occupational displacement comes about as a consequence of job discrimination over the issue of age. The basis for age discrimination in employment is apparent from even a brief examination of cultural values evident in industrialized societies. Using the United States for purposes of illustration, it is possible to see that during the developmental period of the nineteenth and twentieth centuries, emphasis was placed primarily on youthfulness, productivity, the Protestant work ethic, achievement motivation and self-sufficiency. By and large, the American cultural motif shuns references to decay, decline or debility. Partially because of the manner in which most people are channeled into a single occupation or profession, age discrimination becomes much more common as employers need only look to the pool of younger workers to quickly replace workers approaching retirement. Many factors encourage the unitary career, including nonportable pension plans; limited educational opportunities after the twenties; and management values stressing consistency, predictability and the smooth transfer of positions among functionally interchangeable workers. In an effort to counteract the tendency reported by the assistant secretary of labor that unemployment among workers over age 45 costs the American economy one million man years of productive time each year, Congress enacted the Age Discrimination in Employment Act in 1967. Although the law only applies to employers who have 25 or more employees and covers workers between ages 40 and 65, it has nonetheless created the potential for legally abolishing age discrimination. It is of considerable importance, however, that the normative retirement ages have never been seriously challenged by the proponents of the act; hence, individuals who wish or intend to work beyond pensionable age have not been granted similar legal safeguards (Grunewald, 1972).

Work and Self-Image

What possible reactions might a person have as he or she faces either retirement or early job displacement? The combinations are numerous, certainly including such feelings as failure, guilt, fear because no regular pattern of activity exists anymore or even a general denial of aging. While some are able to adjust fairly well to the initial transition, others may immediately search for new work, or retreat into themselves, while still others may internalize society's view of them as too old to be a viable and valuable part of the productive process. A crucial aspect of any of these reaction patterns is the change one's self-concept undergoes. No matter how one rationalizes discrimination, it is personally experienced as somehow reflective of one's own faults or weaknesses. Even if this is natural, the results can be exceedingly destructive. An individual may intellectually apprehend the processes of compulsory retirement policies and yet be emotionally unable to accept them as beyond his or her control. If the older worker incorporates the negative societal stereotypes, a gradual shift in self-image will occur, one which is difficult to overcome in the retirement years. When the negative appraisal summarized in "We see you as a bumbling old fool" becomes internalized to "I am a bumbling old fool," a downward spiral is set in motion that is nearly impossible to break. As workers age they are faced with a recurrent quest for reinforcement regarding their performance on the job, the desirability of their presence and their ability to effect changes in the work situation. Doubtlessly all workers are motivated by the evaluations given them by superiors and other related personnel on the job. Nonetheless, older workers may feel less in control of their own job performance than their younger colleagues. Research based on a sample of older managers has found that, regardless of previous experience, they apparently perceive their initiative and job performance as often unrelated to the outcomes that they desire or expect. Compounding this generally pessimistic view of their personal talents, the older respondents also indicated that intensifying their efforts does not necessarily result in better evaluations of job performance (Heneman, 1973).

It is hoped that a program aimed at sensitizing personnel managers and retirement counselors would help prevent such a cycle of anxiety and poor self-evaluation. More individualized attention could easily be given to workers who appear to be developing anxieties about their performance and their futures. By constructing individual job profiles and offering personalized encouragement in counseling sessions, feelings of inadequacy might be eliminated long before they reached the point of being harmful. It would no doubt help some merely to know that many older workers possess skills in which management places a premium (Stagner, 1971). Adequate adjustment to the retirement role would also be facilitated by preretirement programs sponsored by business or social service agencies. The planning aspects of such programs could aid in alerting workers to potential problems that they will encounter in retirement. Seminars or discussion groups with others approaching retirement not only serve to prepare the workers for the new role, but counseling programs may enable them to retain or transfer jobs. Formal preretirement programs have their greatest value as a mechanism for anticipatory socialization, described more fully in Chapter Nine. The present exercises conducted by unions and employers usually deal only with specific issues, including pension and medical benefits, tax advice, insurance, wills and so forth. Only a few are more comprehensive, covering attitudes toward work and retirement, meaningfulness in life, and potential activities and roles of interest to the retiring worker. Some gerontologists have proposed that social service agencies might well adopt preretirement counseling as an important function, since an agency approach would certainly bring a broader range of alternative choices than those provided under union or company aegis (Monk, 1972).

In Western societies occupational prestige has traditionally been associated with the masculine role. It is interpreted as a negative reflection of a man if he loses his job, becomes ill for an extended period or even retires. As previously suggested, feelings of inadequacy, marginality and possible rolelessness may contribute to ill health to an extent not yet understood (Blau, 1973). Requiring individuals to remove themselves from active participation in the labor force when they may view their participation as the sole or at least the primary legitimation of their existence is bound to create psychological, physical and social problems that might fruitfully be addressed either by changing or flexible retirement policies or by insightful social programming. Flexible retirement programs based on ability and desire have several arguments in their favor. First, they would eliminate the age discrimination inherent in compulsory programs. Flexible policies also offer a better opportunity to utilize the experience and abilities of older members of the work force. There is a possibility that further work would raise the amount of income among retired workers, thereby relieving some of the burden from Social Security and pension programs and reducing the number of elderly living at or below poverty levels. Finally, flexible retirement policies would increase morale and satisfaction among those people who want to remain active in the labor force (Palmore, 1972).

Anticipating the Golden Years

The criteria utilized by researchers to ascertain work satisfaction or life adjustment are a mixture of culturally prescribed values reflecting a dominant emphasis on happiness and high morale at the expense of other equally plausible dimensions. In assessing degree of adjustment among any group of people, and particularly among the elderly, one must carefully distinguish between contentment and that behavior the elderly themselves have been socialized to emulate. As Rosow (1967) points out, industrialized societies have replaced other societal forms in which low productivity is accompanied by a high degree of mutual dependence among members. In the transition, many elderly lost control of property, as well as their prior monopoly on *strategic knowledge*. Increasingly, automation contributes to a reduction of the number of low- to midrange jobs, so that older workers must either face an early but unplanned retirement or an extended period of unemployment prior to reaching pensionable age, since they are seldom seen as possessing skills or training that are readily transferable to new jobs. By contrast, higher status workers may find it easier to apply their general skills in replacement jobs. It has also been suggested that workers in higher status occupations routinely deal with abstract concepts; thus, anticipating the future in retirement may come more easily to them (Simpson, Back and McKinney, 1966). There has been some research focusing on the relationship between status at work and status within the community. Middle status workers occupy the most ambiguous work and community positions and, as a result, often exhibit the greatest amount of uncertainty about retirement. There are also some differences by sex in the attitudes of persons approaching retirement age. The results of a recent study indicate most middle status individuals do not fear lack of income so much as boredom following their retirement. The men in the sample had a more positive attitude toward their life attainments than did women. Interestingly, the desire to leave a mark was important to a quarter of the men, but to none of the women. It is probable that extensive self-appraisals take place for women after children leave home, but for men await the years immediately prior to retirement (Thurnher, 1974).

It may be at this stage of self-evaluation that individuals attempt to balance their perceived attainments with their value orientations. In doing so, they may successfully incorporate any achievements made by their generation into their self-evaluations. By comparing themselves to and appropriating the successes of their peers, they may be able to reduce their anxiety or depression about their own achievements (Thomas, 1970). As will be discussed in more detail in the next chapter, adjustment to retirement may be influenced by positive self-esteem or it may be linked with the relation of retirement activities to preretirement occupation. For some individuals, adjustment to retirement is eased by a continuation of those activities that utilize preretirement occupational skills. For others, focusing on similar skills and activities may rob the retirement years of their intrinsic reward. It is becoming apparent, however, that as life expectancy has increased, and since the technological revolution seems unlikely to slow its pace, one career throughout life, selected at age 22 or so, is an unreasonable expectation for many individuals. It seems at least as efficient and productive to integrate school and work throughout a person's lifetime, enabling midlife career changes and revamped expectations of productivity among older workers. This does not mean that all or even a majority of workers would change jobs or occupations, only that the potential would exist for those who wished to take advantage of it. Similarly, to facilitate adjustment to retirement, variations of the five day, 50 week work year have been proposed. In addition to four day work weeks and longer vacation periods, a work *sabbatical* has been designed for United Steel workers. With every five years of service the worker is entitled to a three month vacation intended to provide time for rest and relaxation. Such a program not only implicitly advocates retraining and relaxation but serves to anticipate the unstructured free time that comes with retirement (Clague, 1971).

A few studies have found that the positive preretirement attitudes toward impending retirement shift toward more negative feelings later. Hindsight is always 20-20; to wit, a significant number of individuals are able to appreciate their own unpreparedness for retirement only after the fact. Of course these results differ by employment status, as well as the nature of the research design. Monk (1971) found in his analyses of professional men in their fifties that their attitudes toward planning for retirement indicated a low valuation of preretirement programs; the participants felt planning was in fact nearly worthless. Their rationales for not taking advantage of counseling programs included beliefs that they would not live long enough to have to worry about it, that rampant inflation effectively negated any possible savings for a comfortable retirement or that retirement was contrary to their personal objectives of remaining actively involved in life until death. As would be expected, however, the weight of the evidence does not bolster their rather naïve perspectives. In the large scale Cornell study of workers approaching retirement, the investigators consistently observed that expectations before retirement were more negative than the subsequent evaluations of retirement (Streib and Schneider, 1971). Further support is lent by the three nation study carried out by Shanas and her associates (1968). American white collar and blue collar workers generally seem to enjoy retirement, with only three of every ten retired workers saying they found little or nothing to enjoy about retirement. Ironically, among retired agricultural workers, traditionally seen in an idealized light, this figure increases to approximately half.

Summary

The experience of older members of the work force is influenced by career patterns and occupational status. Workers who have unstable careers and fill lower status jobs are those most likely to be affected adversely by economic fluctuations. Once unemployed, older workers face tremendous challenges in their attempts to reenter the labor market, even after occupational retraining. Myths proliferate regarding the declining capacities and inefficiency of aging employees, coupled with the costliness of occupational transfer programs. These myths, however, are not supported by research data. In fact, the older person has many valuable skills and traits that could easily be recognized and utilized by personnel managers. Adjustment to retirement is associated with occupational background, willingness to retire and financial security. It is true that many people keenly feel the loss of their work role, yet many others view retirement with favor or equanimity. Flexible retirement programs operated on a trial basis may well provide needed information about morale and life satisfaction when workers are allowed to continue working so long as they desire and are able.

Although many caveats should be noted, it is clear that both advanced industrialized countries and those like Japan that have only recently undergone rapid industrialization will continue to experience similar pressures operating to restructure their work forces. Around the world there are trends to establish increasingly more formalized retirement ages in times of economic strain and governmental incentives to keep older workers employed when economic surfeits cause labor shortages. Generally speaking, in the course of the twentieth century, overall participation in the labor force by the older worker of either sex has steadily declined. The sole exception is seen in the case of middle-aged women, who have significantly expanded their participation over the last two decades. The move toward standardization of compulsory retirement policies plus longer life expectancy creates many potential problems that have not yet been addressed by any integrated, concerted programming. As retirement preparation courses become more widespread and as gerontologists acquire better information, the patterns of previous generations of retiring workers should be changed.

Finally, it is difficult to accurately predict the course for Third World countries just embarking on the industrial road. Their traditional organization and cultural values differ to a great extent from those of the Western world; whether these values will come to reflect technological strategies adopted from Western countries remains yet a mystery. Perhaps Japan provides us with a glimpse of probable value conflicts arising from industrial expansion and technological innovation. Over and above our slight predictive ability, we are presently confronted with major obstacles in planning for economic change, labor force participation and the problems of retirement. To increase our understanding we must turn our attention directly to the benefits and ills attendant with the retirement process and possible alternatives for future change.

Pertinent Readings

BERNSTEIN, M.C. "Forecast of Women's Retirement Income: Cloudy and Colder; 25 Percent Chance of Poverty." *Industrial Gerontology* 1, 2 (1974): 1–13.

BLAU, Z.S. *Old Age in a Changing Society*. New York: New Viewpoints, 1973.

CLAGUE, E. "Work and Leisure for Older Workers." *The Gerontologist* 11, 1, pt. II (1971): 9–20.

DAVIDSON, P.E., and H.D. ANDERSON. *Occupational Mobility in an American Community*. Stanford, Calif.: Stanford University Press, 1937.

DYER, L.D. "Implications of Job Displacement at Mid-Career." *Industrial Gerontology* XVII (1973): 38–46.

Economic Report of the President. Washington, D.C.: Government Printing Office, 1973.

ENGELEN-KEFER, U. "Managing the Older Worker Out of the Labor Market: The West German Experience." *Industrial Gerontology* XVI (1973): 37–50.

FISHER, P. "Major Social Security Issues: Japan, 1972." *Social Security Bulletin* XXXVI, 3 (1973): 26–38.

GRANEY, M.J., and E.E. GRANEY. "Scaling Adjustment in Older People." *Aging and Human Development* IV, 4 (1973): 351–53.

GRUNEWALD, R.J. "The Age Discrimination in Employment Act of 1967." *Industrial Gerontology* XV (Fall 1972): 1–11.

GUSFIELD, J.R. "Occupational Roles and Forms of Enterprise." *American Journal of Sociology* LXVI (1961): 571–80.

HENEMAN, H.G., III. "The Relationship Between Age and Motivation to Perform on the Job." *Industrial Gerontology* XVI (1973): 30–36.

HOSKINS, D., and L.E. BIXBY. *Women and Social Security: Law and Policy in Five Countries*. U.S. Department of Health, Education and Welfare, Social Security Administration, Research Report no. 42. Washington, D.C.: U.S. Government Printing Office, 1973.

JACOBSON, D. "Willingness to Retire in Relation to Job Strain and Type of Work." *Industrial Gerontology* XIII (1972): 65–74.

KREPS, J.M. "The Allocation of Leisure to Retirement." In *Technology, Human Values and Leisure*, eds. M. KAPLAN and P. BOSSERMAN, 239–44. Nashville: Abingdon Press, 1971a.

KREPS, J.M., ed. *Employment, Income, and Retirement Problems of the Aged*. Durham, N.C.: Duke University Press, 1963.

_____ . *Sex in the Marketplace: American Women at Work*. Baltimore: Johns Hopkins Press, 1971b.

LAUFER, A.C., and W.M. FOWLER, Jr. "Work Potential of the Aged." *Personnel Administration* XXXIV (1971): 20–25.

MILLER, D.C., and W.H. FORM. *Industrial Sociology*. New York: Harper and Brothers, 1951.

MONK, A. "Factors in the Preparation for Retirement by Middle-aged Adults." *The Gerontologist* XI, 4 (1971): 348–51.

_____ . "A Social Policy Framework for Pre-retirement Planning." *Industrial Gerontology* XV (Fall 1972): 63–70.

OSIPOW, S.H. *Theories of Career Development*. New York: Appleton-Century-Crofts, 1968.

OSTERBIND, C.C., ed. *New Careers for Older People*. Gainesville: University of Florida Press, 1971.

PALMORE, E. "Compulsory versus Flexible Retirement: Issues and Facts." *Gerontologist* XII, 4 (1972): 343–48.

_____ . "The Status and Integration of the Aged in Japanese Society." *Journal of Gerontology* XXX, 2 (1975): 199–208.

POWERS, E.A., and GOUDY, W.J. "Examination of the Meaning of Work to Older Workers." *Aging and Human Development* II, 1 (1971): 38–45.

REICH, C. "The New Property." *Yale Law Journal* LXXIII, 5 (1964): 733–41.

ROSE, C.L., and J.M. MOGEY. "Aging and Preference for Later Retirement." *Aging and Human Development* III, 1 (1972): 45–62.

ROSENBERG, G.S. *The Worker Grows Old: Poverty and Isolation in the City*. San Francisco: Jossey-Bass, 1970.

ROSOW, I. *Social Integration of the Aged*. New York: The Free Press, 1967.

SHANAS, E., et al. *Old People in Three Industrial Societies*. New York: Atherton Press, 1968.

SHEPPARD, H.L. *New Perspectives on Older Workers*. Kalamazoo, Mich.: W.E. Upjohn Institute for Employment Research, 1971.

SHEPPARD, H.L., and N.Q. HERRICK, eds. *Where Have All the Robots Gone? Worker Dissatisfaction in the '70s*. New York: The Free Press, 1972.

SHERMAN, S.R. "Assets on the Threshold of Retirement." *Social Security Bulletin* XXXVI, 7 (1973): 3–17.

SIMPSON, I.H., K.W. BACK and J.C. McKINNEY. "Work and Retirement." In *Social Aspects of Aging*, eds. I.H. SIMPSON and J.C. McKINNEY, 45–54. Durham, N.C.: Duke University Press, 1966.

SLATER, R. "Age Discrimination in Great Britain." *Industrial Gerontology* XV (Fall 1972): 12–19.

STAGNER, R. "An Industrial Psychologist Looks at Industrial Gerontology." *Aging and Human Development* II, 1 (1971): 29–37.

STEWART, C.D. "The Older Worker in Japan: Realities and Possibilities." *Industrial Gerontology* 1, 1 (1974): 60–76.

STEZHENSKAYA, E.I., and N.N. SACHUK. "Demographic Shifts in Modern Society and Labour Activities of the Elderly Population." In *Main Problems of Soviet Gerontology*, ed. D.F. CHEBOTAREV, 240–51. Kiev: International Congress of Gerontologists, 1972.

STREIB, G.F., and C.J. SCHNEIDER. *Retirement in American Society: Impact and Process*. Ithaca, N.Y.: Cornell University Press, 1971.

SUPER, D.E. *The Psychology of Careers*. New York: Harper and Row, 1957.

THOMAS, H. "Theory of Aging and Cognitive Theory of Personality." *Human Development* XIII (1970): 1–16.

THURNHER, M. "Goals, Values, and Life Evaluations at the Pre-Retirement Stage." *Journal of Gerontology* XXIX, 1 (1974): 85–96.

UNITED STATES DEPARTMENT OF LABOR, Women's Bureau. *Women Workers Today*. Washington, D.C.: Government Printing Office, 1974.

WILENSKY, H.L. "Orderly Careers and Social Participation." *American Sociological Review* XXVI, 4 (1961): 521–39.

Chapter 9

Dilemmas of Retirement

Do we yet know what retirement means? We think we know, but what can be made of the following examples? Clearly, an individual who does not presently work for pay and receives retirement benefits from Social Security or another pension program is retired. How do we classify this same person if he or she returns to work next week? Does it make a difference if the work is only part-time as opposed to full-time? Is a person retired if he or she has not worked for a full year prior to the time of an interview? What if one is unemployed but cannot now claim retirement benefits? Should an individual who was forced out of a lifelong job at age 65, was unwilling to leave and is currently seeking full-time employment be classified as retired? These are anything but easy questions; the answers proposed will vary depending on the criteria by which retirement is defined. We usually decide that someone is retired if he or she is not working full time and derives at least the largest portion of his or her financial support from public or private pension payments. But this is not a universally accepted definition by any means. One alternative strategy suggested to resolve the dilemma inherent in such blanket definitions is to calculate retirement rates based on the number of weeks worked during the previous year (Palmore, 1971). Retirement could then be evaluated as a matter of degree — more or less — rather than as a simple dichotomy.

In the sense that currently applies, retirement is a relatively recent phenomenon. Prior to the stabilization of modern industrialism, people only left the labor force when age or ill health precluded their continued work activity. It was the rarest of instances when the older workers of the last century or before were able to accumulate even a modest nestegg, and there certainly were no widespread social security schemes to assure them a steady income. It is possible to approach the topic of retirement today in a variety of ways. It would be legitimate to focus on it in terms of its societal dimensions: how many people are nearing retirement age, how many are already there and drawing pension benefits of one kind or another, what financial pictures are painted for both the present generation of retired workers and future generations. In addition to these and similar questions, retirement can be looked at from the standpoint of the individual. Although many of the answers will overlap with those for societal level questions, the thrust is slightly different. For the older worker it is just as relevant to analyze retirement as an event, keynoted perhaps by a ceremony of some sort to mark the passage from one status to another. Retirement, though distinct, still represents a continuation of the life cycle, carrying with it many components from earlier years. But at some point retirement implies a new mosaic of roles, complete with their own prescriptions and expectations that are both discontinuous, albeit not always drastically, and vague. Occasionally gerontologists have referred to retirement as a **roleless role** to describe its ambiguities (Shanas, 1972; Burgess, 1960). This is not to say, however, that retired people, or others with whom they interact, do not have some definite ideas about the kinds of behavior and attitudes appropriate to the new role of retirant.

Before reviewing various issues affecting the nature of the retirement experience, it would be well to anticipate certain unavoidable problems. Perhaps foremost, the vast majority of the existing information concerning retirement has only recently become available.

Until the mid-1950s there was relatively little well-founded research despite numerous investigations of the formative and middle stages of the career process. During the last decade, however, analyses of retirement have burgeoned. For the most part these were of the cross-sectional type and, like so many other areas of gerontology, comparisons between different age groups at the same time have been the source of generalizations about how people respond to retirement. Now the results of a few longitudinal investigations are greatly enhancing what is known, offering replacements for many earlier notions. Implicit in the study of retirement and predictions of future patterns are two related variables that merit close attention. First is the question of the centrality of work. We usually assume that it is the most important part of a person's life, but this becomes less likely to be the case for all people in advanced industrialized societies. Second is the contention that retirement presents a dramatic disjuncture in the life cycle, bringing with it a host of deleterious changes. On both counts we may find that retirement does not live up to stereotypic misconceptions.

Embarking on Retirement

Traditional Retirement and Economic Pressures

Legal retirement age was set at 65 in the United States with the enactment of the Social Security legislation in 1935. As was pointed out in Chapter Seven, though, the United States was neither the first to develop health care provisions, nor was its Social Security program ahead of the times. In 1889 Germany under Bismarck established the first large scale program, modeled after a Danish idea, and two decades later England implemented a similar system after Lloyd George and Churchill overcame rather considerable opposition. Initiated as a federal policy for government employees, mandatory retirement soon spread throughout the industrialized sector to affect the hourly and, ultimately, the salaried spheres. In advocating workers' benefits, unions have come to support early retirement programs, not only to provide older workers with a chance for a relaxed life of leisure, but to maximize job opportunities for younger members (Clague et al., 1971). As a consequence, older workers feel the pressure to retire from younger colleagues, unions and management alike. What impact are these trends having? To date no precise answers have emerged; increasingly, though, the evidence indicates many workers will take advantage of early retirement programs only if they are assured an adequate income (Barfield and Morgan, 1969).

Recent experience with older workers who have lost jobs through automation or economic cutbacks reveals many are quite willing to change jobs or even careers in order to remain employed (Dyer, 1973). In order to assess the need for flexible careers, it is necessary to distinguish between jobs and careers. Jobs are specific work positions with related duties, responsibilities and income. An individual may keep the same job throughout his or her work life, yet change employers repeatedly; for instance, a mechanic, teacher or engineer who retains the same duties despite working for different employers. Conversely, an individual might work for the same employer for many years and change jobs as he or she ascends the hierarchy of the particular company. Added to the idea of job change is the notion of a career; the examples in Chapter Eight of an individual progressing from the role of lawyer to banker, teacher to social worker or athlete to small business entrepreneur might be used to illustrate the concept of a career. These considerations, plus internal or external pressures and the availability of job and career opportunities, must enter into any examination of career changes among workers (Murray, Powers and Havighurst, 1971).

The idea of career and retirement flexibility has grown in importance over the past few years because of the character of industrialized employment. Lower status jobs are continually being abolished by automation, while many clerical positions have expanded. Modern technology enables a country to use less human energy in the process of creating more economic surplus, and, in turn, the larger the surplus, the greater the potential for supporting sizeable numbers of nonproductive people. In addition, the health and medical improvements during this century have contributed to longer lives, so that the period of retirement is now averaging as long as 10 to 15 years. It is entirely possible, however, that the advantages of mandatory retirement as far as the industrial sector is concerned may be outweighed by the disadvantages incurred in the personal and social spheres of life. The same values that loudly decry economic waste often seem blissfully ignorant of the ramifications of psychic waste. Tired of seeing older workers dissatisfied and their collective experience underutilized, the idea of flexible retirement has become a rallying point for all those who chose to emphasize human potential and life alternatives as being as crucial as economic growth. Caution must remain the watchword, since the amount of psychological cost levied against those who could no longer explain their retirement as the result of an inflexible system has yet to be determined.

It is entirely feasible that workers in most industrialized countries could retire as early as age 50 or 55 by the 1980s without sacrificing productivity (Kreps, 1970). The unemployment rate over the next few years will probably have more significance than overall productivity however. As unemployment increases, so does the number of applicants for existing jobs; consequently, more pressure is exerted on the extremes of the age continuum to delay their entry or hasten their exit from the labor market. National Social Security regulations have a way of responding to economic pressures, as represented by the three year reduction in the earliest pensionable age for men in the United States in 1961. This change occurred after a period of recession during which unemployment rates averaged 6 percent, up from the 3 percent observed in the early years of the 1950s. Economic growth in America after the middle sixties saw unemployment again drop to between 3 and 4 percent, but the cycle has come full circle and the boom has been succeeded by economic crises and unparalleled expansion in the ranks of the unemployed. One possible outcome will be to place renewed emphasis on expanding flexible and early retirement programs or a general reduction in the mandatory retirement age (Jaffe, 1972).

The Retirement Decision

A wide range of factors influence an individual's decision to retire. Financial adequacy is obviously one of the primary concerns of all over 55 who are contemplating retirement. Health status is usually another. An important issue, and one that may be related to the previous two, is whether or not there are mandatory or flexible retirement policies that are applicable to the person considering retirement. Often workers who are self-employed or occupy upper status professional positions are exempt from the formalized retirement policies prevalent in most other industrial and white collar salaried positions. An additional aspect already mentioned is the availability of jobs for older applicants; when demand is running ahead of the supply of workers, retirement policies are more flexible. Finally, the attitude of significant others may affect a person's decision to retire; these attitudes will undoubtedly shape the worker's reactions to impending retirement.

Retirement Income

One of the most fundamental problems to be faced is the adequacy of retirement income, which may be approached from several perspectives. On the one hand, both state and national governments routinely calculate the minimum income necessary for subsistence survival. This figure provides a useful standard against which retirement income can be judged. On the other hand, individuals make personal evaluations of their own financial situations. A retired person might have income in excess of the administratively determined minimum, yet still feel that he or she is impoverished. The fact that recent surveys of American workers revealed income to be of basic concern to those nearing retirement partially demonstrates the importance of financial security to a sense of personal autonomy and independence. Their concern may also reflect a realistic assessment of the amount of income necessary for a comfortable life in comparison to the amount likely to be available from retirement benefits. The extent of retirement benefits assumes an even greater role among those thinking about early retirement. One survey of automobile workers who retired between ages 60 and 65 revealed that fully 50 percent felt the most influential factor in their decision to retire early was the anticipated level of retirement income (Pollman, 1971). An earlier study found retirement income to be of major importance in the retirement orientation for only the semiskilled portion of the sample; skilled and white collar workers apparently felt their retirement income would be adequate (Simpson, Back and McKinney, 1966b). In contrast, the Cornell longitudinal study of 2000 Americans discovered little relationship between income level and retirement or between subjective evaluation of preretirement income adequacy and the decision to retire (Streib and Schneider, 1971). Of more interest, however, is that while nearly 80 percent of the Cornell sample felt their preretirement income was at least sufficient, nearly as many voiced no complaints with their actual retirement income, though the latter averaged only half of what was earned before retiring. The incongruity may result from the fact that the respondents had been retired for less than five years and financial disadvantage is probably magnified over time as purchasing power relative to the rest of the population declines (Streib and Schneider, 1971; Kreps, 1970).

Despite a radical decrease in income after retirement that leaves one in every five American retirants with incomes less than the current federally established minimums, very few attempt to claim the public assistance benefits for which they qualify. Only a little over 10 percent of those receiving Social Security payments also obtain public assistance benefits — that is, state and federally administered Supplemental Security Income payments — although government estimates suggest 66 percent of those receiving only Social Security payments are attempting to live on incomes less than the minimum set by the federal government (Atchley, 1976; U.S. DHEW, 1975a). A similar pattern emerges in England, where government sources estimate that 10 percent of the elderly British are entitled to Supplemental Benefit pensions but are not claiming them. Furthermore, about half of Britain's pensioners live at or below the governmentally determined poverty level, a figure not out of line with the United States (Wedderburn, 1973). The failure to claim benefits may arise from an ignorance of their availability, but it may also stem from a sense of pride. Many people in their sixties or seventies hold strongly to an ethic of individual responsibility and view governmental assistance programs, and sometimes even Social Security payments, as charity that their self-respect prevents them from accepting (Withers, 1974; U.S. Senate, 1973b). Those who willingly accept Social Security benefits may perceive them as a right, not a privilege, earned by years of hard work and personal contribution. A new proviso of the general Social Security program, intended to furnish retired people with sufficient income to meet minimum subsistence levels, must be noted here, though detailed discussion is deferred until later in this chapter. Like earlier public assistance programs, the benefit rate is determined by family responsibilities and financial resources. Unlike the Social Security criteria, Supplemental Security Income (SSI) payments are not determined by an individual's prior earnings, except to the degree that qualification for SSI indicates the individual does not have adequate income due to either a lack of or minimal Social Security benefit levels. Thus, a person who has not worked for ten years in jobs covered by Social Security will not be entirely destitute in his or her later years with the institution of supplemental benefits. It will be of interest to discover the overall reception given this new program, which has overtones of a "welfare" program.

We might expect older workers to more readily accept benefits as time goes on. For those who entered the labor market after 1940 or so, Social Security was an established, ongoing program. The clearly identified, fully anticipated, yet compulsory withholding from their paychecks should facilitate the interpretation of benefit payments as a right. Coupled with an apparent willingness for early retirement among a large portion of the population, the next few decades will witness an extension of the period during which benefits must be paid to retired workers. There is an inherent misconception in the system, however, as it was not established as the sole source of support after retirement; nonetheless, nearly three-quarters of the retired workers in the United States have no other financial resources aside from their Social Security. Even with minor cost of living increases made in the past few years, the amount paid is often insufficient to meet the growing needs of the majority. When economic recession and deficit spending is balanced by major cutbacks in federal spending, it bodes ill for future benefit increments necessary to keep pace with the rising inflation that has occurred during the 1970s in all industrial nations. In effect, we have further removed control of individuals' lives from themselves to the domain of the public interest; retired workers become dependent for their rights on community determinations of the general good. Overall, it is fair to say that the picture for retirement income in the near future is gray to grim (Atchley, 1976; Bernstein, 1974). It is an accepted fact that reductions in income after retirement in nearly all industrialized countries paralleled the 50 percent figure cited for the United States at least, accordingly, older people are often forced to go without many of the goods and services the rest of the population deems essential.

Pension Programs in Selected Countries

Almost all retired people must adjust to some decline in income, at times to the extent that they become impoverished. While the difference between preretirement and retirement income is indeed large, governments themselves are caught in a quandary of rising costs versus increased benefits. Emerging most clearly in this discussion of retirement plans in various countries are the widely divergent philosophies — some countries, such as Sweden or the United Kingdom, expend vastly more per capita on health and welfare than do most other industrial countries. As described below, American and British systems impose an **earnings test** whereby actual retirement benefits are depreciated by the amount of earned income that the retirant receives. In Britain the test is removed at age 70, but in the United States it remains in effect until age 72. Elsewhere the philosophy is that retirants are entitled to their pensions regardless of any income they may generate; for example, in France, Germany, Canada and Sweden public pension benefits are not reduced in spite of any extra income earned during retirement. Perhaps as a manifestation of their continuing productive growth, Britain, France, Sweden and the Soviet Union provide incentives to older workers who agree to postpone retirement.

Retirement in Britain and France

Older workers in Britain have been able to look forward to a coordinated government-sponsored social security scheme only since 1948. Today approximately 4.5 percent of the national budget is earmarked for pensions or supplemental income benefits over and above that allotted for health insurance. There are three basic plans from which workers of pensionable age, fixed at 65 for men and 60 for women, may draw benefits. The basic National Pension is a flat rate contributory plan covering four-fifths of all former workers. All working residents are eligible for the basic pension, although participation is not mandatory for working but married women, self-employed persons or low income workers making less than $624 annually. During the 1960s, average yearly benefits amounted to $561 for single pensioners and $912 for retired couples respectively, a figure one-third the average family income at the time. The outdistancing of the amount of available trust funds by the number of eligible pensioners created sufficient pressure on Parliament to initiate a new plan. In 1961 a graduated pension plan was instituted to operate in conjunction with the basic National Pension. As of 1972, those workers earning between $21.60 and $79.20 per week must contribute additional graduated withholdings into this second pension program. Thus a worker earning $24 a week paid $1.94 to the pension fund, one earning $72 or more, $4.08. Under this system employers contribute 6.75 percent of their total payroll to the pension fund and governmental subsidies cover the remaining costs. The pensioner's average life earnings are the basis for calculating benefit levels, though after 1972 adjustments are made to incorporate changes in average per capita earnings. Finally, private pension plans in operation in 1975 covered half of the British workers.

Public pension plans apply an earnings test to ascertain benefits for pensioners who have income above a specified amount. In 1970 pensions were reduced for earnings in excess of $14 per week by the amount of additional earnings. Yet earnings for men over age 70 and women age 65 are exempted from any earnings test. Private pensions, on the other hand, have never prohibited pensioners from earning whatever they can. Somewhat paradoxically, there is slight inducement in Britain for workers not to retire at the usual pension age. Men and women who continue working past ages 65 and 60 respectively are eligible for increments to their basic pension for a period of five years determined by the number of weeks retirement is deferred. For various reasons, a number of older workers either do not qualify for basic pensions or do not meet minimum income standards. Accordingly, another program was introduced in 1966 to provide more adequate benefits. Funds for the Supplementary Benefits program are noncontributory, with payments established on the basis of individual requirements calculated from resources, local need scales and the test of essential items. Nearly one-quarter of the elderly are receiving these supplemental pensions, with an additional 10 percent eligible but not claiming the benefits. In spite of the augmented payments, elderly British citizens have a standard of living far below the rest of the population, and almost half live on incomes below contemporary poverty levels. Pensions, including supplemental benefits, only provide from one-fourth to one-half of the weekly income of currently employed older workers (Wedderburn, 1973). On the basis of even this scanty review of pensions among the elderly it is not difficult to understand why both the Labour and Conservative parties in Britain find it incumbent to lobby for new retirement programs on behalf of older constituents. In fact, in mid-1975 the earnings-related pension was suspended and the flat rate National Pension scheme bolstered pending the implementation of a new program (U.S. DHEW, 1975b).

In France the general social security system began in 1930 and presently covers nearly 80 percent of the working population. The fund is financed by employer and employee contributions at a ratio of 2.5 to 1 and anyone who has contributed for 15 years may collect benefits upon reaching age 60. As in Britain, there is a strong incentive for deferring retirement until age 65; for each additional year spent in the labor force pension benefits are increased by 4 percent. To be fully insured a worker must have paid in for 30 years; retirement allowances then amount to 40 percent of average earnings over the decade preceding retirement. Pensions for workers with less than 30 but more than 15 years' coverage are proportionate to the number of years that they have been insured. Other reductions of up to one-half are made for those who elect to retire at age 60. In 1971 French labor unions staged massive demonstrations to press for earlier retirement allowances, permitting workers who are fully insured prior to age 60 to retire at the maximum rate without sacrificing their pensions. The national government has been hesitant about promoting accommodations that allow for early retirement, however, as nearly 50 percent of all wage earners would then be eligible for full benefits before age 65. Granting workers the option of early retirement would not only increase the economic burden borne by the national government, but also create potentially detrimental labor shortages. To counteract union demands, governmental policies were redesigned so that unemployed workers over age 60 may obtain an unreduced retirement if they are unable to secure jobs. Future plans call for increasing the tax base to 50 percent of a worker's salary to offset spiraling prices and the dissatisfaction that has been voiced by labor.

The past 15 years in France have also witnessed a major expansion of supplementary pension programs. These provisions protect many workers in the private sector and parallel the general social security scheme in several respects. Benefit levels are calculated on the basis of a worker's salary, the amount of his or her contribution and the length of covered employment. While the supplemental plans do not guarantee minimum compensation, as in the general program, workers are still encouraged to postpone claiming a stipend until age 65; otherwise, payments under the supplemental arrangement are also reduced for each year earlier payments are made. Unlike British social security, neither program in France utilizes an earnings test. Thus, a worker may seek reemployment following retirement without relinquishing any pension benefits, although the earnings are still subject to withholdings. A final benefit scheme similar to the American Supplemental Security Income program exists for French citizens who have not contributed to pension programs for a minimum of 15 years. The payments such workers receive are not technically pensions, yet they are unobtainable before age 65 in order to discourage their becoming an avenue for early exit from the labor market. Only about one in ten older people draws from the assitance funds, and nearly 80 percent of those who do are women who have had sporadic work histories or are not otherwise eligible for pensions (Morisot, 1970).

Retirement Programs in Other Countries

Germany inaugurated one of the first social security programs in 1889. Pension insurance in West Germany is now universal and is based on a 17 percent contribution rate divided equally between employers and employees. Government subsidies average one-fifth to one-third of the total pension fund expenditures, differing among the three general schemes available. The three, the Manual Workers Pensions Insurance, Nonmanual Workers Pensions Insurance and Miners' Special Scheme Pensions Insurance, cover over four-fifths of the working population. The remainder are self-employed persons who participate in a wide variety of private retirement programs, a few of which overlap with the national compulsory insurance. Since 1973, working men can obtain retirement income at age 63 after 180 months of contribution, although flexible retirement is allowed between 63 and 67. Exceptions to this requirement are made if a worker over age 60 has been unemployed for a full year or if at age 60 a worker with 20 years of coverage elects to receive partial pension payments. Depending upon work experience and individual circumstances, pensions are also available at age 60 to women and the disabled. Pension benefits are calculated from a complex formula that is based on a worker's earnings history and the length and extent of his or her contribution adjusted in terms of the average annual income of all wage and salary workers for the three years prior to the individual's retirement. The purpose of the adjustment is to attempt to maintain benefits at parity in terms of an adequate standard of living regardless of postretirement earnings. The Social Aid plan is a public assistance program designed for support of indigent elderly Germans that is somewhat akin to the British and French alternatives available to elderly people not otherwise eligible for public pensions or with income inadequate to provide subsistence living (Schewe et al., 1970).

Sweden offers yet another example of a universal pension system largely supported by governmental subsidies. Somewhat reminiscent of the British scheme, Swedish workers can qualify for basic and supplemental pensions. Basic pensions received by all Swedish citizens are funded by a surtax on the progressive income tax in conjunction with governmental allotments that comprise nearly 75 percent of the total cost. All recipients irrespective of their actual financial situations claim the same basic pension. In addition, all employed people earning in excess of 6000 crowns annually are eligible for a supplemental pension, which is wage-related. The supplemental system is funded from a 10 percent payroll tax assessed employers by the government. While the usual age for obtaining any retirement payments is 67, a worker may apply as early as age 63. Both the basic and supplemental pensions are reduced for early applicants, depending upon the individual's age. Work incentive exists for those people who defer application until age 70 with increments adjusted for the length of deferment. Under no circumstances is the amount of pension income reduced by subsequent earnings (OECD, 1970).

Japan provides a good example of a non-Western country that has developed an inclusive pension system while in the process of becoming an industrial giant. The Japanese public pension program was one of the earliest Asian social security systems, initiated in 1922. Recent legislative change has affected both of the two major schemes to such an extent that retirement benefits doubled in 1973 alone. These two plans, covering all Japanese workers, have disparate benefits, schedules and philosophies. The Employee's Pension Plan relies on contributions by employers, employees and the national government. The second plan, the National Employment Insurance, is a contributory system designed for the self-employed as well as for those who do not fit into any other category and whose income falls below a certain minimal standard. In the latter case, employee contributions are dispensed with. Workers qualify for either public program at ages 60 and 55 depending on sex. Difficulties arise, however, in the private sector of the economy, where industry has set retirement age at 55. While employees receive a lump sum retirement allowance based on their term of employment, this is inadequate to maintain an average standard of living until public pensions are secured five years later. To remedy this inequitable pattern, the Japanese government now offers subsidies to industry or businesses that raise their retirement age to 60. Monthly pension rates in 1971 under the less generous National Employment plan amounted to $22 for a 65 year old worker who had contributed for 25 years. Because these allotments replace only 5 to 25 percent of previous earnings, the 1973 reforms doubled the benefit rates across the board. Contradictory standards remain in force, nevertheless, as an earnings test diminishes pensions by 20 to 100 percent between ages 60 and 65, though no test is imposed thereafter (Stewart, 1974).

Social Security in the United States

As part of their presidential campaign during the early years of the Depression, the Democrats had as one of their party planks a proposal to institute an old age security program. Three years after the election, a compromise legislative program hammered out in a series of stormy committee meetings finally became law with the establishment of the Social Security Administration. Since 1935 the program has undergone innumerable modifications, yet the basic philosophy remains much as it started. Originally its coverage included only a few categories of employees, but with expansion over the years nearly nine out of ten workers are in covered occupations today. Proponents of the Social Security system are quick to point out that it does not discriminate on the basis of actuarial tables, sex, health status and so forth in providing insurance for unforeseen disabilities and old age. Social Security is not precisely a form of insurance, however, since withholdings are not actually put into trust for later use by the original contributor. Instead, faced with staggering deficits, the program is forced to pay benefits to those presently retired from both the reserve funds and monies currently being collected. As of 1973, the Social Security Administration had only enough in its irrevocable trust account to pay the benefits called for in a normal ten month period (U.S. Senate, 1973b). By 1980 the fund is predicted to fall to less than $24 billion unless drastic revisions are instituted.

Monthly Social Security payments are scaled according to a worker's average earnings computed over the past 10 or 20 years. The base salary upon which employees and employers make matching contributions has steadily risen, up from $3000 in 1950 to $15,300 in 1976, with an increase to $16,500 in 1977. Chances are that further adjustments will be made as more and more operating funds are required to maintain established benefits levels. In 1950 withholdings equaled about 1.5 percent of the stipulated salaries, but this too has given way, reaching a 5.85 percent withholding in 1977, and is likely to become 6.15 percent in 1978. Hypothetically, benefit levels are established to provide a greater relative return for workers in the lower income ranges, but many inequalities prevent an ideal distribution of payments. In 1975 single workers received benefits ranging from a low of $93.80 to a high of $297.60, but as would be expected, the average payment of $164 was far below the maximum. For several years workers have had an option of retiring as early as age 62, but in doing so they must accept lower benefits calculated according to the age at which they retire. Benefits claimed at age 62 are calculated to be 20 percent lower than those received at age 65. Should a worker elect to return to work after retirement, his or her Social Security payments become subject to an earnings test, so that in effect workers are penalized $1 for every $2 they earn in excess of $3000 during 1977, although money earned after age 72 is not subject to the earnings test. The earnings test does not apply to other pension plans and private benefit payments are not included in the earnings schedule.

Unfortunately, quite a number of workers arrive at retirement age only to find they have not worked the requisite 40 quarters in covered occupations or do not otherwise qualify for Social Security. Realizing the hardships imposed upon indigent elderly who are without funds, the Old Age Assistance Act of 1950 (OAA) was enacted to furnish at least a nominal monthly income. Funded out of the federal budget but administered by the states themselves, OAA served as a last resort until it was finally replaced in 1972 by the Supplemental Security Income program. Like Social Security, SSI is not meant to provide total financial support, only subsistence, to the elderly, blind and disabled on the basis of need. Monthly payments of $146 to single persons and $219 for married couples are made where pension income is less than $20 a month and earned income less than $65. If the person has no retirement benefits, exempted earned income increases to a maximum of $85; any income in excess of these amounts will automatically be deducted from the SSI payment. As it is currently operating, the SSI program allows an elderly recipient to retain his or her home and car of reasonable value and resources of $1500 for an individual, $2250 for a couple, and still claim benefits. In 1975 the average SSI payment was $89 with 4.2 million Americans over the age of 65 receiving checks (U.S. DHEW, 1975a).

Only one-fourth of those receiving Social Security also draw payments from private pension programs. For those who do the financial picture in later years is not nearly as bleak as for those with only one source of income, as their total benefits are often double the amount received by recipients of Social Security alone (Reno, 1972). Private pension coverage is extended to a relatively select group of occupations with a large number of workers, favorable unions or responsible management (Graham and Donoian, 1974). The equity of private pension plans is also questionable in light of the absence in over 80 percent of the plans of benefits awardable to the surviving spouse of the pensioner. More often than not, fiscal mismanagement has characterized many private plans in the past few years. Speaking of the problems inherent in private pensions, former Secretary of Labor James Schulz quoted one source as saying:

> In all too many cases, the pension promise shrinks to this: If you remain in good health and stay with the same company until you are 65 years old, and if the company is still in business, and if your department has not been abolished, and if you haven't been laid off for too long a period, and if there is enough money in the fund, and if that money has been prudently managed, you will get a pension. [U.S. Senate, 1973b].

Private pensions are not widespread; currently they are available to only half of the nonfarm employees in the United States. Although the manufacturing sector of the economy employs about one-third of the American workforce, it accounts for over 50 percent of the total private pension plans presently in operation.

Public and private pensions can be contrasted with respect to the amount of previous earnings that they replace. A married man retired with a private pension will collect retirement benefits amounting to 60 to 75 percent of his previous earnings. In comparison, a single man claiming a Social Security pension at age 62 who does not have a private pension will average only 20 to 25 percent of his preretirement income. In general the replacement rate of preretirement income across all income levels for single people is 10 to 20 percent lower than for those who are married. Economists currently estimate that a 75 percent replacement rate is necessary if people are to maintain the standard of living they enjoyed prior to retirement

(Henle, 1972). However, as we noted in Chapter Three, one-fifth of Americans over 65 are impoverished according to governmental guidelines determining adequate income levels. In 1974, single individuals were considered poor if their income was less than $2352; for a couple whose head was over 65 the poverty level was $2958.

A number of criticisms have recently been leveled at the Social Security program. First, the system cannot be realistically expected to insure adequate income for retired Americans. As Figure 9.1 indicates, the amount required to fund the program has increased dramatically, and is far above the expenditures for other areas. It was never intended to be the sole source of financial support, and today averages at best a 50 percent replacement of a worker's previous earnings. Couples of which the wife has never worked outside the home are alloted a dependency allowance. If the husband should die before the wife is 65, she can obtain only half of his benefits; however, if she is widowed after age 65 she is entitled to the full amount. American women who work outside the home are at a particular disadvantage; they are entitled to pensions based on either their own work histories or derived from their husbands', whichever is larger. Once any benefits are claimed on either grounds, there is no possibility of later switching. Critics hold this provision may discourage women from seeking outside employment in the same manner as the earnings test on wages in excess of $3000 punishes those older persons best able or most in need of continuing to work. Since the earnings test is applicable only to wages, not other pensions, interest income or annuities, it effectively discriminates against lower status workers who are least likely to derive income from the latter sources.

Another disconcerting dimension of the system revolves around the payroll tax upon which Social Security is founded. Since 1945 it has risen so rapidly that it has become the largest single tax levied on most individual wage earners, preceded only by income taxes. Although Social Security taxes are intended to yield some of the financial resources necessary during retirement, it seems contradictory to impose so heavy a tax on wage earners at or not far removed from the poverty level. Despite the graduated benefit scale designed to replace a larger share of the earnings of a lower income worker than one in the upper brackets, the payroll tax hits the low to medium income categories appreciably harder than those above them. Workers making in excess of $16,500 might well afford higher taxes, while those below this figure are hard pressed to fulfill their tax obligations as it is. The inequities are also exacerbated by race, as Chapter Thirteen details. At least one observer has proposed that black workers qualify for benefits at earlier ages than whites since the premature mortality of black workers in effect subsidizes white

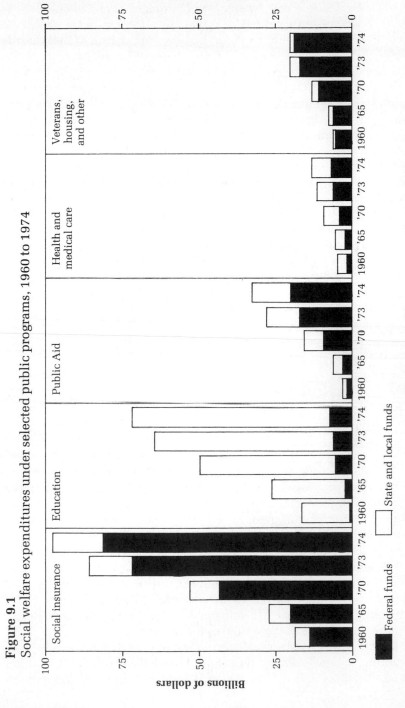

Figure 9.1

Social welfare expenditures under selected public programs, 1960 to 1974

Source: U.S. Bureau of the Census, *Statistical Abstract 1975*, 96th ed. (Washington, D.C.: U.S. Government Printing Office, 1975), p. 276.

retirement benefits (Jackson, 1972). Some view Social Security not as insurance at all, but as a transfer program from those presently working to those presently retired, widowed or disabled. In this light, the wage-earning contributors should be taxed according to their ability to pay. Advocates of reform call for revision of Social Security levies to parallel the theoretical income tax criterion of placing the heaviest burden on those best able to afford it. A form of retirement bonds described in Chapter Fourteen has been created that resembles a mandatory savings program sponsored by the government and administered as an annuity type program where interest-bearing bonds purchased now are redeemable after retirement at a rate above current Social Security benefits. Other reformers have asked for the removal of Social Security payroll withholding, and substituting instead higher income taxes, which would enable the program to be funded out of the general federal revenue (U.S. Senate, 1973b). Critics of the system are taken to task by its proponents on many of the same issues. According to those who have been speaking out in defense of the current method of providing Social Security, the system's strengths lie exactly in the current tax structure of gathering matched compulsory contributions. Former Commissioner of Social Security Robert Ball testified before Senate hearings that the way the program is now operated encourages all workers to appreciate their pension checks as a matter of right, not of charity.

Making the Most of Retirement

Educating for Leisure

During the retirement years, most people find themselves with more time on their hands than their experience or interests can accommodate. As was brought out in Chapter Eight, the amount of time free from the specific demands of the job has and will continue to increase in the coming decades. Unless prepared for the degree of unstructured time attendant with retirement, it is quite possible that older workers released from the pressures of sustaining life will be unable to utilize their retirement as they anticipated during the harried years of work. In fact, instead of overindulging in relaxation and leisure, individuals with more unstructured time than they expected may actually withdraw to a minimum level of participation. Retirement is not automatically a time of leisure any more than days of unemployment can appropriately be called leisure. It is not an easy task to define leisure even by describing what it is not. Leisure is not simply time freed from the demands of a job. Some people may engage in work-related activities, others in pure relaxation, still others in rest. What one person feels are leisure pursuits another may see as worklike. Whatever else can be said about leisure, it is intimately related to the nature of work in modern societies. Herein lies a good bit of the difficulty: Does what we now call leisure retain its same meaning when not integrated into the work cycle?

Adjustment to retirement stems to a significant degree from a worker's prior attitudes toward the event or process. If the individual perceives retirement negatively, fears the loss of work role or friends from the job, or is uncertain for any reason about the future, adjustment may be difficult. In large measure negative attitudes that stem from the lack of knowledge about potential financial, health and psychological problems can be alleviated through preretirement counseling programs. Whether counseling takes the form of lectures or discussion, even minimal exposure has proven to reduce levels of dissatisfaction among participants (Barfield and Morgan, 1969). Facilitating adjustment may result in part from a clarification of the worker's expectations and a sharing of his or her concerns with other participants only to find they too have similar feelings. It often helps just to know that the company, one's supervisors and one's peers recognize the place retirement will have in his or her life. Of course attempts to mold positive attitudes about retirement presuppose that the retiring worker is able to cross a certain financial threshold, thereby avoiding worry over maintaining a sufficient financial cushion. Pre-retirement planning programs go a long way toward identifying alternate roles, activities and strategies that will be rewarding in their own right. While work may not be the dominant source of influence upon self-concept and identity in everyone's life, this does not mean most people do not experience some adjustment problems. Even if the psychological rewards derived from working are not profound, a job is the primary feature lending a structure to life for 40 years. Earlier leisure pursuits may serve as a form of *anticipatory socialization*, preparing the individual to more smoothly accommodate the changes inherent in retiring. Pre-retirement planning sessions may serve a similar function, to a limited degree. When workers are allowed and encouraged to explore alternative roles and activities with others facing the same future, the effect is to facilitate the transition while minimizing any potential stresses.

The most successful transitions to retirement have been found to be strongly related to educational and occupational background. Perhaps a higher level of education enables workers to more easily structure free time, but certainly it fosters the possibility of obtaining further employment after retirement. Likewise, professional or white collar workers may view retirement positively, partially because they have faced a greater degree of control over their life situation; also they are able to anticipate relatively fewer financial constraints. Further, the availability of compatible roles promotes greater access to previous occupational gratifications. A common example is the retired academic who maintains a high level of commitment to occupational and professional activity (Rowe, 1972). This commitment is intimately related to the desire not only to feel useful but to have a purpose in life. Streib and Schneider (1971) report in the Cornell longitudinal study of retirement that satisfaction in retirement is nearly always higher among professionals, or among those workers who manifested a positive preretirement attitude, although more professionals than other workers do continue working. Attributes such as good health, family affection, a stable social environment and definite plans for future activity are also influential in retirement adjustment.

Adapting to Retirement

Analyses of retirement have resulted in a variety of models assumed to lead to successful adjustments. Perhaps the most important implication to be drawn from the fact that no single approach is universally applicable is that individual reaction and adjustment differ to such an extent that one or more models may fit any particular situation. Though the models are intended to be neither theoretically sophisticated, nor mutually exclusive canons, they represent alternative views toward the process of adjustment to the last years of life. It should be borne in mind, however, that many individuals have merely minor problems, having anticipated and accepted retirement (Eisdorfer, 1972).

What may be the earliest model of retirement adjustment emerged from the studies conducted by Friedmann and Havighurst in the early 1950s. Maximum adjustment to retirement was assumed to be characterized by a tendency toward *substitution,* an idea akin to the activity orientation discussed in Chapter Five. It is hypothesized that the loss of the central role in life, in other words the work role, portends the loss of nearly all satisfactions once derived from job-related activities. To adequately adjust to the newly acquired status of retirant, the individual must somehow replace or find substitutes for those satisfactions relinquished along with his job. A major stumbling block with this model has been in the determination of the meaning of and the satisfactions obtained from working. It is becoming more common to find that what retirants miss is the money they had while working, or the friends made on the job, rather than some intrinsic meaning in the work. Another model developed to explain the adjustment process conceives of retirement as a process. Adjustment then becomes dependent on the *accommodation* or adaptation made by the individual to changes in roles, activities and meanings that accompany realization of the imminence of retirement and its continuing unfolding. Since many changes are in most cases inevitable, accommodation occurs throughout life; thus, adjustment to retirement may reflect an ability built up over the years to balance new stimuli (Shanas, 1972).

Some studies have implied that retirement may be an impetus for an emotional or psychological crisis. Accordingly, several strategies for dealing with the disruption of previously familiar relationships are available, though the objective of them all is an attempt to return control over one's life to the individual. If the problems presented by retirement are simply too much and cannot be reconciled by the individual, his or her reaction may take the form of resignation or depression. Still another model describing adaptive patterns focuses on a continuity of environmental factors that serve to *reinforce* appropriate behavior. If the positive reinforcements present during early life and working adulthood are removed by retirement, the likelihood of adjustment is jeopardized. If a worker perceived money to be the most important reward for working, the significant decline in income after retirement will complicate the process of adjustment. If friends or feelings of autonomy were the reinforcing component of work, then retirement may pose markedly fewer problems. Although leisure has been acknowledged as a legitimate reward for workers, leisure during retirement has never been accorded the same value. As leisure becomes more positively defined throughout the life cycle, it may assume the position of one of the primary reinforcers of the retirement years. Finally, a perspective that focuses on an individual's efforts to maintain a consistent emotional state by interacting in such a way as to resolve feelings of *dissonance* may be helpful in addressing whatever discrepancies are created or compounded by retirement. Two distinct elements enter into promoting adjustment through a reduction of dissonance. For a worker who perceives no alternative to retirement despite a strong work ethic, only minor dissonance may be generated if the decision is seen as beyond his or her control. Similarly, a worker dissatisfied with work may welcome the chance to withdraw gracefully, without undue guilt for walking away from a socially valued role. Dissonance arises when retirement presents no positive prospects, or in the event the retirant believes he or she is personally accountable for the decision. In situations similar to the latter examples, adjustment may await a rationalization of retirement and the resolution of defensive attitudes (Eisdorfer, 1972).

The Government's Role in Retirement

A concomitant of urban industrial growth has been a significant diminution in the oral transmission of culture and knowledge, a consequence of which has been to reduce the esteem and respect accorded to the elderly in more primitive societies. At the same time, the nature of valued resources has shifted away from individually held real property to corporate holdings and more ambiguous forms of wealth. Add in the disappearance of productively meaningful roles available to the bulk of the elderly and the last remnants of financial independence are also relinquished. This leaves most of the older people in industrialized societies in a one-sided relationship of economic dependence on their government. How well the nation responds to the challenge, providing needed resources to its elderly, is as good a way as any of evaluating the humanitarian elements of its philosophy.

In many instances, governments around the world have been slow to acknowledge their responsibility for alleviating the social needs of the elderly, even when there is no question of providing medical services or pension programs. In most cases governmental policy toward the elderly does affirm a recognition of the necessity to protect their rights. However, with severe economic woes, programs aimed at furnishing rather basic services often seem to be singled out as expendable. In the United States, a series of small scale projects have operated for the last decade seeking meaningful roles for those elderly who are not content to simply withdraw. The utilization of their skills fulfills social service obligations to other groups. The ACTION program previously administered by the Office of Economic Opportunity, but now an independent citizens service corps, is probably the most familiar example. Clustered under the ACTION umbrella, the Foster Grandparents, Senior Aides and Retired Senior Volunteer Program have all experimented with the retired as service workers involved in social projects. OEO has also provided funds to promote search programs like Medicare Alert or Project FIND to identify and isolate areas where the elderly are particularly in need of assistance. Since the passage of the Older Americans Act (OAA) in 1965, support for government intervention on behalf of older Americans has risen dramatically, from $7.5 million the first year to over $130 million just nine years later. Although the identification of needs and service delivery to the target population has the highest priority, funds have also been allocated for training professional gerontologists and for retraining programs open to lower income workers over age 55.

Despite these invaluable contributions from the federal government, state and local agencies largely responsible for dispersing the money have not always carried through in a comparable manner. Since the mid-1960s federal monies have been available through Social Security legislation which would pay up to three-quarters of the costs of delivering social services to the elderly, if the state would supply the remainder either in cash or in nonmonetary contributions. States could in turn contract with voluntary or private agencies to administer the services, thus avoiding the need to establish expensive state bureaucracies to meet the needs of the elderly. Many states made little use of these matching funds until 1972, when expenditures under welfare titles increased $281 million over the previous fiscal year to reach $777 million. Despite this increase, the percentage spent on privately contracted service delivery barely climbed from 11.1 to 11.3 percent. For a variety of reasons, most state governments were more involved with developing their own bureaucratic networks than in utilizing this federal program to meet a portion of the needs of the elderly, blind or disabled (Gold, 1974).

Other Issues in Retirement

Retirement brings with it several constraints that affect many spheres of life. One of the contributors to the emotional stress experienced by the elderly is the expenditures that continue unabated in the last years of life. It has been pointed out several times that total income decreases by half for most people in retirement, while, with the exception of clothing, all other expenses increase in terms of available money. Of course many people try to save a little for their old age; two-thirds of those approaching retirement have savings, but usually they manage to accumulate very little. Not surprisingly, those who find themselves most in need of financial support are the least prepared for retirement. On the average, less than 60 percent of the elderly on the lower end of the income scale actually have savings they can draw on, and in the case of lower income minority elderly this percentage falls to just over one-fifth (Harris, 1975). Even worse perhaps is the fact that what the disadvantaged are able to save does not really grow in relation to the escalating consumer price index. Regardless of detailed planning, retired people simply do not participate in the increases in actual income experienced by those who are still working. Those who work are the recently retired, yet the elderly represent a wide age range. After age 72, few people are actively involved in the work force or able to supplement their incomes; further, when they were employed, the salaries upon which their Social Security is computed were far below contemporary levels. What money these people do have is spent entirely on subsistence needs; there is seldom room for luxuries.

It is costly to retire these days. An average retired couple will find themselves facing expenses that are 10 percent higher than before retirement. The cost of medical attention is the biggest culprit, amounting to more than three times what younger people pay for health care (Mueller and Gibson, 1975). Food and housing do not exhibit such large increases, but still cost more for older people. Because of consumption patterns that center around restaurant meals and convenience foods bought in small quantities, older people on the average pay 5 percent more for food, not to mention the poorer nutritional quality of what they do eat. Housing and shelter expenses vary more than food, depending upon physical capacity as well as locale. For the retired over age 75, shelter expenditures are nearly 10 percent higher than what the recently retired pay and one-quarter higher than for the preretired. Popular opinion has it that the equity held by most older people in their homes will furnish them a comfortable cushion, but like so many other myths, equity in substandard inner city homes does not usually amount to very much, nor is it easily convertible. About 60 percent of the elderly own their own homes and usually receive a break on their property taxes, but the saving is often consumed by repair bills and maintenance costs. While the exact expenditures differ for other countries, the pattern remains fairly stable. In Britain, for example, medical costs are for all practical purposes nonexistent for older citizens. Nonetheless, they still pay more of their incomes for necessities than do younger families. In 1970 it required over 53 percent of a retirant's financial resources to purchase basic necessities; younger people paid barely 45 percent of their income to buy equivalent goods and services (Wedderburn, 1973). The figures cited for both the United States and Britain are based on intermediate income levels; obviously, the comparisons would be somewhat different for their richer or poorer counterparts. In the case of the latter, medical expenses would remain the single most overwhelming budgetary item.

In view of the strength of popular stereotypes about retirement going hand in hand with ill health, it is worth reiterating the point made originally in Chapter Seven. Until people reach their late sixties or seventies they express little perceived change in their health status. They experience a gradual decline, of course, for the reasons alluded to earlier, but these have little to do with the realities of retirement. Previous research findings of a widespread incidence of poor health preventing postretirement employment now appear to be the result of either an unconscious or an unwilling retreat to the sick role in order to legitimate the status displacement of retirement and absence of either familiar or rewarding social roles. It is just as likely that informal retirement procedures were easily circumvented so that only the people in ill health actually did retire. More reliable studies have found that this is certainly not the case today; not only do a large majority of the retired report at least nominally good health, but there is some evidence to suggest that health status may even improve a bit during the early years of retirement (Streib and Schneider, 1971; Atchley, 1976). Chances are the overall medical profiles on retirants will show an upturn over the next several decades as new generations come to retirement viewing it as a hard-earned, legitimate respite from their work. The same thing applies to the question of mental health. Retirement may exacerbate existing conditions, but there is no evidence to indicate the personality characteristics of a lifetime will suddenly fall by the way after a person retires from the labor force. Stable, passive types will remain that way, just as hostile or aggressive people will maintain their personality patterns, perhaps shifting their targets slightly. Retirement may contribute to the anxiety in a person's life as it promotes a separation from familiar routines; at the same time it may truncate job-related frustrations and lead to a more satisfying life (Lowenthal and Berkman, 1967).

Summary

While retirement may be viewed from the standpoint of either the larger society or the individual, this discussion places a greater emphasis on individual reaction and adaptation as conditioned by societal demands and expectations. Despite many popular myths that when individuals lose control over their central life role — work — they see retirement in a predominantly negative light, or that retirement brings on feelings of uselessness, ill health or early death, scant scientific evidence can be found to support such assumptions. There are, of course, instances of negative consequences to retirement, but in general people neither avoid retirement nor find it worse than they had anticipated. Instead they react as they have learned to do over the course of a lifetime. Chronic health conditions do occur among the retired; however, these do not have a direct link to retirement per se, as the ills experienced are also incurred by those who are still working.

Pension programs in selected countries reveal disparate philosophies behind the provision of social security. Most countries have a two step scheme consisting of a general coverage, compulsory system as well as private or supplemental public programs designed to meet more specific needs. Earnings tests on postretirement employment are imposed in Britain, the United States and Japan, effectively discouraging many older people from working to fulfill their financial needs. The age at which people become eligible for pensions also varies by country, but is most frequently between 60 and 65. Without exception, public social security fails to provide the amount necessary for subsistence requirements. For example, a comparison of expenditures for a retired couple and a younger family in the United States reveals that the older couple spend approximately 5 percent more for food, 10 percent more for housing and over twice as much for medical attention.

As a rite of passage, retirement denotes a transition, separating the older person from his or her previous roles and initiating another phase of the life cycle. Adjustments are affected by such factors as financial security, health, education, occcupational status and family and marital relationships. Carefully planned pre-retirement counseling will facilitate adjustments, although the strategies used must rely on the personal characteristics of the workers involved. In recent years support from the federal government has increased dramatically, yet the funds appropriated have not always been passed along in the form of services. The present crunch on Social Security has not only been a long time coming, but unless revisions are made in the system of funding, payments will be even less adequate. By the time the boom babies begin retiring in the first decade of the twenty-first century, the ratio of workers to beneficiaries will have fallen from the current 3.2 to 1 to as low as 2 to 1—posing an onerous tax burden on wage earners. Substantial reforms are in order.

Pertinent Readings

ACUFF, G., and D. ALLEN. "Hiatus in 'Meaning': Disengagement for Retired Professors." Journal of Gerontology XXV, 2 (1970): 126–28.

ATCHLEY, R.C. "Disengagement Among Professors." Journal of Gerontology XXVI, 4 (1971): 476–80.

———. The Sociology of Retirement. Cambridge, Mass.: Schenkman, 1976.

BACK, K.W. "The Ambiguity of Retirement." In Behavior and Adaptation in Late Life, eds. E.W. Busse and E. Pfeiffer, 93–114. Boston: Little, Brown and Co., 1969.

BARFIELD, R.E., and J. MORGAN. Early Retirement: The Decision and the Experience. Ann Arbor, Mich.: Institute of Social Research, 1969.

BELLINO, R. "Perspectives of Military and Civilian Retirement." Mental Hygiene LIV, 4 (1970): 580–83.

BERNSTEIN, M.C. "Forecast of Women's Retirement Income: Cloudy and Colder; 25 Percent Chance of Poverty." *Industrial Gerontology*, 1, 2 (1974): 1–13.

BURGESS, E.W. *Aging in Western Societies*. Chicago: University of Chicago Press, 1960.

CALLISON, J.C. "Early Experience Under the Supplemental Security Income Program." *Social Security Bulletin* XXXVII, 6 (1974): 3–11.

CARP, F.M. *The Retirement Process*. Washington, D.C.: U.S. Government Printing Office, 1968.

———. *Retirement*. New York: Behavioral Publications, 1972.

CLAGUE, E., B. PALLI and L. KRAMER. *The Aging Worker and the Union: Employment and Retirement of Middle Aged and Older Workers*. New York: Praeger Publishers, 1971.

CRAWFORD, M.P. "Retirement: A Rite de Passage." *Sociological Review* XXI, 3 (1973): 447–61.

DONAHUE, W., H.L. ORBACH and O. POLLAK. "Retirement: The Emerging Social Pattern." In *Handbook of Social Gerontology: Societal Aspects of Aging*, ed. C. Tibbitts, 330–406. Chicago: University of Chicago Press, 1960.

DYER, L.D. "Implications of Job Displacement at Mid-Career." *Industrial Gerontology* XVII (1973): 38–46.

EISDORFER, C. "Adaptation to Loss of Work." In *Retirement*, ed. F. Carp, 245–46. New York: Behavioral Publications, 1972.

ELLISON, D.L. "Work, Retirement, and the Sick Role." *The Gerontologist* VIII, 3 (1968): 189–92.

FILLENBAUM, G.G. "The Working Retired." *Journal of Gerontology* XXVI, 1 (1971): 82–89.

FILLENBAUM, G.G., and G.L. MADDOX, "Work After Retirement: An Investigation into Some Psychologically Relevant Variables." *The Gerontologist* XIV, 5 (1974): 418–24.

FRIEDMANN, E.A., and R.J. HAVIGHURST, eds. *The Meaning of Work and Retirement*. Chicago: University of Chicago Press, 1954.

GOLD, B.D. "The Role of the Federal Government in the Provision of Social Services to Older Persons." *The Annals of the American Academy of Political and Social Science* CDXV (1974): 55–69.

GRAHAM, H., and H. DONOIAN. "The Union Role in Administering Collectively Bargained Pension Plans." *Industrial Gerontology* 1, 2 (1974): 34–41.

HARRIS, L. and ASSOCIATES. *The Myth and Reality of Aging in America*. Washington, D.C.: The National Council on the Aging, Inc., 1975.

HAVIGHURST, R.J., J.M.A. MUNNICHS, B. NEUGARTEN and H. THOMAE, eds. *Adjustment to Retirement: A Cross-National Study*. Assen, The Netherlands: Van Gorcum & Comp. N.V., 1969.

HENLE, P. "Recent Trends in Retirement Benefits Related to Earnings." *Monthly Labor Review* XCV, 6 (1972): 12–20.

HOLLISTER, R. "Social Mythology and Reform: Income Maintenance for the Aged." *The Annals* CDXV (1974): 19–40.

HURWITZ, J.C., and W.L. BURRIS. "Terminated UAW Pension Plans: A Study." *Industrial Gerontology* XV (1972): 40–51.

JACKSON, J.J. "Black Aged: In Quest of the Phoenix." In *Triple Jeopardy —
Myth or Reality*, 27–40. Washington, D.C.: National Council on Aging,
1972.

JAFFE, A.J. "The Retirement Dilemma." *Industrial Gerontology* XIV (1972):
1–89.

KATONA, G., J.N. MORGAN and R.E. BARFIELD. "Retirement in Prospect and Re-
trospect." In *Trends in Early Retirement*, Occasional Papers in Gerontology, no. 4, 27–49. Institute of Gerontology. Ann Arbor: The University of
Michigan–Wayne State University, 1969.

KREPS, J.M. "Economics of Aging: Work and Income Through the Life Span."
In *Aging in Contemporary Society*, ed. E. Shanas, 78–87. Beverly Hills:
Sage Publications, 1970.

LOWENTHAL, M.F., and P.L. BERKMAN. *Aging and Mental Disorder in San
Francisco*. San Francisco: Jossey-Bass, 1967.

MILLER, S.J. "The Social Dilemma of the Aging Leisure Participant." In
Older People and Their Social World, eds. A.M. Rose and W.A. Peterson,
77–92. Philadelphia: F.A. Davis Co., 1965.

MORISOT, M. "Flexibility of Retirement Age in France." In *Flexibility of Retirement Age*. Paris: Organisation for Economic Co-operation and Development, 1970.

MUELLER, M.S., and R.M. GIBSON. "Age Differences in Health Care Spending,
Fiscal Year 1974." *Social Security Bulletin* XXXVIII, 6 (1975): 3–16.

MURRAY, J.R., E.A. POWERS and R.J. HAVIGHURST. "Personal and Situational
Factors Producing Flexible Careers." *Gerontologist* XI, 4, 11 (1971): 4–12.

ORBACH, H.L. "Social and Institutional Aspects of Industrial Workers' Retirement Patterns." In *Trends in Early Retirement*, Occasional Papers in
Gerontology, no. 4, 1–26. Institute of Gerontology. Ann Arbor: The University of Michigan–Wayne State University, 1969.

ORGANISATION FOR ECONOMIC CO-OPERATION AND DEVELOPMENT (OECD). *Flexibility of Retirement Age*. Paris: OECD, 1970.

OSTERBIND, C.C., ed. *Income in Retirement: The Need and Society's Responsibility*. Gainesville: University of Florida Press, 1967.

PALMORE, E. "Retirement Patterns Among Aged Men: Findings of the 1963
Survey of the Aged." *Social Security Bulletin* XXVII (1964): 3–10.

———. "Why Do People Retire?" *Aging and Human Development* II (1971):
269–83.

———. "Compulsory versus Flexible Retirement: Issues and Facts." *The
Gerontologist* XII, 4 (1972): 343–48.

———. "What Can the U.S.A. Learn from Japan about Aging?" *The Gerontologist* XV, 1 (1975): 64–67.

PARSONS, T. *Social Structure and Personality*. New York: Free Press, 1965.

POLLMAN, A.W. "Early Retirement: A Comparison of Poor Health to Other
Retirement Factors." *Journal of Gerontology* XXVI, 1 (1971): 41–45.

POLLMAN, A.W., and A.C. JOHNSON. "Resistance to Change, Early Retirement
and Managerial Decisions." *Industrial Gerontology* 1, 1 (1974): 33–41.

RENO, V.P. "Compulsory Retirement Among Newly Entitled Workers: Survey of New Beneficiaries." *Social Security Bulletin* XXXV (1972): 3–15.

ROWE, A.R. "The Retirement of Academic Scientists." *Journal of Gerontology* XXVII, 1 (1972): 113–18.

———. "Scientists in Retirement." *Journal of Gerontology* XXVIII, 3 (1973): 345–50.

SCHEWE, D., K. NORDHORN and K. SCHENKE. *Survey of Social Security in the Federal Republic of Germany*, trans. F. Kenny. Bonn, Federal Republic of Germany: n.p., 1970.

SCHULZ, J.H. *Pension Aspects of the Economics of Aging: Present and Future Roles of Private Pensions*. United States Senate, Special Committee on Aging. Washington, D.C.: U.S. Government Printing Office, 1970.

SHANAS, E. "Adjustment to Retirement: Substitution or Accommodation." In *Retirement*, ed. F. Carp, 219–44. New York: Behavioral Publications, 1972.

SHANAS, E., et al. *Old People in Three Industrial Societies*. New York: Atherton Press, 1968.

SHEPPARD, H.L. *New Perspectives on Older Workers*. Washington, D.C.: Upjohn Institute for Employment Research, 1971.

SIMPSON, I.H., and J.C. MCKINNEY, eds. *Social Aspects of Aging*. Durham, N.C.: Duke University Press, 1966.

SIMPSON, I.H., K.W. BACK and J.C. MCKINNEY. "Attributes of Work, Involvement in Society, and Self-Evaluation in Retirement." In *Social Aspects of Aging*, eds. I.H. Simpson and J.C. McKinney, 55–74. Durham, N.C.: Duke University Press, 1966a.

———. "Orientations Toward Work and Retirement, and Self-Evaluation in Retirement." In *Social Aspects of Aging*, eds. I.H. Simpson and J.C. McKinney, 75–89. Durham, N.C.: Duke University Press, 1966b.

———. "Work and Retirement." In *Social Aspects of Aging*, eds. I.H. Simpson and J.C. McKinney, 45–54. Durham, N.C.: Duke University Press, 1966c.

STEWART, C.D. "The Older Worker in Japan: Realities and Possibilities." *Industrial Gerontology* 1, 1 (1974): 60–76.

STREIB, G.F., and C.J. SCHNEIDER. *Retirement in American Society: Impact and Process*. Ithaca: Cornell University Press, 1971.

U.S. DEPARTMENT OF HEALTH, EDUCATION AND WELFARE. "Current Operating Statistics." *Social Security Bulletin* XXXVIII, 11 (1975a): 49–68.

———. "Social Security Revision in the United Kingdom." *Social Security Bulletin* XXXVIII, 11 (1975b): 32–49.

U.S. DEPARTMENT OF LABOR, BUREAU OF LABOR STATISTICS. *Handbook of Labor Statistics, 1973*, Bulletin no. 1790, 327–33. Washington, D.C.: U.S. Government Printing Office, 1973.

U.S. SENATE, COMMITTEE ON FINANCE. "Staff Data and Materials on Social Service Regulations." 93rd Cong., 1st sess., May 1973. Washington, D.C.: U.S. Government Printing Office, 1973a.

U.S. SENATE, SPECIAL COMMITTEE ON AGING. "Future Directions in Social Security." 93rd Cong., 1st sess., January 1973. Washington, D.C.: U.S. Government Printing Office, 1973b.

WEDDERBURN, D. "Old People in Britain." In *Aging in Contemporary Society*, ed. E. Shanas, 94–106. Beverly Hills: Sage Publications, 1970.

_____ . "The Aged and Society." In *Textbook of Geriatric Medicine and Gerontology*, ed. J.C. Brocklehurst, 692–717. London: Churchill Livingstone, 1973.

_____ . "Old People in Britain." In *Aging in Contemporary Society*, ed. E. Shanas, 94–106. Beverly Hills: Sage Publications, 1970.

WILLIAMS, R.H., and C.G. WIRTHS. *Lives Through the Years: Styles of Life and Successful Aging*. New York: Atherton Press, 1965.

WITHERS, W. "Some Irrational Beliefs about Retirement in the United States." *Industrial Gerontology* 1, 1 (1974): 23–32.

Chapter 10

Family Life and Living Arrangements

The kinds of living arrangements in which people are involved may not often be given much thought by the majority of people: nonetheless, they constitute one of the more critical factors in maintaining a sense of well-being throughout life. Although no hard and fast connections can be drawn between housing patterns, family relationships and satisfaction in later life, there are some relatively clear indications that they are often associated. For instance, gerontologists are convinced people who live in isolation and are also without family ties generally encounter more serious problems in their later years. They are also in a disadvantaged position financially, more often live in substandard housing, have more serious health problems and are more likely to experience a sense of loneliness and despair than their peers who are part of a family. Traditionally, research has tended to focus on social isolates, although significant attention is now being paid to the means by which nearly all elderly, whether living alone or with others, might be enabled to remain independent members of the community instead of becoming institutional residents. Currently, roughly one in twenty older people live in one or another kind of institution. A number of observers assert even this represents too large a proportion compared to the aged actually requiring those services obtainable only in an institutional setting.

Apart from a person's immediate housing, the neighborhood is of major importance to old people. Anyone who has lived for a long time in the same area obviously becomes accustomed to the surroundings. This is not to say, however, that he or she necessarily feels happy or secure or, in fact, wishes to remain there. At times, either because of this sense of familiarity or because of health, financial or mobility constraints, an older person will maintain a residence far longer in unsuitable or difficult situations than might be desirable or expected. Part of the problem of lack of alternatives also arises from the lifestyles of younger adults who normally do not have the resources to support older relatives in their homes. To add to the burdens, the public in general sees institutionalization as a last alternative, one step removed from death, thus signaling a final passage to many of the elderly who find they must enter an "old age home." Regardless of the validity of this view, it persists in the eyes of both the elderly and the rest of us. Fortunately, there is a growing recognition of the wisdom underlying auxiliary programs that would allow older people to remain in their communities for as long as possible, necessitating only the gradual use of institutional services. Projects ranging from day care centers, high rise apartments for older citizens, intergenerational public housing, college dormitory conversion plans, retirement centers and integrated concentric communities with a variety of housing arrangements are becoming increasingly visible around the country. Couple with these the enlightened provision of community health clinics for both physical and emotional attention, and living arrangements for future generations of older people need not be as bleak as is often predicted. However, before examining any of the above alternatives, it would be wise to first acquire an overview of the family relationships of older people.

Family Relations in Later Life

Family Patterns

For decades, the impact of family life on the present circumstances and future adjustments of all individuals regardless of age has been readily acknowledged. Almost without exception, societies around the world have a fairly rigid clear-cut kinship structure, although provisions for alternate family systems have generally existed alongside the normative pattern. The most pervasive unit is the **nuclear family** — that is, the immediate family consisting of parents and children. **Extended families**, including the nuclear family plus various blood relationships spread over more than two generations, are also found in many parts of the world. As described in Chapter Two, extended families are customarily prevalent where the nuclear unit is not able to supply sufficient economic and emotional support. The twentieth century has witnessed many alterations in family structure derived in part from greater life expectancy, tendencies toward earlier marriage and fewer children. In its own way, each of these contributes to the likelihood that more people than ever before will have at least one living grandparent during their early adulthood. Among the elderly themselves, family structure has also changed; women usually outlive their husbands, and in recent years have shown a slightly higher rate of remarriage. Nonetheless, a large percentage of the older population is not now married, being either widowed, divorced or single. In such countries as the United States, Denmark or Britain, at least two-fifths of the elderly are not spending their final years with a spouse (Shanas et al, 1968). In the discussion of relative aging patterns among minority groups in Chapter Thirteen, it is noted that ethnic background is an important consideration to keep in mind when talking about family life. Still, across all ethnic groups the usual pattern is nearly twice as many women as men have lost a spouse while, on the other hand, only about one in ten older people have never married. Because of differences in longevity and possibilities for remarriage, the proportion of older men who are married is double that of older women. In 1975, of the 42 percent of the older Americans who lived alone, more than three-fourths were women. While the presence of an extended family structure may serve both economic and labor roles in rural areas, it may be more indicative in urban areas of the loss of a spouse and a resulting dependency upon one's children. In the cross-cultural studies of Shanas and her associates elderly parents were found more often to live with daughters rather than sons, and in general widows are more likely than widowers to live with adult children.

Family Support: Nuclear versus Extended

The long debate over whether or not industrialized societies have corrupted the extended family, insuring isolated nuclear family units out of either economic or practical necessity, has been partially resolved for the time being. In her comprehensive review of research findings at least tangentially related to various aspects of the family in later life, Troll (1971) finds that most evidence points to the existence of a modified extended family structure in modern societies. Although few households, less than one in ten, are actually composed of three generations, the vast majority of older people, almost 80 percent, live within an hour's distance of their children and manage to see them weekly or oftener. There are, however, a few differences by social class (Harris, 1975). Adult children of middle class backgrounds are likely to live somewhat further away from their parents than their working class counterparts, yet patterns of mutual aid and contact are equally viable in both cases. The primary reasons for middle class children not being in as close physical proximity to their parents are more a reflection of their occupational statuses than of any desire to disassociate themselves; they are simply willing to live apart in order to pursue careers. It is true that greater distances do result in fewer visits; nonetheless, when made, the visits are of longer duration than those experienced by working class families. Judging from the best data available, some compensation for the absence of one's children may be provided by the pride elderly parents take in the accomplishments of their children (Shanas et al., 1968; Rosenberg, 1970).

The extended family structure in mass societies can thus be described in terms of the type and extent of interaction, the residential propinquity and the exchange of values and services among its members. The latter category encompasses mutual aid, often measured in economic terms or by the provision of tangible services from childcare to household assistance. A more difficult variable to measure, but one equally integral to the family, involves the emotional meaning and support of family relationships. With a minimum of reflection, it is possible to appreciate that the older generations give and receive a variety of benefits both necessary and incidental to family life. It should not be surprising that family members who live some distance apart must forego most nontangible support exchanged by families who see each other weekly; instead they usually confine their offers or requests for assistance to monetary or material help from either parents or children. By contrast, working class families living in closer proximity are able to assist one another by caring for grandchildren or performing a variety of housework tasks for one another. As might also be expected, middle-aged children in the working classes face a far greater likelihood of having to support their aging parents through different types of help. One of the more common forms of mutual aid in all family units, without regard to social class, concerns the needs that inevitably arise when a family member becomes ill. In Shanas' (1968) cross-cultural analysis of family life, it was discovered that 80 to 90 percent of all old people who are faced with serious health problems receive assistance from family members. There does, however, appear to be a distinction in the nature of interaction and the types of mutual aid that is dependent on the sex of the family members involved. Some data point to the tendency for kin relationships to be focused more closely on the female side of the family. Daughters seem to be more willing to suppress their value conflicts with aged parents in order to participate in activities and the sharing of resources than their brothers. Also, there are fewer men who remain widowers than women remaining widows, so that upon remarriage older men are once again incorporated into a family setting. As will be shown later, older widows more often live alone, although those who find their situations impossible to handle by themselves will generally move in with their adult children. Widowers are more inclined to stick it out by themselves.

Since less than a third of the elderly are currently living with their offspring, some researchers have placed great emphasis on the breakdown of the family by pointing to what is often called the generation gap. Recent longitudinal investigations are calling this idea into question. While it is true each generation has its own particular interests, with older members perhaps concentrating on consolidating and preserving their lives while the youthful are concerned with expanding their horizons, the tensions that emerge may be transitory and the schism itself illusory. Indeed, it may well be the case upon careful analysis that unrelated individuals of the same generation exhibit greater diversity in terms of cultural and personal values than do family members from different generations (Bengtson and Kuypers, 1971; Bengtson, 1975). This is not to say intergenerational interaction does not engender conflicts, for the evidence suggests it does, but merely that too much has been made of an idea that has yet to be validated over time. Upon close questioning, it frequently turns out to be the case that the elderly themselves prefer their intimacy at a distance, not because of the headaches that come of living with their children, but out of a desire to retain their independence (Rosenmayr, 1972). In point of fact, three generational households may be only an economic expediency or social necessity rather than a sign of emotional strength within the family in industrialized societies.

Coupling the recognition that sharing a home with adult children is usually more a stopgap measure than a true desire for the majority of older people with the reality of the lopsided sex distribution among the elderly, the need for providing new living arrangements becomes readily apparent. Among younger people, conventional monogamous marital ties have already been supplemented with a host of marital or interpersonal options. In spite of their problems, older people have not yet reached the point where they are willing to adopt any of the alternatives in significant numbers, although they may be less likely to express their ire about them than previously. As Cavan (1973) suggests, it is a societal disservice to dismiss or underestimate the possibilities of everything from simple heterosexual cohabitation to group marriages, communal enclaves and homosexual relationships, built on either Platonic or sexual grounds, to add to human happiness in any phase of the life cycle. Popular misconceptions about the needs and desires of older people, especially older women, are rampant. Fortunately the elderly themselves are becoming more vocal about the denial of their sexuality and the constraints of a value system in which marriage is of paramount importance. It is doubtful whether older people could really escape the values of their own upbringing, but if they are able to acknowledge the artificial barriers to attempting novel living arrangements, innovation may eventually come with less psychological cost.

Elderly Families

Today one-fifth of the heads of all American households are over the age of 65. In relative terms there has been little change in the past decade, though this is largely a reflection of the growing numbers of young families. The actual number of household heads in the older age range has increased by about 16 percent. Despite this, more older people are spending their last years either alone or, out of economic or social necessity, living with groups of unrelated individuals; in all likelihood this contingent will continue to grow. Irrespective of the demands for change by vocal elderly, it is improbable that a sizeable portion of the widowed, divorced or separated elderly will take on any new form of interpersonal commitment in the near future. Most of what we know about the family life of the elderly is derived from census information gathered from those household heads over the age of 65 who are living with kin related by either blood or marriage. Of course there is a built-in fallacy in this procedure, since chronological age and role distribution within the family are not always comparable, nor does it necessarily reflect the nature of kinship structures. In the United States, for example, roughly one-third of the elderly consider themselves members of four generational kin networks, a rate almost twice as high as observed in either Britain or Denmark. However, the 44 percent of Americans who perceive themselves to be in a three generational network is less than the half found in each of the other two countries (Shanas et al., 1968).

The marital status of Americans over age 65 as shown in Table 10.1 is illustrative of patterns found in most industrialized countries. There are a few significant differences that can be observed by both sex and age. Approximately an equal number of men and women in the two oldest age ranges are single, but when compared to the younger group, only about half as many elderly over 75 are currently divorced. The greatest disparities arise among elderly people who are either married or widowed. Among the men, eight of ten of the younger group are married, a figure that declines to two-thirds for those 75 or over. Women, as mentioned earlier, are far less likely to still be married; less than half of the younger and only a little over one-fifth of the older women have living spouses. It should be evident that the information in Table 10.1 does not really address the question of how many older people have ever been widowed; instead, it only describes the number who are currently widowed or remarried. As might be expected, 95 percent of all elderly families have no adolescent children and over half have no family members between ages 18 and 64 living at home. The largest group of elderly white families, about 83 percent, is composed of only two person

Table 10.1
Marital Status of Older Americans, 1975*

MARITAL STATUS	AGE:	MEN		WOMEN	
		65−74	75+	65−74	75+
Single		4.3	5.5	5.8	5.8
Married, spouse present		81.8	68.3	47.3	22.3
Widowed		8.8	23.3	41.9	69.4
Divorced		3.1	1.2	3.3	1.5

*Percentage distributions

Source: U.S. Bureau of the Census, *Current Population Reports*, series P-20, no. 287 (Washington, D.C.: U.S. Government Printing Office, 1975), p. 8.

households, while among blacks two-thirds of the older families are of this size. Another significant difference is the presence of children under 18 in almost one-fifth of the older black families, though less than half of these represent the elderly couple's own children. Even so, this is four times greater than the rate for elderly white families. Apart from these differences, older families in most industrialized countries are very much alike. Husbands are usually the same age or older than their wives and most couples have children from whom they live apart. While the mythical May-December wedding does occasionally take place, it is a statistical rarity. Only 1 percent of the men over age 65 are married to women 20 years or more their junior, while this is true even less frequently among women. Approximately 10 percent of the wives age 65 or older have husbands younger than themselves, although the usual age difference is limited to less than five years. By comparison, more than 80 percent of the men in this age bracket have wives the same age or younger (U.S. Census, 1975a).

Not all elderly households in the United States are headed by men; in roughly 10 percent of them, the primary responsibilities fall to woman. Racial or ethnic factors are associated with certain variations in terms of locale, size and composition, just as they are in those households headed by men. For instance, one-third of all households in which white women are considered to be shouldering the duties of head are located in the suburbs, while half of those in which black women assume the responsibility are found in inner city locations. The size of the family unit is also related to racial characteristics; black and other minority households are larger in most cases. Interestingly, significant variations become apparent when successive cohorts are examined for the timing of major events in the family life cycle. As demonstrated by Figure 10.1, with one exception, the age at which women are first married has been steadily declining. The exception is that aggregate of women born after the turn of the century who married during the Depression; for them economic and social insecurities forced a slight postponement of wedding plans. Similar patterns can be observed for the age at which women give birth to their first and last child and their age at the time the last child marries. For the most recent cohort shown, hardly enough time has elapsed for some of the transitions to have occurred, but predictions based on previous trends, shown by the dotted lines, indicate a further reduction in the median ages at which these events take place. One of the important things to note in Figure 10.1 is the extension of what is sometimes referred to as the *empty nest* years, when married couples once again live alone. Over the life span of the cohorts born from 1880 to 1939, this period has expanded

Figure 10.1

Stages of family life cycle for six cohorts of American women

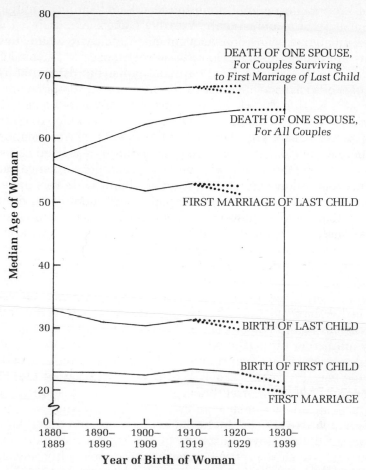

Source: P.C. Glick and R. Parke, Jr., "New Approaches in Studying the Life Cycle of the Family," *Demography* II (1965): 189.

to the point at which today husbands and wives can anticipate about 16 years together after fulfilling the responsibilities of raising and launching their children. In spite of these gains, two-thirds of all married women are likely to spend as long as the last 18 years of their lives as widows (Glick and Parke, 1965).

Separation and Widowhood

Needless to say, the emotional turmoil caused by the death of a spouse is an experience that is not easy to communicate to others.

For most couples, a mutual dependency develops over the years, so that suddenly finding oneself alone naturally evokes feelings ranging all the way from grief, loneliness and confusion to guilt, anger and a sense of abandonment. With the current attention being focused on myriad behavioral facets of death and dying, many new insights are coming to light about a subject most of us consider not only private but unique. First hand accounts, supplemented by the findings of social scientists, have recently provided a poignant new look at what life is like for the surviving partner (Lopata, 1973; Caine, 1974; Glick et al., 1974). Obviously, the emotional aftermath of a spouse's death will depend on the state of marital relations in the period immediately preceding death, but in nearly all cases, the suddenness of the death will have a profound influence on the trauma that follows. Some investigators claim widowers appear to retain their levels of social participation and mobility in more instances than widows; however, the evidence tends to be inconsistent to say the least (Berardo, 1970). Still, widowers do show a greater tendency to remarry within a relatively short time. Without meaning to imply death is ever easy, among those couples who were able to anticipate the summons of death and who have a secure financial picture, adjustment for the surviving partner is relatively easier. Ironically, the same cannot be said for those who had accommodated themselves to the empty nest or to life after retirement; generally they are harder hit by the death of a spouse. In Chapter Eight, the large numbers of women now entering or returning to work after midlife was discussed. Over half of the women in their late forties and early fifties are currently employed, which, in addition to the financial advantages of such an arrangement, also supplies a potentially supportive network in the event one's husband dies. The kinds of jobs held also prove indicative of subsequent readjustment patterns; professionals or retired professionals more readily get back on their feet than their blue collar counterparts (Atchley, 1975).

In several parallel studies of American widows a variety of adjustment modes emerge that are affected by such factors as ethnicity, personality, husband's occupation and income, marital relations or family ties. A primary component of the disorientation following the death of a spouse hinges on the extent of their interdependency in various roles and whether or not the partner was able to develop outside interests. For example, much of a widow's social isolation is clearly a reflection of psychological recovery, yet at the same time it stems at least in part from earlier patterns of social contacts while her husband was still living. The woman whose friendships were based on the entrée furnished by her husband's job or social activities will naturally feel considerably more alone when his death cuts off, or is perceived to cut off, the continuation of meaningful interaction. Voluntary support from family members certainly helps, although in-laws often pose additional problems. A widow sometimes feels that among her husband's family she can rely on her brothers-in-law, while a widower often turns to his sisters-in-law; neither usually seeks extensive help elsewhere in the spouse's family. In contradiction to what is often thought, the presence of children in the home of the bereaved does not appear to either lessen the jolt or hasten the recovery process (Lopata, 1973; Glick et al., 1974). Among the 7.7 million elderly widowed persons, four-fifths of whom are women, the vast majority express a desire to continue an independent lifestyle without becoming dependent on relatives or friends. About one in five widows or widowers still face the responsibility of caring for family members living with them, but three-quarters of all widowed persons live alone. Of the small percentage who are not heads of their own households—in other words, those moving in with others—women outnumber men four to one (U.S. Census, 1975c).

Widowhood presents the single most disruptive crisis of all the transitions in the life cycle. Death most often occurs among elderly couples after they have adjusted to the departure of their children, the introduction of grandchildren, retirement for one or both partners and innumerable other changes unique to the later phases of family life. Perhaps part of the reason for the frequent preoccupation with health matters that is characteristic of older people is the implicit recognition of the inevitability of death and the uncertainty of everyday life. Despite the deeply felt intimacy of grief and mourning, individuals who experience a type of "recovery" seem to follow more or less predictable avenues. Ordinarily, these range from reentry into marriage or nonmarital commitments to extended kin supports and isolated lifestyles. Of course, nonrecovery remains a real possibility, although total inability to cope is usually observed among only a small minority of the widowed. The initial stage of acute grieving gradually dissipates within less than a year or so and life again assumes some outward semblance of normality. Whatever the reactions expressed by the widow or widower, the continuing impression of years of contact with a lover, co-parent, confidant, ally or foe is indelible (Glick et al., 1974).

Family Authority and Grandparenthood

The nature of family relationships in most modern societies differs in the extent to which they insure an active and meaningful role for older people. In his classic analysis of the elderly in preindustrial societies, Simmons (1945) asserts older people were granted an esteemed position only when their numbers were relatively limited and when they dispensed valued folk wisdom or practical knowledge. As has been said, in the absence of written history, the elderly often occupied the role of seer or wiseman, exercising seemingly magical powers and fulfilling an age-old desire for continuity. When social conditions are fairly stable, as in agricultural societies, or where the winds of social change are mild at best, the probability of older people deriving prestige from their seniority status is enhanced. None of these conditions are especially prevalent in industrial societies today, and even a cursory examination of the situations of older people in various countries reveals the family ties of older people to be far from uniform. Before turning to the place of elderly people in American families, let us look briefly at the changes that have taken place over the past few decades elsewhere around the world.

Japan is frequently cited as an archetypal culture in which old age has been held in time-honored reverence. From the Meiji restoration in the last century until the changes wrought by World War II, the vertical age structuring of Japanese society endured with little challenge and nearly iron-clad authority. Religious doctrines emphasized filial piety as the first expression of veneration for the emperor and, by extension, all one's ancestors, thus insuring a remarkable degree of security for the elderly. Realistically, altruism can only carry so far, though bolstering it was the Japanese system of inheritance whereby one child was selected to receive the entirety of a family's wealth or holdings and was therefore duty-bound to shoulder the complete responsibility for the aged parents. Following World War II many aspects of the vertical society were replaced; and with the restructuring came a move toward equitable inheritance among children and a sharing of the obligations for looking after parents. In the wake of rapid industrialization, urbanization and social or geographic mobility, a number of the traditions regarding older people have become perfunctory or in some cases have simply disappeared. Today older Japanese are faced with making major adjustments to a world based on principles alien to their traditional socialization, with only a few remnants of the age-graded hierarchy of the past remaining. As their society in general has become more open, Japanese families have undergone their own form of democratization, which sometimes presents an added stress for older people. This is not to imply the elderly enjoyed a completely idyllic old age in prewar Japan, but only to say that many important supports have been either diminished or removed in the establishment of a more horizontal society. Nevertheless, with the transcription of religious tenets into a simple creed of respect for one's elders, older Japanese do continue to receive some deference. As testimony to their importance, all of Japan observes an Honor the Elders Day each September, while the national assembly continues to enact laws requiring lineal descendants to support their elderly relatives. As a consequence of tradition plus legal sanctions, the classic Japanese extended family remains viable, with eight of every ten elderly living under one roof with children or grandchildren. The remainder are either living with a spouse, live alone or else are institutionalized. Compounding the financial woes discussed in the previous chapter is a dearth of governmental programs designed to alleviate the burden that often falls on families that can ill afford them. Even so, the potential for a positive old age is generally within reach for the elderly in Japan (Plath, 1972; Palmore, 1975).

It is far from rare in Japanese families for both husband and wife to work full time because there is a grandmother in the family who assumes major responsibilities for childcare and housekeeping. In other countries undergoing rapid industrialization, the Soviet Union being an outstanding example, a similar arrangement is often followed. Despite the insistence that children are the salvation of the future, older Russians are also accorded a great deal of admiration for having managed to defeat great odds in reaching their later years. Literature, the arts and everyday life abound with reference to the Russian *babushka*, or grandmother. She is acknowledged as a cornerstone of family stability in a country where seniority in itself is seldom a source of authority in public life, dominated as it is by party membership and service criteria. Conflicting conclusions about the role of older people in the Soviet Union are commonplace, and skeptics often point to the growth of daycare centers as attempts to remove children from the traditional patterns of socialization by an older generation, while more favorable observers note that these centers are frequently staffed by older people operating in a paraprofessional capacity. With the lack of housing units sufficiently large to accommodate even a normal-sized family, it is of little surprise that daily tensions exist in multigenerational families. Yet even these are not enough to detract from the recognition granted older Soviet citizens (McKain, 1972).

Ireland furnishes an interesting comparison to Japan and the Soviet Union. Still largely an agrarian economy, only recently experiencing a significant degree of economic expansion with its attendant urbanization, Ireland's elderly continue to command both approbation and deference. Although the percentage of elderly Irish has nearly doubled in the present century, younger cohorts of the population have maintained a stable proportional representation.

The population as a whole has declined by nearly one million since before the turn of the century, in large measure as a consequence of emigration. Recent developments are sure to alter the picture, however, as traditionally family life in Ireland has been marked by two rather unique conditions. Marriage occurs much later here than in nearly any other country in the world. Also, a larger proportion of the Irish remain single throughout their lives than elsewhere. Among middle-aged Irish a third of the men and approximately one-fifth of the women are unmarried; for those people over age 65 the rate is roughly one-quarter. In either instance this is several times the percentage of Americans who have never married. The lateness of marriage—men are usually over 30 before taking their vows—combines with the realities of small scale farming to foster, at least in rural areas, a degree of filial obedience. Most Irish farms are relatively compact, able to provide subsistence for only a limited number if they are to remain economically feasible. Generally speaking, the family farm passes to the eldest male offspring when the father decides to turn over its operation. Until that time he exercises unquestioned control and domination over his holdings. Upon retirement, the older couple moves out of the central area of the house as the son and his family move in and gradually assume the reins of power. Under the circumstances it would be unusual if the transition were accomplished without some friction. It has been suggested by some investigators that the strong influence of the aging mother over her sons, in combination with the inheritance scheme, contributes greatly to the lateness of marriage. Furthermore, the economic domination of the father and the paucity of other opportunities for younger men prompt some of the waves of emigration in search of a less restricted way of life. Be this as it may, those who remain at home continue to defer to the authority of older people, though, as is the case the world over, the role of the elderly is no longer as clearcut in urban environments as it may have been in a rural setting (Streib, 1972).

The family life of older people in Britain has been the subject of a series of intensive studies over the past decade. Although the conclusions drawn by various researchers are by no means identical, they do offer important insights concerning the place of the elderly in English families. As is the case in the United States, relatively few older people are institutional residents; the largest majority remain in close contact with their children and the rest of their families. Judging from the evidence available, over half of the old people are in touch with their children on a daily basis, while another quarter engage in get-togethers at least weekly. Referring to the definition of an extended family cited earlier, it is safe to assume a very small percentage of elderly Britons are old and alone, only about one in five, while most openly exchange services, live in the same locale and have regular interaction between the generations. In fact, three generation extended families are becoming increasingly familiar as successive stages of family life are occurring earlier than in the past, following trends similar to those shown for American families in Figure 10.1. Of course the exact staging of the family life cycle or the physical proximity of elders to their children is related to social class in Britain, the same as it is in the United States and elsewhere. On the average, white collar English families have fewer children, live further apart and display distinctive patterns of financial and service support when compared to their working class counterparts. In all classes, however, a modified form of the extended family proves to be more often the case than not, though undoubtedly it cannot resolve the innumerable problems encountered by the elderly themselves (Townsend, 1963; Tunstall, 1966; Shanas et al., 1968).

Like their counterparts abroad, many American elderly find a great deal of solace in their role as grandparents, claiming it offers a sense both of renewal and of continuity. For the first time in history, middle-aged couples around the world are becoming grandparents, and in recent years a goodly portion of them have been able to look forward to meeting their great-grandchildren. As Erikson implies by the very labels in his developmental model discussed in Chapter Six, taking an active interest in the lives of youngsters is a healthy sign. In reality, grandparents do participate to some extent in the transmission of values, wisdom and general cultural knowledge, depending on family structure and interaction patterns, but only rarely do they assume a primary role in the socialization of their grandchildren. An analysis of styles of "grandparenting" carried out by a research team in Chicago reveals five seemingly typical models. First there are the tradition-oriented *formal* grandparents who adhere to what they assume to be the prescribed role relationship between themselves and the grandchild. Normally these are the older grandparents, who were reared in an era that stressed reserve and dignity in intergenerational interaction. Among those grandparents who were relatively younger and who perceived themselves as thinking and acting younger than their own parents at the same age, the *fun seeker* is a more common style. For this group, grandchildren offer a pleasurable leisure activity and playfulness tends to predominate in their interaction. In contrast to the formal types, fun seekers were oblivious to authority lines, preferring instead to have mutually satisfying relationships. Other roles can be typified as *surrogate* grandparents, mostly women who undertake daily responsibilities in caring for the child. The *reservoirs of family wisdom*, typically men, are the grandparents who dispense culturally valued knowledge or perhaps their own largess for the benefit of the youngsters. Like the formal type, this role tends to be associated with patriarchal family structures. Finally, there are the *distant figures*, those grandparents who appear infrequently, usually only on holidays. While authority issues seldom come to the fore, the relationship is still constrained, if only because the interaction is so fleeting. Like the fun seekers, distant grandparents are fairly young and may even partially avoid contact because the role is as yet incongruent with their self-image (Neugarten and Weinstein, 1964).

The type of "grandparenting" engaged in is quite clearly dependent on the complex of roles within the nuclear family and on the role accorded the elderly person by his or her adult children. Part of the deference shown to grandparents no doubt hinges upon the process of adult socialization, or the anticipatory look older people provide in the sense of being a role model for their children's own old age. The way old age is viewed will influence the manner in which aged parents are evaluated and will likely as not determine the broad outlines of old age for the children. For those adult children who adopt a kind of *role reversal*, treating their parents as if they were children, it is inevitable that old will be shadowed by a negative light. On the other hand, those adult children who can be characterized by an attitude of *filial maturity* freely give comfort and support to their parents without depriving them of their own identities and probably have a much more positive outlook on what their own later years will be like (Blenkner, 1965). These dimensions of the role of grandparent are far from unique to the American scene; rather, they are indicative of the patterns imposed on aging by various social contexts (Kahana and Kahana, 1971).

Living Arrangements

At the outset of this chapter, a few introductory comments were made regarding the complex interrelationships between living arrangements and the daily adjustment of the elderly. Having spent some time examining the social location of older people within the family structure, a look at the physical environment is also warranted. In most respects, the physical ecology of aging is certainly as multifaceted as the social. It is often subtle, almost always powerful and as fascinating as it is frustrating to those who might wish to effect some alterations in its appearance or impact. A statistical picture of where older people live is not sufficient in itself; a graphic description must also entail close attention to the way individual personalities and ecological factors interact with one another. It is, however, a beginning from which general implications may be drawn and applied to localized settings.

Where the Elderly Live

It should be remembered from Chapter Three that there are considerable variations in the concentration of elderly Americans by geographical region. During the 1960s the population as a whole expanded by one-fifth, with the number of people over 65 accounting for roughly 10 percent of the total. Some states, however, experienced a growth rate among the elderly population many times the national average. The most dramatic increases took place in Arizona, Florida and Nevada, where the number of elderly climbed by nearly 70 percent. Further back, but still far in advance of the average, were additions ranging from 31 to 38 percent in states such as California, North Carolina, Texas and New Mexico. Since this expansion reflects a combination of natural population increase, outmigration of younger people and inmigration of the elderly, it may not accurately depict the current proportion or number of older residents. States with the highest percentage of elderly would include Florida, at over 15 percent, and Arkansas, Iowa, Missouri, Nebraska and Kansas, all of which have aged amounting to more than 12 percent of their populations. Logically, the two largest states, New York and California, have the largest absolute numbers of elderly, over two million each, while Florida, Texas, Pennsylvania and Illinois all have approximately one million, though their proportions are not exceptional.

Willingly or not, older people are likely to find themselves concentrated in rather predictable residential areas. Earlier discussion pointed out the migration of younger workers, first to the cities and then out to the suburban developments, has left behind a disproportionate number of elderly in rural and central city locations. Today nearly one-quarter of all older people reside in rural areas, one-third live in inner cities and another 40 percent occupy housing in older working class neighborhoods on the fringes of central cities. As might be anticipated, their residences are usually older, lower cost and less well-equipped homes or rental apartments. Although housing built prior to World War II is fairly roomy, it presents its own inconveniences such as difficulties in heating and cleaning. The living conditions of elderly Americans are fairly typical of the situations found in other industrial countries. For example, elderly Austrians spending their retirement years in Vienna live in roughly comparable conditions, the possible exception being the larger percentage who live in apartments, over a quarter of which lack running water or bathroom facilities (Rosenmayr, 1972). Perhaps one of the more uncommon aspects of the living arrangements of older Americans compared to the elderly abroad is the preponderance of single family homes, most of which are either owned or being purchased. These are generally older dwellings; 8 percent lack the amenities of complete indoor plumbing and have been lived in by the aged residents for an average of 25 years or more. By and large, those who rent their housing do not have any newer or better kept dwellings, and they often live in even more unstable neighborhoods. In either event, rent or household maintenance requires in excess of 35 percent of an older couple's income, compared to the 25 percent a younger family pays for the same purposes. Even those people who desire a change are often unable to afford a move on their limited budgets; in fact, if the recent trends illustrated in Figure 10.2 are any indication, it would appear that less than one-fifth of the elderly are likely to relocate in any five year period (U.S. Census, 1975b).

The Trauma of Relocation: To Move or Stay

Why is it that some older people are disinclined to move even when it might improve their living accommodations? To begin with, there is the issue of money, or rather the lack of it, to use in securing newer or at least less dilapidated housing. The irony, however, is that the elderly with the least money move most frequently, not because they want to, but often as a consequence of condemnation proceedings or urban renewal, which forces them out of the deteriorated sections of town where they can afford the rent. Second, not everyone welcomes change even if it is for the better. Simply because someone is dissatisfied with the present situation does not necessarily inspire a desire to move that will actually be carried through. Despite the nuisances, inaffable social conditions or perceived lack of safety, all of which undeniably affect morale, the thought of uprooting for new and unknown places may cause even greater consternation. Relocation is a traumatic event; it means leaving behind neighborhood ties and friendships built on long years of living in the same place. Familiar surroundings furnish a sense of security or stability, and even those elderly who might really have wanted to move and who enjoy their new environment may end up grieving for their lost home. The losses mourned are both physical and social-psychological, since the move brings a separation from one's heritage and the cues that bolster old memories (Birren, 1969; Fried, 1972).

Figure 10.2
Percent of the American population moving to, from and within standard metropolitan statistical areas by age, 1970–1975

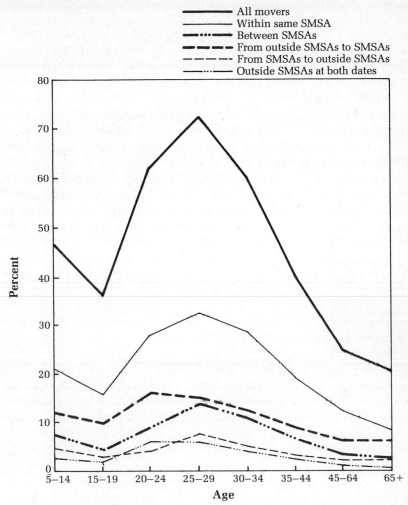

Source: U.S. Bureau of the Census, *Current Population Reports*, series P-20, no. 285 (Washington, D.C.: U.S. Government Printing Office, 1975), cover.

In the past there has been some convenience in living in older residential areas; they were easily accessible and close to shopping facilities and physicians. Of course the increasing commercial and professional exodus to suburban plazas and malls has made transportation a necessity, when being able to avoid owning or driving a car was one of the primary attractions in remaining close to downtown areas in the first place. A move intended by business and professional people to promote efficiency and reduce costs is actually working just the opposite for many elderly requiring their essential services. In evaluating their current housing situation, a majority of the elderly refer to critical distances from medical and shopping facilities as a primary consideration, followed by proximity to relatives, climate, privacy, help with housekeeping or meals, and recreational services. Unable to obtain the necessities, exacerbated by the primitive state of public transportation in the United States, being dissatisfied with their living arrangements, yet unwilling or unable to move is bound to exacerbate the sense of isolation and deprivation felt by many of the elderly (Hamovitch and Peterson, 1969; Lawton, 1975). Until recently many public housing projects discouraged elderly tenants, asserting that their facilities were intended for economically disadvantaged younger families. Strangely enough, even the advent of government-sponsored housing subsidies aimed at remedying some of the problems of older people have not had an appreciable effect. Despite many incentives, including low rent public housing projects, nonprofit schemes or government-guaranteed mortgage plans, there has not yet been a significant alteration in the living arrangements of older residents. Relocating older people involves more than the mere provision of new physical space, as moving threatens the elderly's entire life world. Agencies responsible for housing the elderly must be sensitive to their particular concerns if the move is meant to improve life satisfaction (Niebanck, 1965; McGuire, 1969).

The prospect of a move does not affect all elderly in the same way; therefore, the question becomes one of accounting for the differences. To date there are few longitudinal studies that attempt to discern the true impact of housing changes on morale, but what little evidence is available offers some important practical suggestions. As one would expect, personality and friendship patterns play a major role in determining whether a move is viewed with foreboding and dread or as a welcome relief. So, too, does anticipation, knowing far enough in advance to prepare oneself for the move, and, if possible, making preliminary visits to the new apartment or house, facilitate adjustment. The expectations an older person has regarding the new location and the nature of the situation being left behind inevitably contribute to the effects of the move. Unsurprisingly, physical health is also a major factor. Given sufficient preparation and sensitive handling of the change, new housing often has a positive impact on morale and life satisfaction. One study of applicants to a public housing project in Texas failed to reveal significant differences on several indices of well-being at the time of the change between those elderly who actually moved in and those who decided to remain where they were. However, a year later the new tenants scored higher on a variety of measures of housing satisfaction, morale, perceived health and other salient activities than did their peers who maintained their original situation (Carp, 1966). Similar results are reported by other studies of elderly people who become residents of several types of new housing. With positive expectations, the move is characterized by perceived improvement in health, higher morale, greater participation in voluntary activities and unexpected new friendships (Hochschild, 1973; Lawton and Cohen, 1974).

Institutionalization and Its Alternatives

Becoming Institutionalized

What are older people to do if there comes a time when, even though they are not seriously ill, they can no longer fend for themselves in what may be an unaccommodating environment? For those who have families or financial reserves they can draw upon, there are a number of alternatives that may be pursued. There is, however, an undeniable segment of the older population who have neither family ties nor adequate resources. For them, entering an institution may be the only possible way of getting the help they need. In Europe the availability of domiciliary homes for the elderly goes back to sixteenth century "alms houses" for the indigent old in England and on the continent. During the Middle Ages, care of the elderly was sporadic, generally perceived of as a moral obligation of the church. In England, the Poor Law of 1601 settled the responsibility of caring for the poor and infirm on the shoulders of each community. Based on a localized system of taxation, the law was intended to equalize the burdens of supportive services by requiring each community to contribute only its proportionate share of money and assistance. This was one of the earliest nationally sanctioned measures of relief. Ironically, 375 years later many of the difficulties inherent in such a program are still being addressed by societies. It is only in the present century that similar facilities have been provided in the United States, and many of these came about as a consequence of social legislation during the Depression. At the present time there are almost a million elderly lodged in various kinds of institutions, about 4 to 5 percent of the population over age 65. Comparable proportions of the elderly in Britain and on the continent are also institutionalized. This figure may be slightly misleading though, since it represents only those elderly institutionalized at any given time. It reveals nothing of those who may have been in an institution in the past or may find themselves in one in the future. Among the younger elderly, in the 65 to 75 age range, the percentage is far less, but in the years after 75 it climbs rather precipitously, reaching a rate at least four times the average by the eighth decade. If the scope is broadened somewhat and place of death is considered as evidence of institutionalization, then over 85 percent of the elderly live at least some portion of their later years in institutions (Shanas et al., 1968; Kastenbaum and Candy, 1973).

Who are the elderly most likely to find themselves residents of institutions? Contrary to many popular misconceptions, they are not generally people who have been deposited there by uncaring families. There are exceptions no doubt, but if anything, the majority of families wait far too long before seeking more adequate care for their elders. In the eyes of young and old alike, institutionalization represents the ultimate personal failure for the aged and their family. In fact, two-thirds of the elderly view institutions as the least desirable alternative possible, a sort of confession of final surrender, a halfway stop on the route to death. Often, the older people living out their years in some kind of institution are those who have no other recourse. They are the socially and economically disadvantaged who had previously lived alone and were without close family ties, although serious health problems may lead to the admittance of other residents. Entry normally follows increasing mental or physical incapacity which might not necessarily spell institutionalization but for the absence of supportive networks. Most are white rather than nonwhite older people, excepting those in mental hospitals, and women tend to outnumber men, if only because they are still alive. Thus, most residents come from the generation over the age of 75 who are unable to maintain their independence on the outside or who have otherwise become social isolates (Riley, Foner et al., 1968; S.J. Brody, 1973; Shore, 1974).

The institutions in which older people are confined vary from old age homes that provide little more than custodial care or general supervision to state mental hospitals and skilled nursing facilities. Unfortunately, a latent function of the federal legislation aimed at strengthening health care services has been the increased reliance on institutionalization to solve relatively minor problems of aging. At the same time it has promoted the propagation of proprietary nursing homes, whose profit motives may be at variance with the best interests of their residents. Standards maintained in the different types of institutions have been established by federal legislation resulting in a labyrinth of regulations imposed by successive laws governing their operation. Homes for the aged, sometimes called *domiciliary care* homes, provide protective living accommodations to residents who require minimal supervision in a sheltered environment and who are able otherwise to take care of their own needs. In the event serious illnesses develop necessitating medical attention, residents are transferred to more appropriate facilities, either *personal care* homes with nursing services or, for those who can see to their own medical regime, personal care homes without nursing facilities. Most retirement communities and elderly residential hotels or apartments fall into these categories, which comprise overall nearly one-fourth of the institutional alternatives. *Skilled nursing facilities* may offer complete or intermediate levels of care. In either case, they must furnish around-the-clock nursing service based on personal need and provide medical and dietary supervision. Such institutions may be an extended care facility serving as a convalescent unit for general hospitals or they may admit residents without prior hospitalization. As outlined in Chapter Seven, Medicare requires at least a three day stay in a hospital plus certified medical need if financial assistance is to be supplied by the federal government. Today there are nearly 25,000 nursing homes in the United States; close to 80 percent of these are commercial operations where sizeable profits are occasionally made. Housing two-thirds of all institutionalized elderly, the business potential of such homes is indeed glamorous (U.S. Dept. of Health, Education and Welfare, 1974). Unfortunately, unscrupulous owners have found ways to hedge services in order to enhance the return on their money (C. Townsend, 1971; Butler and Lewis, 1973). Despite the establishment of an Office of Nursing Home Affairs within HEW to oversee enforcement of governmental regulations, the task is formidable. Dissatisfaction with the commercial nursing home industry is so widespread that during 1975 a series of investigations were launched in several states, led by New York, to determine the extent to which profiteering results in both misappropriation of government and private funds and resident abuse. Nonprofit status should not in itself be interpreted as the best solution; whether by intention or lack or training, many religious, fraternal, or governmentally supported homes are not immune from the same kinds of problems encountered in commercial facilities.

A portion of the elderly also find themselves in mental hospitals, though their conditions may not actually justify such treatment. Aside from those who have clinically significant functional or organic disorders, there are elderly in mental institutions, some say nearly half, who have simply become slightly disoriented, but who have no place else where they can go. With the development of supportive services in the community, such as neighborhood mental health clinics or daycare centers, no doubt the aged population in state mental hospitals could be drastically reduced. On the heels of the 1975 Supreme Court decision restricting unwarranted confinement for custodial purposes, there is at least the possibility of large scale discharges from mental hospitals. If this eventuality comes to pass, it might force the development of community services that would allow many of the poor or black elderly to secure the help they need without transferring to another institution. If nothing else, this will surely add to their life expectancy, since mortality among those in all forms of institutions in the United States, Britain and elsewhere exceeds the rate for those who remain at large, especially during the first year. The exact causes of the abnormally higher rates cannot now be pinpointed; certainly higher death rates might be a consequence of physical ills, but other unexplored factors, including the trauma of relocation, would be easily implicated (P. Townsend, 1963; *Preparation for Relocation*, 1973).

Institutional Environments

While there is no denying that many older people could benefit from a sheltered environment, the extent to which the various forms of institutionalization satisfy emotional needs of the elderly is another question. Too many institutions deprive residents of their sense of integrity by depersonalizing the environment to the point where staff find it highly efficient. Residents on the other hand have almost all personal property taken from them, a logical result of a milieu cast in a strict hospital mold. Despite the need for a portion of the setting to be oriented to adequate, sometimes efficient, and extensive medical service, there is no real reason why the remainder cannot be made more flexible. An awareness of psychological needs and residents' rights should be just as strong an element in the architectural design, expecially in old age homes, as the technical aspects of health care. In actuality it would easily be possible to achieve a warmer feeling in all geriatric institutions; most gerontologists agree there is no justification for elevating institutional expediency over the provision of something approximating the residents' own unique life space. Both physical layout and functioning could easily incorporate more resident input, thereby gratifying a desire to continue to exercise some element of control over their living arrangements (E. M. Brody, 1973; Kahana, 1973; Gubrium, 1975).

As a consequence of what is sometimes referred to as *psychological railroading* within highly routinized environments, some older residents are prone to a kind of **institutional neurosis.** Chief among its symptoms is a gradual erosion of the uniqueness of one's personality traits so that residents become increasingly dependent on staff direction for even the most mundane needs. Visitors often complain about the sense of distance between themselves and the resident or the latter's seeming lack of attendance to events outside the institution. It isn't necessarily that personnel in the institution are insensitive to the older person's plight; rather, that the operational procedures themselves breed a kind of docility leading in turn to a leveling of character attributes. In attempting to counter the hospital constraints insofar as practical and to set up the institution as an extension of the community, some investigators point out that many of the negative connotations of institutionalization could be minimized. With the number of older people over 75 expanding far more rapidly than the older segment of the population in general, the need for some kind of supportive environments will continue to expand in the near future. If indeed part of our value framework is the humane treatment of the elderly, ways must be found to restructure institutions to emulate the normal rhythms and needs of the residents. Building in opportunities for the elderly to have a sense of active participation in their own affairs is the first step (E.M. Brody, 1973; Butler and Lewis, 1973; Lawton, 1975).

Institutional Alternatives

In view of the negative aura surrounding institutionalization and by virtue of the fact that in many cases placement is made because no other remedies are readily apparent, there is an obvious need to maximize alternative arrangements. It is estimated that roughly 15 to 40 percent of those people already living in institutions could handily be maintained in the community if adequate supplemental home care could be obtained. Similarly, in her survey of five industrial countries, Shanas suggests at least one-fifth to one-third of the noninstitutional aged in various countries could benefit from these same services to such an extent that institutionalization might be avoided (Shanas, 1971; Morris, 1974). As others have pointed out, the idea of alternatives to institutions has been with us for some time. Alternative may not be the best word, as the proposed programs are basically designed to encourage and facilitate community living and to relegate institutions to the supplemental role they were initially intended to fill. The point is not simply to keep people at home because it seems like a better thing to do, but to ameliorate those conditions pressing them into institutions in the first place. Presently there are approximately 3000 organizations qualified under Medicare regulations to offer home health care, and since proprietary agencies are allowed to offer therapeutic services to noninstitutionalized elderly, this number is likely to increase rapidly. The problem will be in making sure that the target population of needy elderly are fully aware of the choices they have available (Reader, 1973).

Day hospitals where older people can go to secure medical and social services have existed in Britain for two decades, while in America the idea of daycare centers for the elderly has attracted attention only in the past few years. Generally, day centers focus on the provision of social services; however, they are beginning to offer a complete range of facilities, paralleling those furnished by institutions themselves. Among the more important elements of alternative services are health maintenance, housekeeping and shopping services, transportation help, meals, and financial and general counseling. Not only are these options financially feasible compared to institutionalization, they are practical in terms of manpower requirements. The biggest obstacle appears to be the bureaucratic red tape in the federal agencies and the bias in favor of institutional services. Rather than viewing institutions and their alternatives as either-or propositions, the two could be made to work in conjunction, so that the elderly might exercise some freedom of choice in deciding which is the more desirable (Bell, 1973; Kistin and Morris, 1972).

One intermediate arrangement containing elements of both institutional and home maintenance is the retirement community or residence organized on a graduated or concentric basis. Normally these programs are designed to provide a minimally sheltered environment for those who are no longer satisfied living in the community, but who do not yet require any extensive assistance. Residents either purchase or rent living accommodations and make use of other facilities as they desire. There is an element of risk under the purchase plan, with the result that longevity, treatment and profits may be indirectly related. As one observer characterizes the plans, the administrators count on a stable death rate — hence, sufficient turnover — to meet their mortgage commitments. On the other hand, the residents wish to maximize their investment by living long enough to get a good return on the stiff entrance fee without running out of money to meet monthly payments (Marshall, 1973). Usually there are programs for elderly who prefer to live elsewhere but to come to the center during the day for meals or other services. In addition, there is a team that visits the aged person to provide homemaker assistance or to deliver hot meals. For those in need of more help than is practical under independent living arrangements, a second level of care exists where more complete personal attention is given in an intermediate nursing facility, though there is still a full measure of independence. Finally, there is a unit for the nonambulatory older people requiring close nursing supervision. The support systems of these facilities are intended to bridge the continuum from guarded independence to long-term care for the frail elderly.

Ideally, the multipurpose day centers, outreach programs, congregate or independent living accommodations, and the long-term nursing facilities can offer a total service program in which the elderly individually select only the assistance they desire, feeling as though the choice is indeed theirs to make. Part of the problem with the present state of community services springs from the lack of integration among agencies and the underrepresentation of elderly clients. Community mental health programs, for instance, are less involved with their potential elderly clients than would be indicated in terms of their needs, though it may well be that services enabling the older community resident to remain active at home make up for some of the deficiencies left unaddressed by mental health agencies. Such programs as free transportation, contact with health care facilities, and mediation between the elderly resident and social welfare agencies, landlords and local governmental bureaucracies have been deemed crucial by community planners. Organizations that facilitate resident involvement in the community also serve the important function of sensitizing other community members to the needs and desires of the elderly, who often constitute an invisible and fragmented sector of the population (Bennett, 1973; Blonsky, 1973; Shore, 1974).

Summary

One of the more pervasive myths about old age is that the elderly are abandoned by their families to face life's challenges solely through their own devices. In our brief look at the social and physical situations of older people in the United States and a few selected countries abroad, little evidence was found to support such a view. On the contrary, a network of extended families appears to be alive and well, if somewhat modified. At least half of all older people would appear to be incorporated into three generational families who live in close proximity. If the staging of family life cycles continues to advance to even earlier ages, there is reason to believe that four generation networks will become more common as middle-aged people begin to assume the role of grandparents. The place of grandparents in family life is invariably tied to the cultural traditions of a country, but these too seem to exhibit certain patterns that cut across national boundaries. While fewer older Americans share the same physical living space with their children than their counterparts abroad, the majority participate in kinship networks providing emotional and material supports to one another. Over 80 percent of the elderly in the United States and in other industrial countries see their children on a weekly, if not a daily, basis, generally living within easy commuting distance of each other. The housing characteristics of older people in the countries surveyed show some variation in terms of single family homes as contrasted to congregate living arrangements, with the former predominate in America. In most respects, however, very similar patterns emerge. In all cases, the elderly tend to live in older, less desirable accommodations which, while being fairly sizeable, often present serious maintenance problems. Despite the inconveniences involved, relatively few are willing to move away from neighborhoods that they have considered home for an average of 25 years. For those who do move, there is often a period of mourning for the lost residence and for all it symbolizes. If the relocation was voluntary, morale usually does take a turn for the better. Confronted by the supposedly cleansing forces of urban renewal, or simply out of a desire to lighten the burdens carried by some of the elderly, upgrading existing housing provides an important opportunity for intervention, where real and immediate benefits may be realized if the whole matter is handled in a sensitive fashion.

With the differences in life expectancy, the average woman is likely to be widowed for an extensive period. Under the circumstances, it is reasonable to assume that alternative lifestyles for the elderly will evolve. What shape these will take cannot yet be predicted with any certainty, but several possibilities including old age communes, are already gaining attention. As a highly individualized event, the death of a spouse might not appear at first glance to result in any predictable consequences. Once again, researchers are finding the avenues to recovery are not nearly as unique as those involved usually believe. Traditions against remarriage for women are gradually lessening, though widowed men have long shown a greater tendency to take another spouse. Without intending to paint too bleak a picture, older women are more likely to become socially isolated, and therefore more dependent on their children, than are men. For the widowed and the elderly in general, families play a major part in promoting satisfactory adjustment and satisfaction during the later years.

For almost everyone, the thought of residing in an institution is chilling. Like so many other facets of aging, the probability of institutionalization is little understood. At any given time, about one million of the elderly are living in institutions. For those between the ages of 65 and 75, the probability of such an event is less than for those over 75, when the chances increase with each additional year.

Even though only 4 percent of the aged are institutionalized, far in excess of that proportion face entry into an institution at some point, if only for the last days of life. Since it is the oldest age group that is growing most rapidly among the elderly, the nursing home industry should continue to expand in the future unless alternatives can be worked out whereby parallel services are available to those in need. Anyone who reads of a fire sweeping through a geriatric institution or hears of the profiteering of some segment of the industry cannot help but appreciate the feelings of impotence and frustration felt by people who are more intimately involved. Federal legislation or local licensing procedures should not be seen as a panacea, for what is really needed is the provision of more viable options. At present, efforts are just beginning to be made in this direction, with the establishment of stepwise centers that facilitate a sense of independence, allowing their clients to select only those services and assistance they feel they require. In many respects the United States lags behind European countries in offering a full spectrum of social services for the elderly. The American emphasis on self-sufficiency in an age where no single individual can control all the forces that impinge on his or her life has resulted in an underdeveloped and nonintegrated service delivery system stressing remedial measures for problems that might be fairly easily prevented. The question of ameliorative versus preventive programs is not likely to be resolved by one program, but as the number of the very old continues to increase it cannot be ignored.

Pertinent Readings

ATCHLEY, R.C. "Dimensions of Widowhood in Later Life." *The Gerontologist* XV, 2 (1975): 176–78.
BELL, W.G. "Community Care for the Elderly: An Alternative to Institutionalization." *The Gerontologist* XIII, 3, pt. I (1973): 349–54.
BENGTSON, V.L. "Generation and Family Effects." *American Sociological Review* XL, 3 (1975): 358–71.
BENGTSON, V.L. and J.A. KUYPERS, "Generational Difference and the Developmental Stake." *Aging and Human Development* II, 3 (1971): 249–60.
BENNETT, R. "Living Conditions and Everyday Needs of the Elderly with Particular Reference to Social Isolation." *Aging and Human Development* IV, 3 (1973): 179–98.
BERARDO, F. "Survivorship and Social Isolation: The Case of the Aged Widower." *Family Coordinator* XIX (1970): 11–15.
BIRREN, J.E. "The Aged in Cities." *The Gerontologist* IX, 3 (1969): 163–69.
BLENKNER, M. "Social Work and Family Relationships in Later Years with Some Thoughts on Filial Maturity." In *Social Structure and the Family:*

Generational Relations, eds. E. Shanas and G.F. Streib, 46–59. Englewood
Cliffs, N.J.: Prentice-Hall, 1965.

BLONSKY, L.E. "An Innovative Service for the Elderly." *The Gerontologist*
XIII, 2 (1973): 189–96.

BRODY, E.M. "A Million Procrustean Beds." *The Gerontologist* XIII, 4 (1973):
430–35.

BRODY, S.J. "Comprehensive Health Care for the Elderly: An Analysis." *The
Gerontologist* XIII, 4 (1973): 412–18.

BUTLER, R.N., and M.I. LEWIS. *Aging and Mental Health: Positive Psychosocial Approaches.* St. Louis, Mo.: The C.V. Mosby Company, 1973.

BYERTS, T., et al. "Housing: International Research and Education in Social
Gerontology; Goals and Strategies." *The Gerontologist* XII, 2, pt. II (1972):
3–10.

CAINE, L. *Widow.* New York: Morrow, 1974.

CARO, F.G. "Professional Roles in the Maintenance of the Disabled Elderly in
the Community: A Forecast." *The Gerontologist* XIV, 4 (1974): 286–88.

CARP, F.M. *A Future for the Aged.* Austin: University of Texas Press, 1966.

CAVAN, R.S. "Speculations on Innovations to Conventional Marriage in Old
Age." *The Gerontologist* XIII, 4 (1973): 409–11.

FRIED, M. "Grieving for a Lost Home." In *People and Buildings,* ed. R. Gut-
man, 229–48. New York: Basic Books, 1972.

GLICK, I.O., R.S. WEISS and C.M. PARKES. *The First Year of Bereavement.*
New York: John Wiley & Sons, 1974.

GLICK, P.C., and R. PARKE, JR. "New Approaches in Studying the Life Cycle of
the Family." *Demography* II (1965): 187–202.

GUBRIUM, J.F. *Living and Dying at Murray Manor.* New York: St. Martin's
Press, 1975.

HAMOVITCH, M.B., and J.E. PETERSON. "Housing Needs and Satisfaction of the
Elderly." *The Gerontologist* IX, 1 (1969): 30–32.

HARRIS, L. and ASSOCIATES. *The Myth and Reality of Aging in America.*
Washington, D.C.: The National Council on the Aging, Inc., 1975.

HOCHSCHILD, A.R. *The Unexpected Community.* Englewood Cliffs, N.J.:
Prentice-Hall, 1973.

KAHANA, E. "The Humane Treatment of Old People in Institutions." *The
Gerontologist* XIII, 3, pt. I (1973): 282–89.

KAHANA, E., and B. KAHANA. "Theoretical and Research Perspectives on
Grandparenthood." *Aging and Human Development* II, 4 (1971): 261–68.

KALISH, R. ed. *The Dependencies of Old People.* Ann Arbor: Institute of
Gerontology, University of Michigan, 1969.

KASTENBAUM, R., and S.E. CANDY. "The 4% Fallacy: A Methodological and
Empirical Critique of Extended Care Facility Population Statistics." *Aging
and Human Development* IV, 1 (1973): 15–21.

KISTIN, H., and R. MORRIS. "Alternatives to Institutional Care for the Elderly
and Disabled." *The Gerontologist* XII, 2, pt. I (1972): 139–42.

LAWTON, M.P. *Planning and Managing Housing for the Elderly.* New York:
Wiley-Interscience, 1975.

LAWTON, M.P., and J. COHEN. "The Generality of Housing Impact on the Well-being of Older People." *Journal of Gerontology* XXIX, 2 (1974): 194–204.

LOPATA, H.Z. *Widowhood in an American City.* Cambridge, Mass.: Schenkman, 1973.

MARSHALL, V.W. "Game-Analyzable Dilemmas in a Retirement Village." *Aging and Human Development* IV, 4 (1973): 285–91.

MCGUIRE, M.C. "The Status of Housing for the Elderly." *The Gerontologist* IX, 1 (1969): 10–14.

MCKAIN, W.C. "The Aged in the USSR." In *Aging and Modernization,* eds. D.O. Cowgill and L.D. Holmes, 151–66. New York: Appleton-Century-Crofts, 1972.

MORRIS, R. "The Development of Parallel Services for the Elderly and Disabled." *The Gerontologist* XIV, 1 (1974): 14–19.

NEUGARTEN, B., and K. WEINSTEIN. "The Changing American Grandparent." *Journal of Marriage and the Family* XXVI (1964): 199–204.

NIEBANCK, P.L. (with the assistance of J.B. Pope). *The Elderly in Older Urban Areas: Problems of Adaptation and the Effects of Relocation.* Philadelphia: University of Pennsylvania, Institute for Environmental Studies, 1965.

PALMORE, E. *The Honorable Elders.* Durham, N.C.: Duke University Press, 1975.

PLATH, D.W. "Japan: The After Years." In *Aging and Modernization,* eds. D.O. Cowgill and L.D. Holmes, 133–50. New York: Appleton-Century-Crofts, 1972.

POSNER, J. "Notes on the Negative Implications of Being Competent in a Home for the Aged." *Aging and Human Development* V, 4 (1974): 357–64.

Preparation for Relocation, Relocation Report No. 3. Ann Arbor: Institute of Gerontology, University of Michigan, 1973.

READER, G.G. "Types of Geriatric Institutions." *The Gerontologist* XIII, 3, pt. I (1973): 290–94.

RILEY, M.W., A. FONER et al. *Aging and Society, Volume One: An Inventory of Research Findings.* New York: Russell Sage Foundation, 1968.

ROSENBERG., G. *The Worker Grows Old.* San Francisco: Jossey-Bass, 1970.

ROSENMAYR, L. "The Elderly in Austrian Society." In *Aging and Modernization,* eds. D.O. Cowgill and L.D. Holmes, 183–96. New York: Appleton-Century-Crofts, 1972.

SHANAS, E. "Measuring the Home Health Needs of the Aged in Five Countries." *Journal of Gerontology* XXVI, 1 (1971): 37–40.

SHANAS, E., et al. *Old People in Three Industrial Societies.* New York: Atherton Press, 1968.

SHORE, H. "What's New About Alternatives." *The Gerontologist* XIV, 1 (1974): 6–11.

SIMMONS, L.W. *The Role of the Aged in Primitive Society.* New Haven: Yale University Press, 1945.

STREIB, G.F. "Old Age in Ireland: Demographic and Sociological Aspects." In *Aging and Modernization*, eds. D.O. Cowgill and L.D. Holmes, 167–82. New York: Appleton-Century-Crofts, 1972.

SUSSMAN, M.B. "Relationships of Adult Children with their Parents in the United States." In *Social Structure and the Family: Generational Relations*, eds. E. Shanas and G.F. Streib, 62–92. Englewood Cliffs, N.J.: Prentice-Hall, Inc., 1965.

TOWNSEND, C. *Old Age: The Last Segregation.* New York: Bantam Books, 1971.

TOWNSEND, P. *The Family Life of Old People.* Baltimore: Penguin Books, 1963.

TROLL, L.E. "The Family of Later Life: A Decade Review." *Journal of Marriage and the Family* XXXIII (1971): 263–90.

TUNSTALL, J. *Old and Alone: A Sociological Study of Old People.* London: Routledge & Kegan Paul, 1966.

U.S. BUREAU OF THE CENSUS. *Current Population Reports.* Series P-20, no. 276, "Household and Family Characteristics: March 1974." Washington, D.C.: U.S. Government Printing Office, 1975a.

———. *Current Population Reports.* Series P-20, no. 285, "Mobility of the Population of the United States: March 1970 to March 1975." Washington, D.C.: U.S. Government Printing Office, 1975b.

———. *Statistical Abstract 1975.* Washington, D.C.: U.S. Government Printing Office, 1975c.

U.S. DEPARTMENT OF HEALTH, EDUCATION AND WELFARE, PUBLIC HEALTH SERVICE. *Health Resources Statistics: Health Manpower and Health Facilities, 1974.* Washington, D.C.: U.S. Government Printing Office, 1974.

WEISS, J.D. *Better Buildings for the Aged.* New York: McGraw-Hill, 1971.

Chapter 11

Aging: Everyday Concerns

Aside from puzzling over the meaning of the world, the nature of retirement or financial matters, what are older people concerned with as they go about their normal routines? Like everyone else they generally worry about day-to-day occurrences. Idle moments are occupied in reflection — wondering about oneself, friends, marital relations, what to do tonight or tomorrow, even the nearness of death and the purpose of religion. Having lived lives unduplicated by others, we all speculate from time to time whether anyone thinks the way we do or handles life in the same manner. Yet believing ourselves to be somehow exceptional — not necessarily better but unique

— it is difficult to fathom that others might have quite similar thoughts and concerns. This chapter focuses on selected aspects of the everyday lives of older people. It looks at the way they view themselves, their friends and what they do. To approach a comprehensive coverage, an examination of this sort must also deal with sexual interest if it is to depict the true nature of daily experience. There is remarkable consensus among social commentators about the pervasiveness of sexuality as a matter of conversation, consideration and mythology. To shed light on its place in the lives of the elderly, the discussion will include a somewhat clinical look at sexual functioning in the hopes that if it is better understood the vagaries can be dispelled. Thoughts and fears of impending death are allegedly the impetus behind whatever disengagement is observed among the aged. While death is undeniably a salient topic, the degree of apprehension manifested by the elderly has been largely overplayed. Religiosity over the course of the lifespan is another topic surrounded by a host of illusions, just as are sex and death. For some people religion is of the utmost importance, providing a sense of meaning and uplift to their lives. There is little support, however, for the belief that vast numbers of people become more religious as they realize the time remaining to them is limited.

Self and Social Involvement

Reflections from Inside

What do we mean when we ask how old a person is? Chronological age is the customary measure used to formulate a response, but, as noted much earlier, it is likely to mask wide variations. Physiologically, separate components of the body age at different rates; thus, it is entirely possible to have the eyes of a young adult, the lungs of an older person, yet show middle age on the calendar. Asking people how old they feel might not provide any better information, since chances are their answers will be phrased in relative terms. "Do you mean compared to my children? To others who have lived the same length of time? Or, to whom?" Usually they will offer two or three responses: "Last birthday I was . . . , but I feel . . . years younger. No different than I did when I was . . . . I've still got my health, so I'm in better shape than Joe, who is . . . years younger than I am." It is quite common for adults over age 25 or so to report they actually feel younger than their birth certificates indicate. In fact the majority of us, up to and including the very old, often hold a more youthful self-concept than our years would indicate.

Even those in their seventh and eighth decades frequently express their contempt for "old folks" — meaning individuals either older or less healthy than themselves. As many researchers have discovered, the elderly consistently exempt themselves from the reprehensible qualities attributed to others who are at a comparable point in life (Guptill, 1969; Rosow, 1974).

Personal conceptions of one's own age are always subjective, though they may include a complex interweaving of objective criteria such as stage of family life cycle, career and employment patterns, health or socioeconomic background. Self-concepts are never, in themselves, singular; people have as many facets or selves as they have social roles and none ever remain static. At the same time, nearly all see themselves as original and exceptional; indeed, it is true, no one else has the same biography. But the sense of uniqueness goes beyond individuality to encompass a belief that although our age mates are obviously becoming older, we alone are possessed of a particular youthfulness. The person we appear to be to someone else is not necessarily the one we are for ourselves. The real "me" is the one inside. Externally age may show, but these signs are generally dismissed as merely superficial. Compared to the inner person, outward appearances are hardly proof positive of anything. No amount of reality testing will suffice to bring about a complete congruence between our own and others' conceptions of us, primarily because it is impossible to climb out of our bodies for an "objective" look. In a sense, the process of *psychological distancing* implied by self-perceived youthfulness is a protective device, insulating our self-image from derogation. As de Beauvoir (1973) observes, this may be part of the reason behind the under-utilization of medical facilities or the failure to follow a physician's orders that others, little understanding the purpose it serves, find so irksome about many older people.

Percentages vary from one study to the next, however; anywhere between half to two-thirds of those over 65 continue to think of themselves as no more than middle-aged, a perception actually well-established by the third decade (Riley and Foner et al., 1968; Kastenbaum et al., 1972). Approximately the same factors are operative in terms of personal age as influence subjective evaluations of health or estimated chances of survival. Just as social involvements, social class, sex and so on play pivotal roles in shaping the latter, so too do they offset personal images of age. In constructing and maintaining self-concepts, men tend to rely more on external events; women, on the other hand, modify their self-images to bring about a closer correspondence to their personal feelings or abilities (Back, 1974). Most find from their internal point of view an intuitive sense of sameness about themselves. In any event, those who perceive themselves to be younger demonstrate higher morale, greater satisfaction, better health, less somatic concern, increased mobility and more optimistic frames of mind than their age peers who feel somehow older. On the opposite side, only a fifth or less of the elderly regard themselves as being older than their chronological age. Usually these people are recovering from a serious bout with illness or some other displacing events and have not regained their equilibrium. Among additional phenomena contributing to older self-images, researchers have also counted the sudden removal of social props, the absence of friendly reinforcers, and institutionalization and its corresponding stigma and devaluation. The consequences for this group, who view themselves as old beyond their years, are predominately negative — resulting in lower morale, increased dependency, ill health and even earlier deaths. From a practical standpoint it makes a great deal of difference whether individuals consider themselves to be old or not so old.

One of the primary distinctions between those who think of themselves as younger and those older, relative to their years, incorporates their acceptance of stereotypes about the aged and what is considered to be age-appropriate behavior. Younger-thinking people are more prone to personal definitions of life changes than to complete acceptance of socially prescribed norms. This is not to imply any special strengths on the part of those who perceive themselves to be younger; rather, a built-in flexibility and perhaps a more secure sense of self. Positive reinforcements, friends and social involvements may help curtail the negative connotations young and old alike attribute to the later years, thereby abetting the chances for life satisfaction among all the elderly. Subjectively defined age is as powerful a concept as chronological age and, as was illustrated in connection with personal evaluations of health, may in itself prove a reliable predictor of future survival. The means of appraising perceived age are only now beginning to receive attention, not merely as a curiosity but as another tool for assisting older people to maximize the opportunities of their later years.

Old Friends

Along with their memberships in various voluntary organizations, friendships potentially shield the aged against negative self-evaluations. Sometimes more than family ties, intimate friends are a great source of strength, since they provide reference points from which adaptive reformulations of one's self-concept can be forged. By having several or even a single close friend with whom they can share their thoughts, fears, interests or objective problems, older people are protected from many of the negative definitions imposed by the larger society and from some of the protean liabilities growing out of the attrition of their social roles. Peer groups as socializing agents form the basis for the subcultural perspective discussed in Chapter Five and, as such, they are influential and highly salutory for all people, the elderly being no exception. For this reason the value of friends is apt to redouble during adult life; at the same time, the nature of friendships also changes. As indicated in the previous chapter, older people's reluctance to move to improved housing stems partly from neighborhood ties, based on long-term residency and friendship bonds that are often very deeply rooted. Given the opportunity to relocate, many elderly prefer to stay put because that is where their friends are.

As a personal resource, friends play a less significant role as long as there are children to raise, jobs to perform and places to go. Relieved of many full-time family obligations, middle-aged people discover that their friends become a major source of satisfaction. Since friends are usually at a similar point in the family life cycle and have many of the same concerns and interests, there are ample grounds for solid, intimate relationships to take root. With the narrowing of the social life space beginning in late middle age, ties are strengthened; consequently, those most often cited by older people as trusted friends have usually been involved in long-standing relationships carried over from the middle years. Interaction or visiting back and forth is regular, weekly at least, and is apparently unassociated with the frequency of contact among parents and children except among the most disadvantaged. For this latter group, Rosow (1970) reports he and others have found what amounts to an inverse relationship between contact with friends and neighbors on the one hand and children on the other. Greater interaction with one or the other portends less in the opposite realm. For those not severely affected by the hardships of age or by the absence of children in the immediate vicinity, however, the two sets of relationships are thought to be largely independent. There is no doubt about the salience of familial bonds; they continue to play the single most important role in the lives of most elderly. But by themselves family members have a difficult time sustaining morale. Friends also boost morale, and their presence or absence may in fact be an overriding consideration among interpersonal factors contributing to a sense of well-being. Interestingly, the aged almost never turn to their friends for financial assistance; they look only to family for monetary help, though in the case of illness, friends and neighbors constitute viable substitutes for family (Rosow, 1970; Blau, 1973).

While friendships play a major role in sustaining psychological adjustment, it should not be inferred that isolated individuals *necessarily* fare less well. In some cases lifelong isolates have been reported as having average or even higher morale and are no more disposed to psychological distress requiring hospitalization. For example, remaining unmarried throughout life does not automatically impose a particular handicap. Single elderly do not suffer from excessive longliness even though they are clearly more solitary. It is mostly those who have tried and failed to make friends or else have lost their intimate ties who are particularly susceptible to emotional upset. The majority of the elderly do experience fewer contacts with their friends as they enter the further reaches of old age for reasons not solely attributable to death rates. Some evidence reveals that social networks based on work or marital status are the most susceptible to dissolution, although middle class elderly have a greater retention of friends compared to their working class peers. Not only do they have a larger number of friends, but unlike their less advantaged age mates, they augment older friends with those only recently met. Localized friendships also reflect class patterns; here working class elderly are more prone to having a preponderance of friends who are also neighbors. Perhaps as a consequence of their greater sociability, married people more often have intimate friends than nonmarrieds, while women feel they have a greater number of friends than men. In all cases, friends resemble one another fairly closely; thus married people's friends are usually married, and of the same social class, age and sex (Rosow, 1967; Rosenberg, 1970; Gubrium, 1975).

Contrary to popular expectations, intergenerational proximity does not automatically breed more friendships across generational lines. The research data tend to run counter to the common notion — older people in age-integrated residential settings seem to be more isolated than those in age-segregated environments. Propinquity is an obvious component of all friendships, although contiguity must be social as well as physical, and too much of the latter may prove to be dysfunctional. In advocating age-homogeneous enclaves, Rosow (1967, 1974) notes the more segregated the housing the more integrated people are within it. Undoubtedly there are a variety of situations where such a plan would be unsatisfactory over the long run, but for some older people it may be conducive to the insulation so vital to their well-being and self-concept. Structuring neighborhoods or other residences by high age densities may allow a larger proportion of elderly to be immersed in supportive social systems. As brought out in the previous chapter, most elderly are concentrated in urban areas and inner city neighborhoods. Though this may often be by default, there may be latent benefits by having ready access to their friends. In any situation where personal identity is called into question, all people are more sensitive to the influence of those with whom they feel close. Neighboring thus assumes a mutually compensatory function as both parties become helpful role models in maintaining positive self-esteem. The happiest and the healthiest older people are those who are involved in close personal relationships that act as buffers against many social decrements and role losses. With even one close confidant in whom they confide, the aged can face many problems that otherwise prove physically or mentally debilitating (Lowenthal and Haven, 1968).

Voluntary Alliances

Well over a hundred years ago, de Tocqueville graphically described Americans as a nation of joiners; indeed, the penchant for voluntary participation has become part of the pluralistic aura and ideology of the United States. From an analysis of participation rates in six Western democracies, Curtis (1971), however, deems the assumed uniqueness of the American propensity for joining voluntary associations to be overrated. According to his research, approximately half of the American population belongs to various nonunion associations, yet the extent of affiliation in the United States is second to Canada's. In Great Britain and West Germany the number who participate in at least one voluntary organization is roughly one-third, followed by Italy at 25 percent and Mexico at 15. Including union membership does not alter the ordering even though the percentages are somewhat inflated. The proportion who belong to a multiple number of associations is less, of course: one-third in both Canada and the United States, 11 percent in Britain and less than 9 percent in the other countries. Hardly surprising, such factors as sex, social class, marital status and age are important variables in every instance. Except for the United States and Canada, where men are only slightly more likely than women to join various kinds of nonunion organizations, the rate of membership for men is two to three times that of women. People of higher social class backgrounds and the married more often claim involvement in voluntary organizations. In terms of age, affiliations approximate a normal curve, reaching a peak in the middle years, between 36 and 50, remaining at a plateau until the sixties and slowly declining thereafter.

Turning to group memberships of older people, a block of smaller studies specify and provide a closer look at participation rates. Although affiliation with voluntary associations is usually contingent on other roles, Rosow (1974) points out that expressive memberships may help cushion the loss of instrumental roles. Also, Erikson's developmental model with its emphasis on generativity and leaving a legacy implies that older people might find deep satisfaction by participating in meaningful voluntary pursuits. With a proliferation of voluntary associations running the gamut from recreational to civic organizations, there is ample opportunity for older people to be active if such is their desire. Under the aegis of the federal government, the last few years have marked the birth and growth of several voluntary opportunities intended specifically for older people. The ACTION series now includes such adjuncts as a Retired Senior Volunteers Program (RSVP), Service Corps of Retired Executives (SCORE), Foster Grandparents, Senior Companions and avenues for contributing personal services through VISTA. In various areas there are innumerable similar local programs, all of which attempt to provide alternative roles to older people with minimal financial compensation. Some traditional voluntary agencies are also heavily staffed by the elderly, but in many instances they represent volunteers who have grown old. Most involvement is probably derived from local memberships in church, fraternal and social organizations of which the elderly may be but a part. There is near unanimity among gerontologists that voluntary organizations form an important mechanism for maintaining communal and social integration of older people. Membership is thought to provide a sense of efficacy while countering the tendencies toward a narrowing of the social life space, thereby prompting higher morale among the participants. Since there is a definite self-selection process operating, caution must be exercised before drawing any causal inferences. Doubtless those older people with higher voluntary involvement are also more active in every other realm of their lives, manifesting better adjustment overall. Insofar as membership is a reflection of socioeconomic conditions or subjective evaluation of health, the latter, rather than voluntary participation per se, may be the significant contributor to life satisfaction (Cutler, 1973; Bull and Aucoin, 1975).

It is difficult to say what proportion of our older population is actually involved in voluntary associations, since most of the studies focusing on this question have been cross-sectional analyses unlikely to include the truly isolated elderly. In addition, most people are cognizant of societal norms endorsing participation in voluntary groups, and in all probability they exaggerate their reported activity (Wilensky, 1961). Estimates of participation rates for those in their sixties and beyond vary, ranging from a low of one-fifth or so to a high of over 48 percent. Although the evidence is scanty, for every three memberships retained, older people apparently cancel two, generally those most closely linked with earlier stages of the life cycle (Smith, 1966). However among the elderly as among the general citizenry, membership is closely tied to socioeconomic background; hence, the more advantaged are represented in disproportionate numbers. Since most organizations are comprised of a small nucleus of the dedicated surrounded by a few regular meeting goers and a large number of nominal dues-paying members whose commitment is more ideological than concrete, who is active and who is not is a debatable issue.

One of the many paradoxes of voluntary membership is that, socioeconomic and contingent roles notwithstanding, blacks are involved far more extensively than whites or members of any other ethnic group. In their study of voluntary affiliations in Texas, Williams and associates (1973) found structural variables explained the lower participation of Mexican-Americans and the middle level rates among whites, but did little to clarify why blacks are so active. Further, in contrast to global trends, black and Mexican-American women participate more than their male counterparts even when age, the presence of children, education and other variables are taken into account or controlled. In a study of lower income black and white elderly in Philadelphia, church affiliations were found to predominate among the activities of black respondents — followed by social and recreational memberships — but this was not sufficient to explain why so many more elderly blacks remain highly engaged (Hirsch et al., 1972; Clemente et al., 1975). Ad hoc explanations tend to emphasize the compensatory function served by active membership, offsetting those needs unmet by the larger society, but these are seldom generalizable to the elderly of other minority groups.

Regardless of ethnic or racial backgrounds, for those who do choose to retain active memberships in voluntary associations the rewards are most beneficial. For one thing, in many respects there is either an explicit or implicit age grading in the majority of organizations; therefore, older people are brought into close contact with others their age. Out of their interaction, friendships blossom and a mutual exchange of information and opinion takes place. As might be expected, those expressing the greatest involvement also derive the highest degree of satisfaction. Voluntary groups furnish one situation that older people can avail themselves of in order to talk over aspects of their lives not easily discussed with their adult children. They serve a consciousness-raising function, permitting the elderly to realize they are not alone in their problems nor personally to blame for all their hardships. What will be the picture for voluntary membership in the future? Rising educational levels and socioeconomic improvements may supply the foundation for increased activity, while the publicity focused on "new roles" for the elderly might provide the motivation. For many older people who have an inclination for becoming involved this is all to the good. It must not be overlooked, however, that it is undesirable to force all elderly into accepting an activity model. Furthermore, the potential for exploiting their willingness to voluntarily contribute to essential social services cannot be ignored. As discussed in the next chapter, one of the reasons their participation is so important is that it carries over into other dimensions of activism, such as the political arena.

Diversionary Recreation

Chapter Nine emphasized the need to educate people for a meaningful appraisal of time freed from work. The earlier discussion did not, however, concentrate on what people actually do with their free time. Not everyone welcomes or even views retirement as an opportunity for what is commonly called a life of leisure. Though it is an acknowledged actuality in modern societies, the current generation of older people is among the least prepared, practically or socially, to take advantage of its "leisure." Two-thirds of the elderly participants in the Duke longitudinal studies found greater satisfaction in their work than in leisure activities. Asked whether they would like to continue working if they felt no economic necessity to do so, the proportion answering in the affirmative is as high or higher among the retired as in any other age group (Pfeiffer and Davis, 1974). Regardless of the legitimacy of free time as a replacement for work, it is nonetheless a reality for the aged that cannot be treated lightly. While the general spectrum of activities in which the elderly engage does not differ from that of younger people, only occasionally do the two groups do things together. For the most part, there is a fairly rigid segregation operative in leisure pursuits — due either to generational preferences or perhaps to what has been labeled the **portent of embarrassment,** resulting in the avoidance of situations where older people might expect failure (Miller, 1965).

On a daily basis, television, visiting and reading are the most regular forms of diversion, which also occupy the greatest amount of time. Participation rates for all three are higher among elderly people than their younger counterparts; together these account for somewhere in excess of six hours every day. An average of three hours is spent in front of the television set, two hours in visiting and approximately an hour is given over to all kinds of reading. Not unexpectedly, a relatively small number of older people are active in sports, less than 5 percent both in the United States and abroad, and when they do participate, fishing and comparable passive sports are the most prevalent. Walking and gardening are more characteristic forms of exercise, though they are less than half as popular as idleness and contemplation. Other leisure pursuits include handiwork, home repairs, involvement in meetings of church and social organizations, and so on. Few of today's aged attend the theater, concerts or museums; in fact, nearly two-thirds have never been to any of these at any time during their lives. Movies are a more frequent pastime, but are rarely part of preferred leisure routines. Whether because of the changing values reflected in the films themselves or their own visual or auditory difficulties, half the elderly do not go as often as they used to. The number and extent of vacations and outings also decline after age 65 for a variety of reasons, not the least of which is financial. Despite the publicity, adult education courses find little favor with middle-aged and older people; less than 10 percent customarily take advantage of the offerings. Interestingly, there is a close resemblance in the patterns of leisure reported for most industrialized countries. In France, for example, parallel participation rates appear to be the case across the age span (Riley and Foner et al., 1968; Dumazedier, 1974).

Leisure pursuits are quite obviously conditioned by a whole range of demographic, social and personality variables; thus, predicting future patterns among the elderly is risky business. At present, men and women, especially in the middle years, do not have equal opportunities to engage in leisure. As the proportion of middle-aged women returning to work increases, the inequities could conceivably become even more noticeable, yet changing role definitions may effectively offset such tendencies. Future generations of older people will also have had a lifelong exposure to commercial and mass media forms of entertainment, and their leisure will likely incorporate this fact. Improving health maintenance may bring rewards in the leisure and recreational sphere to people who previously might have been unable to participate due to nagging disabilities. This is not to imply that the most significant leisure pursuits entail activities per se; passive leisure may be equally gratifying. An orientation to work still predominates, although there is evidence to indicate that more and more people are recognizing equally important values in other realms of life. Flexible retirement policies, if they are instituted, will help reinforce the wisdom of becoming as capable a leisurite as worker, since larger blocks of time will be available to those who prefer to realize themselves outside of their work role (Havighurst, 1961).

Sexuality in Later Life

Given the important role sex plays throughout life, it is too bad that it is an area of behavior more riddled with misconceptions than most. A generation ago sexuality did not create problems of the same magnitude for older people, as life expectancy seldom exceeded by much the reproductive years. With advances in longevity came the emergence of certain sex-related enigmas. One of the major impediments to a thoughtful appreciation of the place of sex in successful aging is that in nearly everyone's mind people tend to become neutered with the passing of the years. How many can imagine their grandparents engaging in sex? From the guffaws and general expressions of surprise the question often evokes, precious few; unfortunately neither can the grandparents. They see themselves as somehow beyond sex, but frustrated nonetheless because the idea still appeals to them. Most people openly acknowledge the value of basic sex education for adolescents or young marrieds, but what about later on, for the middle-aged and elderly who are just as much in the dark about what sex should be like at their ages? The taboos concerning the sex life of older people are ill-founded; after all, many of those who responded to the famous Kinsey studies after World War II, which told us so much about sexual practices, are themselves now past middle age. Yet cultural stereotypes continue to enforce a fictional view in the face of which the reality of the situation provides a substantial contrast.

Undoubtedly, physiological changes do alter sexual capacities in later life, yet their influence is vastly exaggerated. Psychological elements are probably far more consequential in determining the character of older people's sex lives. The myths proliferate, affecting women and men alike. Common opinion has it that middle-aged men fare somewhat better than women as far as sexual opportunity is concerned; they are allowed to seek out companions considerably younger than themselves — a prerogative not granted women. This is certainly true, but as long as they are presumed to be sexually active, older men are burdened with the onus of performance standards better suited to men 30 years their juniors, which they may be hard pressed to meet. Failing to recognize the basic facts of aging causes them, as well as their partners, to castigate themselves for falling short. Paradoxically, another ingredient of the myth of male sexuality is the widely held belief that the loss of a man's erective capacity is a natural concomitant of aging. While men do indeed experience some delayed reactions in their sexual response cycle, the changes are functionally minimal compared to other physiological involutions. Most importantly, men do not naturally lose their capacity for erection as a result of these changes. An equally inappropriate stereotypic notion is that sex has lost its appeal to women by the end of their procreative years. Menopause is viewed as the great divide, and women on the other side are not supposed to be interested in sex. Again, the facts are quite the contrary. Among current generations of older women, concern with sex never seems to have been as prominent as with their male counterparts, though neither does it stop with their menses. All too often women fall into the trap of equating sexuality with reproductive ability. Like men, older women find themselves surrounded by sexual fallacies so strong they are hesitant to admit to anything other than socially prescribed norms. Physically, women retain their capacity to enjoy sex far more satisfactorily than men, and with mild hormone therapy there is no reason why postmenopausal women cannot remain active so long as they desire (Masters and Johnson, 1970). As one well-known authority phrased it when remarking on society's tendency for "hocusing" older people out of their sexuality in the same way they have been hocused out of other valuable activities:

> . . . old folks stop having sex for the same reasons they stop riding a bicycle — general infirmity, thinking it looks ridiculous, no bicycle — and of these reasons the greatest is the social image of the dirty old man and the asexual, undesirable older woman (Comfort, 1974).

Incidence and Interest

One indication of the recency of scientific recognition of sexual interest and activity among older people is provided by the brief, two page summary made in the Kinsey study (1953). Only with the clinical investigations carried out by Masters and Johnson and the data gathered as part of the Duke longitudinal studies of aging has sexual activity among the elderly been given a significant measure of attention. Subsequent research has begun to augment these initial reports, although for basic information the earlier studies remain the most reliable and complete. Despite older people being enormously underrepresented among Kinsey's respondents, he reports an increasing incidence of male impotence over the years, coupled with declining activity levels. Notwithstanding this, the oldest men do not relinquish their activity levels with any greater speed than younger men. Sexual intercourse occurs less frequently among older women than their younger sisters; however, Kinsey suggests this is more a reflection of male than female processes. The Masters and

Johnson and the Duke research illuminate what Kinsey barely implied. Together they provide a fairly broad overview of the effects of age on sexual interest and responsiveness. The following discussion is based largely on the information made available from these studies. It will focus first on incidence, then on some of the factors associated with male and female sexual functioning.

Sexual interest and involvement are clearly related to a host of variables, yet the single best predictors of whether or not older people will maintain their sexual activities turn out to be continuity and past behavior. Among both men and women, those who have enjoyed a long and recurrent sex life without lengthy interruption are most likely to remain active far longer than their age mates who have not experienced a similar history. Despite declines in the late sixties and seventies, there is no decade this side of 100 in which sexual activity is completely absent. As a rule, men are more active than women at every age. At 60 few men have ceased to engage in sex; by age 68 somewhat less than three-quarters continue to have sexual intercourse, although some portion of those who abstain are still interested — talking and speculating even when they are prevented from actual participation. By the time they reach their late seventies, only 25 percent of the men are still active, and will continue to engage in some form of sex for the rest of their lives. In fact, there is even a moderate increase in the proportion of 80 and 90 year olds who acknowledge sexual activity; the slight upturn is probably a function of greater survival of the more biologically fit. Marital status apparently does not have much of an impact on men's activity levels; unmarried men are nearly as active and certainly as attracted as men who live with their spouses (Verwoerdt et al., 1970).

For women the situation is somewhat different. As with men, sexual interest is greater than actual incidence, even though sex is less often a topic of contemplation. Marital status proves to be the crucial factor in continued involvement; women who do not have a spouse have far fewer sexual outlets than their married counterparts. On the other hand, the number of outlets they have established persists far longer than for married women. Previous enjoyment more than simple frequency of sexual relationships is of particular importance for women in determining how they currently feel about sex — while for men both factors are equally relevant. A woman who has enjoyed her sexual experiences in earlier years, regardless of their regularity, will generally persist in those activities in her later years. Above all else, the presence of a sexually capable, socially sanctioned partner is particularly reflected in a woman's level of sexual involvement. In middle age, the years around 50, seven-eighths of all married women regularly engage in coitus with their husbands. Ten years later, participation has declined to about 70 percent, and by age 65 only about half still engage in marital intercourse. Both members of the older couples in the Duke studies tend to attribute the cessation of intercourse to the husband, due to illness, lack of interest or impotence. Clearly coitus is not the only form of sexual activity, and reports issuing from the Duke investigations suggest masturbation is an alternative practiced by approximately a quarter of the women responding to the sexual questions (Christenson and Gagnon, 1965; Pfeiffer, Verwoerdt and Wang, 1970).

Among that portion of the older population who are sexually involved in their later years, the frequency of intercourse gradually diminishes. The patterns shown in Table 11.1 were exhibited by participants in the Duke studies, yet they do not differ substantially from data reported elsewhere. What such overall trends generally mask is that married people, those from lower socioeconomic statuses and blacks are many times more active than are singles, those from the upper classes and whites (Newman and Nichols, 1970). Judging from these data, there appears to be a slight increase in the occurrence of intercourse for the cohorts listed over what the Kinsey team reported nearly 30 years ago. One possible interpretation of this upward shift entails the presumed changes in sexual

Table 11.1
Frequency of Sexual Intercourse in Later Life*

GROUP	NUMBER	NONE	ONCE A MONTH	ONCE A WEEK	2–3 TIMES A WEEK	MORE THAN 3 TIMES A WEEK
Men						
46–50	43	0	5	62	26	7
51–55	41	5	29	49	17	0
56–60	61	7	38	44	11	0
61–65	54	20	43	30	7	0
66–71	62	24	48	26	2	0
Total	261	12	34	41	12	1
Women						
46–50	43	14	26	39	21	0
51–55	41	20	41	32	5	2
56–60	48	42	27	25	4	2
61–65	44	61	29	5	5	0
66–71	55	73	16	11	0	0
Total	231	44	27	22	6	1

*Percentages

Source: E. Pfeiffer, A. Verwoerdt and G. C. Davis, "Sexual Behavior in Middle Life," *American Journal of Psychiatry* 128, 10 (1972): 1264.

morality, implying that present generations of elderly are less conservative about sex than previous generations. Such an explanation would certainly be in keeping with Kinsey's (1953) own conclusions regarding generational differences in proclivity for orgasm and declining frigidity in women. It also implies that if contemporary trends toward more openly sensual relationships prove durable, future cohorts of older people should be even more sexually active. Despite the paucity of data on sexual functioning among elderly people, small scale research projects conducted around the world affirm the Duke findings and reiterate the call for more intensive counseling programs. For example, one Italian study reports a pattern of current sexual activity among older people almost identical to what has been observed in the United States (De Nicola and Peruzza, 1974).

Sexual Response Cycles

In terms of the physiology of sex, Masters and Johnson (1970) indicate men experience more of an age-related deficit than women, though in neither case are the changes serious enough to interrupt the sex lives of the elderly. Clinically speaking, the four stages of the sexual response cycle begin to change sometime during middle age. The *excitation stage*, marked in men by the achievement of an erection and in women by vaginal lubrication, gradually requires more time than in previous years. The erection, which used to be achieved in seconds, takes minutes in later life, and even then it is neither as full or demanding as that of a young man. Because of hormonal changes and the involution of the vaginal lining, postmenopausal women do not lubricate as thoroughly, sometimes resulting in painful intromission. The *plateau* stage in older men is lengthened, preejaculatory emissions are reduced and seemingly there is less urgency to reach organism. Women seemingly experience fewer age-related changes in the plateau phase. In spite of a modest reduction in the size of the clitoris with age, there is not any apparent loss of sensitivity. The *orgasmic* phase is roughly analogous in both men and women. For men, ejaculation can be divided into two steps. The first brings a sense of urgency marked by psychological readiness and recurring contractions of the prostate gland. In young men contractions come in regular intervals of less than one second, lasting up to four seconds. With advancing age this first step of the ejaculatory process may become less distinguishable; it can be either shorter or longer and might also include irregular contractions. The second step of the orgasmic phase is actual ejaculation. The normal pattern among younger men is a series of contractions that are relatively steady through actual emission. In men over the age of 50, however, the expulsive contractions may change rhythm earlier or be less severe, while seminal emissions are reduced. Middle-aged or older women may experience a shorter orgasmic phase compared to that of younger women, though hormonal treatments often inhibit significant alterations. As with men, women experience several contractions during orgasm, but among the aged these are of shorter duration or may even take the form of spasms accompanied by some abdominal pain.

Finally, the *resolution* phase is again characteristic of both male and female cycles. For men over age 40, the refractory period may be considerably extended. During this time a man remains physically unresponsive to sexual stimulation and is unable to establish coital connection regardless of his emotional involvement. In young men the resolution phase transpires in only a matter of minutes and a limited erection may be maintained throughout, while for the middle-age or older man erections disappear more swiftly and hours may pass before intercourse is again possible. At any age the refractory period for women is far less than for men. Among middle-aged and postmenopausal women, return to a physiological equilibrium is fairly rapid and in many respects parallels that of the older male. For the man, reduced ejaculatory demand may translate into little need to ejaculate at all, thereby prolonging both immediate and long-term sexual functioning, and shortening the resolution phase as well.

Unfortunately, most people have little appreciation of their own bodily processes and any alterations in sexual functioning signal the beginnings of distress. Impotence is the most common sexual disorder among men over 45, precipitating serious emotional turmoil accompanied by health or mental problems on occasion (Kent, 1975). There is some evidence that men in their later fifties or sixties experience a kind of *climacteric* that is somewhat equivalent to menopause; as yet, however, little solid information is available with even less to indicate such a change might interfere with sexual activity. More likely, psychological predisposition plays a far greater role in declining sexual interest. Based on their extensive analyses, Masters and Johnson (1966) have isolated several integral components of male sexual inadequacies. Lack of prowess is often related to disenchantment and marital monotony, preoccupation with extraneous pursuits such as a career, emotional or physical fatigue, overindulgence in either food or drink, mental or physical infirmities, and, finally, fears regarding sexual performance. All can effectively preclude any kind of sexual response. Another commonly expressed fear arises in the aftermath of heart attacks. People sometimes assume once a man has had cardiovascular problems, he should abstain from further sexual relations. Like many other ideas, this misconception finds little medical support and ought to be abandoned. Actually, sex requires no more exertion than taking a brisk walk or climbing a flight of stairs. Along with the cultural views of older people's sexuality, the lessening need and frequency of ejaculation contributes an additional personal strain insofar as a woman may inadvertently feel threatened by a partner who does not ejaculate. Both partners should understand changing sexual functions, learning to take more time to be emotionally demonstrative if they are to avoid confounding their relationship with unrealistic expectations (Masters and Johnson, 1970).

Of all the aspects of human sexuality, the female menopause is a leading candidate for the most maligned. Why the termination of the menses is such a clouded issue is a complex question, yet overriding all other considerations is the fact that cultural conditioning is so pervasive. Behaviorally, the changes attributed to menopause are in many cases merely an accentuation of already existing tendencies previously held in check. Even the clinical features of the so-called menopausal syndrome are far from uniform. In the Western world, hot flushes, emotional turmoil, chronic fatigue, occipital headaches, neckaches, plus myriad other subjective factors are commonplace complaints. Externally there is a drying of the skin, changes in hair color and alterations in secondary sexual characteristics such as breast size and shape. Because of hormonal changes in the reproductive system, additional changes include an introversion of the vaginal walls and a loss of lubricating secretions which may occasionally result in painful intercourse. Lest the many fallacies surrounding menopause be reinforced, it cannot be stressed too strongly that psychological factors are equally, if not more, important with hormonal factors in influencing subsequent sexual interests and functioning. Although depressed sex-steroid levels can be easily corrected by replacement therapy, sexual responsiveness, on the other hand, cannot be restored without appropriate psychological counseling. A woman's subjective perception of herself is most often what damages her sexual outlook; if she believes herself to be unattractive or too old, sex will in all probability become a thing of the past. On the physical side, menopause, or even a hysterectomy for that matter, has little effect on sensate pleasure — in fact many women experience a heightened sense of satisfaction once they are freed of the pressures of preventing pregnancy (Masters and Johnson, 1970).

It is improbable that future generations of women will repeat the sexual patterns of today's elderly women. As Masters and Johnson (1966, 1970) have noted, they will be exorcised of the Victorian belief that women should be sexually passive — sure to be a boon to men as well since the double standard of male dominance is an imposition on both partners. Women will also benefit from the advent of contraceptive security and estrogen replacement procedures developed over the past two decades; thus, menopause will mean neither new-found freedom nor hardship. Even the death or incapacity of male partners will not necessarily spell the end of sexual activity; already there is evidence to suggest masturbation is increasing among women in the 50 to 70 age range, and as social proscriptions against autoeroticism are eroded, more people will feel free to seek their own forms of sexual gratification. It should be remembered that intercourse is not the only means of expressing emotions, and it is a grave mistake to think of its termination as the end of sensuality. At all ages coitus is but a single element in the communication of love. It is not at all unusual for it to be of less importance than other manifestations of the sexual bond. For older couples, being physically or spiritually close, showing tenderness or respect can be valued in such a way that intercourse is hardly missed.

Time, Religion and Death

In the course of the everyday scheme of things, many people ordinarily pause and reflect about what lies ahead. Death is an incontrovertible part of life; the cliché is threadbare by now, though for older people the quandaries it evokes should no longer be side-stepped as they were for so many years. Questions like what is death, where do they go, who is next, what do I do, become relevant topics for daily concern. Looking to the future has always had an uplifting effect, tomorrow is the promise held out for getting through today, but over the years tomorrow becomes less of a sure thing. Time, religion and death are all very much part of the day-to-day frame of reference for older people. Each assumes new meanings and none is completely independent of the others. In addressing death attitudes among the elderly, the discussion will not delve into the meaning it has for those immersed in the final trajectory. Rather, it will serve as a brief look at how those who have not already been separated from the ongoing stream of life feel about death.

Time and Prospect

In Chapter Four the idea of entropy was introduced as one way of conceptualizing the physical process of aging over time. Time is also a basic constituent of the theoretical frameworks proposed by social gerontologists to interpret progressive changes over the life cycle. Recalling Cumming and Henry's disengagement model, it will be remembered that their entire scheme is predicated on personal and societal recognition of a foreshortening of the future as the impetus for withdrawal. Empirical forays into subjective perceptions of temporal duration have generally found that the aged are indeed sensitive to the fleeting character of time and how little appears to remain. As people age they sense time is somehow speeding up: the past recedes ever more swiftly and the future becomes now all too soon. Yet a paradox exists, for on a personal level *futurity* is foreshortened as individuals age. For some, this is cause for anxiety as they realize all their tomorrows are quickly becoming history; others are content with just being — living one day at a time, with little regard for temporal horizons. This is not to imply, however, that cognitively the future cannot be an abstract concept insightfully employed as a means of categorizing experience. Within these two dimensions the question becomes: How do older people view time and tomorrow?

A fundamental component of temporal experience is an awareness of a sense of motion. Children probably become cognizant of time as they come to recognize before and after relationships. Gradually they are able to distinguish memory from now and to differentiate anticipations of what is yet to come; by early adolescence most youngsters have attained a mature sense of time and are able to conceive of themselves in the future. Futurity for them is a circumscribed reference; they know they are in the process of *becoming,* of moving away from and toward something, but their future is very near. In a sense it is as though they recollect the future; what is going to happen to them is no more than what has happened, and, consequently, their thoughts about the second half of life are nearly barren. Strangely enough, at the same time, adolescents seem to *blank out* the past unless asked, giving little thought to what is behind them. The emphasis on future extensions continues to grow until middle age, when most people admit to themselves that they have become whatever it is they are going to be and begin to concentrate on reinforcing their positions. The future is still out there, as the time between now and death, but the *real me* already is (Kastenbaum and Aisenberg, 1972). Whether or not from an awareness of the scarcity of time left, the cumulative impact of experiences and memory or something else, the rate of temporal passage is perceived as if it is speeding up. Experimental studies of time estimation with few exceptions report that successively older respondents consistently underestimate measured time intervals. It should be emphasized, however, that intelligence, socioeconomic status, education, activity levels and morale have also been found to exercise discrete influences over subjective temporal estimates. Some of these factors themselves may be closely related to advancing age. Aside from various possible physiological explanations, a recurrent theme rests on the value ascribed to time by those doing the judging. As long as older people place greater importance on time than other respondents, their judgments will tend to reflect a quickened tempo (Surwillo, 1964; Wallach and Green, 1968; Cottle and Howard, 1972).

Many people learn early in life to defer gratification, to think of the future. It is those forward-looking individuals who are most often extolled. Through at least middle age people can think of the promise of the future as being better than the present, which is in turn an improvement over the past. It encompasses events, goals and aspirations set for oneself and planned toward accordingly. It may or may not entail an explicitly chronological schedule. Having a broad conception of what is to come is helpful, often promoting emotional and practical adjustment. Some researchers have suggested a natural decline in futurity is a concomitant of the aging process and this is the reason so many elderly seem to dwell in the past. To support such a view observers point to the amount of time older people spend reminiscing — perhaps because the past is very much brighter than their future prospects or as a way of bringing about a reintegration of their self-concepts and of achieving a degree of self-validation. Besides, the elderly say, what is there to talk about in the future? If it exists at all in a personal sense, it is the counterpart of the adolescent's view — not extending much beyond the near tomorrow and focused primarily around mundane considerations. In point of fact, close attention to how people respond to temporal considerations should reveal efforts to garner their forces in order to face what comes next. Restructuring the past may be a necessary preliminary step prior to turning to face tomorrow. Only those who have settled past experiences and have found the appropriate pigeon holes in which to categorize their memories can let bygones be bygones and focus more on living out their years. On the practical level of daily life, assisting people to work out and accept their personal time frames presents itself as crucial if they are to maintain their social adjustment and personal autonomy (Kastenbaum, 1976).

The Meaning of Religion

Essential to all Judaeo-Christian religions is a belief in the existence of an afterlife when humankind will be delivered from the trials and tribulations of life on earth. Throughout history, the importance of religious attitudes has ebbed and flowed with the fortune or hardships of the times, reaching high points wherever people sought solace to ward off troubles or misfortune. One of the more durable stereotypes about the elderly is that they too turn to religion as they age. So common is this idea that is has become part of the folklore of aging (Maves, 1960). But as with so much other folk wisdom about the elderly, notions of the place of religion in the lives of older people are open to extensive debate. While only 3 percent of the elderly claim they have no religious preferences, opinion in the gerontological community is divided on whether religious interest or activities increase with age and whether or not religion is beneficial as far as promoting life satisfaction. Although many studies have shown both increases and better adjustment in the later years, others have found little association between religious involvement and daily functioning. In his review of literature bearing on both sides of the issue, Moberg (1968) concludes there apparently is a positive connection between adjustment, religious interest and activities, though it may in turn reflect the presence of other factors. As a result, he is unwilling to draw any causal inferences. In general there does not seem to be any widespread tendency toward greater religiosity with age. Patterns found among today's elderly have either persisted from earlier times or else are indicative of broad social currents.

Those gerontological perspectives stressing the supremacy of expressive roles for the elderly, as well as many of the developmental models emphasizing a constriction of the social life space with compensatory attention directed to ethical or transcendental questions, support the conception of a heightened religious consciousness in old age. One of the reasons so many contradictory positions about the meaning of religion in later life have emerged has to do with the complexity of the issue. Scholars have been defining and redefining religion and what it is to be religious for hundreds of years, yet since it implies so many different things to so many people, little consensus has been achieved. With regard to practical measures of religiosity, many researchers have found it convenient to utilize a five dimensional framework developed in order to lend some coherence to various aspects of religious involvement (Glock, 1962). The most conspicuous dimension of religiosity is the *ritualistic* — the way people actually practice their beliefs. Church attendance or membership is the customary criterion for gauging participation, since each is easy to ascertain. More older people belong to churches or synagogues than to all other voluntary associations combined, and most researchers agree their attendance shows little decline until the late sixties or seventies. From a low point during the thirties, church and synagogue activity gradually increases until old age, when it falls off again as a consequence of a variety of factors. Alternative explanations have been offered, suggesting that atttendance may not in fact decline or, if it does, it is the result of changes in family life cycles or perhaps tendencies to disengage. No one view is applicable across the board to all older people (Bahr, 1970; Wingrove and Alston, 1971).

In summarizing the research on religious practices Moberg (1970) finds that while church-related activities outside the home do indeed diminish in the later years, the elderly compensate by reading the Bible more, listening to broadcasts of religious programs or praying in their own homes. Obviously, practical considerations such as ill health or lack of transportation cannot be dismissed. Nor can the feelings expressed by some older people that churches are guilty of neglecting them be glossed over. Religious organizations have addressed themselves to the plight of the old for centuries, but few modern-day clergy have received pastoral training appropriate for dealing with elderly parishioners. One small study in the midwestern United States revealed that less than 30 percent of the ministers had been given specific advice on meeting the needs of older people and that fewer still felt their training as adequate — this in spite of the fact that one-third to one-half of their work is directly tied to older people (Moberg, 1975). Attendance among elderly Jews does not decline, lending additional support for this view, since their religion has traditionally done more for its elderly than most Catholic or Protestant denominations. Also, among lower income people in a study conducted in Philadelphia, older blacks maintained their church affiliations far more extensively than whites. One possible explanation offered by the authors is that local black churches are more responsive to the needs of the aged (Hirsch et al., 1972).

The *experiential* dimension refers to the subjectively perceived interest in religion. While age trends may be equivocal, most investigations report religious conviction becomes more salient over the years for those who already believe. Two cautionary comments are in order, however. First, societal norms about religion are so strong that it is unlikely many people would openly express feelings of dis-affiliation even if they felt religion was useless. Second, since the majority of religious studies are cross-sectional, the assumed inten-sification of religious sentiment may be an artifact of the research methodology. It might well be that religion itself is a generational phenomenon; indeed, today's elderly were reared at a time when re-ligious involvement was more widespread. As an example, during the 1950s there was a revival of formal religion in the United States for all age groups. In the decade of the 1960s, the Jesus People movement notwithstanding, there were marked declines in church attendance and other indications of religious involvement; therefore, any conclusions based on studies using data from these periods which purported to represent long-term patterns would be some-what misleading (Wingrove and Alston, 1971). Still, the elderly do say the importance of religion has grown for them over the years, with both black and white women expressing the greatest interest. The third, or *ideological,* dimension focuses on doctrinaire beliefs. Again, there may be a generational effect, but older people tend to adhere to more orthodox or conservative religious viewpoints than younger people. Belief in immortality is also more prevalent among older people, as are literal interpretations of the scriptures (Moberg, 1970).

Knowledge about the teachings of one's faith constitutes the *in-tellectual* dimension of religiosity. Here, also, the findings are rather ambiguous. The elderly spend more time reading the Bible and can cite its books more accurately than younger people, but it is a differ-ent matter to conclude that their views are more valid. Whatever the implication, religious study courses do attract people in their fifties and beyond much more regularly than nearly any other form of adult education. In addition, religious questions are frequently the pre-ferred topic of conversation among many groups of hospitalized older people (Moberg, 1968). Finally, the *consequential* dimension includes both the attitudinal and concrete benefits derived from re-ligious involvement. Despite the objection of many researchers (Palmore, 1970), the weight of the evidence is in favor of a correla-tion between religion and a more abundant sense of life satisfaction. It might be inferred that, aside from the spiritual benefits religion has to offer, it does provide a sense of emotional security, perhaps through the provision of an immediately accessible reference group — often lacking to those not closely affiliated with a church. In the face of death, religion seems to infuse its adherents with more posi-tive attitudes so long as they are confident of their own redemption.

Yet as Moberg (1968) and others have repeatedly admonished, adjustment may be due to other factors and it is impossible to say if the adjusted simply belong to churches or if belonging to a church promotes adjustment. Either way, affiliation with an organized religious body is a reliable sign of greater rates of participation in other realms of life.

Anticipating Death

Sooner or later life inevitably becomes a terminal affair. Prior to middle age, few people have reason to reflect on their own finality; after all, none of life's challenges have yet proven insurmountable, horizons have always receded to reveal ever broader vistas and health has rarely presented much of a problem. With the onset of those physical and social changes that characterize middle age, the mode of *bodily transcendence* that had previously predominated gradually dissipates and, as Erikson points out, people quietly begin reckoning how much time they have left. Parental deaths, which today may be postponed until children are in their forties or even older, bring mortality into personalized relief that becomes increasingly more distinct. Throughout the remainder of life, the possibility of death is often a matter of reflection, though not necessarily consternation. In fact, as pointed out in Chapter Seven, after middle age it is less a cause of anxiety than are thoughts of illness and dependency. The death literature is also replete with ambiguities stemming from the diffuse nature of the topic. One consistent theme, however, in the vast majority of studies is that elderly people seldom express serious fears over their own demise. In most instances their views are more realistic, accepting the inexorable more easily than all who still see their own natural deaths as far away in the future. Despite the tenacity of the assumption that those closest to death are the most fearful, there is little evidence to indicate older people are particularly apprehensive (Jeffers and Verwoerdt, 1969; Kastenbaum and Aisenberg, 1972).

It is an enlightening experience to talk with older people about death. In many cases it furnishes a welcome opportunity for them to discuss their feelings and to look back upon things past in order to reach a new understanding of themselves. Unfortunately, they are reluctant to raise the issue with younger people, whom the elderly assume are uncomfortable in such a conversation. Their assessment may be correct, since they often find younger relatives and friends attempt to change the subject when death becomes the focus of conversation. Contrary to popular opinion, those people living in nursing homes or retirement housing, where death is an obvious fact of life, are not more disconsolate over their impending demise than their age mates living in the community. In fact, residents of various forms of congregate living facilities may have an advantage because they are able to socialize one another into a positive or at least an accepting attitude. Few older people living alone or with a spouse have a similar opportunity readily available (Swenson, 1965; Marshall, 1975b). Despite the initially higher death rates resulting from the psychological disruption precipitated by relocation, institutionalization may provide the kind of stable environment that allows an examination of personal values and a comparison of one's own view with that of others in the same situation. Once overcoming the reticence natural in a new environment, the elderly openly acknowledge the imminence of their own deaths, and thereafter willingly discuss various facets of the issue (Marshall, 1975a).

There are older people, just as there are people at every age, who do seem to worry a great deal about dying, yet age itself is a poor indicator of who is most likely to experience marked death anxiety. As is the case with other psychological adjustments, attitudes toward death will reflect reaction patterns long integral to one's personality. Religious beliefs, higher educational levels, long-standing social relationships and an overall sense of security also exert an ameliorative influence over whatever anxiety death may potentially induce. The impact of religion must be qualified to a certain extent; to be beneficial, religion must be accompanied by a certainty of salvation, for those who are not free of fears of retribution may not experience any greater calm (Jeffers and Verwoerdt, 1969). Generally speaking, only a small minority of the elderly openly verbalize a heightened sense of fear. Among the factors seemingly characteristic of the most fearful are physical and social isolation, minimal educational levels or chronic depressive states. Contrary to popular assumptions, seriously impaired health does not of itself portend feelings of dread or fright. Quite the reverse; those who are laboring under sickness and long-term ailments may actually be more accepting — death may be perceived as a welcome relief. What is interpreted as fearfulness perhaps results from the situations in which most people die. Hospitals, where every task is originally intended to preserve life, have become the place where most everyone goes to die. No one dies at home anymore; the vast majority are banished to demoralizing impersonal wards where their questions are met with a conspiracy of silence. As death draws near, the terminal patient is literally avoided, for the priorities lie with those who will live. Physicians visit less frequently and for shorter periods. No wonder the dying are afraid, though it is not death they fear but abandonment, pain and confusion. What many desire most is someone to talk with, to tell them their life's meaning is not shattered merely because they are about to die (Sudnow, 1967; Kubler-Ross, 1969). A general discussion of terminal care would lead too far afield; however, there is a burgeoning library of insightful research that carefully addresses this issue. The crucial point here is simply that death is not the cause of many of the fears attributed to it. Innovative terminal care facilities are just beginning to emerge in the United States. Modeled after the long-established St. Christopher's Hospice in London, St. Luke's Hospital in New York and the New Haven Hospice in Connecticut were the first American efforts oriented specifically toward terminal care. Each maintains patients outside the hospital for as long as is practical, and then arranges a transfer to a supportive medical setting where an interdisciplinary team supplies counseling to patients and families along with appropriate medical attention. Early indications are that dying becomes much easier and fears are of little more than passing concern.

If those near death are not totally consumed by anxiety or preoccupied with denying its imminence, what do they think about? They worry about staying involved, about finishing their tasks and about the future for those close to them. If possible, they prefer a quick death, and hopefully a painless one, but beyond that their thoughts are concentrated on their survivors. A sizeable majority, in excess of three-quarters, attempt to resolve the practicalities of putting their affairs in order, making a will, prearranging the funeral, leaving instructions and talking it over with family (Riley, 1970). Two-thirds of the elderly have wills, far above the national average of one-fourth of all adults (American Bar Foundation, 1976). Much of their attention is given over to minimizing the hardships faced by those they leave behind. While there is no question of the traumatic consequences of a death, here, too, emotional stability is more often the case than is commonly assumed. Most participants in the Duke studies, for example, adapted themselves rather well, without disrupting their lives or sacrificing their health as a result of a spouse's death. Of course, individuals exhibit wide variations. As a rule, women tend to suffer greater distress than men, though both often express relief — for themselves and for the deceased. Having an opportunity to work through the welter of psychological reactions — grief, guilt, confusion, hostility and so on — prior to the actual death normally has a hastening effect on subsequent "recovery." The exception is the illness drawn out over several months; under these circumstances **anticipatory grief** may not prove particularly helpful (Heyman and Gianturco, 1974; Gerber et al., 1975).

Summary

On a daily basis, the thoughts of the elderly reflect an admixture of practical and existential concerns. Seemingly, a nearly universal trait of all adults is an inherent feeling of relative youthfulness compared to others of a similar chronological age. A number of factors contribute to subjective estimations of age, but far from being some kind of psychological abnormality, up to two-thirds of those over 65 continue to think of themselves as no more than middle-aged. Interestingly enough, those who feel younger than the calendar indicates are also in better health, physically and emotionally, than the 20 percent of their age mates whose self-conceptions are old beyond their years. Friends, valued involvement in some sphere of life and a continuity in living patterns are all associated with a more youthful self-image. Despite the fact that we each see ourselves as younger on the inside than our friends, they are integral to our self-concept. More than family ties, friendships are a precious personal resource utilized in maintaining morale and life adjustment. The presence of even a single intimate friend can offset a whole range of hardships imposed on the elderly. In general, friendships are strengthened after the years of heavy family obligations have passed. Patterns of friendships vary by social class, but are seldom affected by contacts with children or other family members. Contrary to many popular notions, intergenerational friendships play a comparatively minor role in the lives of the elderly. Under the circumstances presently existing in most intergenerational neighborhoods, elderly residents usually find themselves more socially isolated than would be the case if they lived in age-segregated housing. Intergenerational friendships are the exception; instead friends tend to resemble each other in terms of age, sex, marital status, social class and so on.

Aside from friendships, voluntary participation in a wide range of organizations is also an important source of satisfaction for the elderly. With the exception of church affiliations, the number of memberships begins to decline in the years after age 60. For those who do remain active, however, their participation carries with it a tendency to greater involvement in other areas of life. For the majority, as well as for some minority groups, socioeconomic factors are the best predictors of associational patterns, although they are of little value in explaining why blacks exhibit higher rates of participation than anyone else in voluntary activities. In addition to friends and organizations, older people occupy many hours in various forms of diversionary recreation. The elderly spend more time in front of the television set or with reading materials than their younger counterparts, but less frequently engage in strenuous pursuits. Regardless of their own interests, idleness and contemplation are the most common forms of leisure among today's older people. Because leisure is so contingent on generational and social history, the recreational realm for tomorrow's elderly will, in all likelihood, assume a quite different character.

Sexual functioning in later life is influenced by biological, social and emotional factors. Pervasive stereotypes allege that people cease being interested in or capable of sex in later middle age. The facts are quite the reverse: on a biological level men manifest more changes than women, yet compared to other involutions these are hardly sufficient to interfere with their ability to engage in sex. Probably the greatest constraint for the present generation of elderly women is the lack of socially sanctioned partners, since physiologically, menopause has little to do with continued sexuality. With age both men and women have somewhat slower response cycles, though this is complemented by the appreciation of more varied and thoughtful sexual interaction. While hormone therapy may occasionally be required, without counseling it cannot by itself bring about the reestablishment of satisfactory sexual relations. The lack of privacy encouraged by institutional design is just one indication of the common assumption that older people are entirely sexless.

Time, death and religion are often topics for reflection in the daily lives of older people. As we grow older, time seems to speed up; anticipating the future holds less attraction for those whose past offers a longer span of contemplation than does what lies ahead. Many explanations have been advanced to account for the changing pace of time, but one of the more persuasive has to do with an awareness of death. This same awareness is also a strong element in the stereotype that older people are more religious than they used to be. Once again, the evidence lends little empirical support to such a widely held view; at best it affirms that for those who already believe in religion, it provides comforting reference in later life. Fears of death have also apparently been overplayed. Few older people are particularly apprehensive about dying, and in most cases they have a more realistic perspective than younger people. What they are afraid of is dying alone, in a strange environment without someone to talk to. The majority of elderly have given attention to the practicalities involved in dying and have spent some time discussing it with those they love in an effort to make the grieving a little easier.

Pertinent Readings

AMERICAN BAR FOUNDATION. "Survey of Legal Needs: Selected Data." *Alternatives* 3, 1 (1976): 1–23.

BACK, K.W. "Transition to Aging and the Self-Image." In *Normal Aging II,* ed. E. Palmore, 207–16. Durham, N.C.: Duke University Press, 1974.

BAHR, H.M. "Aging and Religious Disaffiliation." *Social Forces* XLIX, 1 (1970): 59–71.

BLAU, Z.S. *Old Age in a Changing Society.* New York: New Viewpoints, a Division of Franklin Watts, Inc., 1973.

BULL, C.N., and J.B. AUCOIN. "Voluntary Association Participation and Life Satisfaction: A Replication Note." *Journal of Gerontology* XXX, 1 (1975): 73–76.

CHRISTENSON, C.V., and J.H. GAGNON. "Sexual Behavior in a Group of Older Women." *Journal of Gerontology* XX, 3 (1965) 351–56.

CLEMENTE, F., P.A. REXFORD and C. HIRSCH. "The Participation of the Black Aged in Voluntary Associations." *Journal of Gerontology* XXX, 4 (1975): 469–72.

COMFORT, A. "Sexuality in Old Age." *Journal of the American Geriatrics Society* XXII, 10 (1974): 440–42.

COTTLE, T.J., and P. HOWARD. "Temporal Differentiation and Undifferentiation." *Journal of Genetic Psychology* CXXI, 2 (1972): 215–33.

CURTIS, J. "Voluntary Association Joining: A Cross-National Comparative Note." *American Sociological Review* XXXVI, 5 (1971): 872–80.

CUTLER, S.J. "Voluntary Association Participation and Life Satisfaction: A Cautionary Note." *Journal of Gerontology* XXVIII, 1 (1973): 96–100.

DE BEAUVOIR, S. *The Coming of Age.* Trans. P. O'Brian. New York: Warner Paperback Library, 1973.

DE NICOLA, P., and M. PERUZZA. "Sex in the Aged." *Journal of the American Geriatrics Society* XXII, 8 (1974): 380–82.

DUMAZEDIER, J. *Sociology of Leisure.* Amsterdam: Elsevier, 1974.

GERBER, I., et al. "Anticipatory Grief and Aged Widows and Widowers." *Journal of Gerontology* XXX, 2 (1975): 225–29.

GLOCK, C.Y. "On the Study of Religious Commitment." *Religious Education* LVII, 4 (1962): 98–110.

GUBRIUM, J.F. "Being Single in Old Age." *Aging and Human Development* VI, 1 (1975): 29–41.

GUPTILL, C.S. "A Measure of Age Identification." *The Gerontologist* IX, 2, pt. I (1969): 96–102.

HAVIGHURST, R.J. "The Nature and Values of Meaningful Free-time Activity." In *Aging and Leisure,* ed. R.W. Kleemeier, 309–44. New York: Oxford University Press, 1961.

HEYMAN, D.K., and D.T. GIANTURCO. "Long-term Adaptation by the Elderly to Bereavement." In *Normal Aging II,* ed. E. Palmore, 180–85. Durham, N.C.: Duke University Press, 1974.

HIRSCH, C., D.P. KENT and S.L. SILVERMAN. "Homogeneity and Heterogeneity among Low-income Negro and White Aged." In *Research Planning and Action for the Elderly: The Power and Potential of Social Science*, eds. D.P. Kent, R. Kastenbaum and S. Sherwood, 484–500. New York: Behavioral Publications Inc., 1972.

JEFFERS, F.C., and A. VERWOERDT. "How the Old Face Death." In *Behavior and Adaptation in Late Life*, eds. E.W. Busse and E. Pfeiffer, 163–81. Boston: Little, Brown and Company, 1969.

KASTENBAUM, R. "Time, Death and Ritual in Old Age." In *Studies in Time*, vol. 2, ed. J.T. Fraser. New York: Springer Verlag, 1976.

KASTENBAUM, R., and R. AISENBERG. *The Psychology of Death*. New York: Springer Publishing Company, Inc., 1972.

KASTENBAUM, R., et al. "The Ages of Me." *Aging and Human Development* III, 2 (1972): 197–211.

KENT, S. "Impotence: The Facts Versus the Fallacies." *Geriatrics* XXX, 4 (1975): 164–69.

KINSEY, A.C., et al. *Sexual Behavior in the Human Female*. Philadelphia: W.B. Saunders Co., 1953.

KUBLER-ROSS, E., *On Death and Dying*. New York: The Macmillan Company, 1969.

LOWENTHAL, M.F., and C. HAVEN. "Interaction and Adaptation: Intimacy as a Critical Variable." In *Middle Age and Aging*, ed. B. Neugarten, 390–400. Chicago: University of Chicago Press, 1968.

MARSHALL, V.M. "Age and Awareness of Finitude in Developmental Gerontology." *Omega* 8, 2 (1975a): 113–29.

——— . "Socialization for Impending Death in a Retirement Village." *American Journal of Sociology* LXXX, 5 (1975b): 1124–44.

MASTERS, W.H., and V.E. JOHNSON. *Human Sexual Response*. Boston: Little, Brown and Co., 1966.

——— . *Human Sexual Inadequacy*. Boston: Little, Brown and Company, 1970.

MAVES, P.B. "Aging, Religion and the Church." In *Handbook of Social Gerontology*, ed. C. Tibbitts, 698–749. Chicago: University of Chicago Press, 1960.

MILLER, S.J. "The Social Dilemma of the Aging Leisure Participant." In *Older People and Their Social World*, eds. A. Rose and W. Peterson, 77–92. Philadelphia: F.A. Davis Company, 1965.

MOBERG, D.O. "Religiosity in Old Age." In *Middle Age and Aging*, ed. B.L. Neugarten, 497–508. Chicago: University of Chicago Press, 1968.

——— ."Religion in the Later Years." In *The Daily Needs and Interests of Older People*, ed. A.M. Hoffman, 175–91. Springfield, Ill.: Charles C. Thomas, 1970.

——— ."Needs Felt by the Clergy for Ministeries to the Aging." *The Gerontologist* XV, 2 (1975): 170–75.

NEWMAN, G., and C.R. NICHOLS. "Sexual Activities and Attitudes in Older Persons." In *Normal Aging*, ed. E. Palmore, 277–81. Durham, N.C.: Duke University Press, 1970.

PALMORE, E. "The Effects of Aging on Activities and Attitudes." In *Normal*

Aging, ed. E. Palmore, 332–41. Durham, N.C.: Duke University Press, 1970.

PFEIFFER, E., and G.C. DAVIS. "The Use of Leisure Time in Middle Life." In *Normal Aging II,* ed. E. Palmore, 232–43. Durham, N.C.: Duke University Press, 1974.

PFEIFFER, E., A. VERWOERDT and G.C. DAVIS. "Sexual Behavior in Middle Life." In *Normal Aging II,* ed. E. Palmore, 243–62. Durham, N.C.: Duke University Press, 1974.

PFEIFFER, E., A. VERWOERDT and H.S. WANG. "Sexual Behavior in Aged Men and Women." In *Normal Aging,* ed. E. Palmore, 299–303. Durham, N.C.: Duke University Press, 1970.

RILEY, J.W., JR. "What People Think About Death." In *The Dying Patient,* eds. O.G. Brim, Jr., et al, 30–41. New York: Russell Sage Foundation, 1970.

RILEY, M.W., and A. FONER et al. *Aging and Society — Volume One: An Inventory of Research Findings.* New York: Russell Sage Foundation, 1968.

ROSENBERG, G.S. *The Worker Grows Old: Poverty and Isolation in the City.* San Francisco: Jossey-Bass, 1970.

ROSOW, I. *Social Integration of the Aged.* New York: The Free Press, a division of the Macmillan Company, 1967.

_____ . "Old People: Their Friends and Neighbors." In *Aging in Contemporary Society,* ed. E. Shanas, 57–67. Beverly Hills, Cal.: Sage Publications, 1970.

_____ . *Socialization to Old Age.* Berkeley: University of California Press, 1974.

SMITH, J. "The Narrowing of the Social Life Space." In *Social Aspects of Aging,* eds. I.H. Simpson and J.C. McKinney et al., 226–42. Durham, N.C.: Duke University Press, 1966.

SUDNOW, D. *Passing On.* Englewood Cliffs, N.J.: Prentice-Hall, 1967.

SURWILLO, W.W. "Age and the Perception of Short Time Interests." *Journal of Gerontology* XIX, 3 (1964): 322–24.

SWENSON, W.M. "Attitudes Toward Death among the Aged." In *Death and Identity,* ed. R. Fulton, 105–11. New York: John Wiley & Sons, Inc., 1965.

VERWOERDT, A., E. PFEIFFER and H.S. WANG. "Sexual Behavior in Senescence." In *Normal Aging,* ed. E. Palmore, 282–99. Durham, N.C.: Duke University Press, 1970.

WALLACH, M.A., and L.R. GREEN. "On Age and the Subjective Speed of Time." In *Middle Age and Aging,* ed. B. Neugarten, 481–85. Chicago: University of Chicago Press, 1968.

WILENSKY, H.L. "Life Cycle, Work Situation and Participation in Formal Associations." In *Aging and Leisure,* ed. R.W. Kleemeier, 313–43. New York: Oxford University Press, 1961.

WILLIAMS, J.A., N. BABCHUK and D.R. JOHNSON. "Voluntary Associations and Minority Status: A Comparative Analysis of Anglo, Black and Mexican Americans." *American Sociological Review* XXXVIII, 5 (1973): 637–46.

WINGROVE, C.R., and J.P. ALSTON. "Age, Aging and Church Attendance." *The Gerontologist* XI, 4, pt. I (1971): 356–58.

Chapter 12

The Aged in the Political Arena

The structure of American politics can be characterized in various ways. A few view the political arena as the domain of interested individuals taking the time and making the effort to have their voices heard. Others see it as dominated by the wealthy corporate associations wherein the individual is relegated to a subordinate status. Still another scenario of widespread currency rests political power in the hands of organized interest groups who compete and cooperate among themselves to further their own vested interests. Thus groups, not individuals, forge public policy, and as was clearly demonstrated in the early 1970s, these groups may escape strict accountability for the actions they authorize. It is within this framework that the potential power of the elderly is to be established. The political stage is witness to the efforts of numerous interest groups to influence governmental processes. For any group, the issue of power depends in part on whether it is able to adopt a uniform stance on any particular question. This is of pressing concern to groups dealing with or representing the elderly. Specific reference to age-based political movements oriented primarily toward improving the lot of older people carries with it rather distressing presumptions of the alleged conservatism of the elderly, their increasing lack of opinionation about contemporary social problems, and what is frequently cast as a reduced level of participation across the entire political spectrum. Paradoxically, such views persist in the face of growing public recognition of the as yet unrealized political clout of the emerging interest groups composed of or concerned with elderly citizens. As will be seen, a number of the old assumptions have been largely discounted or at least challenged by new research. Nonetheless, stereotypes about the politically apathetic elderly have been popularized in the eyes of the public. Rather than fixing chronological age as a major factor significantly affecting political behavior, it may be more meaningful to consider the various circumstances under which age might or does make a difference in political activity. It would be quite deceptive simply to look at the results of a poll in which the opinions of youth and elderly are very different and to label one group as more conservative than the other. While this has often been the case in many public opinion surveys, we should be aware of the fact that numerous other variables also play a role and must not be overlooked in any interpretation of the relationship between age and political views or activities. Attitudinal and behavioral variations are apt to reflect not only the historical epoch during which an individual was reared, but also the peer influences of his or her own age cohort, in addition to those factors that can be attributed to the results of aging (Mannheim, 1952; Riley, 1973). Thus we would be hard put to account for differences in the political arena solely by the criterion of age; we must investigate further in order to clarify even the initial relationships that emerge.

The Elderly as a Social Movement

Age Groups in the Political Arena

Over the last decade there has been much controversy concerning the likelihood of age ever serving as the catalyst for the evolution of a viable political movement. On the one hand, a wide-ranging diversity of opinions has been observed among age groups in various polls. Also, many elderly encounter experiences analogous to those of other minority groups, complete with the stereotyping, prejudice and discrimination associated with minority status. Therefore, according to the advocates of an age-based political movement, the aged are theoretically opportune candidates for developing an age group consciousness. There is, of course, the alternative reality: the very heterogeneity of the older generation insures a divergence in the attitudes, expectations and goals of older people. Perhaps the best example of this multiformity is presented by the membership of political organizations whose primary objective is to provide assistance to the elderly. It is not at all unusual to find division among the ranks on such fundamental issues as income security or health care. Since an integral part of the conception of the pluralistic nature of American politics concedes that the political arena is not occupied only by concerned citizens, but, more importantly, by organized interest groups representing various constituencies, no group can wield much power unless its members are of a common mind. These groups then shape public policy through a process of conflict and compromise between and among themselves and governmental agencies. With the continual press of political business, our elected officials tend to rely on interest groups to articulate the desires of their constituents; consequently, the more vocal and powerful the groups, the more responsive the politicians. The role such interest groups play in the political process is sometimes offered as an explanation of the relative powerlessness of the aged, since they have thus far rarely been organized or represented by outspoken advocates. Many studies have previously shown that the political attitudes of the elderly themselves are quite disparate, thereby prohibiting a unified stance. Yet once established, older people do tend to exhibit stable political affiliations. Some data have revealed a greater affinity in their attitudes regarding topics that directly affect them as an age group; nevertheless, that similarity has not yet proven sufficient to transform aged voters into a cohesive political bloc.

According to some analysts, extensive political participation among the elderly will ultimately be founded on the development and utilization of interest groups or on what was referred to in Chapter Five as an aged subculture. In formulating the idea of a subcultural model applicable to the elderly, Rose (1965b) noted:

A subculture may be expected to develop within any category of the population of a society when its members interact with each other significantly more than they intereact with persons in other categories. This occurs . . . [either where] (1) the members have a positive affinity for each other on some basis or (2) the members are excluded from interaction with other groups in the population to some significant extent.

Among those who argue the opposite, that older people will not in fact become an identifiable subculture, the general absence of a sense of group identification among the elderly is often highlighted. It is contended that older people do not develop a lifestyle based on the concrete realities of old age, nor is there much systematic or overt prejudice and discrimination attributable to age itself. Finally, Streib (1965), one of the more vocal opponents of Rose's position, points out that age is not actually an *ascribed* status, an essential component in his view if a distinct cultural grouping is to evolve. The application of any analysis based on either perceived minority group status or the notion that elderly people are in the midst of formulating a definite interest or political pressure group is still in the theoretical stages. If data on income, employment histories or educational achievements are examined for the past 30 years, it is evident that today's older generations earn less, work less and are clustered in relatively lower status occupations when compared to their younger counterparts. In large measure, the near future portends further distinctions between older and younger people. Some argue that the resulting inequalities are, in all likelihood, indicative of those conditions conducive to the evolution of a minority group composed of the aged (Palmore and Whittington, 1971).

The potential for a politically involved group of older citizens has yet to be realized, perhaps because of the absence of any generalized age group awareness. Among those older people who do exhibit a sharpened degree of age consciousness, there is also a desire expressed for continued or heightened interaction with their peers, more organizations for older people and increased political participation, through either voting or other collective action (Rose, 1965a). Until recently, however, an overriding sense of age-identification among the elderly has not been observed for a variety of reasons. To begin with, an active interest group tends not to focus on a single trait; instead, it usually rallies around a set of interrelated or homogeneous characteristics. Hence, it seems that chronological age alone would not be sufficiently binding for any group. To be effective, interest groups must also exhibit responsible organizational structures, some financial stability and, for any national influence, widely dispersed membership. The political impotence of earlier movements organized by or for older people stemmed in part from their failure to fulfill these criteria, from low levels of age group consciousness and especially from the competition waged among themselves for members drawn from a limited population (Cottrell, 1960).

The Advent of Age-Based Social Movements

The first age-based, politically oriented interest groups to take shape in America came about as a result of the economic deprivation and social upheaval of the Depression of the early 1930s, yet few of them managed to outlast the decade. For example, in California alone, several age-based social movements amassed sizeable followings, flourished briefly and disappeared just as rapidly. At its peak during the Depression, the Utopian Society had attracted around half a million adherents; Upton Sinclair's End Poverty in California (EPIC) movement was equally popular in the years preceding his defeat in the 1934 gubernatorial contest. However, by the waning years of the decade few members of either group could be found. Although EPIC was among the first of the coalitions to propose a pension program, it remained for the McLain and the Townsend movements to speak directly on behalf of the elderly as a disadvantaged segment of the population. Named after the physician who founded it, the Townsend Plan was a spinoff from an earlier group that called itself "Old Age Revolving Pensions, Inc." At its peak in 1936, the movement attained a national membership in excess of a million and a half elderly, organized into local clubs. Their primary goal, providing a monthly pension of $200 funded through sales taxes, was met to some extent by the implementation of Social Security legislation. As soon as Townsend and his followers were deprived of their mission, the organization went into partial eclipse, though alternative proposals continued to attract some devotees until the group finally disappeared after World War II.

The McLain Movement, which competed with the Townsend Plan for members, did not fare much better. Originally it was part of an association with the homely title of Ham and Eggs which sought the establishment of financial benefits for older citizens through a referendum in the 1938 California elections. George McLain led a faction more intent on exerting political pressure on local legislatures to improve conditions for the elderly. Eventually, the McLain Movement boasted about 250,000 members spread over 31 states and was represented by both a National and a California League of Senior Citizens. It looked for a time as though McLain and his followers had indeed become a force to be reckoned with, but the economic upturn after 1940 spelled doom for them, just as it had for the Townsend people. McLain himself remained politically active until his death, running for public office as late as 1964, but he was never able to appeal to a broad enough segment of the population to advance in either state or national politics. In California his personal charisma did continue to attract supporters, but elsewhere the grassroots organizations he helped found languished and eventually succumbed. McLain's regional branches tended to become isolated, without local involvements beyond the opinions expressed by a small coterie made up of a few concerned elderly partisans. But even they were so heterogeneous a mix that a unified position on their own self-interests was nearly always absent. Interestingly enough, despite their popular appeal, neither the McLain nor the Townsend movements are viewed by most social historians as responsible for the advent of Social Security or any other significant legislation. Most knowledgeable observers instead see the efforts of more general labor organizations and the influence of Socialist politics in general during the 1930s as being the prime movers behind the lobbying that led to the enactment of Social Security (Pinner, Jacobs and Selznick, 1959; Carlie, 1969).

Today there are numerous national organizations dedicated to the needs of the elderly. The most significant change is that the majority of these groups do not exist solely for the aged; rather, they are groups that have a tangential, though sincere, concern for the elderly, oriented around labor, professional, fraternal, service and community action affiliations. According to a recent count, there are, however, at least ten national groups with varying degrees of effectiveness that are currently involved in the field of aging and political action (Binstock, 1972). Three of these are associations with general memberships, four are trade associations and the remainder are composed of members from a professional society, of social welfare workers and of specialists concerned with the black elderly. The three with the largest memberships are the National Council of Senior Citizens (NCSC), the American Association of Retired Persons combined with the National Retired Teachers Association (AARP-NRTA) which act as a single association, and the National Association of Retired Federal Employees (NARFE). Together these organizations have an approximate membership of over eight million, though it is difficult to say with certainty how much overlap exists. In any event, they do hold the potential of wielding substantial power on behalf of older citizens.

The National Council of Senior Citizens has thus far been more closely involved with partisan politics than any of the other groups. Born in the 1960s in an effort to lend support to the drive for Medicare legislation, NCSC was fostered by the labor unions and on many issues has found itself aligned with policies espoused by the Democratic party. In the beginning, financial support was derived almost exclusively from funds provided by the labor unions, but in recent years membership dues have enabled the organization to become financially independent. Although the majority of members and directors still represent unions or are former union members, this is not a requisite of membership and anyone may join. Another, and perhaps the best known of the organizations supporting older people, is the successor of what began as the National Retired Teachers Association. The parent organization, the NRTA, was founded in 1947 by a retired California teacher, Ethel Percy Andrus, who initially sought legislative reform of pension and tax programs affecting elderly teachers. In the later 1950s, Andrus and Leonard Davis, an insurance agent, joined forces to offer group life and, ultimately, health insurance to NRTA members, a plan so popular that the American Association of Retired People was developed to cover retirants who were interested in participating but who had not been teachers. Today the combined forces of the AARP-NRTA share staff and programs, so that for all intents and purposes they function as one organization with a membership in excess of seven million, making it one of the largest organizations of its kind in the country. While NRTA has been fully involved in the development of AARP, it has steadfastly attempted to maintain an identity in its own right as a teacher-related interest group. Beginning in the late 1960s, both groups moved beyond their initial service orientation to become politically and socially active on the national scene. In contrast to the NCSC, the AARP has, until recently, been nominally identified with Republican political ideologies through its representation of white collar and professional status retirants. Following the 1971 White House Conference on Aging, AARP has deliberately sought to free itself from close identification with either party. Leaders of the two organizations deny such labels, claiming they strive for broad representation to lend credibility to their descriptions of the needs and desires of older Americans (Pratt, 1974). The third organization, the National Association of Retired Federal Employees (NARFE), draws the majority of its 182,000 members from the Washington, D.C., area and only became active on the national scene after 1970. Since its inception in 1921, NARFE has focused primarily on pragmatic issues of immediate relevance to retired federal employees, rarely venturing into the broader realms of social and legislative policy questions. Even though overt sponsorship of political candidates would be grounds for forfeiture of their tax-exempt status, several of the groups are nonetheless able to engage in partisan politics through lobbying and informal cooperation with political campaign workers.

Brief mention must also be made of several service-related organizations that have recently become vocal proponents of the causes of the elderly. Three of the associations are concerned almost exclusively with long-term institutional care of the aged. They include the American Association of Homes for the Aging, the American Nursing Home Association and the National Council of Health Care Services. The guiding interest of each of these groups lies in securing federal funding and having some control over the development of regulations with which old age facilities must comply to retain their financial backing. Many of the smaller affiliates that make up these larger associations are commercial enterprises, one example being the chain of nursing homes owned by Holiday Inns. Quite naturally their primary concerns revolve around the business aspects of providing goods or services to the elderly. Most of the fiscal support behind these three associations derives from the dues of affiliate members and from voluntary contributions. Several other organizations have also become active on behalf of the elderly. A relative newcomer is the National Association of State Units on Aging (NASUA). Membership in this group is comprised of the administrators of the state and territorial agencies serving the elderly, most of which are funded at least in part under the various titles of the 1965 Older Americans Act. NASUA's membership is augmented by personnel from technical and advisory positions in governmental agencies whose concerns tend to focus on the delivery of governmentally supported services. The National Council on the Aging (NCOA) is a general service agency that has evolved over the last decade to a relatively strong position as technical consultant to any organization that addresses itself to problems facing the elderly. The NCOA currently has over 1400 members representing a wide range of health, social work and community action agencies who devote their energies to the dilemmas of the elderly in American life. The National Caucus on the Black Aged, organized in 1970 by professionals concerned with advancing the position of black elderly, is one of the more politically activist groups in the field of aging. Finally, there is the Gerontological Society, with its 3000+ members, which has become increasingly visible on the political scene since the late 1960s. From diverse professional and academic backgrounds, members of the Gerontological Society combine their separate perspectives on the processes of aging to formulate policy suggestions, but, like most professional societies, the major thrust of their efforts is focused on research and training programs aimed at preparing future gerontologists in their search for solutions to many of today's problems (Binstock, 1972).

Although the early voluntary associations have gradually been replaced by more sophisticated interest groups, the potential for political activism has yet to be realized. To date no particularly radical proposals have been offered for such things as income redistribution or maintenance schemes. Instead, the Gerontological Society and its sister organizations have either advocated modifications in existing programs or assumed the role of intermediary between the funding agencies and older recipients (Pratt, 1974). By virtue of their claims to represent the interests of millions of older Americans, concerned professionals and interest groups have often acquired ready access to Congress as well as to other officials in public and private agencies. Accordingly, the groups have been most vocal up to now in the realm of improving benefits within the existing frameworks of Social Security, Medicare and the Older Americans legislation (Binstock, 1974). As the number of elderly continues to expand, it is to be expected that relevant associations will also grow in size, thereby enlarging their probable sphere of influence. Older people already account for roughly 15 percent of the voting public, and if the appropriate consciousness-raising does indeed take place, they may yet mold themselves into a cohesive political bloc, at least on certain issues. Until that time, changes will continue to be incremental and circuitous at best. Politicians have become more aware of the needs of the aging, and in some cases more responsive. Perhaps one ironic indication of the growing visibility of organizations for the elderly in national politics is illustrated by the fate of the NCSC during the heat of the 1972 presidential campaign. Partially as a consequence of its political activities, the NCSC found itself placed on the infamous White House "enemies list," and according to depositions filed in federal courts, the Internal Revenue Service was approached in an attempt to acquire the names of important contributors, presumably to head off further political involvement by the group (Butler, 1974). In some quarters, however briefly, certain older people's organizations were apparently perceived to have come of age, meriting just a bit more attention than otherwise might have been the case.

Attitudes and Political Participation

Aging and Sociopolitical Attitudes

As a consequence of the ubiquitous sociological surveys and opinion polls fielded since the 1930s, many claims have been put forth about the assumed conservativeness of older people. Reflecting a bias easily dating back to Aristotle, the popular notion is that the elderly, who are miserly, crabby and overly cautious, are also politically conservative, if not outright reactionaries. Unfortunately, there are some well-intentioned yet ill-conceived studies that tend to reinforce such a view. For example, surveys conducted in the 1950s and early 1960s report that the older people become, the more rigid and less willing they are to accept change, nonconformity or even governmental intervention in order to control societal institutions (Stouffer, 1955; Rokeach, McGovney and Denny, 1955; Campbell, 1962). While it would make the study of aging infinitely simpler if the relationship between age and attitudes was even half as straightforward as such findings suggest, like everything else we have learned about age changes, it really is not so easy. To begin with, surveys attempting to isolate conservative opinions tend to ask questions about controversial social issues likely to elicit polarized responses from almost any sample. Quite obviously, those people who have little knowledge or experience of the events in question will often express opinions that reflect the nature of the experiences they have had — in short, conservative opinions that affirm the traditional values of the status quo. Nevertheless, in a sense age may still be indicative of what could be called a traditionalist stance on certain political issues. However, as a few researchers are pointing out, it is not because the majority of older people are especially hidebound, but rather that their attitude changes have not been as rapid or liberal as those articulated by the larger proportion of younger citizens (Glenn, 1974). This is a far stretch from saying that the processes of aging are associated with increasing political conservativeness.

As opinion polls have become more sophisticated, attempts have been made to winnow out the effects of age per se from other factors in the formation of conservative attitudes. We already know that socioeconomic status, education, social mobility and even sex differentiate opinions held on various issues. Recently it has also been noted the proximity of the question to people's lives influences the opinions they hold. In other words, if an issue actually impinges on an individual's life, striking close to home, affecting his or her family or community as opposed to the country or someplace else in the world, the opinions he or she expresses will vary from those held about issues farther removed. An equally relevant yet often overlooked consideration is what some researchers label the generational effect. In essence, those who emphasize the need for generational analysis maintain the attitudes individuals hold toward the events taking place around them have been induced, in part, by the history they have lived through. This is not to say that everyone born of an era will have exactly the same world view. Sociological differences still count, but those who underwent comparable experiences or were exposed to fairly analogous values as they moved into adulthood will exhibit a marked similarity in the views they express throughout the remainder of their lives (Mannheim, 1952; Foner, 1972). The question of American involvement in wars waged on foreign soil offers an excellent case in point. Until the late 1960s, the older generations tended to hold less supportive views of international aggressiveness and war than their younger counterparts. In her analysis of opinion polls covering a forty year period, Erskine (1973) found people over age 50 to be generally more opposed to violence than those under the age of 30. However, with the intensification of American involvement in Indochina, a reversal took place; younger generations began expressing marked opposition to war. Explaining why the negative attitudes of the older ages suddenly paled in comparison to the antiwar sentiment expressed by younger people is necessarily post hoc, yet the reversal may reflect the prevailing social attitudes during the formative years of each generation. Following America's involvement in World War II, the postwar generation was more accepting of the need to wage war than the previous generation had been, but as the Cold War became less foreboding, the next generation was not exposed to a similar rationale for maintaining an aggressive posture and subsequently the protests of the 1960s signaled a further shift away from a militaristic frame of reference. When this happened, one of the dominant themes in the country tended to become crystalized or incapsulated in the attitudes of the people who were just then coming to a political consciousness(Jeffries, 1974).

Still another common misconception about the political consciousness of elderly people is that they become less attuned to the important questions facing society as they become older. To some extent, early gerontological studies of opinionation among older people tended to perpetuate this idea by suggesting that the process of disengagement was revealed in part in one's political awareness as demonstrated either by the frequency of neutral or no responses in opinion surveys or by the expression of extremist views calculated to shock the interviewer (Gergen and Back, 1966b). Later analyses which took the average educational level of various cohorts into account found not only that older people continued to hold strong political beliefs, but that in many cases they actually held stronger opinions than younger people with comparable educations. In his reanalysis of a series of 35 public opinion polls, Glenn (1969) found that controlling for education and racial background, as well as for sex — in the past women more often offered neutral responses — eradicated any differences in the propensity toward diminishing opinionation with age. In terms of opinions and, as we shall see below, voting behavior, the most reliable evidence available indicates that political interest not only does not dissipate, but in all probability increases throughout most of adult life. Until gerontologists are able to report the results of their longitudinal panel studies, conclusions about changes in political awareness or involvement must necessarily be based on less than optimal data gathered in cross-sectional surveys. Despite this, the conflicting evidence does not overwhelmingly support the idea of a decreasing political consciousness among older people (Glenn, 1974).

This is not to say there is no distinction between the opinions expressed by the elderly and by younger adults, merely that they cannot be explained wholly because one group is older than the other. In a national survey conducted by the National Opinion Research Council inquiring about the perceived appropriateness of federal allocations for education, health and environmental protection, obvious differences were discovered, with older people expressing quite liberal attitudes on those issues that directly affected their own self-interest. On the question of health, for example, a majority of the young adults and nearly an equal proportion of their elderly counterparts felt too little was currently being spent to maintain the country's health. Preserving the environment is an abstract idea not readily identified by many people as being personally important; hence, when the same study asked about monies for environmental protection, three-quarters of the younger group, but only a little more than 40 percent of the older respondents, felt more should be apportioned for environmental programs. A similar pattern emerges over the issue of educational funding. Important as it is in the lives of families with school age children, over half the younger respondents supported greater fiscal support, while among the older group, whose children are normally far beyond their school years, only about one-third saw any need for increased spending (Clemente, 1975). What findings such as these seem to indicate is that the distance of the issue in question from the life of the respondent probably does have an impact on the opinions a person expresses. Further testimony is provided by two additional studies which asked people how they felt about drug use, abuse and the penalties levied for convictions on drug charges. When the national Drug Abuse Council (1975) asked people about specific alternatives to current legal sanctions covering drug use, it found younger adults and those who had smoked marijuana previously to be more likely to favor either making the penalties more lenient than at present or abolishing them altogether. On the other hand, among older adults, or those who had never experimented with marijuana, the desire for establishing tougher penalties prevailed. Looking at the left side of Table 12.1, only minor differences by age appear among those who favor maintaining the laws currently on the books. The divergence occurs on the right side, where we see two extreme proposals of either decriminalizing use completely or making penalties tougher than they are now. Among the youngest adults, almost 30 percent favor legalizing sale and use of marijuana, while only about 7 percent of the oldest respondents expressed a similar willingness to endorse a reversal of current policy. On the question of tougher penalties exactly the opposite trend is observed. Half of the older people but less than one-fifth of the youngest would impose stiffer sanctions. In another study of drug attitudes, involving older people, students and policemen, the older people voiced the least favorable attitudes regarding drug use, but overall they were not the most punitive. Among the younger respondents, attitudinal differences hinged on characteristics other than their age. Not surprisingly, policemen were more in favor of punishing drug users than either graduate students of approximately the same age or the older respondents. Here, too, it is difficult to say that age per se had a definitive impact on attitudes, since personal knowledge, experience and values obviously influenced the responses given by all three groups (Ross, Greenwald and Linn, 1973).

Despite the caveats accompanying most cross-sectional attitude surveys, a poll commissioned by the Senate Committee on Government Operations (1973) provides other interesting insights into the association between age and political orientation. When the pollsters asked people how they personally felt about such commonly heard complaints as tax laws being intended to help the rich and special interest groups, or the corruption of governmental officials, nearly three-quarters of each age category from the youngest to the oldest expressed serious feelings of alienation from the political process. Whether these results would have been found a few years earlier is certainly debatable, since Watergate was fresh in the minds of all respondents. It is interesting to note both the youngest (18–29) and the oldest (50+) people surveyed expressed the strongest feelings of discontent, even though neither group was willing to admit they felt powerless to effect changes. Somewhat over half of the respondents on either end of the age continuum continued to believe it was within their power to do something about unjust corrupt officials, while only one-third of their number felt there was little possibility of personally doing anything to bring about needed changes. In terms of actual attempts to make their opinions known, there was

Table 12.1

American Attitudes Toward Alternative Penalties for Sale and Possession of Marijuana, 1974

AGE	CURRENT LAW REMAINS UNCHANGED	POSSESSION OF SMALL AMOUNTS SUBJECT TO A CIVIL FINE	POSSESSION OF SMALL AMOUNTS LEGAL	SALE AND POSSESSION OF SMALL AMOUNTS LEGAL	TOUGHER PENALTIES SHOULD BE IMPOSED
All adults	13	10	13	16	40
18–25	11	10	28	28	19
26–34	11	12	18	23	29
35–39	17	13	10	11	41
40–49	15	10	11	12	44
50–59	9	10	7	11	54
60+	15	9	4	7	54

Source: Drug Abuse Council, *Annual Report, 1975* (Washington, D.C.: U.S. Government Printing Office, 1975).

a remarkable uniformity between oldest and youngest as far as routine activities were concerned. Two-thirds of each group had signed petitions, one-third had written their congressional representative and about a sixth had written local officials or visited a state legislator. Somewhat fewer had actively campaigned for a presidential candidate, but again both groups were almost equally involved. Although more older people had contributed money to a political cause, it was only when it came to picketing or street demonstrations that any significant disparities between the two groups appeared. While only about a fifth of the younger group had engaged in such activities, this was three times the number of older respondents who had been involved in this particular form of activism. It is worth pointing out that both older and younger respondents were generally somewhat more estranged than those in the middle generation, perhaps reflecting what has been labeled as their peripheral position in society's scheme of things (Cutler and Bengtson, 1974).

Voting and Participation in the Political Process

Simply making one's opinions known about various issues is seldom enough to bring about many significant changes. To effectuate such change, it is generally necessary to be able to wield some form of power over the political process in order to implement new direction or to exert control over the behavior of others. There is some truth to the old cliché about a velvet glove veiling an iron fist; raw power in the form of physical force is generally irreconcilable with the philosophies ascribed to by democratic political orders. There are exceptions, of course, when naked force is construed to be legitimate, but under normal circumstances the only power most people are willing to sanction is that which carries with it the mantle of authority acquired in the political arena. Aside from the supposedly counterbalancing interest groups, which attempt to lobby directly with the nation's lawmakers on behalf of their members, the most widely accepted avenue for exercising our political franchise is through the voting booth. Among political scientists, the question of quantity of participation in the electoral process versus quality of participation is still being contested. Usually, however, most believe that involving the largest number of people possible is the best means of insuring unbiased results. Taken together, opinions and voting patterns do furnish some valuable indicators that the potential for interceding in the political process clearly exists. To begin with, voter turnout rises steadily with age, at least into the retirement years, and even then it does not decline among the better educated, the actively involved or for those who are not hampered by ill health or immobility. Already older people are overrepresented in the ranks of the voters, accounting for roughly 15 percent of those who turn out on election day. Future trends point to even greater levels of participation into the far reaches of life as successive generations of older people are better educated, have more time free from work and overcome such impediments as transportation problems (Glenn and Grimes, 1968; Olsen, 1972). Examining voter turnout in a recent presidential election will provide an overview of the trends that are approximated in nearly all elections. While the figures shown in Figure 12.1 may vary to a minor extent, the pattern revealed has been observed for quite a number of years. Among both women and men, the proportion voting increases until retirement, at which time there is modest decline; still, more 75 year olds voted in 1972 than did the youngest eligible voters. It is interesting to note that prior to age 45, slightly more women than men voted, although this tendency is reversed from then on until a significant gap appeared among people in their late 60s and early 70s. On the average, presidential election years usually prompt slightly more than 70 percent of the population to register to vote, with about 10 percent less ultimately going to the polls. In comparison, the 1974 congressional races saw just over 60 percent register, while about half the population actually turned out on election day. In the generation over 65, however, somewhere around 90 percent of the people are registered to vote, with nearly two-thirds of this number voting on a regular basis. The greater gap between the number of older men and women who participate in the electoral process has not been satisfactorily explained at this time, though it may have something to do with a less activist political orientation among the older women (Butler, 1974; U.S. Census, 1975).

Voting patterns reflect not only age and sex, but a whole range of other demographic and social characteristics as well. In the 1974 congressional elections about half the white population voted, compared to approximately one-third of the blacks and slightly more than 20 percent of the population of identifiable Spanish origin. In some instances, marital status also makes a difference. In an analysis of the 1972 race, the proportion of married voters over the age of 45 was greater than the widowed or divorced, who in turn voted in larger numbers than those who had never married. Generally, it is only after such factors as sex, race, health, education, and social or financial resources have been taken into account that chronological age can be said to have even the slightest impact on voting (Glenn and Grimes, 1968; U.S. Census, 1973). Another question that cannot now be answered is whether older voters have always exercised their political prerogatives or only do so as they acquire more time and

Figure 12.1
Who voted in the United States, November 1972

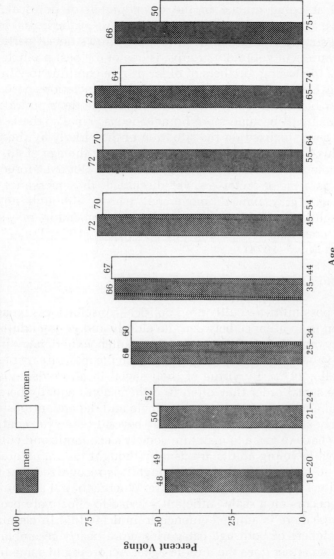

Source: U.S. Bureau of the Census, *Current Population Reports*, series P-20, no. 253, "Voting and Registration in the Election of November, 1972" (Washington, D.C.: U.S. Government Printing Office, 1973), p. 22. (Adapted from numeric data)

fewer distractions. Depending on which of the two possibilities eventually proves to be the case, the likelihood of the elderly constituting a powerful voting bloc able to deliver votes will vary. In either instance, it is important to point out that the characteristics of older voters are exactly those that students of social movements have identified as being crucial in the development of political consciousness. For example, political mobilization, at the initial levels involving simply voting, which apparently grows out of participation in a variety of voluntary groups, is one of the best predictors of voting. As increasing numbers of older people continue to join voluntary organizations or any of the age-graded associations described in Chapter Eleven, there is some basis to assume their political interpretations will become more homogeneous. Finally, the current attention being focused on the situation of the elderly by the mass media, plus the growing number of people over the age of 65, may also promote an awareness of their own affinity. Not to be forgotten, however, is a major factor not yet discussed, the emergence of a rudimentary "gray power" movement which, although not yet proven highly effective in attracting a broad membership, may serve a definite consciousness-raising function (Olsen, 1972; Trela, 1972; Ragan and Dowd, 1974).

Politics and a Generational Alliance

One possibility for cultivating political consciousness broached quite often is an alliance between the elderly and young adults. As previously mentioned these two groups often experience similar feelings of alienation and estrangement from the mainstream of society (Agnello, 1973). By virtue of their social location vis-à-vis the rest of the social order they often find themselves equally bereft of firm social anchorages and in subordinate and dependent postures. The elderly are often considered to be beyond whatever contributions they have to make to maintain society's economic and cultural growth, while young adults are usually thought too immature, not yet ready to make a life choice, although it is recognized that their contributions will come with the future. Whether or not any unification ever occurs on a scale sufficiently broad to effectively propose alternatives, there is ample evidence to indicate that in certain respects members of both age categories more nearly resemble one another than either does the middle-aged. According to some in the field, their feelings of relative powerlessness and structural marginality may be coalescing to the point where older people are now on the verge of an emerging age group consciousness similar to that which swept through much of the world's youth in the late 1960s

(Laufer and Bengtson, 1974; Martin, Bengtson and Acock, 1974). Some have even forecast, perhaps wistfully, an actual alliance between old and young, initiated most probably by the old, although many students of aging predict any intergenerational political movement as unlikely (Kalish, 1969; Cameron and Cromer, 1974; Cain, 1975).

The Gray Panthers is an example of one organization drawing its members from both old and young that has attempted to meld an intergenerational unity through action. Founded in Philadelphia in the early 1970s, the group first took its cue from the so-called radical activists whose goal was to awaken white and black alike to the existence of racism in its innumerable guises. Realizing age biases cut across sex and racial boundaries with equal devastation, the Gray Panthers dedicated themselves to the abolition of prejudice on the basis of age wherever it is found. Although federal laws are now in force prohibiting age discrimination in the world of work — up to age 65, that is — they are difficult to enforce and encompass only a relatively small part of the problem. *Ageism*, or what was defined in Chapter One as a pejorative evaluation and labeling of older people simply because of their age, seems to be evident in nearly every realm of modern society, especially in America, where traditionally youthful vigor has been highly esteemed (Butler, 1969). Illustrative of the insidiousness of age discrimination, in their 20 year survey of employment, Palmore and Manton (1973) found few improvements between the sexes in terms of occupational equality. The advances that did take place primarily encouraged racial equality in work, with blacks registering modest gains. However, when a comparison is made on the basis of workers' ages, the evidence shows that the inequalities have become worse over the last two decades. It is their conclusion that while some portion of the declines among older workers can be attributed to mandatory retirement policies that have been accepted on a widespread scale, the feeling that older workers neither need nor desire equal opportunities is the primary culprit. It is exactly this kind of issue that concerns groups intent on developing power among the aged, but as far as the Gray Panthers and others are concerned, to attack ageism it is first necessary to challenge the negative attitudes held toward and by the old. According to Maggie Kuhn, founder of the Gray Panthers, bringing both ends of the age continuum into close association with the avowed purpose of convincing everyone else that older people are indeed valuable members of society will have its effect on the participants as well as upon those for whom their message is intended. Initially the Gray Panthers have been content to advocate alternative lifestyles for older people — unions with younger partners, mutual sharing, interaction and so on — in order to facilitate a communal consciousness. Of course we are not yet in an era when militant septuagenarians are about to become commonplace; nevertheless, from protesting our conceptions of propriety to welding a political consciousness among the elderly is not nearly as great a leap as it might seem. Older people have already engaged in isolated demonstrations: recall the 200-odd elderly Philadelphians who accosted then Vice-President Agnew in 1972 to decry the inequalities of threatened Social Security cutbacks, or the 2000 older Bostonians who successfully demonstrated a few years back over fare increases in the city's transportation system and who thus succeeded in speaking with a single voice. And what of the Sun City residents who filed suit in the Arizona courts to block young people from settling in their community? If these initiatives and others like them succeed, and if preliminary contacts with opinion leaders do indeed result in new opportunities for affirmative action, then clearly more political activity is in the offing (White House Conference, 1971).

Summary

In recent years considerable attention has been focused on the potential role of the aged in the political arena. While not a unified or powerful group at the present time, future developments emphasizing the common predicament of older people may shape them into a political force to be reckoned with. During the 1930s, the Depression spawned a variety of social movements that looked for a time as though they would indeed serve the needs of older people. With the advent of Social Security, however, most of the groups were deprived of their primary purpose and soon fell into decline. Today there are once again several national organizations dedicated to maintaining the viability of America's elderly. Although there is little consensus among these groups as to the most expedient means of securing a better shake for older people, there is no denying their importance on the national political scene. Paradoxically, many of the new interest groups set up on behalf of the elderly have become closely allied with administrative agencies, serving as intermediaries between government and client. Students of organizational growth are quick to point out that in a situation such as this, voluntary associations tend to become bureaucracies that eventually solidify to the extent that those whom they intended to represent are sometimes left behind, their interests relegated to a secondary position for the sake of the organization's own livelihood (Freedman, 1973).

In addressing the role of age in determining political attitudes, care must once again be exercised before attributing causal significance to any of the factors involved. Differences observed between the political outlook of old and young may not reflect age changes at all, but stem instead from a generational bias cast under particular historical circumstances. Popular interpretations of opinion polls often portray the elderly as politically conservative, yet a closer look at the issues in question is needed before any such general conclusions can be drawn. Familiarity, experience and proximity are in themselves enough to alter the opinions expressed by respondents of various ages. Another misconception about the elderly is that they are less attuned to current events because of the social dislocations they have undergone during retirement or widowhood. However when important sociological variables are brought into the picture, older people are no less informed or more apathetic than many younger people; in fact, just the opposite in many cases. The marked similarity that is sometimes found between the opinions held by our oldest and youngest generations of adults has led some investigators to note their analogous position relative to the mainstream of society, giving rise to the possibility of an intergenerational alliance between the two ends of the adult age continuum.

With respect to voting as a form of political participation, no significant declines occur until quite late in life, and even then, lower turnouts seem to be the result of either mundane problems having to do with transportation difficulties or declining health. As future generations of the elderly are increasingly better educated and able to devote more time to community and voluntary activities, there is reason to expect they will become even more involved in the political process. Already the generation that Neugarten (1974) terms the *young-old* — those aged 55 to 75 — shows signs of being more politically aware than its predecessors. Evidence of growing political concern is also furnished by the rudimentary gray power groups that have formed around the country, with the most active of these, the Gray Panthers, seeking the eradication of ageism through an amalgamation of old and young for the mutual benefit of both.

Pertinent Readings

AGNELLO, T.J. "Aging and the Sense of Political Powerlessness." *Public Opinion Quarterly* XXXVII (1973): 251–59.

BENGTSON, V.L. "Inter-age Perceptions and the Generation Gap." *The Gerontologist* XI, 4, pt. II (1971): 85–89.

BINSTOCK, R.H. "Interest-group Liberalism and the Politics of Aging." *The Gerontologist* XII, 3, pt. I (1972): 265–81.

_____."Aging and the Future of American Politics." *The Annals of the American Academy of Political and Social Science* CDXV (1974): 199–212.

BUTLER, R.N. "Age-Ism: Another Form of Bigotry." *The Gerontologist* IX, 4, pt. I (1969): 243–46.

_____. "The Public Interest: Report No. 2. Old Age in Your Nation's Capital." *Aging and Human Development* II, 3 (1971): 197–201.

_____. "Pacification and the Politics of Aging." *Aging and Human Development* V, 4 (1974): 393–96.

CAIN, L.D. "Political Factors in the Emerging Legal Status of the Elderly." *The Annals of the American Academy of Political and Social Science* CDXV (1974): 70–79.

_____. "The Young and the Old: Coalition or Conflict Ahead?" *American Behavioral Scientist* XIX, 2 (1975): 166–75.

CAMERON, P., and A. CROMER. "Generational Homophyly." *Journal of Gerontology* XXIX, 2 (1974): 232–36.

CAMPBELL, A. "Social and Psychological Determinants of Voting Behavior." In *Politics of Age*, eds. W. Donahue and C. Tibbitts, 87–100. Ann Arbor: University of Michigan, 1962.

_____. "Politics through the Life Cycle." *The Gerontologist* XI, 2, pt. I (1971): 112–17.

CARLIE, M.K. "The Politics of Age: Interest Group or Social Movement?" *The Gerontologist* IX, 4, pt. I (1969): 259–63.

CLEMENTE, F. "Age and the Perception of National Priorities." *The Gerontologist* XV, 1, pt. I (1975): 61–63.

COTTRELL, F. "Governmental Functions and the Politics of Age." In *Handbook of Social Gerontology*, ed. C. Tibbitts, 624–65. Chicago: University of Chicago Press, 1960.

CUTLER, N.E. "Generation, Maturation, and Party Affiliation: A Cohort Analysis." *Public Opinion Quarterly* XXXIII, 4 (1969–70): 583–88.

CUTLER, N.E., and V.L. BENGTSON. "Age and Political Alienation: Maturation, Generation and Period Effects." *The Annals* CDXV (1974): 160–75.

CUTLER, S.J. "Perceived Prestige Loss and Political Attitudes Among the Aged." *The Gerontologist* XIII, 1 (1973): 69–75.

DOUGLASS, E.B., W.P. CLEVELAND and G.L. MADDOX. "Political Attitudes, Age, and Aging: A Cohort Analysis of Archival Data." *Journal of Gerontology* XXIX, 6 (1974): 666–75.

DRUG ABUSE COUNCIL. *Annual Report, 1975.* Washington, D.C.: U.S. Government Printing Office, 1975.

ERSKINE, H. "The Polls: Pacifism and the Generation Gap." *Public Opinion Quarterly* XXXVI, 4 (1973): 616–27.

FONER, A. "The Polity." In *Aging and Society, Vol. 3*, eds. M.W. Riley, M. Johnson and A. Foner, 115–59. New York: Russell Sage Foundation, 1972.

FREEDMAN, J.O. "The Administrative Process and the Elderly." *Temple Law Quarterly* XLVI, 4 (1973): 511–26.

FRIES, V., and R.N. BUTLER. "The Public Interest: Report No. 3. The Congressional Seniority System: The Myth of Gerontocracy in Congress." *Aging and Human Development* II, 4 (1971): 341–48.

GERGEN, K.J., and K.W. BACK. "Cognitive Constriction in Aging and Attitudes toward International Issues." In *Social Aspects of Aging*, eds. I.H. Simpson and J.C. McKinney, 322–34. Durham, N.C.: Duke University Press, 1966a.

———. "Communication in the Interview and the Disengaged Respondent." *Public Opinion Quarterly*. XXX (1966b): 385–98.

GLAMSER, F.D. "The Importance of Age to Conservative Opinions: A Multivariate Analysis." *Journal of Gerontology* XXIX, 5 (1974): 549–554.

GLENN, N.D., "Aging, Disengagement, and Opinionation." *Public Opinion Quarterly* XXXIII, 1 (1969): 17–33.

———. "Aging and Conservatism." *The Annals* CDXV (1974): 176–186.

GLENN, N.D. and M. GRIMES. "Aging, Voting, and Political Interest." *American Sociological Review* XXXIII (1968): 563–75.

GUBRIUM, J.F. "Continuity in Social Support, Political Interest, and Voting in Old Age." *The Gerontologist* XII, 4 (1972): 421–23.

HOLTZMAN, A. *The Townsend Movement: A Political Study.* New York: Basic Books, 1963.

JACKSON, J.J. "NCBA, Black Aged and Politics." *The Annals* CDXV (1974): 138–59.

JEFFRIES, V. "Political Generations and the Acceptance or Rejection of Nuclear Warfare." *Journal of Social Issues* XXX, 3 (1974): 119–136.

KALISH, R.A. "The Old and the New as Generation Gap Allies." *The Gerontologist* IX, 2 (1969): 83–89.

LAUFER, R.S., and V.L. BENGTSON. "Generations, Aging, and Social Stratification: On the Development of Generational Units. " *Journal of Social Issues* XXX, 3 (1974): 181–205.

MANNHEIM, K. "The Problem of Generations." In *Essays on the Sociology of Knowledge*, 276–320. London: Routledge and Kegan Paul Ltd., 1952.

MARTIN, W., V. BENGTSON and A. ACOCK. "Alienation and Age: A Context Specific Approach." *Social Forces* LIII, 2 (1974): 266–74.

MCKINNEY, J.C., and F.T. DEVYVER. *Aging and Social Policy.* New York: Atherton, 1966.

NEUGARTEN, B.L. "Age Groups in American Society and the Rise of the Young-old." *The Annals* CDXV (1974): 187–98.

———. "The Future and the Young-old." *The Gerontologist* XV, 1, pt. II (1975): 4–9.

OLESZEK, W. "Age and Political Careers." *Public Opinion Quarterly* XXXIII, 1 (1969): 100–02.

OLSEN, M.E. "Social Participation and Voting Turnout: A Multivariate Analysis." *American Sociological Review* XXXVII, 4 (1972): 317–33.

PALMORE, E., and K. MANTON. "Ageism Compared to Racism and Sexism." *Journal of Gerontology* XXVIII, 3 (1973): 363–69.

PALMORE, E., and F. WHITTINGTON. "Trends in the Relative Status of the Aged." *Social Forces*, L (1971): 84–91.

PINNER, F.A., P. JACOBS and P. SELZNICK. *Old Age and Political Behavior: A Case Study.* Berkeley: University of California Press, 1959.

PRATT, H.J. "Old Age Associations in National Politics." *The Annals*, CDXV (1974): 138–59.

RAGAN, P.K., and J.J. DOWD. "The Emerging Political Consciousness of the Aged: A Generational Interpretation." *Journal of Social Issues* XXX, 3 (1974): 137–58.

RILEY, M.W. "Aging and Cohort Succession: Interpretations and Misinterpretations." *Public Opinion Quarterly* XXXVII, 1 (1973): 35–49.

ROKEACH, M., W.C. McGOVNEY and M.R. DENNY. "A Distinction Between Dogmatic and Rigid Thinking." *Journal of Abnormal and Social Psychology* LI, 1 (1955): 87–93.

ROSE, A.M. "Group Consciousness Among the Aging." In *Older People and Their Social World*, eds. A.M. Rose and W.A. Peterson, 19–36. Philadelphia: F.A. Davis Co., 1965a.

_____ . "The Subculture of the Aging: A Framework for Research in Social Gerontology." In *Older People and Their Social World*, eds. A.M. Rose and W.A. Peterson, 3–18. Philadelphia: F.A. Davis Co., 1965b.

ROSS, B., S.R. GREENWALD and M.W. LINN. "The Elderly's Perception of the Drug Scene." *The Gerontologist* XIII, 3, pt. I (1973): 368–71.

SHERWOOD, S. "Conservatism and Age: A Reexamination." *Indian Journal of Social Research* II, 2 (1961): 39–44.

STOUFFER, S.A. *Communism, Conformity, and Civil Liberties.* Garden City, N.Y.: Doubleday and Co., 1955.

STREIB, G.F. "Are the Aged a Minority Group?" In *Applied Sociology*, eds. A.W. Gouldner and S.M. Miller, 311–28. Glencoe: Free Press, 1965.

TRELA, J.E. "Some Political Consequences of Senior Center and Other Old Age Group Memberships." *The Gerontologist* XI, 2, pt. I (1971): 118–23.

_____ . "Age Structure of Voluntary Associations and Political Self-interest among the Aged." *Sociological Quarterly* XIII, 2 (1972): 244–52.

TURNER, B.F., and R.L. KAHN. "Age as a Political Issue." *Journal of Gerontology* XXIX, 5 (1974): 572–80.

U.S. BUREAU OF THE CENSUS. *Current Population Reports.* Series P-20, no. 143, "Voter Participation in the National Election: November 1964." Washington, D.C.: U.S. Government Printing Office, 1965.

_____ . *Current Population Reports.* Series P-20, no. 253, "Voting and Registration in the Election of November, 1972." Washington, D.C.: U.S. Government Printing Office, 1973.

_____ . *Current Population Reports.* Series P-20, no. 275, "Voter Participation in November, 1974 (Advance Report)." Washington, D.C.: U.S. Government Printing Office, 1975.

U.S. SENATE COMMITTEE ON GOVERNMENT OPERATIONS. "Confidence and Concern: Citizens View American Government." 93d Cong., 1st sess. pt. 1, December 1973. Washington, D.C.: U.S. Govenrment Printing Office, 1973.

VINEYARD, D. "The Senate Special Committee on the Aging." *The Gerontologist* XII, 3, pt. I (1972): 298–303.

WHITE HOUSE CONFERENCE ON AGING. *Toward a National Policy on Aging, Final Report.* Vol. II. Washington, D.C.: U.S. Government Printing Office, 1971.

Chapter 13

Minority Groups in the Later Years

The United States is often described as a melting pot in which distinct cultural groups relinquish many unique characteristics in favor of a cultural homogeneity. Of late this view has been challenged by those who emphasize the pluralistic nature of a society in which Americans can be subdivided into identifiable racial or ethnic groups including whites from a multitude of national origins, blacks, Asians, Indians and those of Hispanic derivation. Despite the presence of so diverse a collection of ethnic groups, much of what was written about aging prior to 1965 relied exclusively on data collected from white participants. This tendency was so pervasive gerontologists did not even need a footnote in their studies to re- mind them of the overwhelming preponderance of aged white sam- ples, for the reality was that "any resemblance to the aging non- Caucasian is accidental and unintentional" (Kastenbaum, 1971). At best, studies focusing on minority elderly have been ancillary or sporadic until the last few years. On the one hand, this might be con- strued as indicative of a general preoccupation with the most visible cultural group in American life. On the other, some have suggested the omission possibly reflects an unconscious bias among the major- ity of white researchers. No matter what interpretation is given to the paucity of information regarding minority group elderly, its absence makes generalization difficult and hazardous even when data are in fact available. Yet another dimension of the problems in analysis arises with the application of stereotypes that have been discounted either for the minority in question or by subsequent information dealing with the aged in general. It is true, of course, there are innu- merable situational variants in minority experiences; each group has its own history, subculture and ways of coping. However, a close look at the reality of aging within each of the subgroups may reveal many similarities. In addition, there are commonalities among the elderly that cut across racial or ethnic categories. For instance, the greater number of older women, the higher remarriage rate of males, the relationship among living arrangements and income, isolation or locale all affect white and minority groups alike (Moore, 1971b).

Nonetheless, there are a great many distinctions between the aged of minority groups and the white elderly that must be expli- cated. A significant obstacle confronts one who attempts to talk about minority groups as though they too were homogeneous. Within the black population, for example, why should differences between rich and poor, single and married, rural and urban, North and South count for any less than they do among the white majority? On the whole there are but few studies that treat the entire black population as anything other than homogeneous, and fewer still rec- ognizing the divergent backgrounds of the elderly. Among those who are nominally classified Spanish Americans, 60 percent are Mexican Americans, while the remainder identify their origins in South America, Cuba, Puerto Rico or other Latin countries. Needless to say, such diversity makes broad generalizations impossible and unwarranted, and necessitates close examination of the sample be- fore drawing any conclusions regarding the applicability of reported findings. Although the proportion of the population of Asian or In- dian heritage is much smaller, identical stumbling blocks are en- countered when dealing with data for these groups. Do people of Asian ancestry trace their roots to China, Japan, the Philippines or someplace else, and, in fact, what difference does it make? Following the most recent census in 1970, blacks accounted for 11 percent of the population, while the other minority groups combined amounted to only 1.4 percent of the total. Although this is double the proportion recorded in 1950, the classification of racial and ethnic groups by the census has changed so that actual growth rates for specific minorities may be confounded with the redefinition of categories. One thing is certain: like the rest of the population, the size of each minority is on the increase and older people are becoming more numerous.

Triple Jeopardy — the Minority Experience

Social scientists have begun to represent the position of a population at risk as one of *triple jeopardy*, the reference being to people who are old, poor and members of a racial or ethnic minority. Much of the impact of the aging processes hits especially hard on those who are unable to afford quality goods or services or who, by virtue of their minority status, have always occupied a disadvantaged position vis-à-vis the more advantaged members of American society. In spite of a dearth of research, it would seem logical to predict a closer conformance in the experiences of diverse minority group members than between the dominant and minority group elderly. It is highly unlikely that they will feel the same as their Anglo counterparts about life and their personal circumstances since their experiences have been so very different. In any event, there is a real need for hard and fast data about the nature of aging among older members of America's minority groups. A cautionary note must be inserted here as elsewhere; those trends toward improvements in social, educational, health or other realms noted as typical for successive cohorts of aged in general also hold true for minorities. Today's elderly and the situations they face may not be indicative of what subsequent generations will experience when they reach a similar point in life. Another comment is in order at this point. It should come as no surprise that in the process of collecting information about minority aging, respondents and researchers alike are exposed to what has been described as a credibility gap. As outsiders seeking personal reflections on the manner in which minorities age, researchers are almost sure to be suspect, while they, in turn, may wonder about the accuracy of the data elicited. Indigenous interviewers may not solve the problem, though in most cases minority elderly will respond more favorably to either an age peer or interviewers obviously of their own ethnic or racial group (Kent et al., 1971). The truism, commented on previously, that older people have no more in common than any other aggregation of people is as valid for minority elderly as for everyone else. In discussing the minority patterns of aging, problems with the comparability of data reassert themselves as they have in almost every other chapter. All other things being equal, it would be reasonable to expect minority elderly to be represented among elderly Americans at a rate roughly' equivalent to minorities in the total population. That this is not the case, that minority elderly account for only about 7 percent of the aged, indicates the existence of a differential structure of opportunities for diverse subgroups which will be discussed in detail in the following pages.

Aged Black Americans

Only during the last few years have aged blacks received much attention from the professional gerontological community. In her extensive reviews of the literature focusing on black elderly, Jackson (1967, 1971a) suggests that very little was written in the scientific literature about the black experience of becoming old until the late 1960s. For a group whose size would place it among the two dozen or so largest independent nations of the world, there is a remarkable lack of knowledge about the processes of aging among blacks. The reasons for the neglect are manifold, encompassing everything from personal predispositions to scientific rationales; fortunately, research has been given a strong impetus, so that the omission is now receiving widespread recognition. A fundamental question to be addressed, yet one of the most elusive, is the extent to which racial characteristics, inherent or ascribed, influence the life course. Are blacks, because they are black in a predominantly white culture, encumbered with special disadvantages in adjusting to aging? Any facile or glib answer is likely either to be incorrect or to gloss over the crucial dimensions of the problem, without a careful delineation of which we cannot understand, much less have influence over, the way things are. In preparation for a look at black elderly, a brief overview of the relative position of American blacks in general is apropos.

Demographic Characteristics of Black Americans

At the present time there are slightly fewer than 25 million black people in the United States, constituting about 11 percent of the total population. As is true for the general population, fertility rates among black women have been declining, although the typical rate is still somewhat higher than for American women as a whole.

On the average, black women have 3.10 children, compared to the 2.34 recorded for white women, but among the youngest cohorts, from 18 to 24 years old, fertility rates are nearly identical. The disparity in fertility rates has contributed to an age distribution of blacks that is younger than whites; one-third of all blacks are under 15 years of age, while only a little over a quarter of the whites are that young. At the same time, less than 7 percent of the blacks, but over 10 percent of the whites are 65 or older. Further age differences also become apparent when contrasting women and men in the two racial categories. The median ages of black men and women are 21.7 and 24 years respectively, roughly six years younger than the averages for their white counterparts. The age distributions of three minority groups plus the white population are shown in Figure 13.1. Differential birth rates and life expectancies are reflected in the age structure of each of the groups.

Historically, the black population has been concentrated in the South, which is still the case today. Approximately 52 percent of the blacks live in the southernmost states, where they comprise about one-fifth of the population for that region. Another 40 percent live in northern and northeastern areas, while the remainder reside in western states. Although general patterns of residential location have changed very little in the last two or more decades, a major shift is occurring within metropolitan areas. As Figure 13.2 reveals, from the early 1960s until the present, the percentage of blacks in metropolitan regions grew, until recent estimates place over three-quarters of all blacks in urban environments, with the central cities housing six of every ten. At the same time, the number of whites in central cities has been continually declining so that just a quarter are now living in the inner core of any metropolis. Seventeen percent of the blacks consider suburbia or the fringes of the urban areas as their home, 24 percent less than the comparable proportion of whites. The exodus of whites, who command higher wages, from the more concentrated population centers leaves these areas without a sufficient tax base, an essential component in the provision of social services for all ages.

Differences between blacks and whites also emerge in the realms of income and employment. In 1974 the median income of black families in the United States amounted to $7808, or about 58 percent of what white families earned. Despite significant gains in gross income since the mid-1960s, once income is adjusted to minimize the effects of inflation, blacks experienced no increase between 1969 and 1973. The average income of white families stayed slightly ahead of the inflationary spiral during this time, and consequently, in relative terms, the gap between the two groups has

Figure 13.1

Age distribution of white, black, Spanish and Indian Americans, 1973–1974

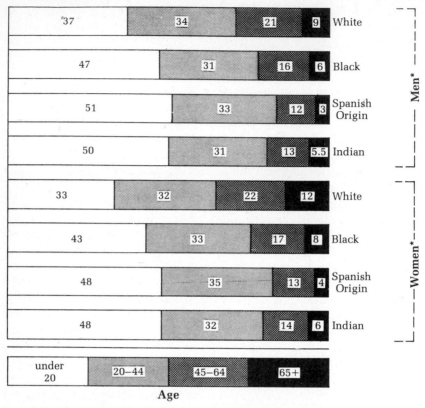

*Totals not equaling 100 percent reflect rounding

Sources: U.S. Bureau of the Census, *Current Population Reports*, series P-20, no. 280 (Washington, D.C.: U.S. Government Printing Office, 1975), p. 24; series P-23, no. 48 (Washington, D.C.: U.S. Government Printing Office, 1974), p. 12; *Final Report*, PC (2)-IF (Washington, D.C.: U.S. Government Printing Office, 1973), p. 2. (Adapted from numeric data)

widened somewhat. Even at that, black families usually required both wage earners to bring in their lower levels of income. Looking at either end of the income distribution, using adjusted dollars to control for inflation, there has been a slight decline for both blacks and whites among those who earn less than $3000 yearly. From 1965 to 1973 the proportion of blacks earning barely enough to survive dropped from one-quarter to one-sixth, while the same period witnessed a decline in the proportion of whites earning equal amounts from 8 to 5 percent. Nevertheless, close to one-third of the black but little more than 8 percent of the white families were below the federally established poverty thresholds in 1973. At the upper end, those

Figure 13.2
Racial distribution of the American population by residence, 1974

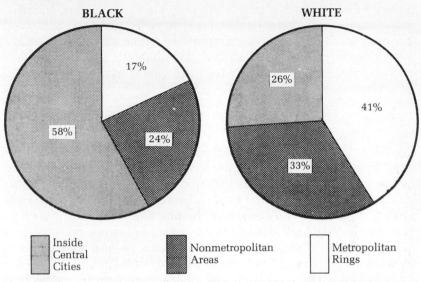

BLACK   WHITE

17% 58% 24% 26% 41% 33%

Inside Central Cities   Nonmetropolitan Areas   Metropolitan Rings

Source: U.S. Bureau of the Census, *Current Population Reports,* Special Studies, series P-23, no. 54 (Washington, D.C.: U.S. Government Printing Office, 1975), p. 9.

earning in excess of $15,000 yearly, blacks jumped from 6 to 16 percent while whites increased from 23 to 38 percent (U.S. Census, 1975a, b, d).

Patterns of labor force participation are seldom stable, being responsive to local as well as national economic trends. Following gradual reductions throughout the 1960s, the jobless rate for blacks has again taken an appreciable upturn, as indeed it has for everyone. In 1970, unemployment idled slightly over 8 percent of the black and 4 to 5 percent of the white labor force. By mid-1975, however, unemployment was hovering around 8.5 percent in general, with a black rate of 14.6 percent. It is suspected by some labor analysts that these figures would be even higher if they took into consideration the hard core unemployed who have grown too weary or discouraged to look for work and are no longer eligible for unemployment benefits. Of the million or more people who fall into this category, perhaps as many as 75 percent are blacks from either end of the age continuum. Of course jobless rates and income figures differ by occupation, education and sex. Considering just sex, income and unemployment, black men are twice as likely to be without jobs as white, while those who are working on the average earn 70 percent of the earnings of white men. Black women are also twice as likely to find themselves in unemployment lines, although when they are fortunate enough to have jobs, they earn wages amounting to 86 percent of those of white women. The purpose in presenting comparative demographic statistics such as these is not to conclusively demonstrate the effects of discrimination, which are well known and have already received widespread documentation. Rather, it is to provide baseline data, required for a discussion of elderly minorities (U.S. Census, 1975d).

Aging and the Black Experience

With relatively few exceptions, the stressful circumstances faced by the black minority are exacerbated among the elderly. Actuarial calculations highlight differential life expectancies between blacks and whites, a partial explanation of why older people comprise little more than 6 percent of the black population. At birth today, whites may look forward to an average of seven more years of life than blacks, though at age 65 the two groups are approximately equal, with remaining life expectancies of between 13 and 16 years for men and women. After the sixth decade, in fact, the tables have turned and the surviving blacks have slightly greater longevity than whites. Why this should be the case is difficult to say, but it probably reflects survival strengths wrought in the face of physical and social adversity (Jackson, 1972a). As is true for their white counterparts, black women outnumber men in the latter half of life. Accordingly, over 60 percent are widowed, while only a quarter are still married. One of the major controversies about black family life has to do with the extent to which it can be characterized as matriarchal. Little in the way of reliable evidence has been forthcoming to settle the imbroglio, yet in view of higher male mortality rates, it is at least possible to appreciate the central role of black mothers and grandmothers in maintaining familial ties. This does not address the question of the alleged dispensibility of black males; instead, it merely suggests, that, in the event of their death, women are fully capable of carrying the familial responsibilities of emotional and physical support (Frazier, 1966; Queen and Habenstein, 1974).

Regardless of racial characteristics, families prove to be the ultimate source of aid for old people, though one difference that has been pointed to by a number of investigators is the seemingly greater prestige accorded black elderly within the family context. For example, if the value hierarchy of the black subculture is found to emphasize survival against all odds, older people, managing to live as long as they have, would naturally be granted a measure of respect not reaped by most whites. Then, too, there are the economic realities of black life in which older people do not experience as radical a decline as their white age peers in terms of falling below the income standards of the rest of the population. Having less throughout life means that one has less to lose in retirement. Further, there is evidence of fewer role losses among blacks in comparison with the experiences of white elderly (Moore, 1971b). The same economic factors also necessitate a greater continuation of employment among older blacks, as many have not been able to accumulate financial reserves. Thus, at the present time a larger share of elderly blacks are still active in the labor force, about 10 percent more black men and 20 percent more black women than white (Rubin, 1974). All aged blacks do not receive Social Security benefits; before enactment of the Supplemental Security Income program in 1974 only 80 percent of elderly blacks, compared to over 90 percent of older whites, received cash payments. This was the result of working at noncovered jobs, and of interrupted participation in and early withdrawal from the labor force. In the last decade and a half coverage has increased significantly, however: over 154 percent for retired black workers. Nonetheless, there remains a differential in the amount of benefits received, and until blacks and whites experience similar work careers, there will be a disparity in their respective retirement incomes. Among workers newly entitled to Social Security benefits, two-thirds of the black men and nearly 90 percent of the black women were concentrated in the lowest economic category characterized by low previous earnings on which benefit levels are based and no second pensions; the comparable rates for white men and women were one-third and two-thirds (Rubin, 1974; Thompson, 1974).

Whether elderly blacks will command high status in their subculture in the future is questionable. In her analyses of black elderly, Jackson (1972a, b) envisions a gradual erosion of the position of older people as they become less essential economically to their families and as the proportion of black elderly increases. All things considered, it is probable elderly blacks are somewhat better integrated into their family groups than whites from equivalent socioeconomic backgrounds. In terms of financial assistance, younger families often have only meager assets themselves and thus are unable to extend their resources to cover the needs of the elderly. In all other respects, family ties are at least as viable as among whites. The issue of money aside, nearly half of those elderly blacks who have children see them more often than once a week. Whether out of economic necessity or preference, aged blacks are less likely than whites to live alone, but like whites there is evidence to suggest that they prefer their intimacy at a distance. Affective kinship relations do appear to be structured on a matrilocal basis, with families living in the vicinity of the wife's mother, although not sharing the same house. Hence it is fair to say a modified extended family represents the norm in urban areas (Hirsch et al., 1972; Jackson, 1972b).

Since blacks are most often residents of inner city locales, it is not surprising to occasionally find large multigenerational households in the same neighborhood. In spite of what was noted earlier about urban renewal programs, older blacks do not move more often than whites and have much less tendency to change residences than the younger members of the black population. Also, despite the fact that older blacks are less likely than white elderly to own their own homes, over half of those over age 60 do live in owner-occupied dwellings. Equity in a home is viewed by a majority of both older blacks and whites as a significant measure of security equaled for some only by close family ties or perhaps a sizeable savings account. The symbolic importance of home ownership transcends all racial and ethnic categories, appearing to be a basic thread in the fabric of the American dream. After a lifetime of lower earnings, it should not be startling that the homes owned by older blacks are less costly than those owned by whites. On the average, their value is at least $5000 lower than for the homes owned by the majority of the elderly. Furthermore, a larger share lack plumbing or other so-called amenities. Similar patterns hold true for the renting population. Blacks not only pay less, but are two to three times more apt to be without some or all plumbing facilities and to live in more crowded units. For purposes of comparison, basic differences in selected housing characteristics of white, black and Spanish Americans are presented in Table 13.1.

Health and Social Adjustment

With almost half the black elderly living in poverty and with a lifetime of inequalities behind them, would it not seem logical for health status to reflect a combination of all these factors? Passing reference was made to various maladies common to the black population in the discussion of health in Chapter Seven, but the extent to which these are a consequence of racial versus socioeconomic background is a question for which no satisfactory answer exists. On one side of the issue, Jackson (1972b) implies that it may in fact be a myth that old blacks are more sickly than old whites, because the former represent a type of biological and social elite, who by virtue of their survival are not prone to as many ailments. Several small scale studies tend to affirm Jackson's assertion but their limited size prohibits any definitive conclusions (Youmans, 1963; Dovenmuehle,

Table 13.1

Does the Housing of Black and Spanish Americans Differ from that of the Average Elderly American?*

HOUSING CHARACTERISTICS	HEAD UNDER 60 YEARS			HEAD 60–64 YEARS			HEAD 65+ YEARS		
	U.S.	BLACK	SPANISH	U.S.	BLACK	SPANISH	U.S.	BLACK	SPANISH
All Occupied Housing Units	45,982,227	4,712,623	2,022,467	5,095,089	453,203	113,536	12,367,434	1,008,415	214,015
Percentage:									
Owner-Occupied	60.7	38.1	41.6	71.0	52.5	56.5	67.5	53.2	57.1
In One Unit Structures	69.7	56.0	58.5	71.9	67.5	66.7	67.1	68.6	67.8
Lacking Some or All Plumbing Facilities	4.4	13.6	5.1	7.0	21.4	9.6	9.1	26.2	12.9
With 1.01+ Persons per Room	10.4	23.3	28.2	2.6	9.2	14.0	1.4	5.7	9.0
Median:									
Income	$9,600	$6,000	$7,600	$7,500	$3,900	$6,000	$3,300	$2,000	$3,100
Value	$18,400	$11,800	$15,600	$15,200	$9,100	$11,900	$12,600	$7,500	$10,000
Gross Rent	$113	$94	$102	$96	$76	$89	$87	$68	$79

*Figures based on 1970 census data

Source: U.S. Bureau of the Census, Census of Housing 1970, Subject Reports, Final Report HC (7)-2, Housing of Senior Citizens (Washington, D.C.: U.S. Government Printing Office, 1973), pp. 517, 540, 563.

1970). However, conflicting data are offered by the National Center for Health Statistics. Coupling blacks with other minorities, trends in health nationwide reveal a prevalence of chronic disabilities almost twice as high as for whites (National Center for Health Statistics, 1971). Besides dying at younger ages than whites, there is some indication that not only do black people feel older than whites at comparable ages but that physiologically they may actually be older. In commenting on the difference, and to offset some of the biological or social inequities experienced by blacks, Jackson has called for a lowering of the retirement age at which blacks would qualify for Social Security. Her reasoning derives from the differential actuarial values for the two groups; since blacks die earlier they ought to be able to draw benefits sooner than whites in order to recoup some fair share of their investment (Morgan, 1968; Jackson, 1972b).

If older blacks tend to remain economically active for longer periods and are more engaged in family life, does this result in higher morale or better adjustment? Once again the evidence is contradictory; this time part of the confusion may be an offshoot of the "happy black" stereotype and the reluctance of older blacks to complain, especially to a white interviewer. It is highly unlikely that race in itself exerts a significant influence over morale; more probably other situational factors have to be taken into consideration before any valid generalizations could be made. With insufficient incomes, inhospitable physical surroundings, poor or at least impaired health and an arduous life overall, it would be unusual not to find some degree of pessimism as a pervasive element in an individual's outlook. However, an exploratory study of majority and minority elderly in Rochester revealed that less than half of the old blacks and whites in that city had serious complaints and those who did expressed desires that are fairly conventional among older people irrespective of race. An interesting sidelight of the Rochester study is the finding that blacks are seemingly better able to accommodate themselves to a racially mixed situation without its having any visible impact on their own sense of well-being. One dimension of morale some investigators feel might have a profound influence on adjustment revolves around the quest for adequate social services. It is often inferred that because of their lack of formal education, misinformation or whatever, older black people are not as aware of or do not utilize agency programs designed to serve them, suffering unnecessarily as a result. Judging from the Rochester data and from similar information derived from a parallel analysis of service provision in Houston, it would appear that, if anything, blacks may be up to twice as knowledgeable about local programs and more than willing to use them to advantage. This may arise partly because whites are more threatened by the need to request assistance, a reluctance which might be dispelled by an educational outreach project aimed particularly at correcting their misconceptions of the services offered. Of course, there are social class differences within each racial category, and inevitably, those most lacking are the least likely to avail themselves of agency supports to meet the demands of their later years. An often neglected facet of the utilization of services is the clients' perceptions of the responsiveness of agency personnel to their needs. Aged blacks rarely view local or state agencies as being willing to meet their personal needs, whether they fall in the area of health, financial or social services. Unfortunately, there may be an element of truth in their perceptions (Ehrlich, 1973; Sterne et al., 1974; McCaslin and Calvert, 1975).

Spanish American Elderly

Next to blacks, people of Spanish origin constitute the largest minority in the United States, yet appreciably less is known about their accession to old age. Two reasons stand out to account for the little systematic information that is available. Since they claim ancestry from at least one of five distinct nationalities, the very heterogeneity of their backgrounds is a major factor precluding ready categorization and generalization. Data gathered from Mexican Americans living in the Southwest are hardly applicable to Cubans in Florida or Puerto Ricans in New York. In addition, the Spanish subpopulation is a very youthful group beset with so many far-reaching problems that the comparatively small number of old people has not emerged to date as a special concern. What little is known has been gleaned from the census and from a few ethnographic studies of particular communities, mostly of Mexican derivation. Accordingly, this overview is by necessity limited to what can be had from these two sources. Larger scale investigations are currently underway in southern California and elsewhere; hopefully, their findings will become part of the professional literature in the near future. For the time being, however, gerontologists must be content with existing, though sparse, data. As with blacks, an overview of Spanish Americans in general will aid in understanding the situation of the elderly of Hispanic origin.

Profile of Spanish Americans

As is shown in Figure 13.3, Mexican Americans predominate among the nearly 11 million persons of Spanish origin, followed by

Figure 13.3
Composition of the Spanish American population

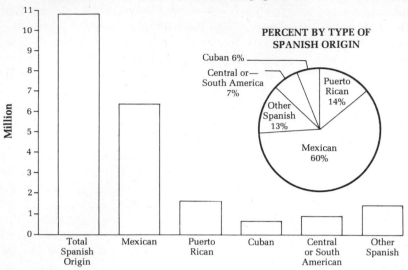

Source: U.S. Bureau of the Census, *Current Population Reports*, series P–20, no. 280, "Persons of Spanish Origin in the United States: March, 1974" (Washington, D.C.: U.S. Government Printing Office, 1975c), cover.

Puerto Ricans, Cubans and those who trace their family history to the other Americas or elsewhere. With so large a percentage originally coming from Mexico, it is reasonable to find the greatest concentrations of the Spanish population, over 58 percent, located in five southwestern states where they account for one of every six residents. Another million and a half are located in New York state. In light of their rural heritage and the stereotypic view of migrant farmers and laborers, it may be somewhat surprising to find over 80 percent living in metropolitan areas with the majority of these being residents of central cities. Referring again to Figure 13.1, it is evident the Spanish population is a more youthful collection of people when compared to the majority or the black populations. One of every eight is not yet five years old and the median age is barely 20 years, a good eight years younger than the norm for the United States. On the other end of the age continuum, less than four percent are over age 65, a figure which is actually lower than it was a decade ago. Cubans provide the sole exception, since their median age is substantially higher, nearly 36 years, with the elderly constituting between 10 and 11 percent of their number.

Why the age structure of the Spanish American minority is so skewed toward the earlier years is a multifaceted phenomenon. In their attempts to formulate some explanation for the distinctive age distribution of the Mexican segment, and by extrapolation of all other Spanish origin people, researchers have offered four plausible and interrelated reasons. To begin with, Spanish Americans, like other minority and poverty-bound peoples, die younger than the general population; from birth onward their life expectancy is less. Fertility patterns constitute a second important dimension; while the birth rate has been declining for much of the population, there has been little change among Spanish Americans. Both the number of children born and family size are greater than the national average, with large families, those containing seven or more members, observed twice as frequently as in the general population. Immigration and repatriation patterns are also important factors that complicate the picture. Traditionally, younger people are those most likely to pull up stakes and move to a new country, and this continues to be the case among recent arrivals of Spanish origin. Once again, Cubans present the exception, as large numbers of professional and white collar workers immigrated to the United States during the period of governmental reorganization under Fidel Castro. While repatriation among Cubans has been negligible, the same is not true of Mexicans. Periodic massive deportations took place during the 1920s, in the Depression of the 1930s and in the 1950s. Furthermore, there is a significant voluntary movement back to Mexico among middle-aged and older members of the population, especially as they near retirement. As future generations come to be increasingly native born, fewer people will return to Mexico, thereby contributing to a moderate expansion of the older population (Grebler et al., 1970; Moore, 1971a; U.S. Census, 1975c).

Despite recent improvements in their income and occupational statuses, it is clear Spanish Americans continue to lag behind the rest of the country. For several years unemployment rates have been roughly 3 percent above national figures, though within the minority incidence varies widely. Puerto Ricans, for instance, consistently face a greater risk of finding themselves out of work than all other Spanish American workers. The same is true of women; not only are they more apt to be unemployed, but even when working their income averages less than half that earned by their male counterparts. Median income for the group as a whole climbed to approximately $8700 in 1974, less than two-thirds of that for the general population. Again, however, Puerto Ricans are relatively more disadvantaged, since their median levels are nearly $1700 less. On the other hand, Cubans and certain other Latin Americans have an income nearly $4500 above the median for the rest of the minority. Although the proportion of Spanish Americans holding professional or technical jobs is half the national average, there are marked differences between subgroups. Cubans and certain other Spanish origin people more frequently hold high-paying positions than their Mexican or Puerto Rican brethren. On the average, one out of 20 Spanish Americans has a job at which he or she earns over $15,000 annually, while at the other end of the scale at least one in five falls below poverty levels (U.S. Census, 1975c).

Aged Spanish Americans

Insofar as what little is known about the aged among Spanish Americans is based almost exclusively on elderly Mexican Americans, any overall descriptions must be viewed as tentative at best. Even though the dependency ratio is one and a half times that of the Anglo population, this is due primarily to high birth rates rather than to an increase in the number of old people. At the present time it is estimated that a 48 year old of Spanish origin exhibits many of the characteristics of aging observed in a 65 year old Anglo (White House Conference, 1971). In most respects, older Spanish Americans are more disadvantaged than successively younger generations, a common theme among older people everywhere. In terms of educational attainment, at least half the elderly have less than an elementary school education, and among Mexican American elderly a larger percentage lack even a rudimentary education. As we might anticipate, income follows a similar pattern, since the two are so closely linked. In 1973, median income for older Spanish Americans was less than half that earned by other members of the minority group. Current data indicate that the next generation of older Spanish Americans will exhibit few changes from those presently aged; indeed, it is quite possible that as much as 30 years will pass before there is anything approaching parity between Spanish and Anglo American elderly (Moore, 1971a). The percentage of black and Spanish-origin elderly who own their homes is nearly the same, although for both groups fewer are likely to than for Anglo elderly. Judging from Table 13.1, it might appear that minority status imposes equally heavy burdens on all elderly. In comparison to blacks, overcrowding is more of a problem among the Spanish American middle-aged and elderly, but there may be somewhat of a trade-off, since their residences are better equipped on the average. These are but general trends; it must be reiterated that Puerto Ricans in New York may differ as much from Mexicans in the Southwest or Cubans in Florida as they do from the rest of the population.

Sex and marital characteristics of older Spanish Americans are roughly parallel to what has been found to be the case among other groups of elderly. Women outnumber men, live somewhat longer and more often remain widowed or live alone. Perhaps it is a reflection of their cultural heritage, but older men in this group are more often married or remarried than any other minority males; 83 percent of the men are currently living with their spouses, though little more than a third of the older women can make the same claim. One interesting group difference is the number of Spanish women who continue to have children into their late forties or early fifties; the middle-aged birth rate is twice as high as that recorded for Anglo women in the same age range. Paradoxically, Spanish Americans perceive the onset of old age as beginning earlier than anyone else; however, job opportunities may have more of a role in this than ethnic status. Clustered as they are in low income tertiary or manual labor occupations, it is not surprising to find a dearth of workers who are old; hence, the enforced unemployment of middle-aged and elderly Spanish American males may make them feel of little value and therefore older (Crouch, 1972). In describing the aging experiences of Mexican American women, Moore (1971a) suggests that fertility patterns may be a contributing factor to their particular modes of aging. The ethnographic studies of Mexican Americans carried out in San Francisco by Clark and Mendelson (1969) tend to affirm this; thus, they imply that the matriarchal power of older Spanish American women is strong enough to keep their adult children in a semidependent status until they are well into their own middle age. Spanish-American families may be unusual in the amount of esteem that they accord older members, but the evidence here is less than conclusive. For instance, conflicting views of the relative standing of older Spanish people is included in the testimony given the United States Senate Committee on Aging (1969) investigating the plight of elderly Mexican Americans. Many knowledgeable sources contend the social bonds between older people, their families and friends are undergoing a rapid transition, bringing them more into line with the majority experience.

Whether the process of acculturation gradually erodes the traditional role of the Spanish American aged or whether they continue to live their lives free of the discontinuities some feel to be characteristic of Anglo aged is debatable; however, at least among the present generation, there is still a place for the elderly person. In fact, one of the more striking aspects of the situation of older people within the Spanish subculture is the manner in which they have remained a central focus for much of the family activity. While all older people continue to exert some measure of authority over the family context, a persistent dilemma involves the relative status of male and female roles. Some researchers have sharply criticized the commonplace observation of male dominance; such a view may betray a certain naiveté since in-depth analyses indicate that women of all ages have a profound influence in the family decisionmaking process. Norms of public decorum discourage open display of this influence, however. With age, women may assume ever more important positions, guiding not only their immediate household but the lives of their offspring's families as well. The significance of these extended family networks cannot be overstated in terms of providing a sense of usefulness among older people. The elderly provide interactional contact for the whole neighborhood, and help with household and childcare responsibilities while serving as what may be the only link to past histories. Adaptation to the dominant cultural mode is extensive among the middle-aged, yet the growth of ethnic pride or *chicanismo* has infused both young and old with a new desire to preserve their cultural roots (Leonard, 1967; Moore, 1971a).

Older American Indians

Indians are among the most rapidly expanding minorities in the United States, although they and the Asian Americans are also among the least visible. In the last three decades the number of native Americans has more than doubled, but even at 793,000 they comprise less than 0.33 percent of the total population. The largest concentrations are found in the southwestern states of Oklahoma, Arizona, California and New Mexico, followed by North Carolina, Washington, South Dakota and New York. Quite unlike other minorities, a majority of the Indians continue to live in rural areas, though the remaining 45 percent are urbanized. Other than for very general trends, less systematic data are available for Indians than for the other minority groups discussed so far. The two federal agencies responsible for collecting basic information, the Bureau of Indian Affairs and the Census Bureau, frequently disagree in their estimates. With high birth and death rates, Indian life expectancy is currently only about two-thirds that of the general population; in fact the Department of Health, Education and Welfare contends that the age distribution of Indians today closely resembles the 1880 profile of the United States population as a whole (Levy, 1967). In view of the diversity among Indian cultures and the scarcity of reliable data, we must hesitate before making a too hasty description of aged Indians. Undoubtedly many commonalities exist, if only because of the governmental regulations under which Indians live out their lives.

The Indian minority stands apart from all other minority groups by virtue of their special history and their relationship with the federal bureaucracy. While most other minorities have attempted to accommodate themselves to the main currents of American life, Indians have been isolated on reservations, cultural islands apart from the rest of the population. In addition, Indians have long been considered wards of the government to the point that the Bureau of Indian Affairs has assumed the responsibility for deciding who may call themselves Indian and who may not. It should not be surprising that, under these conditions, American Indians have become an extremely vulnerable group, filled with mistrust, yet realistically unable to reject the sinecures keeping them dependent on the government. The paternalistic regulations of the Bureau, though intended to insure basic support, have come under serious criticism from Indian and non-Indian alike for their inflexibility and their denial of traditional cultural values. Two examples may suffice to illustrate the main thrusts of these arguments. Under certain conditions, Indians who leave their reservations, for whatever reason, and remain absent for over a year lose their eligibility for many of the social services granted those on reservations. If an Indian seeks a job off the reservation and is away for the specified period, he or she is no longer entitled to medical care in the eyes of the Indian Health Service. Historically, land and grazing privileges have been extended to all tribal members for as long as they desired; today elderly Indians must transfer their grazing rights to their heirs before they can qualify for sorely needed supplemental financial assistance. True, the extra income is a welcome addition, but nonetheless, the way the program operates deprives the old of their traditional position within the tribal structure (Levy, 1967; Jeffries, 1972).

Indians are also a young and an economically depressed population, characteristics that they are likely to retain for some years to come. As shown in Figure 13.1, nearly 6 percent of their number are over the age of 65, though the median age among Indians is barely 20 years. According to reports based on the 1970 census, unemployment is nearly double that of the general population, without even considering those who are not actively seeking work, and it is probable these rates have climbed in the intervening years. As a consequence of their employment picture, it is small wonder that median income for Indians is barely above the poverty threshold, while less than 2 percent earn incomes in excess of $15,000 annually. Among younger adult males in the 25–34 age range, median incomes are around $5100, rising to $5400 for those between 35 and 45 years of age, but falling thereafter with each successive decade. Working women of comparable ages never earn even as much as half of the income for men. It should be noted, though, that despite the importance of wages and other sources of income, there are alternatives to a strictly cash economy on the reservation. This is not to say that Indians are not living on the ragged financial edge, for they are certainly one of the poorest groups economically in the United States. However, barter and other modes of exchange are operative in the rural environments and these are not normally included in the assessments furnished by the government (U.S. Census, 1973b).

The Status of Elderly Indians

To appreciate the situation prevailing among older Indians today, it is necessary to have some inkling of the changes that have occurred since the great Indian wars of the last century. In spite of their subsistence economies, most Indian cultures long maintained a tradition of communal sharing among members of the tribe, occasionally extending similar privileges to strangers passing through their lands. According to Simmons (1945), a sense of family responsibility for the care of the elderly was not uncommon, provided they filled specified roles within the tribe. So long as they were capable of performing minimal, sometimes symbolic labors, old people were treated with respect. Only at the extreme where they became too incapacitated to work were they either abandoned or likely to dispose of themselves. Wisdom was a valued commodity and was often "traded" for food or other goods. Local folklore was usually replete with admonishments about certain foods reserved for the elderly, foods to be eaten at great risk by all but the whitehaired, unless of course nothing else was to be had. Definitions of old age were predicated on tribal custom, but it was a period that began late in life and then usually because of physical decline. If precontact Indians managed to survive until age 50 or so, they probably had a remaining life expectancy greater than that of the general population today, as they represented only the most hardy. Since their number was limited to a scant few, the elderly were held in high regard, and it was not until they were unable to carry on or until the social changes set in motion by the arrival of the white pioneers so restructured Indian life that older Indians began to be disenfranchised or to experience a truly negative old age (Levy, 1967).

Today everything has changed; under the auspices of the Bureau of Indian Affairs, Indians receive social and financial services and live in a way unknown to their ancestors. Keeping in mind the possibility of culturally biased research techniques, the disadvantages of modern life notwithstanding, older Indians do not apparently experience the same kinds of psychological stress common to much of the rest of the population. Instead, as they grow old, they seem merely to switch to a more passive relationship with their world, accepting the changes as a natural part of life (Goldstine and Gutmann, 1972). The adjustment problems older Indians do encounter can probably be traced to a lifestyle dictated by bureaucratic policies. The governmental position on Indian property mentioned earlier offers just one example. Unfortunately, the regulations calling for the surrendering of stock or land in order to receive supplemental financial assistance, in spite of the potential for enhancing financial position, do not bring much of an increase in annual income; median levels for aged men and women combined amount to less than $1500. Without additional governmentally sponsored health programs or social services, older Indians clearly could not survive. A lifetime of hard work does nothing to immunize the elderly against chronic health problems stemming from obesity, gallbladder or arthritic ailments brought on by inhospitable living conditions. Alcoholism, long a problem for Indians, continues to be a major part of life for some segments of the population, though usually it has taken its toll long before old age can be reached. Since 1955, when the Public Health Service undertook the responsibilities of ministering to the health needs of Indians, many improvements have been observed, but it will easily take a generation or more before changes have any significance for the elderly.

As is the case generally, Indian women outnumber men in the years after 65. Consequently, a large percentage of women remain widowed; in fact, over half the women, but less than one-quarter of the men, are without spouses. Also, as is the experience of the majority of elderly, Indians do not exhibit much residential mobility. With advancing age, less than one-quarter move in any five year period, even though more than half live in substandard housing. As the adult children of older Indians are acculturated to dominant American values, they may become more mobile themselves and thereby create additional strains within a family network that has already been overburdened with economic hardship. In the face of such a prospect, further expansion of the health services for older people is required in order to provide adequate housing and nursing facilities. In its report to the delegates at the 1971 White House Conference on Aging, the Special Concerns session addressing itself to older Indians voiced an urgent need for sheltered care facilities, a problem not even being considered in present funding priorities (White

House Conference, 1971). As the situation exists today, life for older Indians has become increasingly onerous; for future aged Indians to have it any better, drastic steps will have to be implemented without additional delay.

Aged Asian Americans

It has become common practice to group together under the general label of Asian Americans all those people whose heritage can be traced to any part of the Orient. No matter that their cultures or their languages are more distinct than a similar collection drawn from Europe, governmental agencies still classify into one category all nonwhites who are not obviously black. In recent years politically active Oriental Americans have taken advantage of this tendency to lay the foundations for a Pan-Asian consciousness stressing the development of a cultural pride based on geographic origin (Kalish and Yuen, 1971). Both because they constitute less than 1.5 percent of the total population and, as a consequence of unexamined stereotypes, because of the importance and viability of filial piety in the Oriental family, the plight of older Asian Americans has received relatively little attention. In fact, the 1971 White House Conference on Aging did not even include a Special Concerns session for aged of this minority until the last possible moment, and then only after a request was made on behalf of concerned Asian Americans. The rationale for not scheduling a special session in the program may have been that everyone knows, at least intuitively, that Orientals always take care of their own, especially the elderly. If, as was shown in Chapter Ten for Japan, traditional familial patterns are being altered in the countries of origin, then no doubt aged minority members are in much greater jeopardy when transplanted abroad. As it turns out, elderly Asian Americans have a whole range of unique experiences in addition to those of simply being old. Since reliable data dealing with elderly Asians are practically nonexistent, it is impossible to state with any sense of confidence either the exact dimensions of their old age or predictions for the future.

While it is true that those who have come to the United States from the Orient derive from widely divergent cultures, with different religions and languages, their experiences in a country dominated by people from European backgrounds reflect a certain similarity. The first waves of male Chinese immigrants arrived in the 1850s to serve as unskilled laborers for the railroads and in the mines of the West. From the outset they faced prejudice and racial discrimination, and by the 1880s, with over 80,000 Chinese on the west coast, there were widespread fears of eventual Oriental domination. Exclusionary laws prohibiting intermarriage, the immigration of women and families, and ownership of real property were passed in the following decades, with the result that the flow of Chinese to the United States had been stopped entirely by the time of the Depression in the early 1930s. The flood of Japanese immigration did not really begin until the 1890s, when large numbers of men arrived from Japan and Hawaii to work in the fields or as unskilled urban laborers. Until the mid-1920s Japanese immigrants were not so strictly regulated as the Chinese; consequently, more extensive familial settlements were established along the Pacific coast. With the passage of the Alien Exclusion Act in 1924, however, new arrivals dwindled to a bare few. Despite a prior "gentlemen's agreement" between the two countries that curtailed the influx of the unskilled, women and skilled men were still allowed entry into the country in sizeable numbers. Filipino migration to the United States was hardly noticeable until after World War I, although Hawaii had been the site of Filipino relocation for more than a decade previously. Like the Chinese, nine out of ten Filipinos traveling to America were men who came for economic reasons and found work in migratory agricultural pursuits or in other low-paying, unskilled jobs. Before the late 1920s, little attention was given to the new entrants; however, in 1929 violent demonstrations erupted in the West because of their high levels of employment at a time when field jobs were becoming scarce. During the same period, a bill was introduced in Congress to bar immigration by declaring Filipinos aliens, though they had been technically considered nationals since the islands were ceded to the United States in 1898. The enactment of the Philippine Independence Bill in 1934 granted commonwealth status to the islands, with independence following ten years later. In the process, Filipinos were reclassified as aliens and immigration quotas were set at a meager 50 per year.

Elderly Chinese Americans

In traditional China, the family was the basic associational unit, with all else, including the state, considered an appendage to it. An individual's identity was based totally on familial membership, and the bond between the two could never be broken. That which was considered good for the family was naturally good for the individual, while personal achievements or failures were always seen as a reflection upon one's family. Although all older people were revered and worshiped by other members, the oldest male exerted absolute authority over business and even emotional matters. Throughout life children were obliged to obey and comfort their parents, to the point of valuing their parents' lives over those of their own children. Ideally, old age was a warmly anticipated, if not welcome, period of life in which people were gradually relieved of burdensome responsibilities without losing any of their security or veneration. Indeed, the position of the elderly in traditional China was so entrenched that the term **gerontocracy** was often used to describe the Chinese social order. In the years since the Communist changeover, other institutions have supplanted much of the family's role and especially that of the elderly. Although family units are still primarily responsible for teaching children to be good citizens, the state rather than the family is now emphasized as that unit most worthy of allegiance. In China, as in much of the Western world, the elderly are of another era and therefore are no longer viewed as a repository of wisdom. At the same time, a redefinition of sexual roles has gradually taken place in which wives are not subordinate to their husbands and both may retain their family names or property after marriage. Divorces were possible in traditional China, though they were initiated almost entirely by the husband. Even if he should leave for the United States on what was to be a temporary absence but from which he never returned, the wife was duty-bound to passively await his homecoming (Welty, 1970). During the last century, immigration obviously exerted a disruptive influence on family life, both at home and abroad. For one thing, it was limited almost exclusively to males, resulting in a lack of men at home and a preponderance in the new country. In 1900 women comprised only 7 percent of the Chinese population in America and today males still continue to outnumber women among the older generations. Responsive to the ideology of material success inherent in the new country, Chinese traditions often have been abandoned in favor of small, economically feasible family units. Hence, the value of filial piety has lost much of its former suzerainty in the lives of native-born offspring.

According to the most recent census, the Chinese population in the United States numbers approximately 432,000, clustered overwhelmingly in urban areas. Median age among Chinese Americans is almost 27 years, nearly the same as for the general population, but only 6 percent are over 65 years old. Most of today's generation of elderly were originally from Canton province. Departing for the United States to earn their fortunes as laborers, they had every intention of returning to their homelands once they had accumulated sufficient wealth. There is also a contingent of Mandarin-speaking elderly from the northern provinces who immigrated as political refugees after the establishment of the Communist government in 1948. In spite of this later influx, the elderly still reflect the predominately male immigration of the early years. Along with the Filipino population, the Chinese display a unique sex ratio, since men outnumber women. Fully two-thirds of the aged men are presently married, compared to about 40 percent of the women, while only about one-fifth of the men, but half of the women, are widowed. Because of their lack of training, old world ways and changing cultural conditions, many of these older Chinese find themselves with perilously few resources to draw upon in their later years. Median incomes for the older segments of the Chinese American population differ by sex: men, at $1950, have an annual income just over one-third that of all other Chinese males, while older women earn about $1200, or half as much as younger women. Part of the reason their financial picture is so bleak stems from the fact that most Chinese Americans have spent a lifetime in low-paying jobs or in employment not covered by Social Security. With no source of income other than what is provided to indigent elderly, the outlook is indeed grim (U.S. Census, 1973b; Wu, 1975).

As the Special Concerns session on Asian Americans pointed out to the 1971 White House Conference on Aging, with suicide rates three times as high among Asian elderly as among their white peers and with over one-third having never seen a doctor or a dentist, there is every reason to believe that serious problems beset the aged. After years of discrimination and living under fear of deportation, they are often reluctant to seek help from any kind of bureaucracy. At the same time, older Chinese are equally loathe to become burdens on their families, since this is not seen as legitimate within the context of their adopted culture. Cultural isolation is a very real problem in the lives of the elderly in any transplanted minority. Among the Chinese it has resulted in an unusually high rate of drug usage, particularly among older men without family or ideological ties to the larger community. The absence of bilingual service personnel or of programs geared to Chinese culture, dietary habits and customs means that even those who are receiving services such as sheltered housing or income maintenance are less than satisfied. Some solutions are undoubtedly at hand, provided an element of flexibility becomes a basic, foundational principle in service delivery. Unfortunately, no extensive effort has been made as yet to accommodate those elderly Chinese Americans who seek assistance. One of the first attempts to deal in a culturally specific way with the difficulties facing the Chinese elderly in the continental United States was launched in San Francisco's Chinatown several years ago. The organization, Self-Help for the Elderly, intends to gather all available resources under one umbrella, making them easily accessible to older people living in the community. Hopefully this will facilitate the search for and provision of services, without imposing the added disadvantage of dealing with outsiders who are perceived as threats. Other programs have since been inaugurated in other west coast cities from Seattle to Los Angeles and in Hawaii. The projects range from the provision of sheltered housing, daycare centers, ethnic meals and outreach treatment to liasons with appropriate governmental agencies. All are intended to meet the distinctive needs of older Chinese Americans as well as the aged of other Asian ancestry (White House Conference, 1971; Kalish and Moriwaki, 1973).

Elderly Japanese Americans

As was observed in Chapter Ten and elsewhere, older people in Japan are finding the exigencies of the modern industrial world to be inimical to the traditional status they have enjoyed. Those who have grown old in the United States face similar challenges coupled with the additional hardship of being a citizen of a country where the Japanese have not always been welcomed with open arms. Though the Japanese faced less overt discrimination than the Chinese during the early years of this century, those over 65 often endured long periods of prejudice prior to their internment during World War II. Actually, many have only been accorded full citizenship privileges since the early 1950s. In the beginning, most *issei*, or first generation immigrants, planned to return home once they had amassed financial reserves, in the same manner as the Chinese. Generally there was no attempt to anticipate their future as American citizens, although by the 1930s family units were already established in the West. Even if the Japanese had known they would remain in the United States, they were prohibited from owning property until 20 years ago and those who desired to do so had to resort to subterfuges such as buying it in the name of an American-born child or a close friend. If nothing else, this stratagem was deleterious to the vertical hierarchy of Japanese life, for the *nisei*, or second generation, were thrust into roles traditionally reserved for their elders. Property purchased or accumulated before World War II was totally confiscated with the relocation drive, and in some instances held until the early 1970s, when Congress finally mandated the return of the remaining bank accounts to their rightful owners, minus compensation for whatever interest might have been earned over the 20 odd years (Kalish and Moriwaki, 1973).

Of the 590,000 Japanese Americans, roughly 8 percent are 65 or older, while 32 is the median age. Because there were fewer restrictions on the immigration of women and families, the sex ratio today among elderly Japanese is more in keeping with general trends, with women outnumbering men and living longer, so that a larger proportion are now widowed. By and large, older Japanese Americans now live in urban areas, having spent their lives in agricultural or small business pursuits within a definite minority community. Median annual income for males over 65 was $2500 in 1970, nearly twice that of aged women. In both cases their earnings are about one-third the income of younger Japanese Americans. Living arrangements among the elderly reflect their *meiwako* values against being an imposition on others, especially on family members; a familiar pattern in which they live an independent life insofar as possible seems typical. Although the responsibility of caring for aged parents does not rest solely on the eldest son as it did in the past, adult children still endeavor to care for elderly family members, and apparently experience serious emotional turmoil if they are incapable of fulfilling their own expectations. In traditional Japan, families occupied the same position of importance as they did in China. The extended family unit was the primary associational and supportive institution, and all members shared individual incomes with the rest of the family. Women, being dutiful, usually deferred to men, and because of the system of inheritance, father-son relationships often took precedence over all others. Marriages were also family affairs, arranged at the behest of the father through an agent who was responsible for maintaining family solidarity. If, for example, a family name was in danger of dying out because of a lack of sons, the agent might ask the groom to assume the wife's family name. With such traditions, the Japanese in America were understandably reluctant to marry an outsider and many made the long trip home to find a wife or, if unable to return, they selected their mates by mail through an agent in Japan. Customary family practices were adapted to a new way of life, but over the years, and with a larger number of American-born, they slowly gave way. Wives became companions, styles of clothing changed and community ties came to resemble local norms, particularly after World War II. The recent advent of convalescent facilities for Asian elderly along the west coast is further evidence of the gradual acculturation of both the older and middle-aged generations, though it is likely that older Japanese will continue their close family ties in spite of the inevitable strains attendant with institutionalization (Modell, 1968; Kitano, 1969).

As pointed out in the discussion of health in Chapter Seven, Japanese Americans display an incidence of cardiovascular diseases approximating that of the general population rather than their country of origin. Other dimensions of health tend to follow a like pattern. Nevertheless, elderly Asians in general are remarkably healthy, exhibiting fewer chronic disabilities than their majority group age mates. Symptoms of psychological distress are not surprising in view of the incongruities in an older person's values, expectations and reality, combined with the strong emphasis the Japanese place on saving face by not admitting to outsiders that serious problems exist. Though a problem for only a small percentage, older males appear to be the most vulnerable and, interestingly enough, their hospitalization rates in Japan and the United States are very similar. The most frequent classification is schizophrenia and defensive withdrawal; however, cultural factors play a major role here, as they do in the diagnosis of emotional problems among all minority groups. The delineation of overt psychopathology can only be carried out within a particular cultural context; what is learned as appropriate behavior under certain circumstances could easily be read as indicative of mental illness under other conditions. Hence the factors resulting in the disproportionate presence of Japanese in California state mental hospitals may not have nearly the same significance in Hawaii or Tokyo. Nonetheless, that the patients are in California and not elsewhere indicates the existence of some disjunctures in their lives whether they originate from within the patients' own psyche or are a function of living in what remains an alien country. As nisei and successive generations of native-born Japanese Americans move into old age there is reason to predict they will manifest physical and psychological symptoms, both in etiology and behavior, closer to the general population than their older relatives have (Caudill and Lin, 1969).

Elderly Filipino Americans

Totaling about one-third of a million, Filipinos are the smallest of the three Asian minorities under discussion. More than half of the population is male, a proportion that increases dramatically with age. Among the 6 percent who are over 65, men outnumber women by more than four to one, higher even than among the Chinese. Under these circumstances, a smaller percentage of the women, about 40 percent, are widows. Median age is over 26 years, with a four year spread between men and women. Income differentials between young and old are similar to those existing in other minority groups. The $2000 median income for elderly Filipinos is sufficient in itself to place them in a disadvantaged position. Due to a highly mobile lifestyle, most Filipinos are employed as agricultural, domestic or other traveling workers. Unlike the Japanese or Chinese, the Filipino community has yet to stabilize; as a consequence, older people more often face their later years without close ties to families or neighborhoods. Many elderly do not have strong bonds to other minority members, but for Filipinos this provokes special anxieties as they were usually reared in a culture that emphasized the social nature of the self. Clinical evidence points to a weaker sense of self when deprived of close ties than is the case for most Westerners. Like the Japanese or Chinese, Filipinos have a long tradition of subjugating their own needs in deference to familial demands; thus, without family bonds they are at loose ends (Marsella and Ouijano, 1974). Another serious problem for the elderly has to do with language barriers, which they have never surmounted due to the lack of formal education. Paradoxically, cultural and linguistic traits stress personal status, and considerable maneuvering occurs between individuals as each ascertains the other's place before their interaction can continue. The older Filipino American who is bereft of traditional appurtenances indicating relative social status is quite reticent about seeking any form of nonfamilial assistance. Unfortunately, there has been no published research focusing on the plight of older Filipinos and, with the exception of the Manilatown Information Service in San Francisco, almost no service delivery systems have been set up to meet their special needs (Kalish and Yuen, 1971).

As is true of other Asian minorities, future generations of older Filipino Americans will present a far different picture. Intermarriage is becoming common among the younger generations, and nearly three-quarters of all those approaching middle age have a high school degree. Native-born people constitute a very small percentage of the current generation of older people, but are in a majority in the younger age ranges. Taken together these two factors — education and birth place — are enough to predict that more adequate financial resources will be characteristic of the future aged as they will have been employed for higher pay in jobs covered by Social Security. Whether family patterns will gradually come to reflect these changes cannot yet be forecast with any certainty, yet if the Filipino minority follows the trends of other Asian peoples who have settled in the United States, we may expect them to work out a middle position between their traditional cultures and the general American patterns. Absent the kind of large scale physical communities characteristic of the Chinese or Japanese, Filipinos may engage in a greater departure from traditional customs.

Summary

Any discussion of aging as a social process would be incomplete without attention directed to the experiences of minority elderly. Regardless of whether the heritage is black, Spanish, Indian or Asian, each of the subcultures described imposes its own distinctive normative structure on the aging individual. Obviously certain dimensions of life, such as psychomotor processes, have little or nothing to do with ethnicity directly. The areas where ethnic status does make a difference lie in that range of behaviors easily shaped by social or environmental factors (Kalish, 1971). One of the more pressing issues involves not so much whether basic patterns are distinguishable by ethnic categories, but rather, how the differences are interpreted by those involved. Suppose both Spanish and Anglo Americans show some age-related alteration in sensory capacities: do both impute the same meaning to the change? Because of the world view implicit in the dominant value structure, the shift in sensory capacities might be cause for all kinds of remedial measures designed to return the individual to an optimum level. The same event might be seen simply as part of one's fate, a natural concomitant of aging, to be accepted and endured, by the Spanish American.

With shorter life expectancy and somewhat higher birth rates among the black population, the proportion of older blacks comprises only about 6 percent. Aged black Americans are not, however, presumed to suffer discontinuities in their lives to the same extent as their white age peers. Perhaps those who do survive as long as 70 years might prove to be in better health than similarly aged white elderly, although evidence remains inconclusive to date. Family ties are a particularly strong source of support for blacks, and from what little data are available, families may accord their older relatives more esteem than is the case in the general population. With lower incomes in old age and throughout life, it is to be expected that the physical surroundings of black elderly will reflect the years of financial hardship. While this is indeed true, it is one of those pervasive myths that all older blacks are in dire straits compared to whites. In many respects the two groups appear to experience equivalent stresses, and even those problems that are linked to race can hardly be considered insoluble. It is difficult to say if what is currently known about the black experience is representative. Studies focusing on racial characteristics were few before the last decade, and the professional literature is replete with contradictions, which in part may stem from those same socioeconomic factors that differentiate other groups of people, coupled with heterogeneous samples that have been treated as a homogeneous entity. It also may be a sign of communication problems between respondents and data gatherers. Increasingly, ethnic communities are wary of responding carte blanche to visiting academics when there is scant opportunity for an immediate or certain benefit in return. In some instances they have even exerted considerable opposition to research studies that have not respected the personal dignity of the minority members involved.

Although Spanish American elderly represent quite varied backgrounds, almost all of the reported information is based on older Mexican Americans in the Southwest. Since they reflect one of the younger age structures among subgroups in the United States, it is understandable that the aged, or aging itself, have not yet received in-depth consideration. In a general sense, Indian aged suffer the same invisibility. In light of their small numbers and the extensive services allegedly furnished by the Bureau of Indian Affairs, their problems have only recently elicited professional concern. Unfortunately, there is some distance between the ideal and bureaucratic reality. The Asian minority, with its Chinese, Japanese and Filipino contingents, plus numerous others not discussed in the present context, is often treated as synonymous, when in fact they are more diverse than most collections of Europeans. Each has had a unique history in the United States and each has developed its own way of coping with the inherent conflicts between traditional and adopted lifestyles. As with other minority subcultures, the elderly in the Asian group exhibit wide variations. Some have spent most, if not all, their lives in the United States; others arrived what seems like only yesterday and have not yet reached a satisfactory accommodation between old and new customs. Of the three Asian minorities, the least is known about the Filipino. It is, however, a reasonable conjecture that Filipino families are not as prevalent as they are in other groups, and that enclaves are small and infrequent, while standards of living are quite low, especially for the old people. The recent acknowledgement of the need for specially designed programs aimed at each segment of the American population is only the bare beginning. Without rapid and extensive expansion, services will be inadequate to ameliorate the inequalities that exist. In addition to socioeconomic disadvantages, the language barriers cannot be overemphasized. Programs that ignore cultural and linguistic background are not only inefficient, but unlikely to benefit the target groups. It should be evident that the elderly deserve better. As crucial as this initial glimpse of the general outlines of minority aging is, it does not provide sufficient grounds on which to formulate conclusive opinions — to do so would indeed be premature.

Pertinent Readings

CARP, F.M. "The Mobility of Older Slum-Dwellers." *The Gerontologist* XII, 1, pt. I (1972): 57–65.

CAUDILL, W., and T.Y. LIN. *Mental Health Research in Asia and the Pacific.* Honolulu: East-West Center Press, 1969.

CLARK, M., and M. MENDELSON. "Mexican-American Aged in San Francisco: A Case Description." *The Gerontologist* IX, 2, pt. I (1969): 90–95.

CROUCH, B.M. "Age and Institutional Support: Perceptions of Older Mexican Americans." *Journal of Gerontology* XXVII, 4 (1972): 524–29.

DOVENMUEHLE, R.H., E.W. BUSSE and G. NEWMAN. "Physical Problems of Older People." In *Normal Aging,* ed. E. Palmore, 29–39. Durham, N.C.: Duke University Press, 1970.

EHRLICH, I.F. "Toward a Social Profile of the Aged Black Population in the United States: An Exploratory Study." *Aging and Human Development* IV, 3 (1973): 271–76.

FRAZIER, E.F. *The Negro Family in the United States.* Rev. ed. Chicago: University of Chicago Press, 1966.

GOLDSTINE, T., and D. GUTMANN. "A TAT Study of Navajo Aging." *Psychiatry* XXXV, 4 (1972): 373–84.

GREBLER, L., J.W. MOORE and R.C. GUZMAN. *The Mexican American People.* New York: The Free Press, 1970.

HIRSCH, C., D.P. KENT and S.L. SILVERMAN. "Homogeneity and Heterogeneity Among Low-Income Negro and White Aged." In *Research Planning and Action for the Elderly: The Power and Potential of Social Science,* eds. D.P. Kent, R. Kastenbaum and S. Sherwood, 484–500. New York: Behavioral Publications Inc., 1972.

JACKSON, J.J. "Social Gerontology and the Negro: A Review." *The Gerontologist* VII, 3 (1967): 168–78.

_____ . "Negro Aged: Toward Needed Research in Social Gerontology." *The Gerontologist* XI, 1, pt. II (1971a): 52–57.

_____ . "Sex and Social Class Variations in Black Aged Parent–Adult Child Relationships." *Aging and Human Development* II, 2 (1971b): 96–107.

_____ . "The Blacklands of Gerontology." *Aging and Human Development* II, 3 (1971c): 156–71.

_____ . "Aged Negroes: Their Cultural Departures From Statistical Stereotypes and Rural-Urban Comparisons." In *Research Planning and Action for the Elderly: The Power and Potential of Social Science,* eds. D.P. Kent, R. Kastenbaum and S. Sherwood, 501–13. New York: Behavioral Publications Inc., 1972a.

_____ . "Black Aged: In Quest of the Phoenix." In *Triple Jeopardy — Myth or Reality,* 27–40. Washington, D.C.: National Council on Aging, 1972b.

_____ . "Social Impacts of Housing Relocation upon Urban, Low-Income Black Aged." *The Gerontologist* XII, 1, pt. I (1972c): 32–37.

JEFFRIES, W.R. "Our Aged Indians," in *Triple Jeopardy — Myth or Reality,* 7–10. Washington, D.C.: National Council on Aging, 1972.

KALISH, R.A. "A Gerontological Look at Ethnicity, Human Capacities, and Individual Adjustment." *The Gerontologist* XI, 1, pt. II (1971): 78–87.

KALISH, R.A., and S. YUEN. "Americans of East-Asian Ancestry: Aging and The Aged." *The Gerontologist* XI, 1, pt. II (1971): 36–47.

KALISH, R.A., and S.Y. MORIWAKI. "The World of the Elderly Asian American." *Journal of Social Issues* XXIX, 2 (1973): 187–209.

KASTENBAUM, R. "The Missing Footnote." *Aging and Human Development* II, 3 (1971): 155.

KENT, D.P. "The Elderly in Minority Groups: Variant Patterns of Aging." *The Gerontologist* XI, 1, pt. II (1971): 26–29.

KENT, D.P., C. HIRSCH and S.K. BARG. "Indigenous Workers as a Crucial Link in the Total Support System for Low-Income, Minority Group Aged: A Report of an Innovative Field Technique in Survey Research." *Aging and Human Development* II, 3 (1971): 189–96.

KITANO, H.H.L. *Japanese Americans: The Evolution of a Subculture.* Englewood Cliffs, N.J.: Prentice-Hall Inc., 1969.

LEONARD, O.E. "The Older Rural Spanish-speaking People of the Southwest." In *Older Rural Americans: A Sociological Perspective,* ed. E.G. Youmans, 239–61. Lexington: University of Kentucky Press, 1967.

LEVY, J.E. "The Older American Indian." In *Older Rural Americans: A Sociological Perspective,* ed. E.G. Youmans, 221–38. Lexington: University of Kentucky Press, 1967.

LIPMAN, A. "Conference on the Potential for Japanese-American Cross-national Research on Aging." *The Gerontologist* XV, 3 (1975): 248–53.

MARSELLA, A.J., and WALLER Y OUIJANO. "A Comparison of Vividness of Mental Images Across Different Sensory Modalities in Filipino and Caucasian Americans." *Journal of Cross-Cultural Psychology* V, 4, (1974): 451–64.

McCASLIN, R., and W.R. CALVERT. "Social Indicators in Black and White: Some Ethnic Considerations in Delivery of Service to the Elderly." *Journal of Gerontology* XXX, 1 (1975): 60–66.

MODELL, J. "The Japanese American Family: A Perspective for Future Investigations." *Pacific Historical Review* XXXVII, 1 (1968): 67–81.

MOORE, J.W. "Mexican-Americans." *The Gerontologist* XI, 1, pt. II (1971a): 30–35.

———. "Situational Factors Affecting Minority Aging." *The Gerontologist* XI, 1, pt. II (1971b): 88–93.

MORGAN, R.F. "The Adult Growth Exam: Preliminary Comparisons . . . by Age and Sex." *Perceptual and Motor Skills* XXVII (1968): 595–99.

NATIONAL CENTER FOR HEALTH STATISTICS. *Health in the Later Years.* Washington, D.C.: Department of Health, Education and Welfare, U.S. Government Printing Office, 1971.

QUEEN, S.A., and R.W. HABENSTEIN. *The Family in Various Cultures.* 4th ed. Philadelphia: J.B. Lippincott, 1974.

RUBIN, L. "Economic Status of Black Persons: Findings from Survey of Newly Entitled Beneficiaries." *Social Security Bulletin* XXXVII, 9 (1974): 16–35.

SIMMONS, L.W. *The Role of Aged in Primitive Society.* New Haven: Yale University Press, 1945.

STERNE, R.S., J.E. PHILLIPS and A. RABUSHKA. *The Urban Elderly Poor: Racial and Bureaucratic Conflict.* Lexington, Mass.: D.C. Heath, 1974.

THOMPSON, G.B. "Blacks and Social Security Benefits: Trends, 1960–73." *Social Security Bulletin* XXXVIII, 4 (1974): 30–40.

THUNE, J.M., C.R. WEBB and L.E. THUNE. "Interracial Attitudes of Younger and Older Adults in a Biracial Population." *The Gerontologist* XI, 4, pt. I (1971): 305–10.

U.S. BUREAU OF THE CENSUS. Census of Housing, 1970, Subject Reports. *Final Report* HC(7)-2, Housing of Senior Citizens. Washington, D.C.: U.S. Government Printing Office, 1973a.

——. Census of Population, 1970. *Final Report* PC(2)-IF, American Indians. Washington, D.C.: U.S. Government Printing Office, 1973b.

——. Census of Population, 1970. *Final Report* PC(2)-IG, Japanese, Chinese and Filipinos. Washington, D.C.: U.S. Government Printing Office, 1973c.

——. *Current Population Reports.* Series P-60, no. 97, "Money Income in 1973 of Families and Persons in the United States." Washington, D.C.: U.S. Government Printing Office, 1975a.

——. *Current Population Reports.* Series P-60, no. 99, "Money Income and Poverty Status of Families and Persons in the United States: 1974." Advance report. Washington, D.C.: U.S. Government Printing Office, 1975b.

——. *Current Population Reports.* Special Studies, Series P-20, no. 280, "Persons of Spanish Origin in the United States: March 1974." Washington, D.C.: U.S. Government Printing Office, 1975c.

——. *Current Population Reports.* Special Studies, Series P-23, no. 48, "The Social and Economic Status of the Black Population in the United States, 1974." Washington, D.C.: U.S. Government Printing Office, 1975d.

U.S. SENATE, COMMITTEE ON AGING. *Availability and Usefulness of Federal Programs and Services to Elderly Mexican Americans.* Pts. 1–4. 90–91st Cong. Washington, D.C.: U.S. Government Printing Office, 1969.

WELTY, P.T. *The Asians: Their Heritage and Their Destiny.* Philadelphia: J.B. Lippincott Company, 1970.

WHITE HOUSE CONFERENCE ON AGING. *Special Concerns Sessions Reports: Asian American Elderly, Aging and Aged Blacks, the Elderly Indian, Spanish Speaking Elderly.* Washington, D.C.: U.S. Government Printing Office, 1971.

WU, F.Y.T. "Mandarin-speaking Aged Chinese in the Los Angeles Area." *The Gerontologist* XV, 3 (1975):271–75.

YOUMANS, E.G. *Aging Patterns in a Rural and an Urban Area of Kentucky.* Bulletin 681. Lexington: University of Kentucky Agricultural Experiment Station, 1963.

Part IV

LOOKING AHEAD

Chapter 14

The Prospects of Aging

A factual description of the situations confronting today's elderly presents only a partial view of the aged in mass society. To justify the concentration of efforts and hopefully stimulate the imagination, your attention must also turn to the future, to a pondering of the place of today's young adults, the elderly of the next century, and to what it will take to render their lives as satisfying as possible. As has been stressed repeatedly, the process of aging envelops both unique, highly personalized phenomena and dynamic structural changes generalizable to relatively large numbers of people. While neither facet of aging can meaningfully be isolated from the other, there are certain patterns and projections that naturally fall closer to one or the other end of the continuum. In every case, the various ingredients of the aging process resemble a complex interrelated chain of molecules — combining basic elements, with each maintaining its own individualized character. Because all people share fundamental physiological features and interact in more or less predictable familial, occupational, political and other spheres, the possibility of fruitful intervention clearly exists. Yet these in no way exhaust individual potentials for creative aging.

The elderly of tomorrow and the day after will present countless characteristics unlike those discussed in previous chapters. Even in demographic terms, the general population of the future will be distinct from what we currently observe. Thus, programs intended to deal specifically with the problems of the aged in years to come must be responsive to many challenges that will inevitably be raised. The most knowledgeable scientific thinkers of today have reached little consensus about what will be the fate of humankind in the twenty-first century; their prognostications range along every point from total annihilation to lives of leisure supported by advanced technological wizardry.

Depending upon which assessment of the future is utilized, vastly different pictures of the roles to be played by old people emerge. If one subscribes to a view of Armageddon, the elderly will likely be even more disadvantaged and disenfranchised than presently. On the other hand, a nearly idyllic lifestyle can be prophesied in which the dominant societal myths of productivity and youth orientation have been tempered by humanistic winds carrying the seeds of alternative flexible lifestyles, careers and family relations. In a similar vein, access to power centers may be diffused among larger segments of the citizenry, with one possible consequence being the valuation of older people in their own right. Any portrayal must of necessity be speculative and, hence, somewhat hazardous. Although a variety of forecasts have been made to provide some sense of what old age will be like for young adults today, what comes to pass will depend in very great measure upon their commitments and actions.

The Elderly of Tomorrow

General Projections

Despite the slowing rate of expansion among industrialized populations, if zero population growth was attained immediately, the effects would not be observed for 50 to 75 years. Those people who will be aged at the turn of the century have already established secure lifestyles, while the large groups of post—World War II boom babies will only be entering the so-called empty nest phase in the year 2000. The numerical size of these cohorts is not in question except insofar as the extent to which mortality rates will reduce their numbers. If mortality trends remain comparable to those of the present, the aggregate of Americans over age 65 in the year 2000 will exceed 26.5 million, nearly one-fifth higher than presently is the case. Projections that foresee reductions in mortality of approximately 2 percent per year, however, envision as many as 35.5 million elderly, or roughly three-fourths more than in the mid-1970s. The lower death rates, if they indeed occur, would be indicative of significant improvements in personal and societal health, coupled with more favorable environmental inputs ranging from pollution control to better educational programs aimed at nutritional, safety and medical advances. Reflections of the possible refinements in health maintenance would be most dramatic among those over age 75. While contemporary mortality rates will result in increasing that portion of the elderly population by half, only a small reduction in mortality would serve to double the size of the very old group. If a slight decline in death rates is observed, average life expectancy would be five years longer for persons aged 65 in 2000 than for those who are 65 today.

Physiologists and other biological scientists do not yet agree on whether the natural processes of aging will be arrested in any way during future decades. Speculations about diminishing mortality rates rely primarily upon health breakthroughs which would check the known diseases now limiting the life span, such as atherosclerosis and various forms of cancer. Research on cancer will undoubtedly spawn important spinoffs, as many of the factors associated with malignancies seem to be particularly common among the aged. Already, extensive research is underway to investigate basic immunological systems perhaps involved in aging and the disruption of the body's internal communication processes which enable it to discriminate between inherent and foreign elements. Additional studies are being carried out on DNA encoding, enzyme synthesis, inhibitory agents for lipofuscin and collagen accumulations plus long-term nutritional requirements and drug effects. The answers to life's questions are still somewhere beyond the horizon, but the search will impart valuable new evidence which will help fill out the mosaic that is today still a mystery. There is less hope among scientists that physiological functions themselves will be unraveled to such an extent that intervention will spell a prolongation of the life span. Although a more healthy old age appears certainly related to greater longevity, there is not a clear or simple causal linkage between the two. Innumerable factors mediate, and there is a growing awareness of the role of social variables affecting life expectancy, from housing, nutrition and sanitation to smoking, alcoholism and relative affluence. It should not be expected, however, that the experience of disability in very old age will be substantially altered or removed; at best this time of life will continue to be constrained by physical and in some cases mental decrements. The crucial question posed to all of us is whether we really want to add years to life without significant changes in the quality of life available to old people (Hayflick, 1971; Neugarten, 1975).

Just as overall health status is likely to shift gradually in the next two decades, so too will the proportion of people who live in or are associated with multigenerational families. Recalling Chapter Ten, individuals are marrying, becoming parents and grandparents at ever younger ages, thereby creating a considerable probability of four and even five generational family structures in the near future. Women whose children were born during the postwar baby boom will be 65 or older around the year 2000. They will have more adult children than women in previous generations as a result of their higher fertility rates. The obvious implications arise in part from previous findings that 80 percent of all elderly today reside in close proximity to their children and generally are able to see them more than once a week. The majority of old people do not *live* in extended families, preferring to maintain an independent status so long as feasible. Nonetheless, all families turn to their own members when they are in need of assistance — a trend not apt to change in the coming years unless there are dramatic alterations in the delivery of social services. Although existing patterns and types of mutual aid differ by social class and subcultural background, there is a definite tendency for those parents who do live with adult children to be more often female, sick or over age 75. This will remain the case in the future as the numbers of the *old-old* slowly expand. A quite plausible forecast is an increase in the proportion of very old adults who share accommodations with their young-old children. Despite the fact that twice as many elderly currently live with adult children or other relatives as live in nursing homes, governmental appropriations already exceed $3.5 billion for support of various types of institutions. It would be unreasonable to expect institutions to care for an ever larger clientele without thoroughgoing modifications in orientation when the standards of care are not only in question but under attack for permitting profits at the expense of human integrity (Mendelson, 1974).

Related trends may be predicted for other facets of the lives of those who will become old in the twenty-first century. Earlier retirement, greater experimentation with second careers and perhaps more equitable pension plans will have a profound impact on the complexion of the retirement years. It is quite possible that age 55 will become the new age for formal retirement from a single career in which one has *vested* a specified number of years. Alternatively, two or more careers may be pursued by those who wish to work well into later life. By the turn of the century, the majority of older people will have a high school degree, plus many will have additional educational experience that may not lend itself necessarily to conventional academic ranking. One effect of this extension of the educational process will be to diminish some portion of the differences currently observed between young adults and the elderly. Another development may be more active and vocal involvement in the political and social arenas, an outgrowth of advancements in average educational levels and rising expectations during times of societal affluence. Glancing back over the magnitude of change that has taken place during the last 25 to 50 years, it is not difficult to appreciate why our grandparents sometimes express awe at the world they see around them. Projecting at least the same magnitude of change into the future, since there are few who envision any possibility for slowing the rate of technological growth, we can acquire a better grasp of the way life may appear to those who will become elderly early in the twenty-first century. A closer look at some of the areas of change for the old of tomorrow is warranted.

Work, Income, Retirement

Some optimistic observers of the national scene foresee the near elimination of extreme poverty among the aged by the turn of the century. The virtual replacement of state-sponsored welfare programs in 1974 by the federally directed Supplemental Security Income (SSI) plan is felt to be the initial step in societally mandated and enforced levels of income adequacy in the United States, though as presently operating, SSI will not be the final answer. Given the number of years that were required before the ramifications of the Social Security Act were fully explored, it becomes evident that it is far too early to foretell the future of SSI. While Social Security was never intended to be the sole source of financial support after retirement, its monies have frequently been utilized in that manner and found to be sorely deficient. This could prove to be the case for SSI, though it attempts to alleviate the plight of elderly at the lowest reaches of the income scale and, as with other governmental pro-grams of late, includes provision for cost of living adjustments. In general, however, for the four-fifths of the elderly population who are above federal poverty guidelines, more comprehensive pension coverage, expanded opportunities for investment to deflect the de-structive potential of the inflationary spiral and higher level Social Security benefits should contribute to if not a comfortable, at least an adequate retirement income. Clearly, many of the problems in pre-dicting the future of retirement programs stem from the unknown social and economic priorities to be forged in the coming years. How the business sector evaluates its needs will influence to a large ex-tent the prospects of retirement, as well as related areas of life. The fact that most people now experience a radical decline, usually around 50 percent, in income after retirement bodes ill for economists and policymakers who must formulate measures to re-dress the inequities in the face of staggering economic turmoil (Havighurst, 1975). There are many indications that the majority of the aged population would be able to manage if their financial re-sources following retirement were equivalent to two-thirds to three-fourths of their preretirement earnings.

As the service and tertiary sectors of the economy develop further in response to societal demands, flexibility in retirement policies might become more common. If declining fertility rates are sustained, the number of younger workers will be stabilized; con-sequently, older individuals may be given more options in terms of career changes and the timing of retirement. One innovation might be the sharing between young and old of those tasks that cannot be automated. The need to provide entry into the labor force for young adults will be less intensive, presumably creating some incentive for retaining and retraining older workers. At the same time, workers themselves may insist on less arbitrary and inflexible programs. De-pending upon the pressures for older workers to remain active in the labor force, flexibility may appear in the guise of either earlier or later ages at retirement and adaptable work schedules allowing employees to select the hours and the extent of their work weeks. There is no denying that the availability of Social Security benefits at ages 65 and 62 is intimately related to policies of formal retirement. These ages can be changed through legislation, and indeed, as men-tioned in the previous chapter, advocates for some ethnic groups are calling for revisions to grant earlier qualification among blacks and other minorities for retirement benefits or for Social Security credit for the time many elderly Japanese Americans spent incarcerated during World War II. Even though Social Security benefits have been coupled with cost of living adjustments since 1972, these have not kept pace with recent inflationary trends, which take their greatest toll on individuals forced to exist on fixed incomes. The question of income adequacy remains of top priority, and predictions for improvements are tentative at best.

Some observers of the retirement scene, on the other hand, do not contemplate far better days for the aged at the dawn of the twenty-first century. The increased numbers of elderly, especially at the oldest ages, lead them to speculate that proportionately more money will have to be allotted to health and personal maintenance by the very old. Even if some form of comprehensive national health insurance is enacted, as is certain to be the case in the near future, the very old will inevitably incur unforeseen expenses that must be wrested from their already scarce incomes. Because their political clout has yet to be tested — in fact, Rosow (1974) and others wonder if it will ever amount to a weighty force — the relative financial status of the aged might be expected to gradually decline, though this factor may have less impact upon the total elderly population than would severe cutbacks in the extent of pension and Social Security support. Those who do receive adequate retirement incomes from pensions and other sources will be more likely to anticipate their retirement years positively, if not eagerly. Individuals retiring in 20 or 25 years will have been socialized into a world where retirement is a normal feature of one's occupational career, perhaps reducing some of the fears now experienced by those facing an event still not totally understood (Atchley, 1976). One of the manifold gains to be realized from advancing educational levels should be a more satisfying experience, with time freed from the exigencies of earning a livelihood. Legitimate endeavors will not be appreciably different from today, including the utilization of retired people in community and voluntary positions or, for those unhappy with their incomes or with early retirement, new employment. Whether engaged in leisure pursuits or further occupational tasks, acceptance of and adjustment to new roles available during the years of retirement will be more widespread among future elderly.

Working women will, in all probability, constitute an even larger proportion of the labor force in years to come; now four of every ten workers is a woman. As illustrated earlier, the highest participation rates are found among young women in the 20–24 age range and among the middle-aged, half of whom are working outside the home. By the end of this century the latter group will retire with quite a number of years of paid employment to their credit. Two problems come immediately to mind. How will families accustomed to checks from two wage earners adjust to retirement level income substantially below their preretirement earnings? Second, under current Social Security guidelines, women are entitled to benefits either based on their own work history or as dependents, under which they receive an amount roughly half that allotted to their spouses. Not only is Social Security as it presently operates a regressive system of taxation, but it discriminates against women, minorities and others who fill lower-paying jobs and who have interrupted work histories. Legislation establishing Social Security credits based on unpaid household and childcare responsibilities has to date received little support from congressional representatives. It may be however, that remedial legislation is destined to become a reality in the not too distant future. Court challenges, such as the recently adjudicated right of widowers with minor children to the same economic support as widows in a similar situation, will eventually force far-ranging revisions of the Social Security statutes. The Employee Retirement Income Security Act, passed in late 1974, has already compelled legislative review of many discriminatory clauses in private pension schemes. Once the participation patterns of the vast bulk of working women are perceived as firmly established, there is little doubt the eligibility requirements of both private and public pensions will come into closer conformance with women's contributions to societal needs. Shorter vesting periods and abolition of punitive measures for interrupted careers will probably be among the first reforms to be forthcoming. Nevertheless, the fact remains that women's retirement programs will depend in large measure on the political forces actively lobbying on their behalf (Bernstein, 1974; Moser, 1974).

Residence

During the 1960s and early 1970s, most American cities suffered a mass exodus to the suburbs and to smaller towns beyond the urban fringe. A major side effect of the departures was the loss of the most significant segments of municipal tax bases, resulting in a disproportionate squeeze on the resources used to fuel public services oriented to the disadvantaged — those who are left behind. It was noted in Chapter Ten that the growth of urban areas early in this century was at the expense of rural communities whose working age members moved to the cities in search of employment. The present tendency toward suburbanization is taking place at a prime cost to cities that only a generation ago were such drawing cards themselves. In both instances, the aged are among those most prone to remain behind; at first they were overrepresented in the older rural areas, then in inner city locations, and after the latest migratory shift will, by the turn of the century, be highly visible in today's suburban tracts. This does not mean, however, that the concentration of older people in central city neighborhoods will disappear during the coming decades. Most relocations involve young families; once settled, the propensity to move becomes less compelling with age. Consequently, after an initial period of moving about, most people age in familiar neighborhoods. Recalling the earlier discussion, most elderly report living in the same place for over 20 years; hence, there is every reason to expect the middle-aged to grow old wherever they are now living.

Despite the outmigration of the general population or the growth in the proportion of elderly living in the suburbs, during the last decade the number of suburban aged has expanded by approximately 10 percent. The largest share of the elderly will continue to reside in metropolitan areas because this is where their homes are and where social service and part-time employment opportunities exist. The attraction of retirement communities in warm climates with optimum services will not be curtailed, so that before the next century nearly 5 percent of the aged will settle permanently in age-segregated retirement settings, chiefly in the South and the West. There will also be some development of similar communities close to the larger metropolitan areas, thus permitting easy access to urban amenities and children. Nursing and personal care homes will still be a vital option, especially since that portion of the population over age 75 will continue to expand at a more rapid rate than the elderly in general. Service delivery to these and to all older people must therefore be made more responsive, not only to their spatial distribution but to their changing need patterns. With regard to residence, perhaps one of the most crucial points to bear in mind is the folly of attempting to separate older people from their environments. Planning for future generations of elderly ought to incorporate a consideration of their personal necessities and desires with an appreciation of the complexities of the urban milieu. Whatever the problems confronting urban governments, from fiscal to physical, they are often exacerbated among aged city residents — particularly the minority elderly. The issue does not turn on whether cities are viable environments, but on what must be done to facilitate living in areas over which the majority of aged have little control (Golant, 1975; Binstock, 1975).

Preparing the Way — Institutional Reforms

Successful aging is a most nebulous concept, incorporating a variety of attitudes and behaviors, which can in no way be construed as a singular process. There are as many maxims for adequate preparedness for the retirement years as there are advisors, though, obviously, practical antidotes for poor planning are rather scarce. Coupling what is known about the present aged population with predictions about future societal conditions increases the urgency for altered or new programing. The integration of facts and hypotheses is laden with uncertainty, yet it remains one of the most important goals of any study involving such a broad range of problems. Several areas have been consistently identified as crucial for insuring a successful old age, and to these are directed the attention and efforts of gerontologists and social service personnel alike. Improved income, housing, health, nutrition and, more recently, transportation have become the rallying calls of the elderly and their advocates. While interrelationships are multiple and complex, the proposed universal remedy often comes close to a blanket economic determinism. Indeed, without sufficient income, even if it is not the ultimate panacea, all other well-intentioned programs are jeopardized.

Social Security

With an excess of one-fifth of all American elderly falling below minimal income levels, finances present one of the foremost obstacles facing older people in any industrialized country. Replacement rates of preretirement income levels are far from satisfactory, in point of fact, federal social security programs tend to replenish only about half of previous earnings. Income adequacy is a most elusive variable; definitions hinge partly on an individual's feelings of relative need or deprivation and partly on an assessment of the purchasing power of a fixed income as it is affected by economic inflation. Governments generally utilize poverty threshold standards that more closely reflect requirements for subsistence survival rather than simply a low standard of living. In the past decade or two the aged have gained some economic concessions, mainly through increased Social Security benefits, the operation of Medicare programs and, for a minority, favorable tax, pension and investment opportunities. Overall, however, the aged have fared less well than their younger counterparts. The staggering levels of inflation of the last few years were not in sight in 1970, and the impact that this has had upon the aged is still at issue.

The mandated reforms in Social Security derive partly from the changing economic conditions during the past decade. Despite the fact the Social Security trust fund contains nearly $44 billion, beginning in 1976, payments to retired workers outstripped the revenues collected. The initial imbalance is projected at $3 billion, but if sustained, it will rapidly drain the monies held in trust, piling up a deficit of up to $20 billion by 1990. The problem is quite thorny, and the solution far from clear. Merely raising the taxable salary base is one of the most commonly heard suggestions, though this would not correct the regressive nature of the tax. Together, workers and their employers pay nearly 12 percent of all annual wages less than $16,500 into the Social Security trust fund. Doing away with the limited base entirely, making all income subject to equal taxation, would at least lessen the regressive character of the tax. Another proposal is to pool all payroll taxes with general revenues and effectively to eliminate separate Social Security accounts. Yet another idea is to advance retirement age to reflect lengthening life expectancies, thereby reducing the number of years during which Social Security payments are received (Koeppel, 1975). Unfortunately, during a time of economic slowdowns, this might only result in higher unemployment rates and, naturally, in fewer salaries on which taxes could be collected. Lower benefit levels have sometimes been offered as a solution, though without massive expansion of private pension programs such a view is short-sighted, as it would lead to greater poverty and related problems for a majority of the aged, increasing the number who live below subsistence levels by an additional one-third to one-half. Liberalizing the earnings test for the recipients of federal benefits would certainly help the aged, but it would not solve the large scale problem of inadequate resources to meet the growing demands of the Social Security program. Further, one of the drawbacks of Social Security, according to many experts, stems from the fact that general revenue funds are lowered by an estimated $5.7 billion annually through the exclusion of employer contributions and pension earnings from taxable income. But critics maintain that to make retirement benefits dependent upon the general tax revenues in order to keep the program solvent would sacrifice much of the self-help orientation presently cultivated. Others point out, frequently with considerable acrimony, that the tax exemptions available to older Americans alone amount to over $4 billion in lost revenue. Nevertheless, on an individual basis, few elderly personally gain all that much from these favorable and exclusionary dispensations.

Legislative Response

The retired persons who fare best in the United States are those with secondary pension benefits. Added to Social Security, pensions may provide enough to bring retirement income to within 85–90 percent of that earned during full employment. The more than 500,000 pension plans in existence covered only 35 million American workers in 1975. As pointed out in Chapter Nine, this is less than half the number of full-time workers, however, for fully 40 million Americans are either self-employed or else employed where pension programs are not available. One of the most important articles of legislation affecting older persons in recent years was the Employee Retirement Income Security Act of 1974 (ERISA), intended to insure benefits for workers currently contributing to pension programs and to encourage the creation of new plans (Public Law 93-406, 1974). As an inclusive effort to remedy much of what has traditionally been wrong with private pensions, ERISA covers both pension and welfare programs aimed at the provision of medical, vacation, training or other ancillary benefits. Eligibility for existing plans must now be determined no later than the employee's twenty-fifth birthday or the completion of one year of service. The law also establishes a tripartite vesting scheme, with the requirement that any employee with ten years service possess a nonforfeitable right to half of the accrued benefits plus an additional 10 percent for each year of service thereafter. Hence, pensions are payable unconditionally, whether or not the employee is still working for the same employer, if vesting schedules are met.

One of the unanticipated difficulties with ERISA is that it raises by a rather wide margin the expenses involved in operating pension plans. First, it imposes strict limitations on the investment procedures followed by most pension funds, while expanding and specifying in great detail the potential legal liabilities facing the fiduciaries, or trust officers, for poor investments. Second, the stringent reporting compelled by the law increases the amount of paperwork to the point that small funds cannot efficiently or economically comply with the demands. In fact, early reports are that the number of small plan terminations more than doubled in the first seven months following enactment of the legislation — from an average of 900 annually to nearly 2000! Another major provision of ERISA creates the Pension Benefit Guaranty Corporation, an agency within the Department of Labor to protect employees' rights to vested benefits. Many of the private pension programs that are folding did not vest benefits until the employee reached retirement age and, burdened with rising costs entailed in conforming to ERISA's specifications, termination has frequently presented the least expensive alternative. While ERISA may inadvertently encourage discontinuation of small pension plans and enforce more conservative investment procedures, it is unlikely that larger plans will suffer once the plan is fully operational. It is entirely possible however, that the higher administrative costs will be passed on to workers through a reduction in proposed pension benefit levels or supplemental services. A latent function of the legislation will be the likely growth of profit-sharing systems that do not require specific contributions by employers. At the same time, the number of *definite benefit* pensions, under which a certain level of benefit payments is assured regardless of the contribution to and investment history of the programs, will probably diminish. The gravity of the problems engendered by the disclosure and investment prescriptions of the law may eventually mandate revisions of certain stipulations if the discontinuation rate continues escalating.

Another innovative step taken by the federal government in 1975 to help people anticipate their financial needs in later years was the establishment of what is called the Individual Retirement Account (IRA) program. This plan permits those not covered by other pension plans, who wish to supplement their Social Security, to set aside a portion of their annual incomes for retirement. Essentially IRAs are tax-sheltered annuities into which earners may deposit up to 15 percent of their yearly incomes, to a maximum of $1500. The monies thus invested may be used to purchase retirement bonds directly from the federal government or else they can be invested in accounts with lending institutions, insurance companies or mutual funds. The IRA then constitutes an income reduction upon which no taxes are paid either on the amounts set aside or the accumulated interest until the money is paid out as retirement benefits after age 65. In addition to the savings and the tax deferment, the amount of tax actually owed will be less since the wage earner normally will be in a lower bracket, and under present federal tax law double exemptions are granted to people over 65. Furthermore, many local and state tax laws release worker earnings invested in an IRA from current occupational, payroll or state tax obligations. Often they may be avoided altogether in areas where retirement income is not subject to these taxes. If it were not for the opportunity to offer IRA or profit-sharing retirement plans, many small companies might find it impossible to extend to employees any pension programs at all due to the prohibitive administrative costs involved. Because they do provide flexible savings schedules to individuals and marginally profitable businesses, IRAs look as though their future is indeed bright.

It is unlikely that retirement programs will soon alter the basic assumptions of the present system or offer innovative changes. New data must be collected to measure the impact of lengthening years in retirement and of shorter work expectancy, as well as new economic and employment demands, including the possible costs of and incentives for encouraging workers to remain in the labor force. The variable components that enter into the determination of an adequate retirement income must be delineated and will probably be met through multiple projects coupling basic income maintenance with a contributory scheme related to occupational experiences. Finally, the very foundation of the current system must be restructured, as is gradually underway, to reduce and eliminate areas of discrimination between sex and racial groups or on the basis of occupational or marital status. Direct income transfers will continue to be complemented with service programs, such as health care and housing subsidies, although such delivery must be carefully evaluated to appraise its success in creating satisfying environments for aged recipients (Chen, 1974).

Flexible Retirement

Turning now to a consideration of what the future portends in terms of the nature of work careers, the possibilities are indeed broad. The most widely touted themes revolve around flexibility either in the hours and years spent in the work force or in the patterns of employment a person follows. While alternative modes of living, working and "recreating" have been espoused, the simple interspersing of vacation or sabbatical leaves throughout the work span would give rise to some fundamental challenges to organizational priorities. Nonetheless, such possibilities have garnered support from both scientific and nonscientific observers. Of course, there are technical problems that would confront the business and industrial communities, though a few demonstration projects would help alleviate some of the more exasperating misalignments sure to occur when such changes are attempted. Experimental arrangements allowing workers to select their own schedules have been found to be associated with somewhat higher morale and declining absenteeism; other plans maximizing individual choices might similarly improve the productive process. Today the five day, 40 hour work week predominates in America; at least eight of ten workers have known nothing else. But in recent years some unions have recommended less than 40 hour work weeks, with a few even stipulating 28 hours as full time. Although their numbers will grow in the coming years, less than 3 percent of the labor force enjoys such shortened work schedules currently. The changeover will probably proceed rather slowly, but not because such a shift is seen as radical — as the move to the 40 hour week was labeled in the 1920s. At least three identifiable factors are more likely to inhibit a significant reduction of hours in the next 10 to 20 years. The first is the introduction of what is known in Europe as *flexitime* — a program that encourages workers to preselect from several alternative schedules that they will follow for variable but relatively short periods of time. A related scheme, also tried first in Europe and termed *variable hours,* where workers are free to come and go as they see fit provided they maintain the production schedule and clock a specified number of hours each week, will also retard the adoption of shorter weekly work patterns. Finally, any such changes must win the endorsement of the Department of Labor, and thus far the stamp of approval for four day, 40 hour weeks or any other alteration has not been forthcoming (Hedges, 1975). Of course energy conservation, productivity needs and automation may foster the adoption of optional scheduling regardless of union or bureaucratic preferences.

As suggested above, flexibility involves more than a restructuring of hourly or weekly schedules. Career models themselves are equally subject to efforts to introduce greater degrees of freedom into the necessity of earning a living. Second careers, or beginning anew on another job track, have so far been limited to workers in skilled, professional and technical occupations, and to those whose jobs evaporate for various reasons. The near absence of second career opportunities for blue collar workers, and especially the dearth of studies of retraining among the lower echelons of the occupational ranks, should not be interpreted as any indication of lack of interest on their behalf. If ample occasion existed, chances are that people from all walks of life would be similarly open to second careers and retraining (Sheppard and Herrick, 1972). Whether the possibility of new careers at midlife becomes a reality for a sizeable portion of the labor force over the remainder of the century depends largely on prevailing economic conditions, policies and technological innovations. If for various reasons a labor surplus develops in any particular occupational realm, and if punitive sanctions in pension plans are eliminated, then career changes will certainly become more attractive. One of the basic ingredients for second careers to be meaningful alternatives may be a nationwide counseling program, sponsored by federal and state agencies in cooperation with unions and employers. As yet it is too early to make predictions about how extensive second careers might become, but the potentials are certainly not to be dismissed.

Prognosis on Health

Given that future cohorts of older people will both live longer and spend more years in retirement, the issue immediately arising is what their overall situations, including physiological and social parameters, will be like. Will people really benefit from these extensions? Any response must initially consider at least two related dimensions: actual health characteristics and accessibility of medical attention. In reference to the first, experts agree that medical technology has made its most significant inroads in the treatment of the acute illnesses frequently associated with early life. While these advances will probably permit older people to remain free from disease and disabilities longer, the aged will undoubtedly continue to be a population at risk; so long as their numbers are on the increase, so too will be the incidence of impaired functioning. Estimates of future health patterns suggest at least 20 percent of those who become old in the decades ahead will require rather extensive social and health-related attention. Generally, those most in need will be clustered among the *old-old*, over 75 years, whose conditions are the most recalcitrant. Having read Chapter Seven, there can be no mistaking the interdisciplinary appeal for routine, primary preventive care in order to achieve early detection of illness, yet a basic and undeniable paradox exists. In the light of present medical knowledge, the majority of chronic degenerative ailments are still beyond reach because of their multiple etiology; prompt diagnosis is all to the good for tractable conditions, but these are not normally what incapacitates old people (Waldman et al., 1970; Tobin, 1975). This is not to say, however, that major breakthroughs may not be just around the corner.

Research on biofeedback and telemetric monitoring has been in progress for several years. From the studies already reported, there are indications that many people can be trained to recognize when their bodies are malfunctioning and taught to control pulse rates and elevations of blood pressure, as well as numerous other bodily processes. Technological gadgetry evolving partially out of the national space program has brought medical supervision of patients in their own homes within practical range. By means of telemetry, levels of physiological functioning can be transmitted to a monitoring center miles away, enabling a team of paraprofessionals and specialists to evaluate bodily activities — telephoning instructions back to the patient or taking whatever other steps may be feasible. Refinements in electronic instruments are also finding practical application in the secondary treatment of cardiovascular problems. Scientists at the Massachusetts Institute of Technology have been experimenting with sound waves similar to a sonar system to assess the amount of damage suffered in heart attacks. Since the echo patterns of living and dead tissue are distinguishable, physicians in the near future will be able to determine the extent of an infarction, and thus to initiate appropriate life-saving measures much more rapidly.

Even the precipitating factors behind cardiovascular diseases may be on the verge of yielding at least some of their secrets. New techniques are now available to detect the presence of saturated fatty substances in the blood stream quickly and economically, so that many more people can be made aware of dangerously high lipid levels. With the discovery of a biochemical agent referred to as CSA (chondroitin-4, Sulfate A), a naturally occurring hormone found in connective tissues, some researchers are hopeful they will soon be able to reverse the accumulation of fat deposits along the walls of the vascular system. With therapeutic dosages of CSA, lesions and related effects of atherosclerosis might be partially redressed, giving many people a new lease on life. In addition, attempts to repair **aneurysms** have made some headway. Using silicone-iron injections held in place over the point of rupture until the material hardens, it appears it may soon be possible to patch destroyed arterial tissue. Clinical investigation of various forms of cancer is proceeding apace and may shortly resolve some of the questions currently thwarting improved health status among the aged. Notwithstanding dramatic progress, many years of exhaustive study and testing are required before any of these innovations can be adopted for the general public. Certainly they cannot become totally effective until years after widespread usage — until an entire cohort has had the benefit of these procedures for much of their adult lives — yet they do hold out the possibility of even longer periods of optimum health for future generations of the elderly.

A comparative look at health status and the degree of physical incapacities in the United States and selected European countries quickly reveals that even though elderly Americans are and will probably continue to be in better health than their age peers across the Atlantic, there is far greater likelihood they will be admitted to a hospital or other institution (Shanas et al., 1968). The reasons this is the case, why institutionalization of all types is more prevalent among older Americans, can be traced to a fundamental divergence in the philosophies underlying respective health care systems, rather than to individual health histories. From the outset, most European countries have incorporated as a central principle of their service delivery programs that, even if specially designed home health aids are necessary, the best place for older people is in their own homes in the community. As apparent from the earlier discussion, the United States was among the last of the major industrial nations to openly acknowledge governmental responsibility in maintaining the health and material well-being of old people. It was not until the 1973 amendments to the Older Americans Act that any explicit mention was even made of the undesirability of institutionalization or of the benefits to be gained from supporting the elderly in their home environments. But, as will be indicated below, recognition of a problem does not lead automatically to a solution; political negotiation and reconciliation take precedence. It is no secret that the medical profession, together with other interest groups, launched a vigorous campaign to block passage of the initial Medicare legislation, forcing extensive revision of the original proposals. As a consequence of their e forts and of the multilateral compromise deemed essential to secure enactment of a limited health insurance plan, authorities on both sides of the issue now lament the inadequacies and inefficiency inherent in the program.

The tendency to overplay the role of institutionalization in caring for older people in the United States is based in large part on the underdevelopment of alternatives. As Blenkner (1967) so aptly points out, the flow of elderly through the country's health care network results from the particular patterns of funding: that is, where the money is spent. Before passage of the Older Americans Act in 1965 the population of older people lodged in state mental hospitals for custodial care was notably larger than we find today. What brought about the change? In establishing health insurance programs for the elderly, government policy earmarked substantial financial subsidies for nursing homes and related institutions. At the time it appeared, medically related problems among older people could be dealt with most effectively within a protected environment. To spur the growth of a sufficient number of facilities to meet the needs thus created, federal money was made readily available. Priorities formalized, nursing homes began to enjoy considerable popularity in investment circles — witness the rapid increase in proprietary operations and the entrance of at least two large hotel chains into the nursing home business. With the nation's conscience assuaged and the medical profession endorsing, even backing, the construction of a vast network of nursing homes and related institutions, relatively little has been realized in the way of developing community services. From a commercial perspective, as investors seek to protect their interests, further expansion of the nursing home industry may well militate against innovative efforts to keep the elderly at home. This does not mean, however, that institutional accommodations are not or will not be needed in the years ahead; it is merely to note the potentially retarding effect on other care options that increased construction of nursing homes may have. In our haste to provide appropriate avenues for institutionalization of the elderly, scant attention has been paid to structuring the internal relations or overall quality of life experienced by the residents. Since the point of entry for most admissions is through a general hospital, nursing homes have most often been cast from the same institutional mold. Neither nursing homes nor intermediate care facilities have yet manifested a commitment to rehabilitative therapy designed to prepare the elderly for community living once again. What deficiencies exist in this orientation cannot be attributed solely to administrators and staff; indeed, there has been only meager financial support offered for such projects. Financial sponsorship and rewards reflect the historically based ambivalence described in Chapter Two in establishing priorities. Those people regarded as past the prime of life have most often been associated with unfavorable cost-benefit ratios. These conclusions derive from global expectations among younger age groups rather than from appropriate age-specific or individualized criteria (Brody, 1970; Tobin, 1975).

If future generations of older people are to realize adequate health care delivery, it is nearly a foregone conclusion that existing programs will have to be largely revamped. Today's coverage is woefully spotty, leaving over half the medical expenses incurred by the bulk of the elderly to be paid from their personal resources. It is one thing to advocate humane treatment of our aged citizens, and quite another when it comes to carrying through. As part of the recurring attempts to shave part of the federal government's staggering financial deficit, trial balloons have been released to test congressional reaction to tightening fiscal purse strings by raising deductible amounts under Medicare and requiring recipients to pay additional portions of their total medical bill (U.S. Senate, 1975a). At a time when out-of-pocket expenses for medical care are over three times greater for the elderly than for the rest of the adult population, such a move demonstrates little regard for the plight of the elderly. If these trends were to continue, it might not be long before only the rich and the totally impoverished could secure medical attention — the former via their own means, the latter because of benefits received under Medicaid. However, even Medicaid patients find themselves hard pressed since so-called nonessentials such as drugs, dental and optometric care, hearing aids or rental of medical equipment are often difficult items to justify when making claims. Despite the limitations on long-term care pointed to earlier, one-third of all Medicare-Medicaid payments are directed to the elderly in nursing homes. The remainder cover the costs of physician and hospital treatment, while less than 1 percent has been diverted to programs aimed at maintaining the elderly outside institutions. The effect of the Medicare legislation has been coverage of short-term, catastrophic illnesses requiring intensive medical attention, at the expense of support for natural lifestyles in the community. Although comparison is frequently made to the presumably enlightened

British and European health care systems, there are some critics who contend the fragmented *nonsystem of noncare* characteristic of the United States is not without its parallels abroad (U.S. Senate, 1971; Whanger and Busse, 1975).

Forecasting future directions in service delivery is highly speculative; ultimately they will be shaped by an amalgamation of economic, political, health and demand factors all filtered through traditional stereotypes and conceptions of the distribution of responsibilities. Judging from revisions of pertinent legislation, the introduction of a Medicare Reform Act and proposed plans for National Health Insurance, more broadly oriented programs are seemingly within sight. As noted above, recognition of the need for governmental assistance for independent living has now been incorporated under Title III of the 1973 Amendments to the Older Americans Act. Basically, the new provisions call for the development of community service networks that will maximize the opportunities among older people to live more fully in familiar settings. Additional reinforcement for integrated outreach programs was also evidenced in the 1974 edition of the Social Security Act, specifically Title XX, which seeks the articulation of local program expenditures for elderly and low income families. Together, these two amendments should contribute to the design of therapeutic communities wherein the needs of the elderly can be assessed on a decentralized basis, often eliminating the necessity of a trip to a hospital. Programs involving home helpers and household assistance are to be greatly expanded to counteract the normal dependencies arising among the aged that might otherwise lead to institutionalization. Day centers, polyclinics and graduated care facilities are expected to become more numerous under the new guidelines, as will outpatient clinics with interrelated health and social services. Proposed 1975 amendments to the Older Americans Act in the House of Representatives included a new Title VIII, which would have provided special sponsorship for homemaker services, residential repairs and renovations plus counseling programs. Unfortunately, the Senate version of the amendments deleted Title VIII programs, and with existing authorizations far exceeding administration proposals, the future of such new programs in subsequent compromises is unclear ("Senate Adopts 2-Year Extension," 1975).

One piece of legislation is seldom sufficient to accomplish all that is required to address complex issues; when such is the goal the program frequently ends up being so ungainly that it is impractical. As one example, to cover omissions in previous bills and while awaiting the enactment of National Health Insurance, a Medicare Reform Act was introduced in 1975. The aim of this admittedly interim proposal was a reorganization of the major sections of Medicare-Medicaid. Whether or not the bill finally becomes law, it does demonstrate what is likely to occur in the future. As initially presented, the reform bill would extend universal coverage to all old people regardless of work history. It would also abolish the deductible clauses, provide for unlimited hospitalization and merge Parts A and B of Medicare, in addition to other changes (Editorial, 1975). Among the recent proposals, perhaps the most far-ranging are those incorporated into the joint House-Senate National Health Insurance legislation. Without encroaching on the role played by institutions in the provision of social and health services, the legislation mandates the development of nonprofit personal care organizations to help older people avoid premature relocation, yet backs institutionalization when it does become the most viable alternative. Most important, the bill would create a system of total coverage of a wide range of medical needs for all citizens, within a preventive framework. Such a holistic approach, if it is to deal effectively with the nation's health requirements in the years ahead, must also endorse general treatment for emotional or mental health problems in and beyond our institutions through the expansion of neighborhood clinics within the local community (U.S. Senate, 1975a; Kahn, 1975). Of equally significant concern is an expansion of the terminal treatment hospices mentioned in Chapter Eleven. With the vast majority of people dying in medical facilities, those professionals most familiar with the problems encountered by patients and their families see an urgent need to incorporate specialized personnel and suitable environmental settings into the overall social and health service delivery system (Tobin, 1975).

Gerontology as a Vocation

Taking into consideration the increasing size of the elderly population, changing health patterns, emergent governmental policies and the political realities of the situation, the facts add up to more attention being focused on tomorrow's old people. To respond to their needs, gerontology as a vocation offers career opportunities that are not likely to be diminished in the foreseeable future. In accordance with the 1967 amendments to the Older Americans Act, a continuing effort to evaluate current and future personnel needs in the field of aging was initiated. Subsequently, several estimates have been made of blanket personnel requirements, as well as what specific areas of need will exist in 1980. Projections just for the decade of the 1970s have brought to light urgent and immediate shortages, with an expectation of doubling and perhaps even tripling the number of trained specialists available to work with the elderly. At the beginning of the decade there were approximately 330,000 persons employed in occupations primarily oriented toward older people; however, the number in tangential jobs was probably many times higher. In all likelihood, fewer than 10 to 20 percent of those directly working with an older clientele had received formal training for their jobs. Overall deficiencies existed, so much so, in fact, that the Administration on Aging in commenting on the critical deficit of qualified personnel was able to declare: "The gap between the need for trained personnel and the capacities of present training programs is so great that there is no danger of overtraining for several decades" (Birren, 1971). A similar statement was issued by delegates to the United Nations as part of their survey of the national and international manpower picture. In both cases it was reported that unmet needs can only be surmounted if the supply of skilled administrative and managerial personnel is greatly expanded. Yet few advances were made; in 1973 and again in 1975 members of the Special Committee on Aging in the Senate were able to note that hundreds of thousands of workers must still be trained in the next five years or so if the growing requirements of the field of aging are to be satisfied (U.N., 1973; U.S. Senate, 1973, 1975b).

Before turning to a discussion of career opportunities in aging, it is appropriate to pause for a moment to ponder the reasons that training in various areas has lagged so far behind acknowledged needs. In the middle to late 1960s, government estimates placed the number of social workers directly involved with older people at less than 1 percent of the profession. At about the same time, Freeman (1971) found that fewer than half of the medical schools he surveyed included formal courses on aging, and that out of over 20,000 faculty members, a scant 15 thought of themselves as qualified in geriatrics. Among practicing psychiatrists, fewer than 100 reported a specialty in geriatric psychiatry, and surprisingly few more were in training. Around the country a wide range of continuing education courses is offered to practicing physicians and psychiatrists, creating opportunities to upgrade their skills and gain exposure to areas not covered in their years in medical school. In the late 1960s, Verwoerdt (1969) determined that over 2100 such classes were scheduled in any given year. Of these, a total of ten made specific reference to geriatrics or problems related to the elderly. General undergraduate courses in gerontology might be expected to be fairly widespread, but in fact as recently as the mid-1960s there were only 71 taught in the United States. Fortunately this number has since increased manyfold, and today courses in aging are becoming widely available. Although the number of graduate students specializing in age-related programs has also increased many times over, a report prepared for the White House Conference on Aging commented that only a few hundred students were receiving government stipends to stimulate and support their interests in gerontology (Birren, 1971; Seltzer, 1974). The obvious question surfaces: Why have so few people planned careers in aging? In nearly all cases the answer is the same: prospective professionals share the same prejudices and stereotypes as the general population. Furthermore, gerontology has not been accorded much prestige as an academic specialty until the last few years. In addition, the problems with which the study of aging must deal are not easy. They demand long years of research, training and trial application, and even then solutions cannot be assured. Fortunately gerontology's stock has been rising on the academic and governmental marketplace. The last few years have witnessed a burgeoning number of courses on all levels; an influx of federal monies has been attracting many able people and aging has emerged as a bit of a political issue — something to be endorsed and supported. The 1973 amendments to the Older Americans Act gave both education and short-term training special attention under the revision of Title IV and by establishing an office of Research, Demonstration and Manpower Resources as a part of the Administration on Aging ("R & D," 1975). Undoubtedly, financial squeezes are sure to dog the field; even after legislation passes Congress, appropriations for training can be jeopardized by budget cuts proposed by the administration. However, the recent creation of a National Institute of Aging should provide greater respectability, while the maturing of the population will provide the impetus for a significant and continuing expansion of training for qualified personnel.

Careers in Aging

In view of recent trends and future expectations, the time for justifying the study of aging is long past. The facts are imperative: without skilled resource people, aging programs of all stripes will remain underdeveloped or, worse yet, mismanaged, perhaps furnishing little more than custodial care. Education and training must be implemented on all levels — in institutions of higher learning, high schools and in-service programs — to ready young adults, the middle-aged and even the retired to meet the challenges of a substantial need for more workers. During the 1970s projections call for the recruitment of at least 700,000 people to fill newly created jobs, not to mention those who will be required to offset attrition. The number of positions to be filled will of course vary by level, but overall estimates envision two to three times more than were in existence at the beginning of the decade. A limited cadre of teachers, researchers and scientific technicians responsible for professional leadership, for producing new knowledge and for providing advanced training must be recruited. Further, a larger core of people capable of translating knowledge into practical terms is required. These will be primarily managerial, administrative and supervisory personnel or technical experts affiliated with community colleges or vocational institutes. Finally, the greatest growth must take place among those who are in daily contact with older people, those who will make the actual application of what is learned in order to deal effectively with immediate problems and situations (Cohen, 1969; Birren et al., 1972).

The difficulty with measuring future personnel requirements is that all such projections will be influenced by events yet to occur. Take, for example, administrators of nursing and personal care homes. If the present growth rate of these facilities continues, and if the number of beds in each is not increased over the current average of 42, then roughly 44,000 administrators must be employed by 1980 if licensing regulations already implemented are to be met. However, many authorities believe the optimum size might be somewhat larger, say a 60 bed average, in which case, the number of administrators necessary might conceivably be reduced by one-third. Fewer managerial positions would naturally imply fewer training programs, which in turn would mean fewer teachers. An analysis of current and expected personnel needs in selected occupations is presented in Table 14.1. These forecasts are based on calculations made at the beginning of the decade and updated in 1973. Although not all specialities are shown in the table, those presented are indicative of trends in other areas. While limited fluctuations will occur, testimony before the Senate Special Committee on Aging in 1975 reiterated the urgency of developing new sources of personnel (Birren, 1971; U.S. Senate, 1975a).

Meeting the 1980 needs of an older population will be contingent on realizing substantial increments for a host of occupations beyond those listed here. At least double the number of speech pathologists, audiologists, homemaker or home health aides, occupational therapists and so on must be trained if tomorrow's elderly are to be adequately cared for in both institutional and community situations. Special instruction to double the number of social workers prepared to help with family, personal or occupational counseling, adjustment processes and related services for older people is also essential before the decade is out if caseloads are to be kept

Table 14.1
Selected Personnel Requirements for Tomorrow's Elderly

	1973	1978	NEWLY TRAINED	NEW POSITIONS	ATTRITION
Small area planning	300	1,500	1,400	1,200	200
State planning and administration	500	1,250	1,000	750	250
Nutrition project directors	275	3,000	3,225	2,725	500
Managers, retirement housing	8,200	27,000	20,800	18,800	2,000
Senior citizen directors	3,000	3,800	1,800	800	1,000
L.P.N. (nursing homes)	88,000	113,000	50,000	25,000	25,000
R.N. (nursing homes)	73,000	81,000	16,000	8,000	8,000
Physical therapists (aged)	3,300	6,600	3,900	3,300	600
Recreation leaders and specialists	25,000	42,000	24,000	17,000	7,000
Teachers at colleges, universities, community colleges	500	2,100	1,700	1,600	100

Source: U.S. Senate, Special Committee on Aging, "Training Needs in Gerontology," 93rd Cong., 1st sess. (Washington, D.C.: U.S. Government Printing Office, 1973), p. 2.

within reason. By 1980, retirement, or what are sometimes called social insurance, experts will be in heavy demand, and again, at least twice as many as presently available will be needed to help with preretirement planning. Taking into account the growth rate of various old age institutions, assessing the number of physicians necessary to staff these facilities and still service the noninstitutionalized elderly is a difficult task. If current training patterns continue, however, it will not be before 1980 or perhaps later that the supply of doctors will be sufficient to meet those shortages already on the books in the late 1960s. Coupled with the vacancies in the ranks of professional and skilled service personnel, many thousands of nurse's aides, community outreach workers and ancillary personnel will also be a prerequisite for the programs likely to be developed over the next decade (Cohen, 1969; Birren, 1971).

Within the last few years, a great deal has been accomplished toward establishing career-oriented training programs. For the prospective student of gerontology, opportunities for undergraduate majors and basic or applied graduate level degrees are more readily available. From coast to coast, innumerable colleges and universities have inaugurated or broadened their instruction in the field of aging. The nation's first degree-granting School of Gerontology was dedicated in 1975 at the University of Southern California, with others scheduled to follow in the near future. Although the fortunes of the new National Institute on Aging are not yet settled, its existence should contribute substantially to career education in gerontology. Indeed, 1977 budgetary figures indicate support for aging is at an all-time high. An emphasis on the interdisciplinary focus necessary to adequately address the problems and needs of old people is far from universal; however, those centers most intimately involved in the study of aging processes are structured in such a way as to draw on the resources of multiple vantage points. The sometimes fragmented perspectives of the various disciplines focusing on aging must be brought to bear on the totality of the experience of growing old in and for society. There is no disagreement among those familiar with the field that gerontology is indeed a challenging and rewarding endeavor.

Summary

Anticipating what the coming decades hold for the elderly is unquestionably a task fraught with ambiguity. While demographic projections might leave one heady with a sense of knowing the outcome of as yet future events, they hardly tell the whole story. The proportion of older people in the population will continue to increase, and is unlikely to even begin to stabilize until the middle of the next century. Medical science may well extend the period of physical well-being until late in the seventh decade, allowing people to lead full and active lives free from nagging chronic disabilities. Current estimates are for people in the near future to live about as long as now. However, dramatic breakthroughs can never be ruled out. If, for example, mortality resulting from renal or cardiovascular and related heart diseases was to be brought under control, average life expectancies might well approach the century mark. There is no denying the enactment of Medicare and the initial Older Americans Act in 1965 was a historic milestone, helping extend the promise of health care to all older people. Unfortunately, many of the improvements envisioned in the delivery of health services have been whittled away in the political process of establishing priorities. While Medicare started out to be a primary source of assistance, by 1975 it covered slightly over one-third of the health bill of the average older person (U.S. Senate, 1975a). Nonetheless, there is a growing awareness of the need to focus on what it means to become old in the mass societies of an advanced industrial age.

To accommodate the expanded numbers of elderly, certain basic institutional and societal patterns will have to undergo changes. At the present time, Social Security constitutes the financial mainstay for the majority of the elderly; yet it is not uncommon in the United States that whenever economic stability is threatened, cutbacks in the payments to older people are proposed. Although observers feel it is unlikely that tomorrow's elderly will be worse off than at present, a substantial minority will continue to be forced to exist below nationally established poverty levels. Additional sources of income, revised pension programs, even individual retirement annuities will undoubtedly become more widespread; at the same time, the structure of the Social Security system faces the necessity of major overhaul — without it the system appears headed for the financial shoals in the next 10 to 15 years. Retirement benefits for women are likely destined for drastic revision in years to come. As more women participate in the labor force, demands for more equitable retirement schemes will increase. Women who select childcare and homemaking responsibilities as their primary careers may eventually be covered by Social Security, receiving retirement credits for performing necessary roles. Judging from the best contemporary evidence, our whole conception of retirement may be altered, as work life, careers and leisure are redefined to encompass greater flexibility.

In large measure, the fate of the elderly in the twenty-first century rests on adequate preparation today. The usefulness and promise of basic research will be obviated if it is not supplemented by a corps of trained experts who stand prepared to offer a broad spectrum of essential services. Not only will future generations of older people be better educated — high school graduation will be the norm by the year 2000 — but they will have had a lifetime's experience of seeking professional help in time of need. The demand for personnel to work with the elderly will easily outstrip the supply at least through 1980 and, many predict, beyond as well. Occupational opportunities exist on all levels, and while the challenge is great, the rewards are even greater. Specialists are required of course, but they, as all professionals in the field, must also possess a general overview of the aging process if they are to contribute to the well-being of the nation's elderly. Gerontology is itself a young field of study, but one ready for innovation and new perspectives on the inevitable path over which everyone must travel. The potential for meaningful intervention is clearly marked:

> Old age, you lied . . .
> Time measured by the years
> is in no way the measure of our
> days.

— Saint-John Perse (1961)

Pertinent Readings

ATCHLEY, R.C. *The Sociology of Retirement.* Cambridge, Mass.: Schenkman, 1976.

BERNSTEIN, M.C. "Forecast of Women's Retirement Income: Cloudy and Colder; 25 Percent Chance of Poverty." *Industrial Gerontology* I, 2 (1974): 1–13.

BINSTOCK, R.H. "Planning for Tomorrow's Urban Aged: A Policy Analyst's Reaction." *The Gerontologist* XV, 1, pt. I (1975): 42–43.

BIRREN, J.E. "Background and Issues in Training." 1971 White House Conference on Aging. Washington D.C.: U.S. Government Printing Office, 1971.

BIRREN, J.E., D.S. WOODRUFF and S. BERGMAN. "Research, Demonstration, and Training: Issues and Methodology in Social Gerontology." *The Gerontologist* XII, 2, pt. II (1972): 49–83.

BLENKNER, M. "The Place of the Nursing Home Among Community Resources." *Journal of Geriatric Psychiatry* I, 1 (1967): 135–44.

BRODY, E.M. "Congregate Care Facilities and Mental Health of the Elderly." *Aging and Human Development* I, 4, (1970): 279–321.

CHEN, Y. "Retirement Income Adequacy." In *Professional Obligations and Approaches to the Aged,* eds. A.N. Schwartz and I.N. Mensch, 134–54. Springfield, Ill.: Charles C. Thomas, Publisher, 1974.

COHEN, W. "The Demand for Personnel and Training in the Field of Aging." *Congressional Record* CXV, 4 (February 24–March 6, 1969): 4465–68.

EDITORIAL. *Geriatrics* XXX, 6 (1975):15, 18.

EISDORFER, C., and M. TAVES, eds. "International Research and Education in Social Gerontology; Goals and Strategies." *The Gerontologist* XII, 2, pt. II (1972): 1–84.

FREEMAN, J.T. "A Survey of Geriatric Education: Catalogue of the United States Medical Schools." *Journal of the American Geriatrics Society* XIX (1971): 746–62.

GOLANT, S.M. "Residential Concentrations of the Future Elderly." *The Gerontologist* XV, 1, pt. II (1975): 16–23.

GOTTESMAN, L.E. "Long-range Priorities for the Aged." *Aging and Human Development* I, 4 (1970): 393–99.

HAVIGHURST, R.J. "The Future Aged: The Use of Time and Money." *The Gerontologist* XV, 1, pt. II, supplement (1975): 10–15.

HAYFLICK, L. "Quantity, Quality, and Responsibility in Aging Research." *The Gerontologist* XI, 1, pt. I (1971): 68–73.

HEDGES, J.N. "How Many Days Make a Workweek?" *Monthly Labor Review* XCVIII, 4 (1975): 29–36.

HICKEY, T. "In-Service Training in Gerontology: Toward the Design of an Effective Educational Process." *The Gerontologist* XIV, 1 (1974): 57–64.

KAHN, R.L. "The Mental Health System and the Future Aged." *The Gerontologist* XV, 1, pt. II (1975): 24–31.

KOEPPEL, B. "The Big Social Security Rip-off." *The Progressive* XXXIX, 8 (1975): 13–18.

MENDELSON, M.A. *Tender Loving Greed*. New York: Alfred Knopf, 1974.

MOSER, C.H. "Mature Women — The New Labor Force." *Industrial Gerontology* I, 2 (1974): 14–25.

NEUGARTEN, B.L. "The Future and the Young-Old." *The Gerontologist* XV, 1, pt. II, supplement (1975): 4–9.

PERSE, ST.-JOHN. *Chronique*. Trans. by R. Fitzgerald. New York: Pantheon Books, Inc., 1961.

PUBLIC LAW 93-406. "Employee Retirement Income Security Act of 1974." 93d Cong., H.R. 2, 88 Stat. 829, September 2, 1974. Washington, D.C.: U.S. Government Printing Office, 1974.

"R & D, Manpower Office Studies Aging Processes." *Aging*, 247 (1975): 23.

ROSOW, I. *Socialization to Old Age*. Berkeley: University of California Press, 1974.

SCHAIE, K.W. "Training of Trainers to Train Trainers." *The Gerontologist* XIV, 6 (1974): 533–36.

SELTZER, M.M. "Education in Gerontology: An Evolutionary Analogy." *The Gerontologist* XIV, 4 (1974): 308–11.

"Senate Adopts 2-Year Extension of Older Americans Act Authority with Changes; House Voted 4 Years." *Aging* 250 (1975): 3.

SHANAS, E., et al. *Old People in Three Industrial Societies*. New York: Atherton Press, 1968.

SHEPPARD, H.L., and N.Q. HERRICK, eds. *Where Have All the Robots Gone? Worker Dissatisfaction in the '70s*. New York: The Free Press, 1972.

TOBIN, S.S. "Social and Health Services for the Future Aged." *The Gerontologist* XV, 1, pt. II (1975): 32–37.

UNITED NATIONS. *Questions of the Elderly and the Aged: Conditions, Needs and Services, and Suggested Guidelines for National and International Action*. #A/9126. New York: United Nations, 1973.

U.S. SENATE, SPECIAL COMMITTEE ON AGING. "Alternatives to Nursing Home Care: A Proposal." 92nd Cong., 1st sess. Washington, D.C.: U.S. Government Printing Office, 1971.

_____. "Training Needs in Gerontology." 93d Cong., 1st sess. Washington, D.C.: United States Government Printing Office, 1973.

_____. "Developments in Aging: 1974 and January–April, 1975." 94th Cong., 1st sess. Washington, D.C.: United States Government Printing Office, 1975a.

——— . "Training Needs in Gerontology." 94th Cong., 1st sess. Washington, D.C.: United States Government Printing Office, 1975b.

VERWOERDT, A. "Training in Geropsychiatry." In *Behavior and Adaptation in Late Life,* eds. E.W. Busse and E. Pfeiffer, 345–65. Boston: Little, Brown and Company, 1969.

WALDMAN, A., M. WARD and S. YAFFE. "Periodic Health Examinations and Mortality in the Elderly." *Aging and Human Development* I, 4 (1970): 323–32.

WHANGER, A.D., and E.W. BUSSE. "Care in Hospital." In *Modern Perspectives in the Psychiatry of Old Age,* ed. J.G. Howells, 450–85. New York: Brunner/Mazel, Inc., 1975.

Glossary

Acute brain syndrome A reversible form of organic brain malfunction resulting from systemic disease, pulmonary or cardiac insufficiency, high temperature, malnutrition, alcoholism, injury, or other factors. Diagnosis is difficult, with the incidence of misdiagnosis high; symptomatology includes rapid fluctuations in mood and cognitive capacity, confusion, easy distractibility and occasional hyperactivity. Early detection and treatment are essential for full recovery.

Acute diseases   Those illnesses marked by rapid onset, definite crisis and self-limiting aftermath. Usually they are brought on by exogenous factors which result in a traumatic course. The most frequent sufferers of acute illnesses are those in their first half of life.

Affective disorders   Most common psychogenic or functional disorders not involving physical malfunctioning. Affective disturbances found among older people have usually existed for many years. They are marked by personality changes, alterations in normal mood states, lack of self-esteem and psychological turmoil. Reactive depressions and, less often, mania are the two most frequent affective disorders observed among the elderly.

Age dependency ratio   A demographic measure of changing age composition in a particular population. Since it is based on an aggregation of those considered either too young or too old to contribute to their own financial or social well-being, the age-dependency ratio indicates how many dependents every 100 working members of a group must support. Based on simple statistics reflecting age distributions, the dependency ratio can be calculated for various populations and allows for comparisons among diverse societies.

Age distribution   Descriptive statistical measure of the proportional age mix in a population.

Ageism   Negative or pejorative image of and attitudes toward an individual simply because he or she is old. The extent to which the public in general holds a negative view toward the elderly is questionable, though in the past it may have been more extensive.

Age norms   Guidelines of age-appropriate behavior within a given complex of roles. Age norms provide a general definition of acceptable behavior but do not supply detailed stipulations for each and every possible performance.

Age-status asynchronization   An inconsistency which develops when relative criteria employed in different social spheres do not reflect similar standing in terms of age. Asynchronization results in role conflict and ambiguous definitions of appropriate behavior.

Aneurysm   Lesion in a wall of the vascular system resulting from atherosclerosis or other insufficiency. By the fourth decade of life clinical evidence of atherosclerotic lesions in the arterial wall is easily diagnosed.

Anticipatory grief Thought by those who study the behavioral aspects of death and dying to lessen the emotional upheaval associated with the death of a loved one. Knowing in advance that the death will occur permits one to make the appropriate adjustments without the additional interference of acute shock and emotional trauma attendant with actual death.

Anticipatory socialization Learning of the obligations, expectations and rights associated with a new role preparatory to actually assuming it. Throughout most of life an implicit component of most roles is a preparation for subsequent roles, thereby making adjustment much easier.

Autodidactic An individual who is an inner-directed self-teacher and who seldom accepts reality at face value, searching instead for underlying themes and new ways of organizing information. Thought to be a personality characteristic of many creative people.

Chronic brain syndrome Irreversible but not entirely intractable form of organic brain disorder. One type of chronic brain syndrome, senile psychosis, occurs when there is an atrophy of the brain or a loss of neurons. Symptoms include cognitive decline, antisocial conduct, lack of emotionality and ultimately physical incapacity. Cerebral arteriosclerosis is another type resulting from vascular insufficiencies which lower oxygen levels, thereby bringing about tissue death. Symptoms include dizziness, confusion, intermittent lucidity and cognitive declines.

Chronic diseases Lacking in specifiable etiology, chronic diseases involve endogenous systemic disruptions which do not run a short-term course. Because they involve a number of bodily functions, the chronic diseases which older people suffer from most frequently are resistant to cure.

Cohort Those people who share a common characteristic. As used by demographers, *cohort* refers to all those born during some specified period.

Dissociative neurosis A breakdown in cognitive functioning thought by some to be a defensive response to psychological challenges which may be too overwhelming to be dealt with. Perceived loss of identity is an overriding symptom.

Earnings test   Assessment of retirement benefits in which payments are reduced according to a schedule imposed on the basis of current earnings.

Etiology   The science of the causes of disease.

Functional age   An indicator of age based on performance capacities rather than simply chronological age.

Gerontocracy   A political system in which the elders, by virtue of their age and wisdom, constitute the ruling group.

Institutional neurosis   Referred to as a form of psychological railroading, marked by such symptoms as an erosion of unique personality traits, increasing dependency, psychological distance and a decreasing attentiveness to external events. Seen by some researchers as a result of institutionalization and misplaced priorities of staff who fail to treat the elderly with appropriate respect and humane concern.

Involutional melancholia   Depressive reaction occurring without previous history. Normally a disorder which first appears in mid-life.

Life expectancy   The average length of time an individual born at a particular point in history can reasonably expect to live.

Life table   A mathematical table showing mortality conditions for specified age groups within a population. Based on age-specific mortality rates, the life table reveals the probability of dying at any given age.

Morbidity   Any departure from complete physical well-being; the incidence of illnesses.

Nuclear family   The conjugal family composed of parents and children living under one roof. Assumed to be the predominant form of family life today, as compared to the extended family in the past in which the conjugal family plus blood relatives from two or more generations live under one roof. Modified extended families are still very much in evidence where two or more generations live in close proximity and maintain close contact, but not under one roof.

Portent of embarrassment   The expectation of being stigmatized for inferior performance in some defined activity.

Rites of passage   Originally, the ceremonial rites marking transition from one social status to another. Presently used to refer to both explicit and implicit status passage that is denoted by some type of occasion.

Roleless role   Used to describe the ambiguity many find characteristic of retirement, wherein there are few explicit expectations regarding actual behavior or performance.

Senescence   The aging process, particularly in the second half of life, which results in increased vulnerability to displacing stimuli of any type.

Senile psychosis   One form of chronic brain syndrome. Marked by the anatomical involution of the brain itself. (See Chronic brain syndrome)

Terminal decline   A decline in cognitive abilities thought by some researchers to occur shortly prior to death. Perhaps as a result of disruptions within the central nervous system, various investigators have noted a marked drop in intellectual functioning as death draws near.

Index

Developmental aging, 147
Diabetes mellitus, 186
Diastolic pressure, 183
Disengagement theory, 117
Dissociative neurosis, 155
Dissonance, 251
DNA (deoxyribonucleic acid), 88
Domiciliary care homes, 283

Earnings test, 238
Economic resources, historical, 45
Educating for leisure, 248
Education, 69, 389
Ego development, 148
Ego integrity, 149
Embolisms, 183
Employee Retirement Income
    Security Act (ERISA), 396
Employee's Pension Plan, 242
Employment
    postretirement, 390
    preretirement, 68, 210
Endentuousness, 186
Endothelial lining, 182
End Poverty in California
    (EPIC), 329
Entropy and energy, 82
Error catastrophes, 89
Excitation stage, 308
Experiential dimension, 315

Families, elderly, 266
Family
    authority, 271
    extended, 263
    historic, 42
    living arrangements, 261
    nuclear, 263
    relations, 65, 263
    support, 6, 264
Filial maturity, 276
Filipino Americans, 376
Flexitime, 399
Forgetting, 136
Foster Grandparents, 300
Friendship, 296
Functional disorders, 152
Functional impairment, 92

Fun-seeker, 275
Future trends, 386

General visualization, 142
Generativity, 149
Genetic programming, 88
Germany, 58, 241
Gerontocracy, 372
Gerontological society, 332
Gerontology
    advancement of, 19
    School of, 410
    as a vocation, 405
Glomerular filtration, 97
Golgi, 90
Gompertz plot, 81
Grandparenting, 271, 275
Gray Panthers, 343

Health
    the dimensions of, 170
    prognosis on, 399
    and social adjustment, 358
Health care services, 195
Hearing, 133
Heart diseases, 179
Hellenistic period, 30
Hypertension, 183

Identity crises, 149
Impingers, 109
Income, 235, 389
Index of aging, 56
Indians, elderly American, 367
Infarction, 180
Institutionalization, 66
    process of, 281
Institutions
    alternatives to, 285
    reforms, 393
Intelligence, 140
Involutional melancholia, 155
Involvement, self and social, 294
Ireland, 273

Japan, 188, 213, 272
Japanese Americans, 374
Justinian's plague, 31